AMBUSH ON ELK MOUNTAIN

**THE MURDERS, THE MANHUNT, AND
BIG NOSE GEORGE PAROTT**

BY

MAX R. ATWELL

Copyright © 2013 Max R. Atwell
All rights reserved.

ISBN: 978-0-692-33667-0

Library of Congress Control Number: 2013908869
CreateSpace Independent Publishing Platform
North Charleston, South Carolina

<u>Dedication</u>

This book is dedicated to the brave lawmen who served on the frontier

Acknowledgments

My interest in this piece of Wyoming history began when I was in **Velma Linford's** eighth grade Wyoming History class. Not only was she my teacher, but also she had written our text book, *Wyoming, Frontier State*. The book had a relatively small reference to the crime at Elk Mountain and the notorious outlaw Big Nose George Parott, but it captivated my curiosity and began this venture.

A number of others helped and encouraged me along the way, and I thank them:

- **Dennis Shepard**, who nagged me whenever I stalled
- Historian Emeritus **Rance Baker**, who was always willing to share his vast knowledge of Carbon County
- My son, **Max Atwell Jr.**, for believing the story should be told
- My daughter-in-law, **Nanette Stansbury Atwell**, for her review and suggestions
- **Donna Kamper** for her expertise with the maps and photos
- **Russ Harrison** for his friendship, enthusiasm, and technical support as we refined this book
- **Candi Harrison**, who was masterful in editing. Candi's encouragement, support, and occasional arbitration were invaluable in bringing this project to fruition.
- Our friends and family members who were proofreaders and made valuable suggestions: **Sam Gallagher,** whose thoughtful notes led to significant revisions; **Max Atwell Jr.; Lynn Finkelstein;** and **Jim Tripp**

I also would like to thank the staffs of the following organizations:

- **Carbon County Museum**
- **Carbon County Sheriff's Office**
- **Albany County Sheriff's Office**
- **South Dakota State Archives**
- **Minnesota Historical Society**
- **Wyoming State Archives and Historical Department**
- **University of Wyoming American Heritage Center**
- **Montana Historical Society Research Center**
- **Union Pacific Railroad Museum**
- **David Rumsey Map Collection**
- **Missouri History Museum**

And a very special thanks to my wife and best friend, **Sharon Barbee Atwell**, for always being there for me.

Contents

Prologue: Bones in a Whiskey Barrel	xi
Chapter 1: Investigation of Attempted Train Derailment	1
Chapter 2: Passing the Evening at Percy Station	7
Chapter 3: Ambush and Murder on Elk Mountain	13
Chapter 4: Robbery Plans Divulged	23
Chapter 5: Outlaw Gang Captured	31
Chapter 6: Confessions	43
Chapter 7: No Rest for Lawmen	63
Chapter 8: Dutch Charley	75
Chapter 9: Grand Jury Acts	81
Chapter 10: The Minuse Trial	89
Chapter 11: Big Nose George Captured and Returned to Wyoming	97
Chapter 12: Another Necktie Confession	115
Chapter 13: Arraignment	121
Chapter 14: Changes	131
Chapter 15: The Trial	141
Chapter 16: Big Nose George Changes His Plea	171
Chapter 17: Attempted Escape	177
Chapter 18: Another Lynching	181
Epilogue: Medical Studies and New Shoes for the Doctor	185
Author's Notes	189
Photographs and Maps	201
Sources	205
Appendix I: 1869 Laws of Wyoming Territory	229
Appendix II: Posse Comitatus	233
Additional Resources	235
Index	241

Preface

This book is based on years of extensive research and is as factual as I could make it. Many folks — especially those from Wyoming—know the story. My goal was to flesh out the details. I had the opportunity to haunt the Carbon County Museum in Rawlins, as well as the State of Wyoming Archives located in Cheyenne, and I gathered every bit of information I could find. It became an obsession, and this book is the result.

Most of the dialogue is fiction, to help the story come to life. Where I was able to find exact quotes—such as in the trial—I have shown the dialog in italics.

Since this is a story set in the Old West, I've tried to capture the flavor of that time by including words and terms that were common. Some readers may not be familiar with those terms, so I've provided definitions at the end of each chapter.

I encountered some great side stories along the way—stories about the people and politics of the time—and I've incorporated some of them in the dialog. Others, I've put in side boxes throughout the chapters, so they don't interrupt the flow of the story but are available for added perspective. I really wanted to give my readers the bigger picture of life in the Old West at that time.

As you will see, I have a great love for railroads, and the book is full of references to the mechanics of trains and aspects of operating the railroads at that time. I worked for the Union Pacific Railroad, where I was transferred up and down the line between Cheyenne, Laramie, and Rawlins, Wyoming, and I gained a real appreciation for trains and the people who worked on them. Please bear with me, if you don't share my passion. Then again, maybe some of my enthusiasm will rub off on you!

Most of all, I hope this book conveys my deep respect for the brave men who enforced the law in the Old West and the women who supported them. I am in awe of their courage and dedication.

Prologue:
Bones in a Whiskey Barrel

1: Remains of George Parott found in 1950, Rawlins, WY

Thursday, May 11, 1950, noon: Rawlins, Carbon County, Wyoming. Dust and exhaust began to dissipate as work abruptly halted on the new Hested's store basement. Inquisitive workers began to make their way to the northeast corner of the worksite to see what had prompted backhoe operator Mike Gravouc to shut down his machine and jump from the cab. Phil Wallstrom, general superintendent of the Metcalf Construction Company, pushed his way to the source of the disruption and was relieved to see that it was not the result of injury or damaged equipment.

In the cut of the backhoe was a partially exposed wooden object. After removing more soil, it became evident that the item was actually the end of a rotten whiskey barrel. Wallstrom pried open the exposed end of the barrel, releasing a musty smell, and as the noonday Wyoming sun revealed the contents of the barrel, someone in the crowd exclaimed, "Bones!"

2: Dr. Lillian Heath Nelson with George Parott's skull cap

Clearly, the bones were human. A skull with the top of the cranium neatly cut off lay at the bottom of the barrel. The age of the barrel and bones indicated that this was not a recent crime. Someone notified the Rawlins police and the coroner, Dr. Ben Sturgis. Ed Bennett, a local merchant in the crowd, remembered long-retired doctor Lillian Heath Nelson had in her possession the top of the skull belonging to the notorious outlaw Big Nose George Parott. He suggested to the coroner that this may be the rest of George Parott's remains.

Dr. Heath Nelson's husband, Lou, brought the skull cap to the construction site. When they put the two pieces together, it was a perfect fit. The mystery at hand was solved. The human remains in the whiskey barrel were those of the notorious outlaw Big Nose George. Coroner Sturgis declared that there would not be a need for an inquest. Lt. Harry Forney took the contents of the barrel to the police vault for safe keeping awaiting proper disposition.

The discovery of George Parott's bones caught the attention of Wyoming citizens and heightened curiosity about this chapter of Wyoming history. Though Parott was a legendary outlaw, the real story lay in the ambush and murder of Carbon County Deputy Sheriffs Henry H. "Tip" Vincents and Robert Widdowfield, and the manhunt that ensued across the territories and neighboring states.

3: Dr. Ben Sturgis, Carbon County Coroner, and Lou Nelson

4: Sturgis and Nelson with a perfect fit

Chapter 1

Investigation of Attempted Train Derailment

5: James G. Rankin, Deputy Sheriff (later, Sheriff), Carbon County, Wyoming Territory

Saturday, August 17, 1878: Carbon County Deputy Sheriff James G. Rankin was returning to Rawlins Springs, Wyoming Territory, on Union Pacific Passenger Train Number 3 after delivering a prisoner to the Territorial Penitentiary at Laramie City. When the train stopped at Rock Creek Station, a telegraphed message from his boss, Carbon County Sheriff Isaac Lawry, was waiting for him. There had been an attempt to derail a train near a bridge six miles east of Medicine Bow Station by "persons unknown." Rankin was to continue on to Medicine Bow in the express car and await further directions.

At Medicine Bow Station, another message from Sheriff Lawry directed Rankin to meet Union Pacific station agent Joseph B. Adams and accompany him to the bridge so he could investigate the attempted derailment of the train. No sooner had Rankin finished reading the telegram message when Joseph Adams stepped up to him.

"Sheriff Lawry asked me to go with you to the bridge." The two old friends sat down on a bench. Adams said, "Let me fill you in on what happened."

"Please do."

"A section crew working on a track area further south of the bridge was headed back to the station when they noticed that the spikes for a section of rail had been removed. The rail had been left in place so that an engineer looking up the track wouldn't realize there was a problem. A spool of telegraph wire had been taken from a toolshed, tied to the rail, and then spooled out a long distance to an area of scrub brush and trees.

"The section crew cut the wire loose and secured the rail by driving the spikes back into the ties. They never went over to the tree and brush area, for fear that the culprits might still be hiding there. If they had gone to investigate, they surely would've been killed.

"The section crew returned to the station, and the foreman, Erick Brown, reported the situation. I immediately sent warning telegrams to all the stations east and west. Superintendent Dickinson issued a protection order requiring that, until further notice, a guide engine and caboose precede every train."

> *Author's Note: James G. Rankin*
>
> Rankin was born in Indiana County, Pennsylvania. During the Civil War, he served as a sergeant with the 14th Pennsylvania Cavalry. About 1872, he and his brother, Joseph, migrated west and settled in Rawlins. Rankin served as constable and then as deputy sheriff of Carbon County.
>
> In the spring of 1875, Rankin married Julietta Smith. Their son, Edgar Perry, was born in 1877, followed by Jennie Bell in 1879, and Darrell James in 1881.
>
> In 1878, while deputy sheriff, Rankin ran against his boss—Sheriff Isaac Lawry—and won. Rankin served one two-year term and was defeated by another Isaac—Isaac Miller—who served two two-year terms before he was replaced by Rankin, who then served another two years.

Adams continued, "I have made arrangements for horses and food. We can leave at first light and go back and investigate. Maybe we can pick up their trail. If they'd succeeded in derailing a passenger train, a great many people would've been hurt or killed and a lot of equipment destroyed.

"You can bunk here on the station floor." Adams gave Deputy Rankin several wool blankets to lie on and bid him good night.

6: Isaac M. Lawry, Sheriff, Carbon County, Wyoming Territory

Sunday, August 18, 1878: The next morning, the two men were ready to leave by 5:30 a.m. They each had two good horses, plenty of hardtack, antelope jerky, and two canteens of water.

The telegraph operator came in. "Good morning, gentlemen. I see you've found the coffee. I brought you some fried elk sausage and bread for your breakfast."

When the men finished their breakfast, Rankin said, "I'm ready when you are."

It took about forty-five minutes for them to ride to the bridge. When they arrived, Albany County Sheriff Daniel Nottage and two other men from Laramie City were already there.

Nottage greeted them: "Good morning, Jim. I thought we should come up and take a look at this, just in case it took place in Albany County. Are you Mr. Adams?"

"Yes, sir."

Deputy Rankin asked, "What have you found so far?"

"We were just getting started when we spotted you two riding toward us, so we waited for you. The section foreman, Erick Brown, was just showing us where the spikes and fishplate were removed and where they made the repair."

Erick Brown, who had walked over near the bridge to check another fishplate, returned to the group.

After introductions, Rankin told him, "Erick, it was very brave—and probably a little foolish of you and your crew—to stop and make that repair without an armed escort to search the surrounding area. Whoever pulled the spikes could still have been over in those trees."

"My men and I were afraid the whole time we were working. We just had the feeling that someone was watching us. That's why we just left the telegraph wire on the ground when we cut it loose from the rails. As soon as we finished, we took our tools and hightailed it out of here."

"Did you find the tools they used to take up the rail?"

"No, sir. But we never left the track area to look for them, either."

"Let's follow the wire back into the brush and see if we can find where they were waiting. I'd like to determine how many of them there are and what direction they went when they left here."

"Would it be all right if we spool up the wire as we walk down there?"

"Sure. It would be best if we get it out of here so it can't be used again."

Once they were down in the brush and tree area, it appeared from the trampled grass and brush that the culprits probably had been there while the section crew was working on the track. They examined the area for about an hour and a half.

They found the tools the gang had used. Further back—away from the tracks—they found the spot where the outlaws had tied up their horses.

Though everyone agreed on most of the findings of the investigation, they differed on how long the outlaws had stayed in the area and how many of them there were. They concluded that the crime scene was definitely in Carbon County, so Sheriff Nottage and his deputies decided to catch the next freight train back to Laramie.

In parting, Sheriff Nottage said, "Jim, if you track this gang back into Albany County, telegraph me right away and let me know where we can pick up the trail. We'll come back with horses and take up the search. Be sure to let me know what you find."

"Sure will, Sheriff."

"Best of luck on your hunt. Watch your backside."

Sheriff Nottage, his deputies, and Brown headed to a place along the track where they could board an eastbound freight train. Going back to their horses, Deputy Rankin said, "Mr. Adams, let's take a ride."

The two men rode due south for about a mile and a half, where they found fresh tracks. It had rained several hours the night before, making it easy to follow the trail. They continued to track the outlaws for another two miles. Finally, Rankin asked, "Joe, what do you think of this?"

7: Daniel Nottage, Sheriff, Albany County, Wyoming Territory

"It looks like someone is driving stock."

"I don't think it's stock. I think this is the party we are looking for. All the horses are shod."

The men followed that trail for about five miles, going southwest toward Elk Mountain. By then, their horses were tiring, and they decided to head back to Medicine Bow. They dropped off their horses and jumped on a steam engine to Carbon. At Carbon they got fresh horses and continued south toward Elk Mountain.

Picking up the gang's trail about five and a half miles south of Carbon, they rode another two and a half miles, ending up on top of a high hill. The black clouds they had been watching for over an hour cut loose, producing such a severe hailstorm that they could no longer follow the trail.

Rankin asked, "It's the middle of the afternoon…do you think we should try to wait this out?"

"No, Jim. I think we're done for the day. Let's head back."

The return trip took them within two miles of Foote's Ranch at Elk Mountain. They proceeded with little conversation, arriving at Percy just before dusk. At Percy Station, they asked some section hands to take a railroad handcar up to the top of Medicine Hill to see if the trail they were following crossed the railroad tracks.

When the section hands returned, they reported that they'd seen no trail across the tracks. This satisfied Rankin and Adams that the outlaw gang was somewhere south of the track.

Author's Note: Terms You May Not Know

Fishplate: *A fishplate, also known as a splice bar or joint bar, is a metal bar bolted to the ends of two abutting rails to join them together in a railroad track. The top and bottom edges are tapered inwards so the device wedges itself between the top and bottom of the rail when it is bolted into place. Fishplates generally have either four or six bolt holes.*

Names and Places: *During the 1870s, the original names of some towns began to change into the names used today. Examples: Laramie City, Rawlins Springs, and Green River City are now known a, Laramie, Rawlins, and Green River.*

Laramie originated from the name of a French or French Canadian fur trapper, Jacques LaRamie, who—in the 1810s—disappeared and was presumed killed by Indians. He disappeared from the mountains that now bear his name, just east of the present-day city of Laramie.

Now, we have Fort Laramie, the Big Laramie River, the Little Laramie River, Laramie Valley, Laramie County, the Laramie Mountain Range (originally known as "the Black Hills"), and Laramie Peak.

Cheyenne is the county seat of Laramie County, and Laramie is the county seat of Albany County.

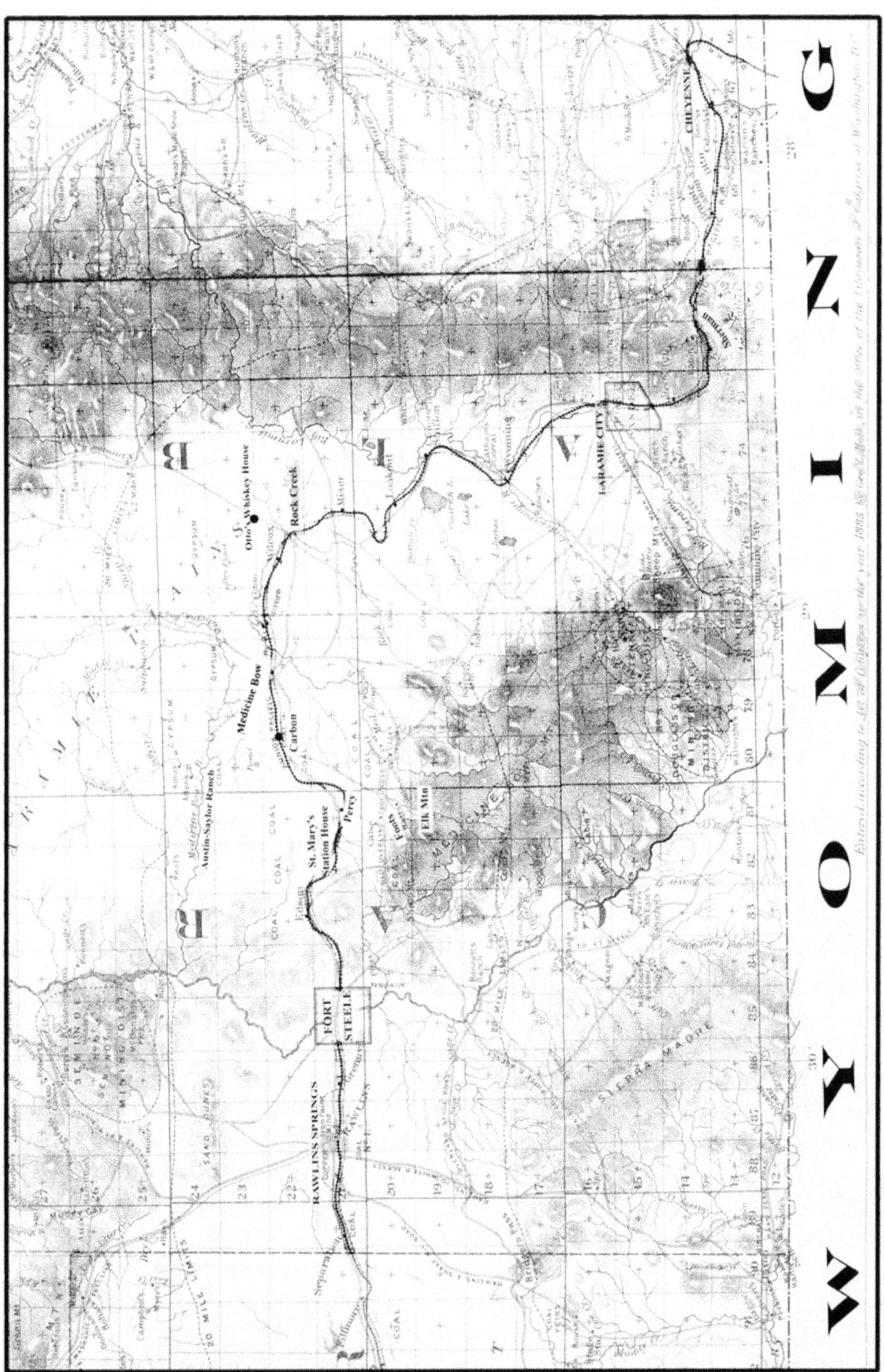

Chapter 2

Passing the Evening at Percy Station

Sunday, August 18, 1878: Rankin and Adams sent telegrams to sheriffs and railroad officials in Rawlins Springs and Laramie, detailing the information they had found. While they awaited responses, the two men took care of their horses and had dinner at the Percy House. Then they went back to the station.

Around quarter to ten in the evening, an eastbound freight train stopped at the small Percy Station, and Union Pacific Special Agent Henry H. "Tip" Vincents came into the building.

"Tip!" Deputy Rankin said, "What the hell are you doing down here so late?"

"Good evening, gentlemen. Superintendent Dickinson asked me to meet him here as soon as possible."

"I didn't know Ed was coming up here. We were just sitting around waiting for further orders."

Vincents said, "He'll be here within a couple of hours to meet with all of us. Uncle Pete—I mean the Union Pacific—is putting a very high priority on trying to apprehend this bunch. It's bad enough to have all the robberies and thefts we've had on the line, but having these bastards intentionally try to wreck a passenger train is the straw that broke the camel's back. My God, if they derailed the train in the right place, it could kill or maim thirty to forty people. Maybe more. The company really wants to catch this bunch and make an example out of them."

"I certainly can understand that."

"Did you know we're running a guide engine and caboose out in front of every train moving through the district?"

"That's what we were told."

Rankin and Adams gave Vincents a full account, even though they knew they would be repeating the story for Superintendent Dickinson.

Rankin said, "Sheriff Lawry told me that the Union Pacific is increasing the number of railroad special agents on the payroll."

Vincents replied, "Seems so. We have such a high turnover in detectives that we're hiring all the time. All the railroad special agents or detectives get deputized in the counties they're working in. That's important, so we can pursue people off railroad property and make an arrest. Are you interested in hiring out, Jim?"

"Hell no! I can't see me being a cinderdick. I'm happy where I am. It gives me a chance to help my brother, Joe, out with our livery stable and other enterprises, in my spare time. I can't see myself out walking the railroad yard at night, sticking my head in empty boxcars looking for tramps to chase. I'm afraid one of you boys are going to get your head knocked off when you stick it in a car and some tramp takes a club to you. Tip, in what capacity are you here? Cinderdick or deputy?"

"Both. Since we have some time to kill, I'd like to hear what happened when Number 3 was robbed right outside here at Percy, last May. I was in Rock Springs, but when I got back, Bill Daley and some other town characters told me all about it. One of them still had the newspaper with the story you wrote. By the way Joe, you're a damn good writer.

"Anyway, Bill told me you scared a confession out of that youngest member of the gang. He said the whole posse was exhausted, and their patience was worn down to a frazzle. They didn't fully appreciate the humor in what you did until much later, when they were rested and just sitting around talking about it. Every time they would start telling me the story, they'd get to laughing so hard, I couldn't make heads or tails of what happened."

Adams jumped in. "I'll tell you because I know that Jim here is too modest to tell it all. It happened on a Wednesday—May twenty-ninth, to be exact. It was about midnight, Number 3 Passenger Train was just pulling out after making its scheduled stop here at Percy Station. Before it could pick up much speed, four outlaws climbed aboard. There were three Pullman sleeping cars on the train, and they came aboard the second car, entering by way of the front door. They fired three shots—two through the roof and one through the side of the car—to wake up and intimidate the passengers before they started robbing them. They hadn't been at their work for more than a minute or two when one of them spotted the porter standing at the end of the car.

"The outlaw shouted, 'Don't you touch that bell cord, or I'll shoot you!' Then he reached up and cut the cord with his knife. What the robbers didn't know was that the porter had already pulled the cord. The train immediately began slowing down. The outlaws knew that they had been found out, so they jumped off the train and disappeared into the darkness.

"Ed Dickinson, who had been working as temporary superintendent since Superintendent Shankland retired, was in the forward Pullman car. He was talking to Conductor Mills before retiring to a berth. They noticed the train slowing down and knew something was wrong. They rushed to the end platform and met Pullman Conductor Huestes, who asked if they'd been robbed, as he had been.

"Huestes reported that the robbers had taken John Cameron's open-face gold watch. It was engraved inside the case with 'Cameron Dondee' and a family coat of arms consisting of a lion rampant. They also took his gold link watch chain, a key, a locket with a red-and-white stone setting, and a hundred dollars in cash. From Conductor Huestes, they took an open-face gold watch, a braided-hair watch chain, and thirty-five dollars in cash. And from William C. Ramsey, they got two first-class tickets from Cheyenne to Ogden and about fifty dollars in cash. They got about five in cash from the Pullman car porter. Fortunately, the outlaws didn't know there was a hundred and twenty thousand dollars in the express car.

"Dickenson's first impulse was to stop the train, form a party, and go after them. But since they had no idea how many outlaws there were, he decided that stopping the train might put the passengers in danger. So Number 3 westbound traveled on to Fort Steel, and Superintendent Dickinson wired ahead to Rawlins to inform Sheriff Lawry of the robbery and ask him to meet them.

"The good sheriff rousted Deputy Rankin's ass out of bed and put him in charge of the operation. Several men were deputized and ready to go. Jim was directed to gather his posse and meet Number 4 eastbound in the morning so they could travel back down here to Percy Station. Sheriff Lawry also wired Deputy Sheriffs Robert Widdowfield and Jens Hanson from Carbon to be ready to board the five-thirty freight train and meet up with the rest of the posse.

"Three soldiers from Fort Steel would be ready to board with pack mules to carry the posse's supplies. The Colonel couldn't let his officers chase outlaws, since the government passed that Posse Comitatus law, but they could offer supplies.

"The stock car for the horses was loaded and ready to be switched onto Number 4. Jim here and his men were seated in the passenger car when the Number 4 pulled out of Rawlins at five-thirty in the morning, Thursday, May thirtieth. At that point, the posse was made up of men from Rawlins, Carbon, Medicine Bow, and Percy, with the soldiers and their mules for hauling supplies.

"When Number 4 reached Percy Station, the stock car was switched out and spotted on a siding. We unloaded the animals, took them over to the corral next to the livery, and gave them feed and water. Superintendent Dickinson told us that the Union Pacific had authorized a thousand-dollar reward for the outlaws, 'dead or alive.'" He said, 'I don't care how you bring them in…just bring them in!'

"I have to tell you, I take my hat off to Ed Dickinson. He hadn't been to bed for at least three days and was running on pure anger and determination. But he still had the ability to think of everything that was needed and then make it happen.

"Counting myself, the posse was made up of twelve men. There was Jim here, Bob Widdowfield, Bill Daley, Jesse Wallace, Webber, McCarthy, Jens Hanson, Tim Wadsworth, Tom Jones, Kirk Calvert, and Bill Aylsworth. We were being supported by the three soldiers and their mules.[1] We had Kirk Calvert, William Aylesworth, and Thomas Jones as trackers…they're as good as they come.

"We thought the outlaws probably would head for Elk Mountain. When everyone was ready, we started toward Fort Steele and figured that we'd pick up their tracks in four or five miles. The trackers took the lead, with Kirk riding on the south side of the tracks and Tom and Bill on the north side. About four miles west of Percy, the trackers stopped. Each one made a circle and then came back together at the tracks, where they had a discussion among themselves. In a minute or two, they motioned for the rest of us to come on up to where they were.

"Tom said to us, 'Gentlemen, here are their tracks. They're not heading south toward Elk Mountain, like we thought they would. They're headed north, in the opposite direction.' Then Tom said, 'There are four of them, and they're on foot. It looks like they're heading toward High Mountain.' We figured they probably had horses tied up somewhere to the north.

"Jim said, 'Let's get going. They've already got more than a ten-hour lead on us.'

"We kept going north. There were many times when we were in rocks where I felt no one could follow tracks, but those three trackers kept going. Every time we'd get back on dirt, there'd be the outlaws' tracks. By the time we were about ten miles from Percy Station, we had completely lost sight of the soldiers and pack mules behind us. We just hoped we were leaving enough of a trail. As we neared the Medicine Bow River, the tracks became more distinct, and we thought we were gaining on them.

"By six o'clock, we reached the bluffs overlooking the Medicine Bow River. We were traveling over cliffs and rocks. Now it was clear they had a raft or boat hid out somewhere in the canyon below and had already taken to the water. By that time, it was night, and we had traveled about fifty miles over some of the roughest country I had ever seen. We picketed our horses to graze. Since our pack outfit hadn't arrived yet, we went to bed tired and hungry.

"The next morning—that would be Friday, May thirty-first—we built a small raft and sent Tom Jones across the Medicine Bow River to scout the trail on the other side. The river was still quite swollen from the spring runoff. Tom had been scouting downstream for about twenty minutes when he found where they'd left the water and retrieved provisions they had previously hidden. It was clear that once they had their provisions, they'd returned to their raft or boat and were again on the water, nearing where the Medicine Bow River runs into the Platte River. We needed to know if they were headed down the Platte River or if they had crossed the Platte to meet confederates. Our chance of catching the outlaws was looking doubtful. We needed to get a man across the Medicine Bow River to see if they had landed on the other side.

"With no materials to build a raft, we had no choice but to go around the mountain to the ford closest to Austin and Saylor's Ranch. We arrived there at noon. But we still had to cross the river. We made several attempts at riding our horses into the river, but those horses wanted none of that cold, fast water. It was four o'clock, and we hadn't eaten since seven o'clock the previous morning. Webber decided to make one more attempt at crossing…only this time, he removed the saddle. To our delight, he made it.

"He rode without a saddle fourteen miles to Austin and Saylor's Ranch, and he returned with provisions and directions to a canoe. With Webber and his mount on the other side, we started ferrying the men across in the canoe. Soon we had several men on the other side to catch the horses when they came out of the water. The remainder of the men drove the horses into the river and clubbed them across. We rode to the ranch and camped there that night.

"At daybreak, we started for the Platte River. But we couldn't pick up the trail. Mr. Saylor, who is very familiar with this country, assured us that the outlaws couldn't have taken a raft or canoe through the canyon ahead because of the rapids, bowiders, and waterfalls. He showed us a pass that would take us over the mountain and around this dangerous canyon.

"We suspected that the outlaws might have another raft or canoe hidden on the opposite side of the canyon, so we rode as quickly as we could to the other side, in hopes of cutting them off. We found what first appeared to be driftwood. It was the remains of a raft. We concluded that if they had attempted to pass through the canyon, they were now dead. No one could possibly go through that canyon and be alive.

"We spent the next hour searching along the shoreline of the Platte River for their bodies. As we searched downstream, we found where they came over the mountain and were traveling alongside the Platte River, on foot. We were certain they couldn't be far ahead of us.

"We rode at a good gait for about three miles, and for the first time, we could see the robbers about two miles in front of us. We spurred our horses up to a full gallop and were closing fast. When we were about a thousand yards from them, they spotted us and started for the river. They were just about ready to jump in when we opened fire on them. All of them—but one—stopped in their tracks, dropped their weapons, and threw up their hands. One of the outlaws was going at a dead run. Old Webber fired a shot at him and missed. He spurred his horse while he tried to reload, but the fired cartridge was stuck in the breech, and he couldn't remove it. He was closing on the robber but couldn't shoot him, so Old Webber rode straight at that outlaw.

"He was almost on top of him when—in one quick motion—he reined in his horse, jumped off, and cracked the robber in the head with the butt of his gun. The robber hit the ground like a hundred-pound sack of flour. He was on the ground, trying to raise his hands above his head, yelling, 'You got me! You got me! You got the drop on me! I'm done!' Old Webber disarmed his prisoner and marched him back to where we had the other prisoners.

"We disarmed and searched the prisoners but found nothing on any of them from the train robbery. Rankin asked them their names, and they identified themselves as John R. Thomas, whose age looked to be about twenty-seven; William A. Gibson, who looked to be about twenty-two; William Henry, who looked to be about fifty-five; and Dick H. Hill, who looked to be about thirty. Jim, here, demanded to know where they had disposed of the stolen property taken from the train robbery. All four professed their innocence. They kept telling us they were gold miners heading for the Black Hills.

"We cuffed and roped them together and then marched them back to our camp. Once we were there, Jim questioned them for another half hour. Then he motioned to Bob Widdowfield to follow him, and they walked out into the darkness to discuss how to continue the interrogation. About twenty-five minutes later, they came back to the campfire. Jim stood there and stared at William Henry. The look on Jim's face was so determined, it almost gave me the shivers.

"Jim figured that William Henry was the leader of the gang, as he was the oldest, and the others kept looking at him to take the lead. Jim reached down, grabbed Henry by the shirt, and pulled him to his feet. He looked Henry straight in the eye, and said, 'I don't want to hear any more of your goddamn lies about being gold miners. I want you to tell me where you hid the loot you stole from the train.'

"Henry said, 'I already told you…we are miners, and don't know anything about any train robbers.'

"Jim told Bob Widdowfield—who was standing beside him—to go get a picket rope. Bob returned and handed the rope to Jim, who tied a noose in the end of it, counting outloud the number of wraps he was making until he hit eight. Jim said to Bob, 'Don't need the traditional thirteen wraps, when eight does the job.'

"He expanded the end of the noose enough to fit over Henry's head and pulled the slack out of it, until it was snug around his neck. Then he said, 'Come on, Bob. We're going to take Mr. Henry over to those trees and give him one more chance to tell me what I want to know.'

"With Rankin pulling on the rope and Widdowfield poking a rifle in Henry's back, the three disappeared into the darkness. No one said a word. We all were straining our ears to hear what was going on over in the trees. About twenty-five minutes later, the two deputies came back. Jim walked over to Dick Hill and motioned for Bob to get another rope. He pulled Dick Hill to his feet and said, 'Your leader was one stubborn bastard.'

"Jim wrapped that rope eight times and fit the noose over Hill's head. 'Alright, you son of a bitch,' he said. 'You have until we get over to the trees to make up your mind if you're going to tell me the goddamn truth.'

"They headed toward another spot in the trees, and twenty minutes later, the two deputies came back alone. They followed the same routine with John Thomas. When the deputies returned to the campfire twenty-five minutes later, Widdowfield immediately went to get another rope.

"Jim began tying up the last noose. When he finished, he said to the group, 'I can't believe those dumb bastards would choose to die and end up wolf shit rather than tell the truth and spend four or five years in prison. But that was their choice.' Then he said, 'Old Man Henry died hard. I thought he never would stop flopping around. Well, we'll cut them down in the morning and leave them for the wolves.'

"By this time, young William Gibson—who was next—was shaking in his boots. When Jim placed the noose around Gibson's neck, he was wailing, 'For God's sakes don't do this! I'll tell you everything! I'll lead you to where Bill Henry hid the watches and the jewelry and the money. I have a family in Cheyenne, and I was out of work. I needed to feed my children. That's when I fell in with this crowd. I've never done anything like this before. I'm not an outlaw. I just needed money so bad to feed my family. Bill hid the money, but I can show you about where it's at. We can find it. I'll help you find it.'

"Jim asked young Gibson, 'Then you're admitting that you were the four that robbed the train?' and Gibson said, 'Yes, sir, we robbed the train!'

"Then Jim asked him if he was willing to turn Territorial evidence and tell the judge all about this robbery, and Gibson vowed he would. So Jim told Gibson that if he showed us where the loot was hidden and told the judge everything, then Jim would recommend lenience. Gibson practically kissed Jim's feet.

"Then Jim asked Gibson where the loot was hidden. He said they hid it close to where we were. They thought they were being followed and hid the money a couple miles away. Henry had told them, if they were caught with it, their fate would be sealed. He thought if they were caught and didn't have the goods on them, they'd be turned loose.

"Gibson told Jim that they walked from Cheyenne to Percy Station, where they robbed the train. Henry told them they'd end up with enough jewelry and money to last for a long time. When they made their getaway, they were going to float a raft down the Medicine Bow River into the Platte River and then all the way to Fort Fetterman. They figured they could use their new wealth to buy passage on a stage back to Cheyenne.

"Jim had Bill Daley and me take Gibson a distance from the main camp so he couldn't see the other three prisoners brought back from the trees. Up to that time, Bill and I and most of the others still thought the other three outlaws were dead. When we were settled at our new camp, Jim pulled us aside and told us the other prisoners were alive. He said Bob Widdowfield and others would go out and retrieve them after we were gone.

"The next morning, at first light, we had young Gibson lead us back a couple miles to where Old Man Bill Henry had hidden the loot. It took about a half hour of searching around the rocks, but we finally found it under the edge of a very large log, covered with leaves. With all the watches, jewelry, and money recovered, we went back to the camp. When young Gibson saw that all three of his partners were very much alive, all he could say was, 'I thought they were dead. I thought they were dead.'

"Tom Jones and Kirk Calvert brought four horses for the prisoners to ride, and we loaded up and took a short cut back to Saint Mary's Station, arriving there about five p.m. Superintendent Dickinson ordered down an engine, stock car, and caboose to take us home. We arrived back in Rawlins a little after eight, booked in the prisoners, and then went home."

"That's a great story!" Tip Vincents said. "I should have known that an old dog like you, Jim, would have all kinds of tricks up your sleeve. Joseph, now I know what you meant in your article when you said something about, 'promises—backed up by a picket rope—induced Gibson to squeal.'"

Adams said, "Well, I enjoy being a freelance reporter. I write an article and sell it to several newspapers. It provides them a good source of information and gives me a few extra dollars. I have a standing agreement with the papers: my articles get printed as written. Of course, I clear my stories with the Sheriff before sending them in. Sometimes the Sheriff wants to hold back information, to prevent jeopardizing a case."

While waiting for Superintendent Dickenson, the three old friends made plans for the fall hunting trip with Bob Widdowfield.

Footnote:
1. Nate Craig was the Western Union manager in Rawlins at the time of this robbery. In his autobiography, *Thrills,* Craig wrote that he was a member of this posse. J.B. Adams's account of the story—published in the *Laramie Sentinel,* June 4, 1878—and other accounts all fail to list Nate Craig as having been there. As Craig's story could be not verified, his autobiography is not included in the Sources or Bibliography sections of this book.

Author's Note: Terms You May Not Know

Guide Engine: *A railroad engine that would run far enough in front of a freight or passenger train to detect any sabotage or other problems with the track, track bed, or bridges. It would probably pull a caboose. If there were trouble, the guide engine either would see it and stop in time or derail. The railroads thought it better to sacrifice a guide engine than an entire train.*

Bowiders: *rocks or boulders just under the surface of fast-moving water, such as a river, capable of tearing the bottom out of a boat or destroying a raft*

Express Car: *Also known as a baggage car or mail car. The railroad officials called it "express car."*

Railroad Special Agent: *a railroad law enforcement officer, also known as a railroad detective or railroad policeman. Other slang terms: cinderdick or fly cop*

Chapter 3

Ambush and Murder on Elk Mountain

Monday, August 19, 1878: Just after midnight, a westbound train from Laramie City came to a stop outside Percy Station. A few minutes later, Superintendent Ed Dickinson walked into the building.

"Good evening, Joseph, Deputy, Tip. Thank you for being here."

Deputy Sheriff Rankin looked at his pocketwatch and said, "Good morning, Ed. It's nice to see you up and about so early."

Dickinson said, "I want to thank you two for all you've done in locating the outlaws' trail. I've been in contact with Sheriff Lawry, and between us, we decided that you should return to Rawlins Springs. You'll be needed up there. Joseph, you can return to Medicine Bow Station.

"We plan on having Deputy Bob Widdowfield come over on the early morning freight train from Carbon. Tip, you go with Bob. He'll have fresh horses and supplies so that you two can continue trailing the outlaws. All we want you to do is follow the trail and locate them. If they're still in this vicinity, we want you to come back. We'll put together a large enough posse to go out and arrest them and bring them in. We don't want you to make contact or do anything that would give away the fact that you are the law. Deputy, were you able to determine how many there are in that party?"

"Somewhere between seven and ten. It's hard to tell, exactly, because they've been riding single file."

Dickinson said, "Bob Widdowfield is very familiar with all the area around Elk Mountain, clear to the other side of Medicine Bow Peak. He'll be bringing provisions for the possibility of two days out and two days back. With the rain and hail we've had in the last few days, the tracks will be a little harder to follow. I'm having the conductor hold the train for you, Jim. Tip can brief Deputy Widdowfield later this morning, when he arrives from Carbon.

"Don't worry about the horses. I'll have some railroad employees take them back. Once again, I want to thank you for your help and the information you have provided."

Rankin turned to Vincents, "You and Bob are both good men. But I want to tell you…don't you take any unnecessary chances. We don't know how dangerous these sonsa bitches are."

"We'll be careful, Jim."

Rankin boarded the caboose, and the conductor signaled with his lantern for the engineer to pull out. Superintendent Dickinson, Joseph Adams, and Tip Vincents bedded down on the floor of the station to await the arrival of Deputy Robert Widdowfield.

A little after seven, the westbound freight train stopped and switched out the stock car with the fresh horses in it. Dickinson and Vincents met Widdowfield as he stepped down from the caboose.

"Good morning, Bob!"

"Good morning, Ed…Tip."

Dickinson said, "I'm going to have the conductor hold the train long enough to get you men ready to go. Then Joseph and I will travel on to Rawlins Springs. Later this afternoon, we'll head back to Medicine Bow Station by train, and I'll go on to Laramie City. As soon as you have the horses unloaded, let's meet at the station."

It took fifteen minutes to unload the horses, walk them back to the station, and tie them up. Dickinson reminded them that they were not to confront the outlaws. "Find them and then come back and put together a posse. When you two get back, telegraph Sheriff Lawry and me what you've found."

Ed Dickinson and Joseph Adams walked to the caboose and climbed aboard. Vincents and Widdowfield waved good-bye as the train pulled out of the station and headed for Rawlins Springs. As soon as the horses were watered and the tack and provisions checked, the two deputies mounted up and started out, following the road to the Foote Ranch, in search of the outlaws' trail.

Thursday, August 22, 1878, 3:30 p.m.: Superintendent Dickinson sent telegraph messages from Laramie City to Sheriff Lawry in Rawlins Springs and all points and stations between, asking if anyone had made contact with Vincents or Widdowfield. They kept Sheriff Nottage advised, in case the outlaws doubled back into Albany County. Sheriff Lawry wired back to Dickinson that no one had yet heard from the men. By sundown, there was still no word from the two deputies. Everyone was apprehensive.

Dickinson wired the agent at Carbon, copying Sheriff Lawry, to request that he contact the Union Pacific Coal Company's mine superintendent to ask for two or three good trackers who could go out to find the deputies' trail. There had been rain mixed with hail at least twice since Sunday, so the deputies' trail would be difficult to follow.

Two volunteers were selected for the task. The trackers were not deputized and were told they should not act like lawmen…just try to find the deputies or their trail.

The trackers left early Friday morning, August twenty-third. They returned Sunday the twenty-fifth, reporting that they had not found the deputies or their trail. However, they had come across a survey party who had told them that they'd seen a large group of men heading for one of the canyons to the south—probably the one known as 'Rattlesnake Canyon'—about a week ago.

The next afternoon, they'd seen two men in the distance, headed in the same direction as the larger party the day before. A couple of hours later, they could not see the two men any longer, but they heard a lot of shooting coming from that general direction. At first, they thought that it was a hunting party, but it seemed to be more shooting than would be necessary to bring down several deer. About three hours later, the survey party spotted seven or eight men off in the distance, leading a horse. They were headed in the direction of the railroad tracks, somewhere near Carbon.

As soon as this information was telegraphed to both Sheriff Lawry and Superintendent Dickinson, they began forming a large search party. Dickinson arranged for a stock car and a special car to be put on a train at Rawlins to bring down as many men as possible. They would meet up with men from Medicine Bow and Carbon. Sheriff Lawry summoned Jim Rankin to his office to brief him on the missing deputies.

As he walked in the door, Rankin said, "Sheriff, I have a bad feeling about this."

Handing him several telegrams, Lawry replied, "So do I, Jim."

Rankin read the telegrams. Then he looked back up at Lawry.

"I'm putting you in charge of the search party, Jim," Lawry told him. "I want you to contact as many good men as you can and prepare them to go with you in the morning. Use some railroad and county employees—they're already being paid. Dickinson will take care of transportation. He's coming up from Laramie to join the search party; he'll provide food and supplies for the group. Take what you feel is necessary from this end.

"Use any of the local boys that are good trackers and familiar with the country. But just remember one thing: you are in charge. I want you to continue the search until Tip and Bob are found."

8: Town of Carbon, Wyoming Territory

Monday, August 26, 1878: By the time Deputy Rankin arrived at the Rawlins Springs station, William Daley, owner of the lumber company and funeral home in Rawlins Springs, was already there, along with Jesse Wallace. Several other men were riding toward the station. As soon as the horses were loaded and all of the men were aboard the special car, the cars were switched onto an eastbound freight train. Earlier that morning, a westbound freight train had picked up the other men in Medicine Bow and Carbon and proceeded to Percy Station.

Rankin took charge of the search party, and they left Percy Station in the late morning. The party traveled on the Foote Ranch road to the place where Rankin and Adams had intersected the road a week before. They left the road at that point, and the two trackers who had searched for the deputies guided the party to the place where they had met the survey team. After familiarizing themselves with the area, they decided to ride back to John Foote's Ranch to spend the night.

John Foote welcomed the party. After the horses were corralled, fed, and watered, the men were shown where they could bed down for the night, under the stars.

Rankin said, "John, let me tell you what's happened."

Rankin and Dickinson took turns recounting the facts of the attempted derailing and the various searches to date, culminating in the present search for Tip Vincents and Bob Widdowfield. Rankin said, "John, you know this country like the back of your hand. I want you to join us tomorrow and guide us up Rattlesnake Canyon and over the pass, if necessary."

"I'll be glad to join you, Jim. We'll get the men fed and be on our way between five-thirty and six."

Tuesday, August 27, 1878: Having finished breakfast, the men filled their canteens. The horses were fed, watered, saddled, and ready to go. The men gathered around Deputy Rankin and John Foote, awaiting the order to move out.

Rankin said to the group, "Men, I don't know what to expect or what we'll find, but I think we have to expect the worst. Those men the survey crew spotted may have been the outlaws. When we get to the canyon, keep some distance between yourselves, in case they've set up an ambush. I doubt they're still in this area, but I don't want to take any chances. Also, remember…if anyone finds anything, fire two quick shots in the air as a signal for everyone to come in. John, would you like to say anything before we get started?"

"Yes. Men, I don't know if any of you are familiar with Elk Mountain or have been up Rattlesnake Canyon and over the pass. There will be a lot of places you can water your horses along Rattlesnake Creek. As we approach the canyon, there is a lot of brush along the creek bed. The further up we go, the more heavily wooded the canyon becomes. When we get there, we will spread out to look for signs.

We'll search both sides of the canyon, as well as along the creek bed. Keep your eyes and ears open. Remember, this canyon is named 'Rattlesnake Canyon' for a reason. With that said, I think we should move out."

"We're not turning back until we've located Tip and Bob. It's been eight days since anyone has seen them. Again, I think we have to expect the worst," Rankin said.

The men mounted and started riding toward Rattlesnake Canyon. By late morning, the search party was at the mouth of the canyon. They had located the main trail, with visible tracks heading up toward the pass and other tracks heading back down. The men spread out so they could cover both sides of Rattlesnake Creek. They were watching for tracks that might leave the main path.

That trail and several secondary trails ran together for some distance, then separated, and then eventually came back together. John Foote was still in the lead as the search party moved slowly and methodically up the canyon. No one spoke.

A little after two in the afternoon, Foote noted that at least eight horses had left the main trail and formed a side trail. He began following this trail. He'd traveled four hundred to five hundred yards when he reined up his horse and looked over at what appeared to be an Indian-style wickiup shelter. The remains of a small campfire was in front. A couple of other men rode up to join him.

"What do you make of this, John?"

"Don't know for sure, but it appears that someone stayed here in the last few weeks. From this vantage point, you can watch the main trail and spot riders coming from miles away. I believe that was the purpose of this camp. Don't see anything else of importance here. Let's continue on up the canyon."

They continued. After about two hundred yards, Foote spotted a body partially hidden under some brush. He reined his horse, squeezed off two shots from his pistol, and yelled, "Over here! Over here!" Out of instinct, he searched the surrounding area before dismounting.

All the members of the search party converged on the site.

Rankin rode up. "Is it one of them?"

Foote and Bill Daley were in the process of removing the brush from the body. The dead man was lying on his back.

Foote replied, "Looks like Bob Widdowfield. Oh…my God–he's been shot in the face. There by his mouth. Looks like it came out through the back of his neck. Has a lot of ashes on him. By the looks of him, he was either dragged through a firepit or fell into one when he was ambushed."

Rankin said, "Keep looking, men. Tip is probably nearby."

Foote and Daley mounted their horses and headed up the canyon. Within fifteen minutes, they found Tip Vincents's body, about 125 yards from Widdowfield's. He had been shot many times. Then a leather strap or buckle-type cartridge belt had been tied around his legs just below his knees and used to drag him over to a brushy area, where the bandits had covered him with more brush.

Some of the men removed the branches that covered Vincents's body. Foote pulled back Vincents's shirt so he and Daley could examine the wounds. The body was in an advanced state of putrefaction and was swollen considerably. Tip Vincents had been shot in the left breast and several other places. The wound to the right breast appeared to be a large exit wound, which indicated that he had been shot in the back. He had two wounds in his leg.

Foote observed, "His boots and hat are gone. These bodies have been robbed."

Deputy Rankin and Ed Dickinson rode up, and they were soon joined by Jesse Wallace, Bill Ike, George Swassor, and Taylor Pannock.

"Is that Tip?" one of them asked.

"Yes, sir," Foote said.

"What kind of a lowlife son of a bitch would kill a man and take his boots?"

The men stared in silence at the grisly sight, some shaking their heads, and others wiping their eyes.

Finally, Deputy Rankin addressed the group: "Men, I want you to spread out and search the area for anything that might be connected to these murders. Try to determine if they went over the pass or if they were the ones that the surveyors reported heading in the direction of Carbon. Remember, if you find anything, make note of the location and bring it in. Ed, stay here with me so we can plan what must be done next."

The search continued.

Rankin said, "The first thing we have to plan is to make arrangements to get the bodies and physical evidence out of here. I don't see any way that can happen before tomorrow. I'll need to stay here with the men until the area is thoroughly searched. Let's give them some time to see if they can turn up anything else. Then we can ride down to Percy and start sending telegrams to all points about what we've found. We want to make sure that Sheriff Lawry in Rawlins, Sheriff Nottage in Laramie, Sheriff Dykins in Green River, and Sheriff Carr in Cheyenne are notified, and that everyone is on the lookout for a group of eight to ten men.

"We'll send out a list of Tip's and Bob's missing belongings, just as soon as we can put it together. The outlaws may very well split into smaller groups. Sheriff Lawry will need to notify Tip's family, and he will probably want me to go on to Carbon and notify Mrs. Widdowfield. This needs to be done right away, before they find out from other sources. That's something I don't relish."

Dickinson said, "Jim, after the initial telegrams are sent, I can handle the arrangements. I'll take care of everything you can't get done."

"I know you will, Ed," Rankin said. "I'm just so damned mad about this. Maybe this wouldn't have happened if I'd gone with them, instead of going back to Rawlins Springs."

"Jim, you can't blame yourself. You were directed to go back to Rawlins Springs. Besides, they were ambushed. If you'd been with them, you'd probably be dead now, too."

"We need to have pack animals and coffins sent down to Percy Station from Rawlins Springs. We can move the bodies to the road from the Foote Ranch to Percy Station. We'll have a team and wagon with the coffins meet up with the pack animals carrying the bodies, and then the wagon can take the bodies to Percy. It will be late tomorrow by the time we get to Percy Station."

Dickinson replied, "That should give Sheriff Lawry and Coroner Edgerton time to plan a coroner's inquest somewhere…maybe Carbon or Ft. Steele. When we put together the list of items stolen from Tip and Bob, we must make sure it includes the missing horses and tack. Their personal property may be the only way we'll be able to identify the sons of bitches that did this."

Some forty-five minutes later, Daley and Jesse Wallace came riding back to where Deputy Rankin and Ed Dickinson stood. Daley carried an old Springfield rifle and an old pair of worn-out boots; Wallace held an old saddle, old stirrup straps that had been cut off, and what looked like a saddle girth strap.

"Jim," said Daley, "we found these items about seventy-five yards east from the three main campfires." The men handed the items to Rankin and Dickinson and dismounted.

Rankin said, "This looks like an old Springfield army rifle…probably a forty-five-seventy, or fifty-four caliber."

"That's my thinking too, Jim. Both are slow, but when they hit, they sure would knock a big hole in a man. Like the shot that went in Tip's back and out his chest."

"Bill, I want you to go to Percy Station with Ed and me. You can be a big help to Ed in making arrangements, if Sheriff Lawry wants me to go to Carbon and meet with Mrs. Widdowfield tonight. Jesse, you and the men stay up here in the canyon. In the morning, either you or Taylor Pannock can ride toward Percy to meet the men with the pack animals and the wagon with the coffins. You can leave the wagon at the road while you lead the pack animals back up here to Rattlesnake Canyon. As long as you men are in the area, it'll keep the scavengers away from Bob and Tip. Thank God they haven't been chewed up already."

"Don't worry about a thing here, Jim," Daley replied. "We'll make sure no further harm comes to our friends. Everyone here has ridden with you and Bob many times, and we all knew Tip."

"When I look at those bodies, it's all I can do to keep from breaking down."

"We all feel that way."

About an hour later, Deputy Rankin looked at his pocket watch and decided it was time to proceed. "Ed, Bill, mount up. We need to go now. If we ride steady, we can make Percy Station before dark. Jesse, let the men know what we're doing. We'll try to be back here by noon tomorrow."

Tuesday, August 27, 1878, 4:00 p.m.: During the return ride, the three men didn't talk until they reached the road between Percy and the Foote Ranch. Deputy Rankin, who had been riding in the lead, slowed his horse so the other two could join him.

Dickinson spoke first. "Let's use this time to discuss the things we need to do when we get to Percy." Rankin said, "Right."

Dickinson went on, "First, I think we need to send a confidential telegram to Sheriff Lawry, and copy the sheriffs of Albany, Laramie, and Sweetwater Counties. We need to tell them we found Tip and Bob murdered and robbed, and that there was a gang of men who were seen in the area. Bill, do you have two coffins at your place? If you do, we can let Sheriff Lawry know."

"Yes, I have two very nice identical coffins in the warehouse."

"We want to make sure the sheriff understands what state of decomposition the bodies are in, and make sure the pack animals are well-seasoned. Putting a dead body on inexperienced animals could cause unnecessary problems."

"We can get a wagon at Percy Station. We also should ask about notifying next of kin."

"Sounds good, Jim. I'll tell the yardmaster at the Rawlins Springs Station to set whatever type of cars the sheriff asks for on a siding, so they can be put on an eastbound train bound for Percy Station. I'll telegraph Omaha to inform the railroad officials what happened and request reward money. The company is really good about things like that. I'm sure they'll match what the County Supervisors put up," Dickinson concluded.

Making plans helped pass the time, and before they knew it, they were coming into Percy Station. Dickinson noted, "We made good time. It's eight-thirty."

They rode straight for the corral at the livery stable. After caring for their horses, they started toward the station.

Dickinson asked, "Are either of you hungry?"

"I honestly couldn't eat anything," Rankin responded.

"Me either, but I'd drink a cup of coffee."

"Come on. We can get that at the station."

Inside, they settled down with their coffee to write their telegrams. Dickinson asked, "Jim, did you know Bob Widdowfield very well?"

"Yes…for a long time. He and his brother, Joe, and my brother, Joe, worked in the mines together. Whenever I was in Carbon, I'd visit their mother, Ann. Bob and Joe absolutely worship their mother. They're a very close-knit family.

"Ann was really Bob's stepmother. She's his father's third wife. The first wife and Bob's mother both died in England. He and his sister were very young when their father married Ann Maugham. She took them under her wing, and no one in this world could have ever treated them better or loved them more. Bob was always given full honor as the oldest son, and he really helped her raise the younger brothers Joseph, John, and Thomas. She will take this news very hard."

About 9:00 p.m., the rhythmic clicking of the telegraph operator's key broke the silence. Sheriff Lawry responded to his telegram quickly, directing Deputy Rankin to catch the earliest train to Carbon to meet with Deputy Widdowfield's family. In addition to breaking the tragic news, Rankin was to get a list of everything Bob might have had with him so that they could provide this information to all the law enforcement officers in the territory. Lawry also asked Rankin to give Ann Widdowfield his personal condolences. Lawry said he'd have a deputy with a wagon meet Bill Daley at the Rawlins Springs Station. Together, they could pick up two coffins at the warehouse and take them to the station to be loaded in the morning.

Dickinson turned to Rankin, "Let's get out as many telegrams as we can before Number 3 Passenger Train comes in. Then Bill and I will go on to Rawlins Springs. I'll assist Sheriff Lawry any way I can, and I'll offer the full support of the Union Pacific Railroad. Jim, you can catch that eastbound freight train due here around one a.m. and go to Carbon. Please give the Widdowfield family my sincere condolences. Tell them I'll stop by just as soon as I can.

"I'll come back down on my way to Laramie, on the earliest train I can get. But you most likely will have already left for Elk Mountain. Just leave the information you get from the Widdowfield family with the agent here at Percy Station. I'll put it with what I learn in Rawlins and send the list of stolen property to all points and stations and the newspapers. You can pick up a copy of the complete personal property list when you get back to Percy with the bodies.

"The rest of the men and pack animals will come down from Rawlins Springs in the morning. I'll have the agent locate us a good team and wagon here and have it ready for the coffins. You can lead the party back to Rattlesnake Canyon. When the bodies are released for burial, I'll come back up to attend the funeral services."

Wednesday, August 28, 1878, 7:30 a.m.: Deputy Rankin spent the remainder of the night in Carbon at Arnold's Wyoming House. He awoke early and left the hotel to go break the news to Mrs. Widdowfield. He walked down the dirt street past John O'Connor's Billiard Parlor and Bill Sutten's Rooming House, then turned and headed toward the Widdowfield house. When he got to the door, he removed his hat and knocked. Ann Widdowfield opened the door immediately. She searched his face and knew the purpose of his visit.

"Mrs. Widdowfield, I'm very sorry to have to tell you this. Bob is dead. He and Tip Vincents were murdered."

"Oh, my God!" she gasped. "Oh, Jim, please tell me it's not true. Not my Bob. Please, dear God, not my Bob!"

She broke down in sobs, and Rankin caught her as she fell forward. He helped her inside to a chair and watched helplessly—holding back his own tears—as she cried. Finally, she asked, "What happened, Jim? What happened?"

"Ma'am, they rode into an ambush. It was the men they were following. They were murdered in cold blood…didn't have a chance to defend themselves. They were shot, and they died instantly. They did not suffer."

"You're sure they didn't suffer?"

"No, Ma'am, they didn't."

Regaining her composure, she nodded. "Jim, thank you for being the one to come tell me. Bob always had such respect for you."

"Can I call in someone to be with you?"

"No, thank you. Joe will be here in a little while. Right now, I just need to be alone and think what I need to do next. When can I have my Bob back?"

"We'll bring them down from Elk Mountain this afternoon and take them to Ft. Steele for the coroner's inquest and examination. That probably will happen tomorrow. Then Tip will be taken to Rawlins Springs, and Bob will be brought back here to his home."

"Thank you for being so kind. You say they died on Elk Mountain?"

"Yes ma'am. In Rattlesnake Canyon, on Elk Mountain. Now I hate to ask this, but we need your help. Bob and Tip were robbed after they were murdered. We need a list of everything Bob had with him—description of his horse and saddle. And ma'am, I hate to inform you they even stole the clothes he was wearing"

The tears came again. "They even took his clothes?"

"Some of his clothes. Yes, ma'am. A good description of what was taken may be the only way we can identify the murderers. We need to get a list out right away in hopes someone will have seen this group of outlaws…maybe identify the horses or something."

"I understand. Can you write down what I tell you?"

"Yes ma'am. I'll write it down."

"Bob was a proud man. They shouldn't have taken his clothes, Jim."

When Joe Widdowfield arrived and saw Deputy Rankin, he knew it was bad news. Rankin repeated what he'd told Mrs. Widdowfield. In despair, the young Widdowfield helped them put together the personal property list.

As Rankin was departing, he turned to Mrs. Widdowfield. "Ma'am, I'd like to stop by the preacher's place and ask him to come by and help you with arrangements. Would that be all right?"

"That'd be nice, Jim. Thanks for your kindness. I know you'll bring my Bob home with dignity."

Rankin informed the preacher and went back to the Carbon depot to wait for the next westbound train to Percy Station.

At Percy Station, the special car was spotted on a siding. The team of horses and wagon had already pulled alongside to unload the coffins. The rest of the party and pack animals were ready to go. Deputy Rankin and Bill Daley walked over to the station to leave the property list for Superintendent Dickinson:

Items the murders took from Widdowfield and Vincent

1. One dark grey mare branded "HL" on the foreshoulder and "A" on the left hip
2. A heavy California saddle
3. Light grey saddle blanket
4. New bridle
5. One light grey mare, eight years old, branded "OC" on left hip and "anchor with cross" on left shoulder
6. California saddle, newly leathered with handholds on the hind tree
7. One bay mare branded "CB" on left shoulder, white spot in forehead, very heavy built and with a great many saddle marks, no saddle

Thursday, August 29, 1878, 11:15 a.m.: Coroner A.G. Edgerton traveled to Fort Steel and held the official coroner's inquest. The bodies were examined and the Coroner's Jury presented its official verdict at 2:30 p.m. Due to the August heat and the deterioration of the bodies, the lids of the coffins were sealed with beeswax before being shipped to Rawlins Springs and Carbon.

Both funerals were held on Saturday. Henry Vincents's funeral was held in the morning, and Robert Widdowfield's funeral was in the afternoon. Dickinson arranged for a special engine, passenger car, and caboose to provide transportation to and from Carbon so that those who knew Robert Widdowfield could attend that service. Railroad and mine employees were given time off to attend. Most of the citizens of Rawlins Springs went to the services for Tip Vincents, and the citizens of Carbon attended Bob Widdowfield's service. Superintendent Dickinson, Sheriff Lawry, Deputy Rankin, and the other deputies attended both funerals.

9 and 10: Widdowfield's grave in Carbon, Wyoming

11 and 12: Vincents's grave in Rawlins, Wyoming

Author's Note: Terms You May Not Know

Wikiup: *a dome-shaped shelter made from brush, originated by Native Americans*

$20,000 REWARD!

Office of the Clerk of Carbon County,
Rawlins, Wyoming, August 29th, 1878.

A Reward of $2,000 each will be paid by the Commissioners of Carbon county, for the arrest and conviction of the parties who murdered Deputy Sheriff Robert Widdowfield and H. H. Vinson, in Big Canyon, on Rattle Snake Creek, near Elk Mountain, in Carbon county, Wyoming, on Monday, August 19th, 1878. The party that committed the murder is supposed to consist of from eight to fifteen persons. All information in the possession of the Commissioners will be furnished on application. The following is a description of the property taken murdered men:

One dark gray mare, branded H. L. on right shoulder, and A on left hip; heavy California saddle, light gray blanket, and new bridle. One light gray mare, eight years old, branded O C on left hip, and anchor with cross on left shoulder; had California Saddle newly leathered, with hand holds on hind tree. One bay mare, branded C B on left shoulder, white spot in forehead, very heavy build, and with a great many saddle marks.

By order of the Board of County Commissioners of Carbon county, Wyoming Territory.

JAMES FRANCE, Chairman.

Attest: J. B. ADAMS,
County Clerk.

13: Wanted poster

Chapter 4

Robbery Plans Divulged

December 1878: Christmas was just days away. Four months had passed since the murder of Deputies Vincents and Widdowfield, and there still was no clue to the identity of those responsible. Law enforcement officials in the seven counties stayed in close communication with each other, looking for any evidence that would help render justice. Every person arrested—regardless of the charge—was thoroughly interviewed in hope that some bit of information might be uncovered. But thus far, it had come to no avail.

Meanwhile, the November 2 elections changed some of the lawmen involved in the case. Three newly elected sheriffs would take office in January: Nathanial Kimball Boswell, Albany County; George W. Draper, Laramie County; and James G. Rankin, Carbon County. One of them replaced an incumbent who was not eligible to run again because he had already served two consecutive two-year terms.

Boswell, a Republican, was a former sheriff, having served as first territorial sheriff of Albany County. Boswell won that county's Republican Party nomination over one-term sheriff Daniel Nottage and then went on to defeat another former sheriff, Democrat John R. Brophy, by thirty-six votes. Rankin was nominated by the Republicans over his one-term boss, Sheriff Isaac M. Lawry. Lawry would never forgive his deputy for taking his job.

In small Wyoming communities where all of the candidates knew each other, personal ambitions were set aside for the good of the community. For the most part, transitions took place in a civil manner. After all, there would always be another election.

Despite the lack of breaks in the Elk Mountain case, clues began appearing that eventually helped the lawmen unravel the mystery.

Outlaws routinely robbed the Cheyenne–Black Hills Stage Line, the Medicine Bow Stage Line, and the Thayer Stage Line. On Friday, September 13, 1878, late in the afternoon, the Cheyenne–Black Hills Stage Line between Deadwood and Cheyenne was robbed.

Twenty-six year old Daniel Boone May was one of the most feared and hated of the armed shotgun messengers. Like many shotgun messengers, he also served from time to time as a deputy US marshal. May and John Zimmerman were the shotgun messengers on the southbound "down" stagecoach.

About six miles north of the fork where Old Woman Creek joined Lance Creek, they met the northbound "up" stagecoach, which had been robbed a few miles back. After gathering all the information they could from the driver and messenger on the northbound coach, May and Zimmerman decided to get off their coach and follow on their horses, which were tied to the rear of the coach. They planned to stay several hundred

> *Author's Note: How Outlaw Bands Formed*
>
> *Outlaws often formed a band, committed a series of robberies, and then broke up and moved in different directions. Later, they would meet up with other outlaws and form new bands in other parts of the territory.*

yards behind the stagecoach when it approached the robbery location, which was four miles south of the Lance Creek fork on Old Woman's Creek, so they could surprise any outlaws that appeared.

Sure enough, the southbound "down" stage was stopped by robbers. May and Zimmerman dismounted and quietly approached the stagecoach. They were within fifteen steps of it when one of the robbers saw them and opened fire. May and Zimmerman returned fire, and one of May's shots hit—and fatally wounded—one of the robbers.

14: Daniel Boone May

While the robbers retreated back to a defensible area, the stagecoach made a hasty escape. May and Zimmerman continued to exchange fire with the outlaws for about a half hour, but they couldn't dislodge them. They also couldn't retrieve the mail sacks that had been dropped in the road, along with May's prized overcoat, which he'd dropped when the shooting started. At dusk, the shotgun messengers decided to go on to the next stage station and accompany the stagecoach on to Cheyenne in the morning.

The outlaw killed in this robbery later was identified as one of the Elk Mountain murderers.

Late Sunday evening, October 13, 1878, a group of outlaws broke into the Trabing Brothers store at Medicine Bow. The Wyoming winter was setting in hard, and the outlaws stole large amounts of warm clothing, food, and camp supplies. Leaving the scene, the outlaws set fire to the store in an attempt to cover up the crime and give them a head start in their getaway.

Some of the stolen goods would turn up in the possession of the Elk Mountain outlaws.

On Sunday, December 8, 1878, a stage driver and shotgun messenger reported to their boss, C. Dana Thayer at Rock Creek, that they had seen several members of a known gang near Fort Fetterman. They noted that the group appeared to be moving in the direction of the Union Pacific Rock Creek Station and the little town that had grown up around it, known as "Rock Creek."

The same stage crew spotted several of these gang members near the Rock Creek Station again and reported the sighting to Dana Thayer on Friday, December 13, 1878. Thayer asked several of his employees, along with some of the townspeople, to keep an eye out for this gang, but they seemed to have left the area. Thayer telegraphed Sheriff Nottage to make him aware if this group was moving toward Laramie City, forty-five miles south of Rock Creek Station.

Some of the members of the gang spotted by the stagecoach crew would prove to be involved in the Elk Mountain murders.

Sunday, December 15, 1878: When Frank Howard came into the Thayer Hotel Eating House, Dana Thayer and one of his employees went over to his table to find out who he was and why he was in the area. Howard said he had fallen on hard times and had taken a job on a nearby ranch as a herder. He had come into town for a Sunday meal and to pick up some supplies for his employer. Since his story seemed genuine, they wished him well and left him alone. John Lafever—an old acquaintance of Howard's—came into the restaurant and walked over to Howard's table.

"Well, I'll be damned! What are you doing here, Frank?"

"It's good to see you, John. I remember you told me you had a place near here and that you sometimes stayed at the Thayer Hotel. I was planning on finding out if you were in town."

"I do have a place not far from here that I'm working on as time permits. I try to come to town on Saturday afternoons to get a hot bath here at Thayer's Hotel. Then I go back on Monday mornings and work on my place," Lafever replied.

"Do you still keep that room at the New York House down in Laramie City?"

"Yes, I do. The rent's reasonable, and it has an adjoining livery stable. It's a great place to spend the winter."

Howard invited Lafever to join him, and they spent the next hour getting caught up. Howard talked about his winter herding job. Lafever explained that he came up from Laramie many times throughout the year to work on lumber contracts. He liked Rock Creek because it was a good shipping point, and it was central to Fort Fetterman, Medicine Bow, Carbon, and Medicine Bow Peak.

"The railroad doesn't buy ties and lumber like they used to when they were first laying track. They haven't bought firewood since they got to Carbon and opened their first coal mine. The Union Pacific Mining Company mines at Carbon and Rock Springs, and the new mines they are opening at Hanna buy lumber and lots of mine timbers. But the big contractors have that business all sewed up. I've thought about doing something else."

"Believe me, I know exactly what you mean. It's been really lean for me too."

The meal over, they agreed to meet again the next time Howard was in town. It wouldn't be long.

Sunday, December 22, 1878: Frank Howard returned to Rock Creek and went straight to the Thayer Hotel. He found Lafever and asked to confide in him. Howard believed he was in a dangerous situation. "A few years back, you said you knew most of the lawmen in Albany County and that you had spent your share of time being deputized."

"Yes, I remember telling you that. Why?"

"I need you to vouch for me and act on my behalf with your law-enforcement friends."

"I would certainly vouch for what I know of you, Frank. What's this all about?"

"Like I told you, I'm doing some herding work on a ranch about six miles northeast of here, over by the south end of Como Bluffs. It's not too far from where the Fort Fetterman Road crosses Rock Creek. On occasion, I stop by Otto Olson's Whiskey House, which is a few miles out of town, near the Fort Fetterman Road. Otto converted his cabin into a small saloon. I have a drink with Otto or anyone else that comes by. It's lonely out at the ranch, so it's nice to have someone to visit with.

"Two weeks ago Friday, when I stopped in at Otto's, a party of men were already there. It turned out to be the same party of men that I had run into up at Fort Fetterman several weeks ago when I was on my way here. They had invited me to camp with them, and I had spent a couple of days enjoying their hospitality. Some of them mentioned that they knew Otto, but I was surprised to run into them at his place.

15: John Milton Thayer

Author's Note: John Thayer

The patriarch of the Thayer family, Brigadier General John M. Thayer served his country in many capacities. He lived in Nebraska for years and served that state in the United States Senate. He was appointed the second Territorial Governor of Wyoming and served from March 1, 1875 through May 28, 1878.

General Thayer, with other family members, had many successful business holdings in the small burg of Rock Creek, including the eating house, hotel, stage and freight lines, and several of the buildings. They also held ranch land in the surrounding area.

The Thayer Hotel was the site of payroll operations for the Thayer business enterprises, the large US Government Warehouse which serviced the territory's military post and forts, and the Union Pacific Railroad.

16: Rock Creek, Wyoming Territory

Author's Note: Rock Creek Station

The Rock Creek Station was twenty-five miles southeast of Medicine Bow and forty-five miles northeast of Laramie City. It was headquarters for 175 different freighting operations that serviced the US Government Warehouse, which supplied the northern military post and forts. It was also on the main stagecoach route to Fort Fetterman and other points north to Junction City, Montana Territory. It was one of the most important cattle shipping terminals in the territory.

Between August and November, some one hundred stock cars were loaded every day, shipping cattle to markets in the East. The cowboys with their great herds from the cattle companies camped out all around the town of Rock Creek, waiting their turn to load. The town boasted three well-stocked saloons and several good hotels, including Tom Garret's Wyoming House and Perry Brown's Brown Hotel. Anything you wanted could be had for a price. By the first week in December, the cattle drive would be over, and Rock Creek would settle into its quiet winter routine.

"When I ran into them at Otto's, they said that they were going to stay in the area for a few days, but then they might need a place to camp for a while. I told them the owner of the ranch was at his Cheyenne house and probably wouldn't return to the ranch before spring. I told them the ranch house was very small, but they were welcome to throw their bedrolls on the floor and stay in there with me.

"They thanked me for the offer and said they preferred to camp out. I told them there's a nice grove of trees with plenty of dead wood for fires, about two hundred and fifty yards from the ranch house. The area was sheltered from the wind and very near Rock Creek. They'd have grass and water for their horses. I told them I'd be going into Rock Creek on Sunday, and when I came back by, they could follow me out to the ranch if they wanted to. I was just returning the hospitality they had shown me.

"When I went by Otto's place Sunday afternoon, they were ready to go. Otto said he'd come out the next day with the supplies he was picking up for them…he said he knew the way, as he had been out to the ranch on several occasions in the past. The men followed me out to the ranch.

"When we got to the grove of trees, they hobbled the horses down by the creek, where there was still a lot of grass showing through the snow. I helped them gather firewood and get three campfires started. We continued to talk while we set up camp. I stayed there until almost dark, and then I went back to the ranch house.

"Monday afternoon, Otto arrived at the ranch with several hemp sacks full of provisions and whiskey. I showed Otto how to get down to the camp. We all stood around the fire and passed a jug of whiskey around and talked. Otto and two of the men went over and stood by another fire. I overheard Otto telling them when the government warehouse employees' and freighter's payrolls would be in, and that the payrolls for the Thayer enterprises would also be at the hotel. I can't remember if he said that the Union Pacific employees' payroll would be at the hotel or at the station. He said just as soon as he could find out the day and train it would arrive on, he'd let them know. It finally dawned on me what these men were really about. They were planning a robbery. I was fearful, but I didn't dare show it, or I'd be killed. Otto and I finally left a little before dark and went to our separate ways. We didn't say much to each other.

"During the next few days, I knew I couldn't act different in any way. So every afternoon, I'd go down and spend several hours with them, just sitting around the fires and talking. Some of the men asked me what I was doing here. I told them I'd been out of work for some time, and this herding job at least gave me a place to stay and something to eat during the winter. I guess they figured I was as desperate as they were to make some money.

"More and more, they took me into their confidence. Eventually, they invited me—forcefully—to join them. I was told that, since I knew who and where they were, I was now considered one of them. They made it clear that if I didn't want to be one of them, there would be a heavy price to pay.

"On Wednesday they invited me to go over to Otto's place with them. I was scared to be among them, but I went along. When we got to Otto's cabin, we tied up our horses on the west side and went in. We ordered up a shot of whiskey to take the chill off.

"As I said, several of them knew Otto and had been friends of his for a very long time. Pretty soon, Otto started telling us, in detail, how he had been fired from his job at the government warehouse.

"One of the men cut in and said, 'You already told me that sorry damned story. What did you expect them to do, you dumb, thieving bastard?' We all laughed at that.

"Otto said, 'I'd still like to get even with those dirty sons of bitches. I liked that job!'

"The other guy fired back, 'Sure you did, because there was always something for you to steal!' They all laughed again.

"As I listened to the various conversations, I learned Otto could get you anything. Now I knew that good ol' Otto was selling a lot more than whiskey. If you were passing through and didn't want to be seen, Otto would go to town, buy anything you needed, and bring it out to you. For this service, he was paid generously. I also learned that Otto would work as a spotter and provide information, for pay. One of them said, 'You can trust old Otto to help you out, and the best part about him is, he knows how to keep his damn mouth shut. Isn't that right, Otto?'

"Otto replied, 'Damn right! I keep my eyes open and my mouth shut.'

"After a while, we all mounted up and rode back to the camp.

"Through the next few days, I kept up my duties around the ranch. I'd go to the camp every afternoon and spend time sitting around the fire, talking with the boys and listening to their stories. Then a week ago Saturday, when I was at the camp, Otto came in with provisions he had picked up at Thayer's Store. He stayed for a couple hours, just drinking coffee and talking to us. I left when Otto left.

"The next day—Sunday—I came into town to get supplies for the ranch and have a meal. That's when I first met Mr. Thayer. He seemed like a very personable man, but he sure did ask me a lot of questions. Everything I told him was the truth, about me and the ranch. But I was too afraid to tell him anything about the men camped up near the bluffs.

"After I had my meal here at this hotel eating house, I walked over to the store to pick up my supplies before heading back to the ranch. While I was in the store, one of the men from the gang came in and bought some tobacco. He nodded his head in recognition of me but didn't say anything. I nodded back. As he left, I looked out the front window, and I could see another one of the men waiting with the horses and just looking around. All the way back to the ranch, I thought about what was going on and how I was going to get out of it. I knew these men were planning something big, and they accepted me as one of them. How can I get out of this alive?"

Lafever interrupted, "Frank, who are these men? How many of them are there?"

"All I know are their first names. Let's see…one is 'Fred.' Then there's 'Joe' and 'Henry'—sometimes they call him 'Hank'—and 'Dutch Charley' and another one they just call 'the Kid.'

"Late Wednesday afternoon, Otto came back to the camp. We all just sat there for a while. Then finally, Otto said, 'Next Monday, the payroll money for the employees of the Union Pacific, all of Thayer's businesses, and the government warehouse will be brought up in the express car on the Number 3 Passenger Train. The money will be kept at the hotel eating house and paid out from there, so the best time to rob the place would be just as soon as the train pulls out.'"

Lafever asked, "Frank, have you told any of this to anyone else?"

"No, not yet. I wanted to talk to you first because I remembered your contacts with the law. I want you to know that I'm damn scared that I can't get out of this alive. During the time I've been in camp with these men, I've picked up bits and pieces about some of their work. I feel pretty sure—from what I've heard—that two or more are part of the gang that killed those two deputies over on Elk Mountain."

"That is serious. Which two?"

"I overheard Dutch Charley and Joe talking about it. Dutch Charley said he couldn't believe they each have a two-thousand-dollar reward on their heads. He was grumbling that all they got for their trouble was a couple horses, a saddle, a gun, boots, and some clothes. He said, 'And we had to steal them off a damned dead man, to boot.'

"John, these are some very bad, cold-blooded sons of bitches. I have no doubt they'd kill me in a heartbeat if they thought I betrayed them. I have no choice but to act like I'm going along with them. It's the only way I can survive."

"What can I do, Frank?"

"I'm in between the outlaws and the law, and I need protection. If you help protect me, and everything goes as I hope it will, I can survive, and we'll share in the rewards. There are several big rewards on these guys—they're all wanted for one thing or another. If we can bring these bastards in, we can get the money, and justice would be served. John, if you and I have an agreement on this, then let's ask Mr. Thayer to join us. We'll tell him everything."

"Don't worry, old friend. I'm with you on this."

They went to the Thayer Hotel Eating House to meet with Dana Thayer. Howard was clearly anxious. Lafever turned to their waiter, "Bill, we need to speak to Mr. Thayer. Would you please let him know we're here and ask him to join us?" The waiter nodded and left to find his boss.

When Dana Thayer arrived at the eating house, he came to their table. "Morning, John. Bill said you want to see me."

"Thanks for coming, Dana. Let me get right to the point. My friend, Frank Howard here, has some important information that we think you need to hear immediately."

"I remember you, Frank. We met last week. You're a herder on a ranch northeast of here."

Howard looked around to make sure their conversation would be private. Then he addressed Thayer. "I have some very serious information for you, but it must be handled properly, or I'll end up dead. I need your help. I invited a group of men that I met over near Fort Fetterman to stay out at the ranch where I'm working. It turns out that they're outlaws intent on robbing the Union Pacific, government warehouse, and Thayer payrolls. I let them believe that I've thrown in with them because…well…they gave me no choice. There's no question they'll kill me if they think that I'm not with them."

For the next half hour, Howard filled Thayer in on the outlaws and their plans. He revealed Otto Olsen's connection, and he gave a detailed description of their camp by the bluffs.

"What I need is for you or John to contact Sheriff Nottage or Sheriff-elect Boswell in Laramie City and tell them what is about to take place here. I hope you'll convey to them how dangerous these men are. I believe that two or more of these men were involved in murdering those two deputies over on Elk Mountain, a few months back."

"How do you know that?"

"I overheard them talking and laughing about it. Be sure to let Sheriff Nottage know about that. I'd like to see the Sheriff arrest Otto first and make Otto guide them to the camp. Arresting Otto first would prevent him from warning them."

"Besides Otto, how many men are there in the camp?" Thayer asked.

"There are five now, and another one, named 'Irwin,' is supposed to come to the camp today. They sent him to Cheyenne to get supplies and told him to take the supplies to a place they have near Fort Fetterman before he comes here. That's where they'll go after they pull off this robbery.

"To keep me safe, we need to make it look like I'm being treated like them. So when the Sheriff and his men get to the ranch, tell them they can tie up on the south side of the outbuildings and then walk around to the house and quietly arrest me. Then they can bring Otto into the house and put a guard on the both of us. It would be best if the Sheriff keeps me under arrest until they're all in jail. If any of them escapes, or their friends find out I had something to do with their capture, they'll kill me to settle the score.

"After they arrest me, it would be best if they approach the outlaws' camp on foot. They'll be able to see the campfires from the house. It shouldn't be hard to encircle the camp, except back by the horses. The Sheriff will want to watch the horses, because if any of them get to the horses, they're likely to ride straight to the cut that will take them up and over the bluffs. Then they'd likely escape. They have nothing to lose, and they won't hesitate to kill as many lawmen as possible before going down.

"Now, as much as I don't want to, I have to go back to the ranch and act as if nothing is wrong, or they may get suspicious. I trust you two, and I know you'll do all you can to make sure the Sheriff knows I'm not really one of them.

"You've done the right thing, Frank," said Thayer. "I appreciate your trust, and I promise you I'll do all I can to honor it. You've saved me and others a lot of grief by coming to me today, and you and John deserve those rewards if we can capture these outlaws."

Before Howard left, Thayer cautioned, "Don't do anything that would put them onto what you've been doing. Be careful, and may God look after you."

Howard left the hotel and climbed up on the wagon. He pulled down his ear flaps, tugged the sheepskin collar of his coat up around his ears, and wrapped his heavy wool scarf around the back of his neck and across the bridge of his nose, leaving only his eyes showing. He whipped the reins and headed down the road.

Chapter 5

Outlaw Gang Captured

Sunday, December 22, 1878: "John, why don't you stay and help me compose a telegram to Sheriff Nottage, Sheriff-elect Boswell, and Superintendent Dickinson? We'll go to the station and have it sent. Then I guess we just wait for an answer from the Sheriff. I'm guessing it'll take an hour or more to get an answer."

"I'll stay right here with you 'til this thing is over, Dana. I won't have anything else on my mind anyway."

They drafted the telegrams. As they walked to the station, Thayer said, "It takes a lot of courage to do what Frank is doing. He could easily get killed if someone starts shooting."

17: Nathaniel K. Boswell, Sheriff, Albany County, Wyoming Territory

"I know. I admire him for the position he's taking."

At the Rock Creek Station, they handed the written message to the agent, who quickly scanned it. "I'll send the wire immediately, Mr. Thayer. Where will I be able to find you when a response comes back?"

"We'll be over at the hotel."

At two p.m., the Union Pacific telegraph operator in Laramie City began receiving the message. After it was transcribed and the key closed, the operator rewrote the message and made three carbon copies. He took the original and two copies to the yardmaster. "This is very important and needs immediate action!"

The yardmaster read the message and then told the crew caller to take one copy of the message to Nottage, one to Boswell, and the other to Dickinson, just as fast as he could.

Boswell received the message at his home. Reading it, he asked the crew caller if he had delivered a message to Nottage and Dickinson yet.

"I delivered Superintendent Dickinson's copy to him at his residence in the Union Pacific Hotel. I'll deliver Sheriff Nottage's message to him at his home.

"When you deliver Nottage's copy, would you please ask him to meet me at the sheriff's office as soon as possible? And when you go back by the Union Pacific Hotel, ask Dickinson to meet with us, too."

"I'll do that right now."

"Thanks."

> **Author's Note: Nathaniel Kimball Boswell**
>
> *Known as "Boz" to his friends, he was one of the toughest and most-feared lawmen ever to serve the Territory and State of Wyoming. Clerk of Court for the Second District, Colonel John Meldrum said of his good friend, Boswell, "He was the only man I ever knew who seemed to be born without physical fear, and this is attested to by (the) hair-raising chances he took in rounding up those notorious desperadoes."*
>
> *Boswell held several jobs as a peace officer in his career, including*
>
> - *Albany County Sheriff (he was the first),*
> - *Officer in the Rocky Mountain Detective Association,*
> - *Laramie City Town Marshal,*
> - *U.S. Deputy Marshal, and*
> - *Chief of Detectives for the Wyoming Stock Growers Association.*
>
> *On December 10, 1869, Governor John A. Campbell signed a bill granting suffrage to the women of Wyoming Territory; as Albany County sheriff, Boswell was the first officer of the court to summon the women jurors for the 1870 Session of District Court held in Laramie City. Judges Howe and Kingman ordered that women be summoned to serve on both the Grand and Petit Juries. The first woman summoned was schoolteacher Eliza Stewart. She was followed by Mrs. Amelia Hatcher, Mrs. Sarah Pease, Mrs. G.F. Hilton, Mrs. Mary Mackley, and Mrs. Agnes Baker, who eventually was excused. Boswell was proud of his role in such a historic event.*
>
> *Boswell was married to Martha Salisbury; and they had one child, Minnie.*

Sheriff-elect Boswell put on his hat and coat and said good-bye to his wife, telling her he was going up to Rock Creek and probably would not get back until late the next afternoon. He picked up the carpet bag where he kept extra warm clothes and headed toward the sheriff's office.

At the sheriff's office, Boswell handed the message to Deputy John T. Donahue and said, "Read this. I'm waiting for Sheriff Nottage and Ed Dickinson to arrive. Looks like we need to make plans and move as fast as we can. Dickinson can help us make arrangements for transportation up to Rock Creek Station."

The deputy read the message and looked up. "I'll be damned. Looks like we might finally have a break in the Elk Mountain murders!"

Dickinson entered. "Good afternoon, Sheriff. Deputy. Maybe fate has smiled down on us this day."

"Hope so," said Boswell.

Sheriff Nottage came in. "Looks like we have a job that needs tending to."

"Yes, we do," Boswell replied.

The men sat around a small table, discussing how they'd form a posse and get them and their horses to the Rock Creek Station. Nottage said, "Since I have so few days left in office, I think Boz should take the lead on this. He'll be more readily available for future court testimony than I will. You are already deputized, so if you agree Boz, I'll give you full rein and just back you up."

"That sounds reasonable to me, Daniel. Here's what I propose. I want to hit their camp in the dark, just before first light. If we keep the element of surprise on our side, we'll have a better chance of capturing or killing them without getting any of our men shot."

Dickinson offered, "Sheriff, if you can get your men ready, they can go up on Number 3. If you can't meet that time line, I'll have an engine and caboose standing by to take you up when you're ready. I'll have the yardmaster spot a special car for your men and another for their horses, along the freight office loading dock. As soon as Number 3 takes on water, we'll switch the special cars onto the train. If Number 3 is on time, the cars should be spotted about ten p.m. at Rock Creek Station on the government warehouse siding. That should make it easier to unload the horses. We'll leave the cars right there until you're ready to come back. Then we'll switch you onto the first eastbound that comes along, for your return trip."

"Thanks, Ed."

"Sheriff, thank you and your men for going after these bastards. I don't envy any of you being out in this cold all night. If last night is any indicator, I think it'll be twenty-five…maybe even thirty below, before morning. I'm sorry Millard Leach, the railroad detective, isn't here to go with you. He's been over in the Ogallala area for the last ten days and won't be back in Laramie City until tomorrow. I want to keep him involved in this as much as possible."

"Don't worry, Ed. We should have no trouble calling out enough of our old standbys to get the job done."

"Very well, Sheriff. I'll go make arrangements for the cars. When your men are ready to load, let me know, and I'll meet you at the freight office. Oh, by the way…tell your men if they get their horses loaded early enough, they should come over to the Union Pacific Dining Room. We'll feed them a good hot meal before Number 3 pulls out. It may be a while before they get to eat again."

Boswell directed, "Deputy Donahue, start rounding up a posse. Get some of the off-duty deputies to help you."

Sheriff Nottage reached into his desk and pulled out a roster of trusted posse members. "How many men do you think you'll need, Boz?"

"The report says there are seven outlaws. By the time we get there, there might be eight of them. I'd like to have at least a two-to-one edge on them, to make sure none of them gets away. Let's try for fifteen to twenty men. If we can't make that, we'll go with what we have.

"Make sure they bring their guns and ammunition, and tell them to dress warm. We'll be outside for a long time. Have the posse assemble here, and we'll go down as a group about five p.m. If any of them needs a rifle, sidearm, or ammunition, they can draw it out of our weapons vault. We'll reimburse them for any of their own ammunition they use."

Deputy Donahue left to get the posse ready. The two sheriffs began the job of listing and securing for transport the guns, ammunition, rope, ten pairs of handcuffs, ten leg shackles, blankets, and equipment.

"Let's pack everything we can in tote bags for the trip up to Rock Creek. We'll use two blankets to roll the cuffs and shackles, so they don't jingle against each other and give away our position. Let's take a dozen empty gunny sacks for evidence we might collect. When we get there, we can leave everything we won't immediately need—like the shackles—in the railroad car."

Boswell turned to Nottage. "Why don't you ride up to Rock Creek with us? After we leave for the ranch, you can catch the next freight back to Laramie City. I think it'd be a good idea if you were here in the office in the morning. We undoubtedly will be seen going to the freight office and then to the hotel dining room and back. Too many people will know something is in the air besides snow.

You can bet Doc Hayford or one of his snoops from the *Daily Sentinel* will be here at first light, trying to find out what's going on. I think the only thing we should tell them is that this party is suspected of robbing Trabing Store at Medicine Bow. We need to play this hand real close to the vest until we know exactly who, and how many, are involved and what other crimes this gang has participated in. The last thing we need is for some of their friends to try to break them out of jail."

At a quarter to five, the office door opened. In walked former sheriff Thomas J. Dayton. "I thought you boys might be able to use some professional help about now."

Nottage nodded, "Sure could, Tom. You know someone you'd like to recommend, you sorry old reprobate?"

Boswell grinned, "If we can get a few more former Sheriffs down here, we won't need a posse."

The men exchanged greetings, and Boswell asked, "So, you going up with us?"

18: Thomas Jefferson Dayton, Sheriff, Albany County, Wyoming Territory

"You bet! If what little I heard is correct, it would be a pleasure to help bring these sons of bitches in."

The door opened, and several more men walked in. Within minutes, Deputy Donahue entered with another seven men. Donahue handed Boswell a list of names. "Here is the posse list as it stands now. I think we'll be joined by two more at the freight office."

"Thank you, Deputy." As Boswell well read the list aloud, he looked up to associate each man with his name: "Thomas J. Dayton, Morgan Knadler, N. Thies, Tom Dougan, Ed S. Kerns, Fonse Metcalf, Jed F. Holcomb, Al LeRoy, Jack Fee, B. Halstead, F. Brown and J. English, Laramie City Policeman Scott, and—of course—Deputy Sheriff Donahue.

"Men, I'll give you a few details now and the rest on the train. We're going to Rock Creek Station tonight in two special cars on Number 3. Our cars will be switched out and spotted on the siding by the government warehouse, where we'll unload our horses.

"Dana Thayer and John Lafever will meet us and tell us how to locate the outlaws' camp. It's on a ranch northeast of Rock Creek Station. When the horses are unloaded, we'll proceed as quietly as possible to the outlaw camp. There'll be virtually no moon tonight, so that's in our favor.

"There's a strong possibility some of these men—maybe all of them—were involved in the murder of the two deputies at Elk Mountain. We also believe they robbed the Trabing Store in Medicine Bow twice and set it afire the last time, to cover up the break-in. We think this bunch has robbed many stagecoaches over on the Cheyenne–Black Hills Road, as well as many of the ranches in that area. Needless to say, this is a real tough party of men, and they'll probably decide to shoot it out with us rather than face the hangman's noose. We'll fare better if we can take them by surprise.

"Any of you men needing a weapon or more ammunition, draw it now. We'll meet up on the south side of the courthouse. Then we'll go together to the freight depot and load our horses off the freight dock. When the animals are secure, we'll go back to the Union Pacific dining room with Superintendent Dickinson. He'll have a meal waiting for us.

"One other thing…I don't want any of this discussed with any acquaintance you meet along the way. If there are no more questions, then let's move out."

The posse loaded their horses and stashed their guns, extra clothing, and tote bags with the cuffs, shackles, and rope in the other car. At the Union Pacific dining room, Dickinson held the door while the posse members—several of them railroad employees—headed to the small private dining room. Dickinson addressed the group, "Men, I would like to take this opportunity to thank you for the task that you are about to undertake. At a minimum, you will stop several major robberies. And maybe—as Sheriff Boswell has already shared with you—you'll help capture some of the individuals that may have been connected to the murder of Deputy Bob Widdowfield and Deputy Tip Vincents on Elk Mountain. I know that many of you were personally acquainted with Tip and Bob and grieve their loss as deeply as do their communities of Rawlins Springs and Carbon.

"Tip Vincents was one of most respected special agents on the Union Pacific Line. The Union Pacific Coal Company will never forget Bob Widdowfield from his days as mine foreman. He was much loved, trusted, and respected by all who knew him. Both men served as deputized Carbon County posse members for a number of years. When called upon in that capacity, they would give it their best effort. The thought of these good men being bushwhacked and shot to pieces gives me nightmares. We cannot rest until their killers are brought to justice. I'll pray for your safe return, with the outlaws in tow.

"I'm going to eat with you and see you on your way. I'll be awaiting word that you have accomplished your task."

Number 3 Passenger Train arrived soon after the men had eaten. The fireman filled the engine's boiler with water. The car toads checked the packing and oil in the journal boxes and topped them off. The lamps had been lit and a fire built in both stoves. Then the two special cars were added to the train. The conductor on one side of the train and the brakeman on the other walked the length of the train, visually checking the trucks, wheels, brake pads, and draw bars, looking for anything that might cause a problem. Finally, Dickinson looked at his watch and said, "It's time to board."

The posse shook hands with Dickinson and filed out the west side door toward the train. In the bitter cold, their breaths rose like the escaping steam from the train.

When they were seated, the conductor called, "All aboard." Assured that no more passengers

19: Union Pacific Depot, Laramie, Wyoming Territory

were boarding, he signaled "all clear" to the engineer. The fireman had the engine's boiler steam up to full operational pressure. Traction sand spewed onto the rail to minimize the slip of the drivers. The engine started to pull the train forward, and each successive thrust to the drivers increased its speed.

The train passed the iron foundry and steel-rolling mills, then the stockyards and the north end of the railroad yard. It crossed the bridge over the Big Laramie River. In three quarters of a mile, the men looked west, straining their eyes to see the gigantic buildings of the new ice house. It was too dark to see the ponds where—by day—ice was harvested by territorial prisoners under contract. As soon as the roof was completed, the facility would be put into full service. It would hold the distinction of being the largest railroad ice house in the world.

Someone mused, "Who would have believed you could harvest vegetables in California, load them into box cars, ice them in Laramie City, and then sell them on the east coast in the middle of the summer?"

In another mile and a half, Number 3 was up to full operating speed. Some of the men discussed strategies with the sheriffs. Boswell explained how important it would be to have two men on each of the outlaws. He reminded them that every bit of evidence had to be gathered and its owner identified. The evidence could connect the outlaws to other crimes in the region.

In no time at all, the forty-five miles slipped by. At 10:15 p.m., the train was pulling into Rock Creek Station. Sheriff Nottage got off the train and walked over to Thayer's Hotel Eating House to wait for the rest of the posse. After its normal stop, Number 3 pulled forward to clear the north end switch. The switch was thrown, and the train backed onto the government warehouse siding, where the two special cars were spotted, braked, and uncoupled. Number 3 pulled onto the main line, and the switch was returned to its normal position. The conductor signaled the engineer, and the train—a little behind schedule—inched forward to finish its run.

The posse put on their heavy coats, hats, and gloves, picked up the tote bags, and left the car. Government warehouse employees placed a gang plank between the stock car and the warehouse dock and held kerosene lamps, while the men—one-by-one—went into the car where their horses were waiting. Each man retrieved his horse and walked it out across the plank, onto the dock, then down the big ramp to the ground level. When all the horses were on the ground and loaded with gear, the men mounted and rode to the Thayer Hotel Eating House. Dana Thayer and John Lafever were waiting to deliver the last few instructions. They'd have several hours to kill before they started their journey.

Thayer greeted Boswell. "Pleased to see you, Sheriff. You know John, don't you?"

"Sure do." Turning to Lafever he asked, "How're you doing? Still brokering lumber?"

"I try to. Business has fallen off some since the Union Pacific stopped buying ties at the rate they used to. Every once in a while, I sell timbers to the Union Pacific Coal Company for their mines at Carbon. We do the best we can.

"So congratulations are in order, Sheriff."

"Looks like I'll be getting some more full-time deputy positions, if you're interested. Why don't you come down to Laramie and see me after the first of the month?"

"Thanks, Boz. I'll give it some thought. Meanwhile, I have my cold weather gear, gun, and horse ready to go. If you don't mind, I'll join your posse. I do have a vested interest in the outcome."

The briefing began. Thayer, Lafever and the lawmen covered all the information Frank Howard had provided. They reminded the posse that Olsen and Howard would be arrested with the rest of the outlaws. Howard's identity as an informant had to remain a secret until all members of the gang were behind bars. Since they didn't know if all the members of the gang would be at the camp when they made their raid, the posse had to protect Howard from the possibility that other associates were at large and would kill him—or have friends kill him—later on.

Boswell addressed former Sheriff Dayton. "Tom, I think the first order of business is to go to Otto's place and arrest the son of a bitch. We need to make him guide us to the outlaws' camp."

"Agreed," said Dayton.

Nottage said, "I don't recall seeing Otto's whiskey shop operation on the tax rolls. At a minimum, you can arrest him for that. But I don't think that would pressure him like arresting him as one of the gang members will."

Thayer turned to the group, "Go out on the street, and you'll see the wagon road to Fort Fetterman. It runs off to the north and then back to the east. You'll have to really watch where you're going because all you'll have is a waning crescent moon for light. The wagon road heads north about a half mile, where it forks. The northwest fork will take you to Medicine Bow Station, and the northeast fork will take you over the Laramie Mountains to Fort Fetterman. The road is well-used between here and Fort Fetterman. It services the lumber camps, as well as all the ranches back in that country.

There are a number of ranch roads and trails crisscrossing the main road. You'll really need Otto to guide you to the outlaws' camp. Don't let him lie to you or take you to the wrong place or warn his friends. I think he is a purveyor of information and, therefore, an accomplice, rather than a gang member. But damn his ornery hide…he's always riding on the edge of dishonesty.

To get to Otto's place—he calls it his 'Whiskey House'—follow the Fort Fetterman road for about five and a half miles. The Whiskey House sits off the road, about 50 yards to the east. You shouldn't have any trouble finding it in the dark. It's real near Boone Creek. After you've arrested Otto and convinced him to cooperate, head on down the road for about five more miles to Sheep Creek. Turn east on a wagon road that heads toward Laramie Peak. In about three miles, you'll start to follow one of the forks of Sheep Creek. I think it's the north fork, but it might be the middle fork. Otto will know. The ranch where Frank is staying and the outlaws are camped is several miles north and east of there. I don't know exactly which road you take to get there, but you'll still be on the north tributary. Do what you have to to get Otto to guide you."

Boswell stood up. "It's time to go. Remember—keep your talking to a minimum until we get to Otto's place. After that, no talking. Only hand signs."

Monday, December 23, 1878: About one-thirty a.m. the posse bid farewell to Nottage and Thayer and left the building. After one last check of their horses, tack, weapons, and tote bags, they mounted up and rode out of town—two abreast—with the sheriffs in the lead. The temperature was already fifteen degrees below zero, and it would get even colder by first light. Their heavy wool scarves were wrapped around their heads. The sound of the horses' shod hooves on the frozen dirt road was all but lost as the wind blew through the sagebrush.

An hour later, the posse neared Otto's Whiskey House. They strained their eyes trying to locate it. Five minutes later, Boswell signaled for the column to halt. He pointed to the northeast, where—in the dim light—the outline of the cabin could be seen. He directed Deputy Donahue to take half the men around the east side, while he led the other half to the west side, encircling the cabin and preventing escape.

The posse advanced slowly and got into position, pistols and rifles ready. Boswell dismounted and tied his horse to the hitching post out front. Then, pistol in hand, he walked to the cabin. He banged on the door with his fist. No response. He banged on it again. This time, a voice came from inside. "Who's there?"

Boswell boomed, "This is Sheriff Boswell from Laramie City, Olsen. I'm here to arrest you. There're fifteen armed men out here, so open the door and show yourself, with your hands in the air. If there is anyone else in there with you, they'd better do the same."

There was a long pause. Boswell tried again. "If you don't come out of your own free will, we will forcibly remove you—even if it means burning down your cabin and roasting you inside. This is the last time I'm going to tell you. Open the door, now!"

"I'm alone, Sheriff. Give me a minute to light a lamp."

"Hurry up. Keep your hands where I can see them."

Seconds later, Boswell heard the dead bolt sliding back, and the door slowly opened. The posse trained their weapons on the door. Boswell commanded, "Otto, step outside and put your hands above your head. Now, turn around, face the cabin, and put your hands on the wall." Olsen didn't hesitate. Putting his hands on the wall, he uttered, "Sheriff, I've done nothing wrong."

"Keep your mouth shut, Otto." Boswell motioned to two deputies to enter the cabin and make sure no one else was inside. The deputies came back outside and signaled all clear. For the prisoner's benefit, Boswell directed, "Take him inside and get him dressed for a nice cold morning ride. If he gives you any trouble, shoot the son of a bitch. I'll be back in a few minutes."

He assigned two pickets to stand at each corner of the building, looking outward, so no one could come up and surprise them. "Morgan…you, Fonse, and Jack go out to the barn and saddle up Otto's horse. Make sure there's nothing that will jingle or make noise on his tack. Jed, you and Al take a position just outside the door. I'm going in to speak with Mr. Olsen."

Then Boswell entered the cabin and closed the door. He surveyed the sparse furnishings and settled his gaze on Olsen, who was sitting in a chair near a small flat top wood stove, struggling to get his boots on. "Otto Olsen, we have come to arrest you and the other gang members that are planning to rob the Rock Creek payrolls."

"Sheriff, I'm not a member…"

"Shut up! I didn't come here to debate your guilt with you. As soon as you're dressed, you will lead us to the gang's camp. Your horse is being saddled for you now."

"I've been trying to tell you. I'm not a member of any gang. I don't know anything about where a gang is hiding."

Boswell narrowed his eyes and called through the door, "Jed, bring me my rope." Holcomb came inside and handed the rope to the Sheriff. The Sheriff threw the noose end over a rafter and handed the loose end back to Holcomb. Looking at Olsen, he said, "I'd prefer to just shoot you, but the sound would carry too far and might betray our position. So if you lie to me again, I'm going to hang you instead. Now, I'm asking you for the last time…are you going to lead us to your gang's camp or not?"

"All right. I'll lead you to the camp. But believe me…I'm not a member of any gang. My only involvement with them is they pay me to get supplies and whiskey."

Boswell pulled the rope back over the rafters and coiled it up. "We'll discuss your involvement with this gang at a later time. For now, finish putting on your cold weather gear, and let's get going. Just remember…you've had your last chance with me. If you try to warn them of our approach, I'll have you on your way to hell before the echo stops."

Boswell gave the posse final instructions before leaving Olsen's cabin. They would tie up on the south side of the ranch house, between the small barn and the house. Former Sheriff Dayton would stand guard on Olsen while the rest of the posse surrounded the house and arrested Frank Howard and anyone else there. Then Dayton would bring Olsen into the house, and he and one other deputy would guard the prisoners. The rest of the posse would split into two groups, spread out, and surround the camp. If all went well, the darkness would help them take the outlaws by surprise.

About three-thirty the posse and their prisoner, Olsen, were riding toward the outlaw camp. The men rode two abreast, with Boswell leading and Olsen on his left. Dayton and Lafever were right behind them. Deputy Sheriff Donahue and Jack Fee followed. The temperature dropped steadily.

By a quarter after five, the posse reached the ranch. According to plan, they quickly arrested Frank Howard. Then they took Olsen inside, and Dayton and Tom Dougan began their guard duty. The posse made a final check of their firearms and ammunition before moving toward the outlaw camp. They could smell the smoke and see the glow of the campfires. At the Sheriff's signal, the posse slowly encircled the camp. It took more than a half hour to get into position.

When they were in place, Boswell moved to within ten yards of one of the campfires, where one of the outlaws saw him. Boswell was pointing a pistol directly at his face. Noting that he'd been seen, Boswell yelled, "Throw up your hands! We have you covered."

Realizing they had been found, the outlaws had no choice but to raise their hands. One of them begged, "Don't shoot! You have the drop on us."

The posse moved in and disarmed the outlaws. Boswell counted noses and concluded at least one of the outlaws was missing. There were only four in camp, and there should have been five or six. Boswell headed northwest to where the horses were tied up. As he approached the horses, he could see movement behind some brush. Pointing his pistol at the brush, he yelled, "Come out of there, you son of a bitch, or I'll shoot you through that goddamn bush."

"You've got me. Don't shoot! I'm coming out."

The outlaw stood slowly with his hands raised above his head. Boswell turned him over to the deputies to be secured and searched. Then he directed one of the deputies to get the tote bag that has the handcuffs, and bring the extra bags to gather up their belongings.

One of the outlaws feigned innocence. "Sheriff, why are you arresting us? We're just camping here while we look for work. We haven't done anything wrong."

Boswell looked him straight in the eye. "I don't know your names yet, but I do know what you've done. We're going to Laramie City, and then we'll talk about it. I don't want any of you sons of bitches to speak to me or to my deputies or to each other, unless I direct you to speak. Take warning—if any of you open your mouth, I'll close it with the barrel of this pistol."

It was now nearly seven-thirty in the morning, and they could see the silhouette of the Laramie Mountain Range against the pink eastern sky, as Deputy Donahue returned with the bags and cuffs. The posse members cuffed the outlaws and stuffed their belongings into the bags. Then Donohue ordered the outlaws to pick up their gear and saddle up their horses. "If any of you need to relieve yourself, you'd better do it now. This'll be your last chance until you board the train car."

They walked the horses up to the ranch house, where Sheriff Dayton and Tom Dougan had Otto Olsen and Frank Howard cuffed and ready to go. A horse had been saddled for Howard, and his belongings were placed in one of the tote bags. The two other horses that had been in the barn would be led back to Rock Creek and placed in the livery stable for safe keeping.

Boswell pulled out his pocket watch, noting it was just after eight a.m. "Ed, I want you and Morgan to ride on ahead. Pick up that pistol Otto has under the bar and that old rifle by the stove. It'll be light by time you get back there, so look the place over real good to see what might be stolen. Keep a close eye out for anything marked 'UPRR' or 'US GOV.' If you find anything like that, bring it along or—if it's too large—make note of it. I suspect there are some folks who'd like to help Otto become a resident of that Big House across the river. We'll meet you back at Rock Creek Station, at the train cars."

Then Boswell gave one final warning to the captives. "We're going to go now. If any of you outstanding citizens would like to make a break for it, please feel free to do so. I really don't give a damn if I bring you in dead or alive. That's your choice." Turning to the posse, he instructed, "All right now. Mount up and form a column. I want to alternate two prisoners riding abreast, then two deputies."

The return trip was uneventful. The wind had stopped blowing, and the lawmen and outlaws alike were thankful for the morning sun on their backs. In the morning light, they could see Elk Mountain in the distance to the west, and to the southwest, Medicine Bow Peak rose to a majestic height of over 12,000 feet. The going was a whole lot easier and faster in the daylight.

When the group rode into town, they headed toward the government warehouse, reaching the train cars on the siding at about ten-thirty in the morning. Sheriff Boswell dismounted and directed his posse, "As soon as you get these men on board the train car, put the leg shackles on them. Keep them well guarded. Half of you stand guard, and the other half get the horses loaded. I'm going to walk over to the depot and make arrangements to have these cars switched onto the first eastbound train. I'll also telegraph Superintendent Dickinson and Sheriff Nottage to let them know we made the capture and ask them to meet our train with a prisoner wagon. Come on, John, you go with me."

As Boswell and Lafever neared the station, they saw Dana Thayer walking toward them. Boswell greeted him, "Good morning, Dana. It's been a long night, but we think we have all of them but one."

Thayer said, "Great news! Are you and your men alright?"

"Everyone's fine—just cold and tired. It came off as we planned. The only loose end is that Irwin fellow who was supposed to show up at the camp. He never showed. When he gets back in the area, he'll probably go to Otto's place to get directions to the camp. Since he won't find Otto, he may come here. Could you have your employees keep an eye out for strangers? If they spot him and can ascertain that it's Irwin, detain him and anyone else with him. Use whatever means are necessary. Come on. Let's all go inside so I can start the arrangements to get us back to Laramie City."

While the agent sent the telegrams, the Boswell filled Thayer in. "I'm concerned about this Irwin. I won't be able to turn Frank loose until we're sure he won't get shot in the back. Since Irwin was supposed to go to Cheyenne, I'm going to telegraph Sheriff Carr. He can contact the city police and have them check around to see if anyone knows of Irwin's whereabouts."

Lafever, who was standing by the window, interrupted, "Sheriff, I see your other two men riding toward the warehouse."

"John, would you please step out and motion them over here?"

"I'd be pleased to, Sheriff."

In a few minutes, Kerns, Knadler, and Lafever all came into the station.

"Did you men find anything of interest?"

"We found a lot of things, but it will be hard to prove ownership. We've got a few items in this tote bag. Would you like to take a look, Sheriff?"

"Not now. I'd like you to go show it to the foreman at the government warehouse. Tell him what else you saw at Otto's place. They need all the information you can give them so they can make a determination about filing charges against Otto. Take care of that business now so we can be ready to be switched onto the first eastbound. I'd like to be back in Laramie before two this afternoon, if possible. We have a lot of evidence to inventory, and I want to get started with the interviews."

The three men warmed themselves by the big cast-iron pot belly stove.

"I think our prisoners were counting on the Thayer enterprises and the Union Pacific to finance their winter stay. I'm just surprised they didn't try to pull off the robberies in late October or early November, while the weather was a little warmer. Well, I'm glad they didn't wait until the end of January, when it could have been thirty-five below zero. I must be getting old. I don't enjoy these all-night winter rides like I used to. I'd better go on over to the government warehouse and check on my posse. I'll keep you informed on what we learn after we've interviewed them."

"I'd appreciate that, Boz. Let me know if you need anything from us."

"Right now, just make sure you have your employees keep watch, in case Irwin shows up around here. Are you going to ride back to Laramie with us, John?"

"I'll come down the day after Christmas. When you turn Frank Howard loose, he can stay with me at the New York House if he wants to, until we see about the possibility of rewards and put in our claim. Then Frank can come back up here and stay out at that ranch."

Back at the train cars, Sheriff Dayton assured Sheriff Boswell that all was going as planned. The horses were in the stock car, and the prisoners had been shackled in the passenger car. The posse members had been taking turns going into the government warehouse foreman's office for hot coffee. Since everything was under control, Boswell went inside and had a cup of coffee, too, finishing just in time to get aboard the passenger car before it was switched onto the eastbound train.

The return trip was quiet. Everyone was tired, and no one had much to say. In what seemed like no time at all, the new ice house and the ice house ponds came into view. About twenty prisoners from the Territorial Prison were busy cutting blocks of ice and loading them on skids for transport. The train crossed the bridge over the Big Laramie River and entered the north end of the Laramie yard. Shortly thereafter, the stockyards came into view. The train was switched off the main line and onto one of the switching tracks on the west side of the depot. Within fifteen minutes, the special cars were switched out and spotted back on the west side of the freight office loading dock.

Sheriff Nottage and Superintendent Dickinson were waiting on the Freight Office loading dock, where they were joined by Boswell and Dayton.

"Your telegram said that all went well. No need to fire a shot."

"That's right, Ed. The only loose end is there's at least one member named 'Irwin' that is still out there, somewhere between Rock Creek and Cheyenne. I telegraphed Sheriff Carr from the Rock Creek Station to see if this Irwin and maybe some of his associates could be located around Cheyenne. If he can find Irwin, I asked him to hold him for us."

All four men trained their eyes on the prisoners, as they were being lead from the passenger car. The outlaws shuffled toward the waiting prisoner wagon. It took less than 10 minutes to get all seven prisoners cuffed and in leg irons, off the train car, and onto the wagon.

Boswell asked, "Do either of you recognize any of these men?"

Nottage said, "I've seen one of them around Rock Creek, and another looks familiar to me, but I can't place where I've seen him. Let me think about that awhile. Maybe it'll come to me."

Boswell told the deputies guarding the prisoners to tell the jailer not to let them talk to each other and to clean them up. "I don't want those stinking bastards to have the jail smelling like an outdoor privy. They all smell bad enough to make a buzzard puke!"

The horses were walked off the car and around to the front of the freight office, where they were tied up east of the building. A small group of citizens and some of the old Laramie loafers had gathered to watch, as the three deputies retrieved their horses.

Someone in the crowd asked, "Who are the prisoners, and what did they do?"

"You'll need to ask the sheriff that question."

The deputies mounted up and accompanied the prisoners to the courthouse, where they were separated and placed in cells to await the booking-in process.

Officer Scott and one of the deputies were excused so they could go get something to eat and some rest, before they had to report back to duty. The remainder of the posse led the horses to the county stable, where they were impounded as evidence. At this point some of the posse members were excused, and some stayed to help the deputies with the task of inventorying the belongings of the prisoners. The sheriff needed a complete inventory before he started to interview the prisoners. Boswell, Dayton, Nottage and Dickinson watched the unloading. Then Dayton said, "I'm hungry, let's get something to eat."

The four walked toward the dining room of the Union Pacific Hotel. They decided to go back into the small private dining room, where they could talk without being disturbed by other patrons. After they'd placed their orders, Nottage said, "I didn't get a chance to tell you…I met with Sheriff Lawry this morning and told him what you all were doing."

"Ike was here in Laramie?" asked Boswell.

"Yes. He telegraphed me from Cheyenne that he and his new bride would be coming through on the morning train. I went down to meet with them while the train took on coal and water. Don't know if you knew that Ike went back east two weeks ago and married an old sweetheart in Moline, Illinois. The wedding was on the eighteenth, I think. His bride is a very lovely woman. 'Fannie Moore' is her name."

Sheriff Lawry was finishing up his two-year term. He had less than a week left before his former deputy, newly-elected Sheriff James Rankin, would be sworn in for his two-year term, beginning in January of 1879.

"Ike didn't say too much about the election. I reminded him that I was a one-term sheriff. But I really wasn't that upset that I didn't get another term.

"He sure was pleased to hear that we may soon have some of the Elk Mountain murderers in custody. He said all of Carbon County would be waiting for your report. I told him we'd let him know just as soon as we had anything positive to report."

Dickinson asked, "Do you think these fellows are all involved in the murder of Tip and Bob?"

Boswell replied, "One…maybe two are. I won't know about the rest until I have a chance to interview them. I'll start with the informant. We need to treat him just like the rest of them, for his own protection. With the information we get from him on the record, and the inventory of the evidence, I hope to shed light on several crimes."

"I'd appreciate it if Special Agent Millard Leach and I could be present when you talk to Howard and any of the men suspected of murdering Tip and Bob. We'd just listen."

"Sure enough," Boswell responded. "I'm pleased that Leach is back in Laramie. His input would be welcome. I was real impressed when he captured Davis Dungford and Albert Spears within a week's time, over near Wood River Station. Everyone thought for sure Dungford was involved in the Elk Mountain murders. Maybe Millard can connect some of this gang to crimes east of here. I know that he, Boone May, and Seth Bullock stay in contact, in case one of them runs into some son of a bitch the others might be looking for. Don't know—Seth is in charge of the Black Hill Detective Agency, now that he lost the election for Sheriff of Lawrence County to Johnny Manning.

"It's frustrating that none of the bastards we've brought in so far can be tied to the murder of Tip and Bob. Back in October, Boone May and Bill Taylor captured Henry Borris, who was going under the name of 'Charles Henry.' We thought he was part of the Canyon Springs robbers and part of the Elk Mountain murderers. But that didn't pan out. He finally confessed that he was supposed to be at Canyon Springs, but he didn't make it because he was drugged out in one of the opium dens in Deadwood.

"Maybe we'll have better luck with this bunch of bastards. I'll send word to you when we're ready to start. It probably won't be much before 9:00 a.m."

Author's Note: Terms You May Not Know

Car toad: *slang for "car man" or "car inspector." Also known as "car knocker or "car whacker," from the practice of tapping on the wheels to detect flaws. The name "car toad" describes the act of squatting while inspecting the wheels and journal boxes.*

Picket: *sentry or lookout*

Shotgun Messenger: *an armed guard with a shotgun, generally sitting next to the driver of a stagecoach. This is where the term, "riding shotgun," comes from. On a treasure coach, there would be one shotgun messenger next to the driver and one or more inside the coach.*

Laramie loafers: *men who have nothing to do but hang around public places such as railroad depots and billiard parlors, to visit with other "loafers"*

Chapter 6

Confessions

December 23, 1878, 6:30 p.m.: Boswell turned his attention to former Sheriff Dayton, "I don't know about you, but I'm ready to go home and get some rest. But first, I'd better telegraph Sheriff Lawry and Sheriff-elect Rankin in Rawlins and tell them what we have here. I'll also send it to Sheriff Thomas Carr, US Marshal Gustave Schnitger, and Town Marshal David McDonald in Cheyenne, so they're up-to-date. I want them to keep an eye open for Irwin and anyone else that might be associated with him."

"I'm with you on that, Boz. Let's go."

"By the way, men…I just want to say this whole affair has been handled very well. I always worry about getting a deputy killed when we're dealing with this kind of back-shooting sons of bitches."

Nottage said, "I'll have the jailer serve them up a little fear with their evening meal by telling them what they're in for tomorrow…maybe have him wake them up a few times during the night, too. We don't want them to sleep too well. Fear might help loosen their tongues."

"Good idea," Boswell replied. "A little apprehension is good for the soul."

At that, the men parted company.

20: Albany County Courthouse,
Laramie, Wyoming Territory

Tuesday, December 24 (Christmas Eve), 1878, 7:00 a.m.: Boswell walked into the Sheriff's Office and greeted the deputy on duty, "Good morning, Deputy."

"Good morning, Sheriff. Did you get a good night's sleep?"

"Sure did. It was hard to get out of that warm bed this morning. Did you get any names out of our guests?"

"I got some, but a couple don't want to give their names. The only thing one of them will tell me is that he's called 'The Kid.' I told him he'd better think long and hard before he tries that 'Kid' bullshit on you. The other one says if he has to give us a name, he'll just make one up. I told him we'd get his name in due time."

"Did the deputies bring in an inventory of evidence and a detailed description of the horses and tack?"

"Yes, sir. The report's on that desk over there. Looks like they did a real good job on it. I also pulled all the missing and stolen horse reports over the last two years. The description of the horses taken from the murdered deputies is lying to the side. I started with that report, and we already have two matches."

"Looks like it'll be a real good day."

"Yes, sir! The way it looks now, five of the horses we've got are on at least one of those lists. Like I said, two were taken from the murder scene at Elk Mountain. A lot of the clothing and camp equipment looks like it could match what was taken from Trabing Store at Medicine Bow. After we have a chance to examine it and book it in as evidence, I'll have one of the Trabing brothers or one of their employees come by and see if they can identify any of it."

Nottage and Dayton arrived. Boswell updated them, "This fine deputy here has already matched two of the horses we picked up yesterday to the Widdowfield-Vincents murders. They're being taken care of at the Albany County stable. How's that for openers?"

"Great news! Anything else?"

"Not yet. We haven't had a chance to look any closer.

"It's twenty after seven. What I'd like to do—if it's all right with Sheriff Nottage—is have all of us go through the evidence, making all the matches we can. About nine, we can start the interview with Frank Howard. He should be able to give us a lot more information on the rest of the gang. With that information, along with the evidence we have, I think we can to start to unravel the Elk Mountain murders and maybe some of the other crimes in the Territory…especially the ones on the Cheyenne–Black Hills Stage road."

"I full well agree, Boz," Nottage replied. "You've got my blessing. Let me know what I can do to help."

"Good. Deputy, would you please have a clerk remind Ed Dickinson that we're going to start at nine a.m? He and Special Agent Leach should come over ten minutes before we start."

For the next hour and a half, the lawmen meticulously analyzed and matched evidence to various crimes. Superintendent Dickinson and Special Agent Leach arrived at the sheriff's office at eight-forty-five and were briefed on the matches they'd already found.

"If everyone is ready, let's get started. Deputy, would you have the jailer bring Frank Howard in? Make sure he's treated just like the others. I don't want to tip our hand that he's our informant. Once we start the interrogations, I want to continue until we're finished with all of them. And I damn sure don't want them talking to each other. We can always bring them back for a second interview.

"I want to get everything we can on the Elk Mountain murders. All other crimes are secondary to that. We'll go all night if we have to, but I'd like to be done by morning. Tomorrow is Christmas Day, and I know you'll want to spend time with your families."

Tuesday, December 24, 1878, 9:05 a.m.: The jailer—with Frank Howard in tow, cuffed and shackled—came back into the room. "Here he is, Sheriff."

"Thanks. You can leave him. I'll let you know when he's ready to return to his cell. Frank, I'm Sheriff Nottage. Here, let me remove those handcuffs. I believe you know Sheriff-elect Boswell, former sheriff Dayton, and Deputy Donahue."

"Yes, sir. I know them, but we've never been properly introduced. I never thought I'd be so happy to see so many lawmen in my life."

"This is Union Pacific Railroad Superintendent Ed Dickinson and Special Agent Millard Leach. They're here because railroad property was involved."

As they shook hands, Howard said, "I wasn't sure I'd still be alive today."

Boswell began, "We have the information you shared with Dana Thayer and John Lafever, but we want you to tell us everything again to make sure that we have it all. Tell us everything you can remember about this group of men, including Otto Olsen. Start with how long you've been with them and how you got hooked up. I want you to tell us who you believe each one of these men is, and what you know about them. From time to time, one of us may stop you and ask you to clarify or elaborate on something you've said."

Howard leaned back in his chair. "Well, let me start by saying I've had some very tough times. I was working over in Cheyenne, and I lost my job. I've done a little bit of everything, from freighting to handling livestock. With winter setting in, I decided I'd go up to Fort Fetterman, buy some supplies, and try to get some work around there. I thought about moving up to Deadwood, where I knew I could get work cutting firewood or working in one of the mines."

Boswell said, "Apparently you changed your mind?"

"Yes I did. When someone told me about a herding job near Rock Creek, I thought that'd be as good a place as any to hole up until spring. It wouldn't pay much, but I'd at least have room and board for the winter. Then maybe I could head over to Salt Lake in the spring. I heard the Central Pacific Railroad and the Union Pacific were doing a lot of freighting up north, in preparation for expanding some of their rail and spur lines."

Howard told the same story he'd told Thayer and Lafever. He said that in time, he had become accepted as a gang member, and he'd feared being killed if he didn't act as though he was going along.

Boswell looked him in the eye. "Frank, we're holding these men on suspicion based on what you've told us. We do have evidence that we believe ties at least some of them to prior crimes. But you understand that, outside this room, we have to treat you the same way we treat them. That's the only way we can protect you."

"Yes sir. I understand and appreciate your caution."

"We don't know how many others are still on the loose. We believe there's at least one more gang member—John Irwin."

Howard nodded, "Sheriff, when I first met up with them over near Fort Fetterman, John Irwin was with them."

"We sent a telegram to Cheyenne about Irwin and requested that he be arrested if he can be located. If he isn't in Cheyenne, we need to find out where he is and who he might be with, and bring him in. Until we're sure we have the whole gang, we can't safely turn you loose. You'll need to plan on spending Christmas and maybe a few more days here with us."

"I understand, Sheriff. To the best of my knowledge, John Irwin is the only other gang member that was supposed to be in on this robbery. But I don't know if he was supposed to be coming back to the ranch alone, or if he might bring others. When he gets to the Rock Creek area, he'd have to go to Otto Olsen's Whiskey House to get directions to where the others were staying. He'd probably stay around Otto's place for a day or two, waiting for him to come back. Then he'd probably go into Rock Creek, looking for Otto."

Boswell assured him, "Dana and his employees will be on the lookout for Irwin, if he shows up there."

"This is one dangerous group of men. I'm damn well afraid of them."

"We understand. Now, we want to associate them with any other crimes they've committed. So, please, tell us what you know."

Howard sipped his coffee and began again, "Well, I heard several of them mention robbing one or another of the Trabing Stores. The last one they robbed was the one in Medicine Bow."

"The one that burned down?"

"They set it on fire to cover up the fact that the store had been robbed. All of them were in on that robbery. They talked about how they could always count on the Trabing Stores to outfit them for the winter, and then they all laughed. Joe Minuse—or John Manuse—I've heard him called both names…he said he sure did like the fine coat he got from one of the shotgun messengers that was following the downstage from Deadwood. I asked him why a shotgun messenger would give him a coat, and he laughed, 'Well maybe he didn't exactly leave it for me. But he did leave it in the road up at Old Woman Creek, on the Cheyenne–Black Hills Road.'

"Then Dutch Charley said to Joe, 'As soon as you're done thanking that shotgun messenger for the coat, I'd like to shoot the son of a bitch for killing our old friend, Frank Towle.'

"Another time, I overheard Dutch Charley talking to Joe about how Frank Towle was the first one to start shooting at the deputies on Elk Mountain. He said Frank shot the one that got off his horse right in the mouth, and he fell dead into the firepit. He said he thought Big Nose George was the first to shoot the other man. Then everyone started shooting him as he rode up the hill, trying to get away.

"They all talked about different stagecoach robberies they'd committed. They said they preferred gold, even though it was getting harder all the time to get into the gold strong boxes. They joked about all the love letters they had read when they searched through US Mail bags for paper money.

"From what I could gather, quite a few of them had ridden with Joel Collins, Sam Bass, and Persimmon Bill, at one time or another. I can't remember which ones exactly. One of them—think it might have been Joe—said Frank Towle told him Persimmon Bill liked to make it look like Indians committed the crimes. Bill said that as long as those goddamned red bastards were being blamed for murders, then they were leaving him alone. Apparently Bill had a lot of acquaintances among the Indians and had spent time with them. Frank said Bill often wondered if he'd sold more horses to the Indians than he stole from them."

Author's Note: Persimmon Bill Chambers

At one time, some thought Bill Chambers might have been involved in the Elk Mountain murders.

H.E. "Stuttering" Brown was the business scout for Gilmer, Salisbury, and Patrick. He negotiated and bought the stagecoach Cheyenne–Black Hill Stage Line for them from Frank D. Yates and Company. In those days, the line just went as far as Fort Laramie and then north to Custer City. Brown served as the division agent north of Fort Laramie, and Luke Voorhees was superintendent of the whole line.

As the line grew in the Black Hills, Voorhees promoted Brown to superintendent of operations north of Fort Laramie, and Voorhees handled everything south to Cheyenne.

In 1876, Voorhees and his party were coming back from Custer City through Red Canyon when they came upon the remains of the Metz family from Laramie. The whole party had been murdered, scalped, and hacked to pieces. The Metzes had been in Custer City starting a bakery and were murdered on their return trip. Voorhees and his companions buried them the best they could, while looking out for the Indians that had committed the crime.

Voorhees had barely returned to Cheyenne when he received a telegram saying that Stuttering Brown had been attacked by Indians. He was not expected to live, and he wanted to pass along some information to Voorhees.

Voorhees left immediately on horseback, but arrived too late. It turned out that Brown had been having a lot of trouble with William "Persimmon Bill" Chambers. He and his gang had been stealing livestock, and Brown had made it known that he intended to stop Chambers's marauding.

As time went by, more people began to believe that Persimmon Bill had murdered Stuttering Brown and the Metz family, making it look as though hostile Indians had done the killing and robbing.

Lawmen went after Persimmon Bill several times, but by the time they would get to where he'd been seen, he was gone. Rumor was that he eventually left his criminal life and went back to North Carolina.

Confessions

Leach interjected, "Excuse me, Sheriff, but I'd like to remind everyone of that stage robbery on Old Woman Creek, near Robber's Roost. Boone May and John Zimmerman were following behind the stage and saw the outlaws stop it. When they approached, one of the robbers saw Boone and began shooting at him. Boone returned fire and hit the robber, who fell to the ground. His friends pulled the robber to the safety of a nearby ravine. Boone and John held off the gang while the stagecoach made its escape. Boone was pretty sure he had killed one of them, but when they went back later to search for a body or grave, they found neither. Do you gentlemen know Boone May and John Zimmerman?"

Everyone nodded in agreement. Boswell remembered, "I met Daniel Boone May and his brothers, Jim and Bill, three or four years after I moved from Cheyenne to Laramie. I was up near Fort Laramie on the Platte doing some work for the Rocky Mountain Detective Agency. If my memory serves me, Boone was the agent at Robbers Roost. Jim and Bill were running the May Ranch, just south of there where Lance Creek and Old Woman Creek come together.

"I think all the May boys have served as deputy US marshals from time to time. Boone still seems to make fairly regular runs as shotgun messenger between Deadwood and Cheyenne. I think he came up from Kansas shortly after J.T. Gilmer, M. Salisbury, and M.T. Patrick hired Luke Voorhees as superintendent of their newly-acquired Cheyenne–Black Hill Stage Line, about the time they were looking for that bastard, Persimmon Bill Chambers.

"Well, to get back to our stagecoach holdup…I've read about that incident in several newspapers, including the *Black Hills Daily Times*. They all mention that Boone left his coat. Boone and Johnny couldn't dislodge the outlaws from their cover or reach the mail sacks or his coat. They finally gave up and went on down to Cheyenne. Believe me…if Boone said he shot some son of a bitch, he shot him! Last time I saw Boone, he was still cussing those bastards for taking his coat."

Boswell said, "We need to telegraph Boone and get him to come over to Laramie and see if he can identify his coat. I'll telegraph Luke Voorhees at the Cheyenne–Black Hill Stage Line office and have them find Boone as soon as they can. He'll be someplace between Deadwood and Cheyenne. That would help convict at least some of them. In the meantime, if we can get a confession out of any of them, we might find out what they did with Frank Towle's body. If we can find Frank's body, Boone would stand to collect a $2,000 reward from Carbon County and $200 from Laramie County. Frank, if we can get a confession and conviction, you'll get some reward money, too."

"That would be real good; I'd split it with John Lafever. But getting a reward wasn't why I turned them in."

"We appreciate that, Frank. Please, go ahead with your story."

"Dutch Charley, the dead man Frank Towle, and possibly Joe Minuse were all part of the gang that killed the two deputies on Elk Mountain. I heard Dutch Charley chide Joe about laying up with some whore in Green River City and not getting back in time to help with wrecking the train. There's no doubt in my mind that Joe was part of that gang, but I couldn't say for sure that he was there when the deputies were murdered. He and Charley talked about it several times. I know—even if he wasn't there—he knows a lot about it.

Boswell said, "Do you recall them speaking of other crimes?"

"Yea, one other thing I remember them talking about…back in March of 'Seventy-seven, Frank Towle was with the gang that held up the stage near Deadwood, when the driver—young Johnny Slaughter—was shot and killed. Joe Minuse said Frank told him it was Reddy McKimie that shot Johnny Slaughter. But I don't know any more about that."

"Do any of you other men have any questions for Frank?"

They had no questions, but they agreed they'd need to press Joe Minuse about the Elk Mountain murders and the killing of Johnny Slaughter.

"Frank, I'm going to send you back to your cell. I think I speak for all of us when I say how pleased we are with your help. Because of you, one big robbery was prevented. And, at last, we may begin solving some major crimes."

"Sheriff, even though I did not do this for the money, if everything works out, and these are the men, I would appreciate laying claim to that reward."

"If everything works out, we'll do everything possible to get you two that reward."

"Thanks, Sheriff."

"You'd better thank Superintendent Dickinson. The money will be coming from the railroad and Carbon County."

Dickinson jumped in, "Frank, when the sheriff releases you, come over to the Union Pacific Hotel. We'll have a room for you. We'll see if we can find you some work while you wait for your reward claim to be processed."

"Thanks, Mr. Dickinson. I really appreciate your offer."

The deputy put the cuffs back on the prisoner. Boswell said, "We'll talk later, Frank," as Howard was led back to his cell.

The lawmen spent a few minutes discussing Howard's story and then turned their attention to the inventory list. Deputy Donahue came back to the room in time to hear the Sheriff say, "Gentlemen, I believe one of the horses we have at the county stable fits the description of one of the horses taken from Deputy Robert Widdowfield."

Boswell picked up the property list from the Elk Mountain murders and read aloud:

"Items the murderers took from Widdowfield and Vincent

"One: One dark grey mare branded 'HL' on the fore shoulder and 'A' on the left hip, a heavy California saddle, light grey saddle blanket, and new bridle

"Two: One light grey mare, eight years old, branded 'OC' on left hip, and 'anchor with cross' on left shoulder; had 'California saddle' newly leathered, with handholds on the hind tree

"Three: One bay mare, branded 'CB' on left shoulder, white spot in forehead, very heavy built and with a great many saddlemarks, no saddle[1]

"The dark grey mare and a California saddle that appear on this list are no doubt the same ones we took from our guest, Mr. Henry Harrington. Frank never said anything about Harrington being a member of the Elk Mountain gang, but I think we should interrogate him first and find out how he came into possession of that horse and saddle. Deputy, would you have the jailer bring Mr. Harrington here, please?"

Tuesday, December 24, 1878, 10:20 a.m.: The door opened, and the jailer escorted Hank Harrington—shackled and cuffed—into the room. He sat in the vacant chair across from Boswell.

After a period of cold silence, Boswell leaned forward: "Mr. Harrington, you know why you are here, so I'll get to the point. We intended to have the whole damn bunch of you on your way to Rawlins Springs on the afternoon train so you could be tried for murder and hanged up there. But the way things are developing outside, I don't think we could get you back to the train depot safely. I guess all the telegrams we sent and all the railroad men we've had to involve, along with the fact we had to bring you right through the middle of town, has drawn a lot of attention. I should've anticipated this might happen."

Harrington was belligerent. "What the hell are you talking about? Send us to Rawlins Springs to be *hanged*? We didn't do anything! We were just camped out at that ranch, and you arrested us and put us in jail for no reason."

"Stop right there. Your friends have already given you up. We know all about the robbery of the government warehouse, Union Pacific Railroad, and Thayer Hotel you were planning. We also know all about Trabing Store in Medicine Bow, and the ranches and stagecoaches you've robbed. And those crimes are minor compared to murdering two deputy sheriffs."

Struggling to remain emotionless, Harrington started, "I didn't have any—"

Deputy Donahue jumped to his feet, pulled out his pistol, and started around the corner of the table toward the prisoner. Pointing the gun at Harrington's head, Donahue yelled, "I'm going to kill this lying goddamn son of a bitch! Widdowfield was my friend. And now this murdering bastard is riding his horse."

Nottage and Dayton jumped up and grabbed Donahue, forcing his gun away from Harrington's head. Nottage shouted, "Get a hold of yourself, man! You can't shoot him in cold blood, even if he does have it coming. Give me that goddamned pistol."

"Ah, shit. Take it."

Nottage growled, "Sit down over there, Deputy. If you can't control yourself, get the hell out of this room and stay out."

Boswell waited as Nottage, Dayton, and Donahue sat down. Then Boswell continued the interrogation. "Mr. Harrington, like I was saying…much as I'd like to have you on your way to Rawlins Springs, it doesn't look like that will be possible. We're getting reports that a mob of vigilantes has formed…a 'citizens' committee.' They have one thing in mind, and that is to come here and deal with the lot of you.

"You see, a few years back, a real cold-blooded son of a bitch terrorized the committee that was trying to form the first city government. Eventually, they all resigned. You boys remember that, don't you? When that committee resigned, Asa Moore proclaimed himself mayor of this fine city and started appointing his thugs to fill every office, including sheriff. The territorial governor sent me here to bring law and order to Laramie. A new 'citizens' committee' formed to back me up. Of course, I never did know who they were, because they all wore masks, but they finally did have one hell of a shootout. They lynched Asa Moore, Con Wagner, and Big Ned Wilson in John Keane's unfinished building. They caught up with Long Steve Young and lynched him from that telegraph pole near the end of the Union Pacific Hotel. I was alone—there was nothing I could do to stop them. What a pity. You still got those old photographs somewhere, Sheriff Nottage?"

"Sure do. Want me to get them?"

"Yes. I think they might interest Mr. Harrington here."

A moment later, Nottage returned with two photographs and laid them on the table in front of Harrington. Pointing at a photograph of three hanging corpses, he asked, "Did you ever see two men hanged with the same rope? The bald one is Asa Moore, and his rope partner is Con Wagner. Big Ned Wilson apparently rated his own rope."

Pointing at the other photograph he said, "That there is Long Steve Young, hanging from the telegraph pole down by the depot."

Allowing Harrington time to take in the photographs, Boswell continued, "Those citizens' committees still show up on occasion when they think the law is not moving quick enough." He glanced at his watch. "I figure we have a little over six hours till dark. I don't think they'll come after you until then. They've got men all around this courthouse, so moving you to the Territorial Prison, or any other safe location, is out of the question."

"Sheriff!"

"Let me finish, Mr. Harrington. I just want you to know that I don't intend on getting any deputies or innocent people hurt or killed. I'm not going to let this new building get shot up and destroyed while trying to protect the likes of you, either. If the vigilantes come—and I do believe they will—I will unlock the front door, drop all the cell doors' keys in the middle of the floor, and leave. Before they hang you, they'll get a confession out of you. They pride themselves in not sending a man to hell with a lie in his mouth. The problem is, we probably will never be privy to the confession. So if you'd just tell us about your crimes now, we can set the record straight later."

Harrington, clearly shaken, glanced at Deputy Donahue and then turned back to Boswell, "Good God, Sheriff! You've got to protect me. You can't let them hang me for something I didn't do. I'll tell you everything I know, but you have to protect me. I had no idea that my horse and saddle ever belonged to that dead deputy. I'll tell you where I got that horse, and I'll confess to everything I've done. I'll tell you everything I know about each member of the gang. But you've got to protect me. You've got to promise you'll protect me!"

21: Lynching in Laramie, Wyoming Territory

22: Lynching in Laramie, Wyoming Territory

"Why is it that, when the chips are down, you sorry bastards always look to the law for protection?" Boswell paused and then asked, "You'll tell me everything? And you'll be prepared to testify against the rest of them in court when called upon to do so?"

"Yes, sir. I will!"

"Very well, then. Sheriff Nottage, will you get a clerk to take down Mr. Harrington's confession? And Harrington, one more thing: if I even begin to suspect you're lying to me or withholding any information, this agreement is off and—as far as I'm concerned—you'll be the first out the door tonight. You will answer for the crimes you've committed. However, if you tell us the truth, and the information we get from you is helpful, then we'll inform the judge about your cooperation. That might figure favorably in the judge's sentence."

"I understand, Sheriff. I'll cooperate."

Tuesday, December 24, 1878, 11:30 a.m.: The clerk recorded the date, time, and subject of the confession. Boswell said, "If everyone's ready, let's begin. For the record, would you state your name?"

"My name is Henry Harrington, but a lot of people call me 'Hank.'"

"Mr. Harrington, would you start by telling us how you came into possession of Deputy Widdowfield's horse and saddle?"

"Yes, sir. In late August or early September, I was in a saloon in Cheyenne when I met up with John Irwin, Fred Ruby, and a man called 'The Kid.' Later, I found out 'The Kid' is Charles Condon. None of us had work or any prospect of finding a job. After a lot of drinking, we talked about how we were going to get through the coming winter. We talked about how we'd all done our share of honest work when we could find it and how we'd all crossed over the line when there wasn't any work.

"We were all low on money, and we had no prospects, so we teamed up together and made plans. We knew there was a lot of gold and valuables moving across the Black Hills road between Deadwood and Cheyenne. We agreed we'd go a respectable distance north of Cheyenne so it'd cut down on the likelihood of us getting caught or recognized. Then we'd start robbing every ranch, stagecoach, freighter, and individual traveling on the road.

"Most of the coaches we saw on the road were the large six-horse Concords that carry twelve passengers. The treasure coaches—the ones we really wanted to find—were generally smaller and had extra shotgun messengers. Generally, they didn't carry passengers.

"We were about a day north of Cheyenne when we stopped a large Concord. Two of us stayed in the bushes, and John Irwin stood in the middle of the road and waved his hands to get them to stop. John Irwin is a game little bastard; I don't think he's afraid of anything. Anyway, the shotgun messenger kept a gun trained on him as he asked if he could get a ride to Cheyenne. Irwin said his horse had stepped in a hole, broke its leg, and had to be shot. He was so convincing that they were about ready to let him board. That's when we jumped out of the bushes and told them to throw up their hands. We told them we had them surrounded.

"They did as they were told. We were disappointed because this coach wasn't carrying a strong box or gold chest, and it had only three passengers aboard. We took the mail sacks, robbed the three passengers, took their ammunition, and sent them on their way.

"The next day, we robbed a northbound stagecoach and took what the passengers had and a mail sack. Later in the afternoon, we stopped a freight wagon, but the bullwhacker didn't have any money to speak of—just thirty-five dollars. He didn't have anything else we could use, so we took his money and let him pass. As we traveled north, we would avoid stage stations. When we camped in the evenings, we'd go through the mail sacks, take the money out, and burn the letters and sacks.

"Two days later…in the middle of Sunday afternoon…I think the date would have been about September eighth…we came upon a party of men resting their horses in a grassy open area alongside the road. There were five of them, and they were giving us a real good looking over. We were doing the same to them, just in case they might be lawmen. These men certainly didn't look like lawmen, so we rode over toward them. They had us outnumbered, and they clearly weren't afraid of us. We exchanged pleasantries, and they asked us to dismount and get acquainted. They said they were going to move back away from the road and set up camp for the night. They said we could join them if we wanted to. We decided to take them up on their invite.

"Those men turned out to be Frank James—he was going by the name 'McKinney' or 'Mack'—Joe Minuse, Dutch Charley, Frank Towle, and Sim Waun. Sim and Mack seemed very close…like close friends, or maybe even relatives.

"We got a fair piece off the road and found a good camp location near a stream. Dutch Charley and Frank rode off toward the west to see if they could find an antelope or deer, and the rest of us worked at setting up camp and getting wood for a fire. They hadn't been gone very long when we heard a single rifle report. Mack said, 'Looks like we eat good tonight.' About thirty minutes later, they came back into camp with two hindquarters of an antelope.

"I helped hobble their horses while they went down to the stream and cleaned up the hindquarters and themselves. A couple of the men fashioned two pikes to skewer the hindquarters, and we roasted the meat above the coals. All we had to do is cut off a piece of meat when we wanted it and give the pike a turn.

"Anyway, it didn't take long to figure out that we all were doing the same thing, and that it'd be better if we worked together. We stayed at this camp for the next three days. We made trips back to the road to wait for the next stagecoach or wagon to come by. John Irwin and Frank Towle both knew this road well, and they recommended that we move our operation further north. Frank said he knew a place on the new cutoff, where the stages crossed the Cheyenne River. He said the banks were real steep, forcing the stagecoaches to go real slow, and there were plenty of trees and brush to hide in. It'd be real easy to get the drop on the driver and shotgun messenger. John said he'd heard freighters and drivers refer to this place as 'Robbers Roost.' He said they didn't like the place because—even though it shortened the trip by many miles—it made sitting ducks out of them.

"This plan sounded real good to everyone except Mack and Sim, who didn't want to go any farther north. They said they were going to head back to…I think they said Missouri or Tennessee, or someplace in that part of the country. They wanted to spend the winter with friends and relatives. We all said our good-byes, and we headed north as they headed south toward Cheyenne. I think they were going to follow the North Platte River to Grand Island, Nebraska.

"There was a lot less tension in the group after Mack and Sim left. Frank Towle and Mack seemed to be vying to be the leader. Dutch Charley started to refer to Mack as 'Frank.' Dutch Charley talked about Frank's exploits—meaning Mack's—and that was not going over very well with Frank Towle."

"Mr. Harrington, do you think this 'Mack' or 'McKinney' was Frank James, the train robber? The cold-blooded murderer that rode with Quantrill's Raiders and Bloody Bill Anderson?"

"Sheriff, I'm not sure, but I think he is. Dutch Charley and Joe Minuse sure thought so. Like I was saying, Dutch Charley seemed to be in awe of Mack. He was praising Mack's plan to derail that passenger train, just like the one they derailed about fifty-five miles west of Des Moines, Iowa…near that little town of Adair, back in July of 'Seventy-three."

Leach interjected, "The engineer, John Rafferty, was killed in that wreck."

Harrington continued, "Dutch Charley said if it hadn't been for that section gang coming by and driving the spikes back in, it would've worked again someplace over near Medicine Bow. He'd say, 'Hell of a good plan. Just bad luck.'"

Boswell wanted to get back on track. "Mr. Harrington, at some point, I presume you're going to tell us how you came to have a murdered deputy's horse and saddle."

"Yes, sir. I'm getting to that. We traveled about half a day when my horse injured its left front ankle. It was swollen up about three times its normal size. I knew I had no choice but to take the first saddle horse that came our way.

"We found a place where the road crosses a creek. John Irwin called it 'Old Woman's Creek.' After looking the area over real good, we figured we could place a picket or lookout to watch north and south and signal us when a stage approached. The rest of us could hide in the brush and trees near the creek and leave our horses in the gulch, out of sight. When we were all satisfied with the location, we rode west of the road about a mile and set up camp for the night. The nights were getting pretty chilly.

"I believe it was Friday—I think it was September thirteenth—we rode back to the road, and The Kid was put out on picket. The other five of us hid our horses in the gulch, and then we hid on both sides of the road. We watched as a large wagon train went by. There were two very large wagons, both pulled by twenty-mule teams, and several smaller wagons pulled by teams of oxen. As they were coming up out of the bottom, those bullwhackers were cracking their whips. It sounded like rifle shots off in the distance.

"A couple hours later, the Kid signaled that the upstage to Deadwood was coming from the south, so we got ready to greet it. The area wasn't as good as Robbers Roost, but there was plenty of cover, and the stage would have to slow down as it came through Old Woman Creek. In about twenty minutes, the stage came over the bank. We stepped out of our cover and stopped the stage without a fight. There were two passengers—a man and a woman. We robbed the man of ten dollars and took nothing from the lady. When we shot open the treasure box, there was a lot of money in it, so we gave the man back his ten dollars.

"We kept the mail sack and sent the stage on its way. We took the mail down into the gulch and passed time going through it, looking for money and reading the letters. Maybe three hours later, the Kid signaled us that another stage was coming. This was the downstage to Cheyenne, and we hoped it would have a large shipment of gold in its treasure chest. In about twenty minutes, we saw the coach through the trees as it came over the bank and began slowing as it approached the creek. We stepped out and pointed guns at the driver, stopping the stage. We set to work robbing one of the two passengers and removing the mail sacks.

"Everyone was busy with the stagecoach and had quit watching our picket. The Kid fired a shot into the air to get our attention. No one had noticed, but two armed shotgun messengers had been riding about two hundred yards behind the coach. They'd tied up their horses and walked up close to us.

"When we heard our picket's warning shot, Frank Towle spotted them and fired a shot at them. One of the messengers fired back and killed Frank where he stood. We were on the other side of the coach, so they couldn't get a clear shot at us. We dropped the mail sacks, grabbed Frank, pulled him off to the side of the road, and ran for the cover of the gulch. One of the messengers yelled for the stage driver to leave, which he did…as fast as he could go.

"We spent probably a half hour exchanging fire from our protected position at the edge of the gulch. The messengers were shooting back from the trees. We had no choice but to stay there and shoot it out with them. They really wanted to retrieve those mail sacks. When they figured out they couldn't dislodge us, they worked their way back to their horses, crossed the creek, and followed the stage. I was glad, because I didn't want to kill anyone, and I didn't want to get killed.

"When we felt like it was safe to come out of the gulch, we walked back to where we had dragged Frank Towle. We could see the mail sacks in the road. We all were really shaken by the ordeal, and we just stood there for a long time, looking at poor Frank all covered with blood.

"Finally Joe said, 'We should've known that the first stage would report our whereabouts. Damn. It won't be long until they're back with reinforcements to retrieve this mail. We need to get out of this area as fast as we can.'

"Dutch Charley said, 'We can't just leave poor Frank here. We can take him back toward the camp and bury him. Then we'll get out of here.'

"John Irwin volunteered to go get Frank's horse to pack him on. That's when I said that—if no one had any objections—I'd trade my horse and saddle for Frank's. The stitching on my saddle was coming apart, and my horse was lame. Everyone agreed that this made sense—no need to bloody up a good saddle. So we packed Frank's body on my lame horse. After we buried Frank, we rode for a while before I threw my old saddle and tack away and turned the lame horse loose."

Boswell asked, "Weren't you afraid someone would find the horse and trace the brand back to you?"

"Sheriff, I said I'd tell you the truth: that horse couldn't be traced back to me because it wasn't my horse. I stole it in Cheyenne. That's the God's truth, how I came by that deputy's horse. I had no idea Frank's horse had belonged to a murdered deputy. Neither Dutch Charley nor Joe said a word about where Frank got that horse. The first I knew that horse belonged to a dead deputy was when you told me this morning. I swear to God."

"Go back a bit. What did you do with the body?"

"Well, we tied Frank across my saddle, and someone—I think it was Joe Minuse—picked up a coat that one of the shotgun messengers dropped in the road along with the mail sacks. We rode west for about a half mile, staying in the rock as much as possible so we couldn't be tracked. We found a sandy place about twenty-five yards south of the creek, near some rocks.

"We didn't have a shovel, so we scooped out a grave about two feet deep in the sand. We took poor Frank's pistol, rifle, and money, since he wouldn't be needing it anymore. We covered Frank with sand and put lots of rocks on his grave to keep the wild animals from digging him up.

"After that, we split up Frank's bedroll and broke camp. We stayed just off the wagon road and rode back to a cabin that Dutch Charley and Joe had, south of Fort Fetterman. We laid low there and took turns going to the fort for supplies, as we needed them.

"We ventured back to the Black Hills Stage road in early October and robbed one coach and a freighter. Then we went back to the cabin. It was getting colder, and there had been several snow storms, so it was nice to get back to the cabin. Dutch Charley and Joe came up with a plan to go over to Medicine Bow and rob the Trabing Brothers Store to get enough money and supplies to last us until we could figure out how to hit the railroad or some other big payroll. Both those guys knew the area real well, so this sounded like a good idea.

"We left the cabin on Friday, October fourth, and took a couple days riding over to Medicine Bow. On Sunday, the sixth, we robbed Trabing's and really loaded up on supplies. As we were leaving, John started a fire. He said it would cover what we had done and keep the citizens busy while we made good our escape.

"It was during this time that I learned that Dutch Charley and Frank Towle were part of the gang that killed those two deputies up on Elk Mountain last August. I couldn't figure out if Joe Minuse was there with them when the killings took place. For sure, he was part of the gang, even if he wasn't there for the killings.

"I never heard if the Trabings' store burned completely down or not. We returned to the cabin and laid low for most of November. We sat around talking and making plans for what we all called, 'The Big One.'"

Boswell interrupted, "Mr. Harrington, before you start telling us about the Rock Creek robbery, I want you to tell us everything you can remember hearing about the Elk Mountain killings, including the names of those who were involved."

"Yes, sir. They didn't say too much, especially when Mack and Sim were still with us. In fact, Dutch Charley and Joe Minuse talked more about the killings after we were camped at the ranch near Rock Creek. I guess that's because where the killings took place wasn't far from where we were camped when you arrested us.

"I remember they said that Frank Towle was the first to shoot. He shot one of the deputies in the mouth, and the bullet came out of the back of his head. Big Nose George was the first to shoot the other deputy, who was trying to ride away. Then they all started shooting at him and kept shooting until he fell off his horse. They said he kept trying to get up and shoot back at them, but they just kept shooting until he fell dead on the ground. I heard them say they robbed them. Got forty dollars, I think, and one of them took a pair of boots and a gun. I don't remember which one of them did that. Sheriff, I never heard them say anything about that horse I got from Frank Towle."

"Tell us their names the best you can remember."

"Well, there was Dutch Charley, Mack McKinney or Frank James, Sim Waun, Joe Minuse, a man named 'Tim,' and one called 'Sandy,' Frank Towle, Jack Campbell, and George Parott. They called him 'Big Nose' George behind his back because he really has a huge nose. But Charley said you don't dare call him that to his face because he just might kill you. Dutch Charley also has a nickname that he doesn't like - 'One-Winged Charley.'

"I never heard some of their last names. I guess after the failed robbery and murders, they rode together for a way and then split up. Big Nose George and Jack Campbell and—I think— Sandy headed north back up to the Powder River Country, where George has a cabin. I never heard which direction the rest headed. No…wait a minute…now, I remember. Joe Minuse said he met them over on the Green River. So maybe they headed west. I'm sorry…I'm just not sure now what they said. All the rest went over to that cabin south of Fort Fetterman, where we met up with them.

"I'm sorry, Sheriff—that's all I know about them."

"If you can remember anything else, you let us know."

"Yes, sir."

"Please proceed with your story, Mr. Harrington."

"From that point on, Charley and Joe did most of the planning. They were familiar with the area around Rock Creek Station, and they knew someone near there that they trusted to get good information about payrolls and such. Turned out, that was Otto Olsen. Dutch Charley seemed to know about when different payrolls would be moved by the railroad for their employees and the employees of the mines in Carbon. If we could hit these, the payroll for the Thayer's enterprises, and the payroll for the government warehouse, we'd end up with enough money to get through several winters.

"The more we talked about it, the better it seemed. Maybe we'd end up with enough money that we'd never have to work again. By the time the second week of December came around, thanks to the Trabings' store at Medicine Bow, we were well equipped for a winter camp and ready to go.

"We left the cabin and took our time riding over the Laramie Range, so as not to tire our horses too much. We rode to a little whiskey shop north of Rock Creek Station. We stayed for a night or two, talking to Otto, the proprietor. Like I said, it turned out, he was the spotter Dutch Charley and Joe had talked about—the one that would furnish payroll information to us.

"While we were there, Frank Howard came in to see Otto. We'd met Frank over at Fort Fetterman in the middle of November, and he came out to the cabin and stayed a few days with us. We told him we were going to be staying for a week or two before moving on, and Frank took the opportunity to repay our hospitality. He invited us to stay out at the ranch he was working at. Of course, we agreed. It was the perfect place to stay while we gathered the information we needed. Well, you know the rest of the story. That's where you arrested us."

A clerk knocked lightly on the door and handed Sheriff Nottage a telegram.

Boswell told Harrington, "I'm going to end our interview for now. But I may have more questions for you later. Deputy, would you return Mr. Harrington to his cell, and make sure he is kept away from the other prisoners?"

Harrington was docile as he left the room with the deputy, remembering this man's former outburst. Sheriff Nottage reported, "Here's the telegram from Sheriff Carr in Cheyenne that we have been waiting for. They've found John Irwin in the city jail, of all places. Seems the town marshal, David McDonald, had him locked up in his calaboose for shooting up the McDaniel Theater. As the telegram was passed around the room, Sheriff Nottage said, "We should retrieve him as soon as possible. I can send a deputy in the morning. Or would you like the honor, Boz?"

"I think it'd be best if I went," Boswell replied, "so I can bring Sheriff Carr and US Marshal Schnitger up to date on what we have here. It'll give me a chance to meet up with Boone May. Besides it'll keep the deputies close to town on Christmas Day; I know they'd appreciate that. Would you have a clerk telegraph Sheriff Carr back? Ask him to meet the morning train. Copy Schnitger and McDonald."

Dickinson joined the conversation, "Your deputy scared the hell out of me! I thought he was going to blow Harrington's brains all over the wall. I didn't know that he even knew Bob Widdowfield."

"I don't know whether he knew Bob or not. We staged the whole thing to get our guest to talk. Worked pretty well, don't you think? Like I always say: do what ya gotta do to get the job done."

"You had me convinced."

Leach grinned, "Boz, I am glad to see you haven't lost your touch at interviewing prisoners."

"Let's take a short break and get something to eat."

Tuesday, December 24, 1878, 1:30 p.m.: "Well, gentlemen," Boswell said, "now that we're all back, which of our charming guests shall we bring in next? The Kid?"

Before anyone could respond, Boswell answered his own question. "Yes, I think we should talk to The Kid next. He refused to give any other name when he was booked in last night. I think we should talk to him next, to help separate the murderers from the stagecoach and mail robbers. What he tells us could help solidify the information we have. Would any of you care to wager how long it will take me to get a name out of The Kid? It may not be his real name, but he *will* give us a name."

Dayton laughed, "I wouldn't be foolish enough to take that bet, Boz. Your stare would scare a dead man."

Everyone had a good laugh, and then Nottage told Deputy Donahue to have the jailer bring The Kid in. They agreed they'd use the same interrogation method they'd used with Harrington.

At 1:55 p.m., the jailer led The Kid into the room. He sat in the chair opposite Boswell. Silence prevailed until Boswell leaned forward in his chair and asked, "What's your name, kid?"

"They call me 'The Kid,' and that's good enough. You had no business arresting me at the ranch. I'm innocent of whatever you think I've done."

Boswell said, "Very well, Mr. Kid. We'll come back to that question a little later. You know why you're here, and I don't have time to play childish games with you." The sheriff recounted the story of the Elk Mountain murders and his desire to ship all of the outlaws to Rawlins Springs to be tried and hanged. "Of course, we hear that a group of vigilantes is forming in town. You know what will happen when they finally come to get your sorry asses? They will hang the lot of you, and we will be powerless to stop them."

The lawmen followed the script, with Deputy Donahue jumping to his feet and the two sheriffs wrestling away his pistol.

The Kid began confessing. "I don't want to hang for a murder I didn't commit. I'll tell everything I know."

23: Joe Minuse

"Well, Mr. Kid, while I send for a clerk to take down your statement, you can start by telling us your name."

"Sheriff, my name is Charles Condon."

Nineteen-year-old Charles Condon told them essentially the same story Henry Harrington had related. When the sheriffs were convinced he'd said everything, he was sent back to his cell. It was a quarter after three.

After a short break, the lawmen discussed who they would talk to next. Boswell mused, "I think we should interview Joe Minuse next, because we know he is one of the Elk Mountain gang members, but he may not have been involved in the murders. Dutch Charley is for sure one of the murderers, and he knows that if he is in any way tied to the killings, he'll hang for it. He'll be hard to crack. But if Minuse wasn't there when the killings took place, we may be able to get a confession out of him. We'll have to go at him with a vengeance to get the truth out of him. Are we all in agreement?"

When they nodded their agreement, Boswell turned, "Deputy, have the jailer bring in Joe Minuse."

Confessions

Tuesday, December 24, 1878, 3:40 p.m.: Joe Minuse entered the room, handcuffed and shackled. The jailer directed him to sit in the chair directly across from Boswell, who fixed his cold stare on him.

"What's your name?" Boz asked.

"John Minuse. Most people call me 'Joe.'"

"Well, Mr. Minuse, I want to congratulate you. Your friends have put a rope around your neck."

"What the hell are you talking about, Sheriff? Camping out while looking for work is not against the law!"

"That's true, Mr. Minuse. Camping out isn't against the law…unless you happen to be trespassing. I see no reason to charge you with the robberies of Trabing's Store and a few stagecoaches. Oh, then there's interfering with the United States Mail. We'll just go for the big one and indict you for first-degree murder. After all, if you're hung for murder, we won't have to waste our time trying you for any of the other crimes we can prove you committed. I like to think of that as letting the tail go with the hide. When they spring the trap door on the gallows, all overdue accounts get settled."

"I don't know what the hell you're talking about! I don't know anything about no goddamned murder!"

"Well, maybe you've committed so many murders you can't keep them straight. So I'll remind you of the two I'm speaking of. Just think back four months ago, when you and your good friends came down from the Powder River country and tried to derail that Union Pacific train. Surely, an intelligent man like you can remember back four short months.

"When you failed to derail the train, you, Dutch Charley, Mack, Big Nose George, Sim Waun, Sandy, Frank Towle, Tim Reed, and Jack Campbell rode up Rattlesnake Canyon on Elk Mountain. There, you ambushed and murdered two deputies in cold blood. Now, Joe, that was not real smart on your part. You traded a charge of attempted robbery, attempted interfering with the US Mail, attempted murder, criminal trespass, and destruction of property for a first-degree murder charge."

"I heard about those killings, and you're not going to pin them on me. I wasn't even in this part of the country. I had nothing to do with that."

"That's odd, Mr. Minuse. I wonder why Charley would say it was you who shot Deputy Widdowfield in the mouth? He said you and all the others—everyone except him—shot Deputy Vincents as he tried to ride up the canyon. Charley claims he didn't fire a shot, and he is willing to turn Territorial Evidence against all of you in exchange for a lighter sentence. What would you think of your associate if I told you that gutsy little bastard even asked about collecting the reward money? After thinking about it for a few minutes, I had to tell him that it might be possible and that I would look into it…if he were telling the truth."

Minuse was clearly unsettled. He said, "I don't believe a damn thing you're telling me. I already told you I wasn't even in that part of the country. I don't know any of those people you named. I just barely know Dutch Charley, and what reason would he have to lie about me? I've heard all about you, Boswell. I've heard how you force men to confess to things they never did. I'm not afraid of you, and I'll not be intimidated by you. I've done nothing wrong. So I suggest that you just give me back my personal things and my horse, and I'll ride out of here."

The room was quiet, as the lawmen anticipated Boswell's next move. Finally, Boswell stood up, walked over to the coat tree by the door, and took down a rope that had been coiled there. He walked back across the room and stopped in front of the prisoner.

"Mr. Minuse, I don't believe we'll turn you loose just yet. No, I think we'll just continue this interview across the street in that old barn. Deputy, remove the shackles from his ankles. Just in case he might try to 'escape,' I wouldn't want him to trip and fall."

Deputy Donahue removed the leg shackles and laid them on the table.

"All right, you tough little bastard. Stand up."

"I'm not going over there with you!"

Boswell slowly expanded the noose end of the rope, placed it around Joe's neck, and snugged it up. "Don't you tell me what you're not going to do, you lowlife son of a bitch. You can go willingly, or I'll tie the other end of this rope to my saddlehorn and drag your ass over there. I don't give a good goddamned if it pulls your head off. That's the only choice you have in this matter."

Minuse grumbled, "At least give me a coat. It's cold outside."

"Mr. Minuse, I'm not giving you your goddamn coat because I don't believe it is your coat. I think that coat you were wearing belongs to Boone May. It matches the description of the coat he lost when you sons of bitches robbed that stagecoach on September thirteenth. Remember…when your partner, Frank Towle, was killed? If that's Boone's coat, I want to get it back to him in the best condition possible. Besides, it's not worth the time it would take to get you a coat. I don't believe you'll be needing one for long.

"Now, if you gentlemen would like to join me, let's get our coats and head across the street."

Sheriff Nottage lingered. "I'll stay here. I have some things I need to get done. Just let me know what happened when you get back."

The group walked out the door, down the steps of the courthouse, and across the street to the old barn. Once inside the darkened building, Boswell looked at the shivering prisoner. "Mr. Minuse, tell me about the Elk Mountain murders."

"I already told you. I don't know nothing about it. I wasn't there!"

Boswell threw the other end of the rope over a roof beam and ordered Deputy Donahue to help him pull it. Together, they lifted Minuse a foot off the ground. The prisoner thrashed around, eyes bulging, until he was about to pass out.

Finally Boswell ordered, "Let him drop."

Minuse fell to the ground, and Boswell reached down and loosened the noose. The prisoner gulped a breath of air and continued gasping until he regained full consciousness.

Boswell looked at Dickinson and Leach. "Gentlemen, feel free to leave if you'd like to."

"No, Sheriff. We'll see this through."

Boswell turned back to Minuse. "Alright, Minuse, you lily-livered bastard. I'm going to give you one last chance to tell me about the Elk Mountain murders. That was your only warning. Next time you go up, we'll tie off the rope. You can go to hell with that lie in your mouth. The grey wolves on the summit will be chewing on your carcass before the sun goes down. I damn well won't waste a spot in Potters Field on an escaped prisoner. Personally, I wouldn't waste my piss on you if you were on fire."

Boswell pulled out his pocket watch and said, "Joe, you have thirty seconds to make up your mind."

Thirty seconds passed, and Boswell pulled the rope taut. Then he turned to Donahue and directed, "Take him up, and tie him off!"

As the men pulled the slack out of the rope, Minuse rolled over and—with the help of his elbows—got to his knees. Suddenly contrite, he begged, "Stop! Don't do this! I'll tell you. I'll tell you everything I know."

Boswell gave the rope some slack. "Start talking, you sorry bastard. And you damn well better tell us everything."

Between gasps, Minuse blurted, "I know what happened. I know everything about what happened, because I was told about it. I was a member of the gang. I was supposed to meet up with them and help rob the train, but I didn't get back from Brown's Park in time. I was helping steal some horses near Green River City. I'd rather go to jail for stealing horses than get hung for a murder I didn't commit."

Boswell said, "Start talking - and you had better convince me you're not lying."

Minuse swallowed hard before he began, "I am not lying. Just give me a chance to catch my breath. It was too late to get back to help with the train, so I stayed in the Green River area with some friends. Six or seven days later, three members of the gang rode over to where I was staying and holed up for several days. That's when I found out that the train robbery had been a failure and that they'd murdered two deputies."

"Who were these men?"

"Big Nose George Parott, Jack Campbell, and Sandy. They told me what happened. They said the group had split up, and the rest of them went back over to the cabin near Fort Fetterman. They said they were going up around the Jackson Hole area for a while and then probably circle back to Big Nose George's cabin near Pumpkin Buttes. They invited me to join them, but I wanted to go back over and work the Deadwood Stage road before winter set in. After they left the Green River area, I headed back to the hideout south of Fort Fetterman to try to meet up with the rest of the group again."

Boswell demanded, "Tell me all the names. I want a complete list."

"There was 'Mack' or 'McKinney,' who was more or less the leader. He talked us into going after a train for its payroll. Sim Waun…I think he and Mack might be related. Mack is Frank James. He just uses the name 'McKinney.' The others were Big Nose George Parott, Tim Reed, Frank Towle—Frank was killed a while back over on the Deadwood Stage road—Jack Campbell, Dutch Charley, and John Wells…we all called him 'Sandy.'"

"What is Dutch Charley's last name?"

"Charley said his last name is Clarke, but I've heard him use 'Bates' and 'Randall.' I'm not certain, but I think it's really 'Clarke.'"

"Have you ever heard him referred to as, 'One-Winged Charley?'"

"Yeah. Several years back, a lot of people called him that. He has tried to discourage that name. He wants to be called 'Dutch Charley.' A lot of the boys use false names to protect their families from shame, just in case they get caught."

Boswell gave a hard jerk on the rope and said, "And there's one other member... you!"

"Sheriff, honest to God, I swear that I wasn't there. I was part of the gang and should have been there, but I didn't get back from Brown's Park in time. I wasn't there when the murders took place. All I know about that is what the other men told me. If you'll give me a chance, I can prove what I say."

"I'm a long way from being convinced, but you've bought yourself a little time. I'm going to take you back to the jail. I'll expect a full statement from you. The first time I even suspect that you are leaving anything out, or lying, I'll finish the job. Do you understand me?"

"Yes, sir."

"And you'll also tell me all about the stagecoaches you've robbed?"

"Yes, sir."

"Tell me, now. Where did you get that coat?"

"I got it at the stage robbery when Frank Towle was killed. One of the shotgun messengers dropped it, and he couldn't get back to it without getting shot. So when the two messengers left, I took the coat. It was much better than the one that I was wearing. I don't know the messengers' names."

Boswell and the deputy pulled Minuse to his feet, steadying him as he shook from fear and cold. Boswell removed the rope from his neck and coiled it up. It was beginning to get dark, and the temperature had dropped to about nine degrees below zero. The party left the barn and headed back across to the courthouse.

Boswell summoned the jailer. "It appears that Mr. Minuse has pissed himself. Take him down and get him a dry pair of trousers. Then bring him back so we can finish our interview."

As the men hung up their coats, Dickinson asked, "Would you have really hanged him if he hadn't talked?"

Boswell turned toward his friends and winked, "He talked. So I guess we'll never know, will we?"

Around half past five, the jailer brought Minuse back into the room and walked him over to the same chair. Following jail policy, Deputy Donahue picked up the shackles and put them back on the prisoner. Boswell ordered, "Please send a clerk in to take down Mr. Minuse's statement. And get him a cup of coffee. He looks like he could use it."

As the clerk entered the room, Minuse sat quietly, all of his bravado gone. Sheriff Nottage came back into the room. "Well, it looks like Mr. Minuse did not escape."

"If everyone is ready to proceed, then let's get started."

Joe Minuse's version of the crime filled in gaps in the information they'd already gathered.

"How did Harrington come by that horse and saddle?"

"Frank Towle took the horse and saddle from one of the dead deputies. When Frank was killed, we all agreed that Harrington could have them."

"Did Harrington know that the horse and saddle were taken from the dead deputies?"

"No, I'm quite sure he had no idea where Frank got that horse and saddle."

"Who took the newly leathered California saddle?"

"Dutch Charley took it. He was still using it when you arrested us."

"What happened to Deputy Widdowfield's boots?"

"I ran into Big Nose George, Sandy, and Jack Campbell over on the Green River a few days after they killed those deputies. Jack Campbell said he was wearing the boots he pulled off the man Frank shot…the one they said fell dead into the firepit. When I finally did meet up with Frank Towle and Dutch Charley, they told me pretty much the same thing. They said Frank shot the first man, and George Parott was the first to shoot the second man. Then all of them started shooting him, until he was dead. They said that after the killings, Sim Waun led them out of that country. Later, they split up and went different ways."

Leach questioned Minuse about Frank Towle's version of the murder of Johnny Slaughter, just a few miles out of Deadwood. The prisoner told him that Frank Towle had identified Robert "Reddy" McKimie as the one who had shot Slaughter. He'd shot him through the heart with a shotgun during the attempted robbery of the Cheyenne-Black Hills upstage. Towle had said that the gang members were angry with McKimie for killing young Slaughter, but they'd figured McKimie had murdered Johnny because he was afraid the young driver would recognize his red hair, since McKimie had known Slaughter and his father, the city marshal, when he'd worked as a utility man at the Inter-Ocean Hotel back in 1875.

When asked about other gang members involved in that crime, Minuse said Towle had named Joel Collins and Sam Bass as the leaders. Towle, McKimie, and either Jim Berry or Heffridge were the other members. They'd stepped out on the road and ordered the driver to stop. McKimie had shot Johnny Slaughter, who'd fallen from the coach boot and was dead when he hit the ground. The team of six horses spooked and took off running, headed for town. Towle had told him they'd shot at the coach several times, but with no driver, nothing could stop it.

At six-thirty, they returned Joe Minuse to his jail cell.

Sheriff Nottage said, "Well, that certainly is some story. With the information he gave us, it's hard to believe that he could know that much about the murders without being there in person."

"I know what you mean," replied Boswell. "Part of me believes he wasn't there, and part of me believes he was. Anyway, the information we got from him sure gives us a picture of what took place. Tomorrow, I'll go to Cheyenne and pick up Irwin and bring him back here so we can continue the interviews on Thursday. I don't think we'll get much out of Dutch Charley. He obviously knows that there can only be one outcome for him, and that's a hangman's rope."

"Are you sure you want to go to Cheyenne tomorrow…on Christmas?"

"I know it's Christmas, but I think I'd better go. We want to keep the momentum on this case. I should be back in the early afternoon. And it gives me a chance to see my old friends Sheriff Carr, US

Marshal Schnitger, and possibly Sheriff-elect George Draper. I can bring them up to date. They may be able to clear up a lot of ranch and stagecoach robberies that have taken place the length of Laramie County and all the way to Deadwood.

"I hope Boone May is in—or on his way to—Cheyenne. I'd like him to come to Laramie to identify his coat and get directions to where these bastards buried Frank Towle. That could be worth some real money to Boone.

"Millard, you have a connection to this McKimie fellow, as I recall. Am I remembering correctly?"

Leach responded, "In early November last year, I got a tip from one of my sources that a man who was possibly connected to the Big Springs, Nebraska train robbery was living in Hillsboro, Ohio. It was Robert McKimie. He was spending a lot of money. There was somewhere between forty and sixty thouand dollars taken in that robbery, so—needless to say—I'd been chasing every lead I received. When I heard about this man and his extravagant spending, I thought I'd better go check him out.

"I went to Hillsboro and quietly gathered information on the man. I learned he'd returned to Hillsboro in September with a large sum of money. Of course, that cleared him of the Big Springs Robbery, because it took place in October 1877. However, it's not likely that a man like McKimie would have earned that kind of money legally. On my way back, I ran into Seth Bullock in Ogallala, Nebraska. You probably know that Seth has been the chief defective of the Black Hills Detective Agency since he lost the election for sheriff.

"I gave Seth the best description I could of McKimie. Seth said he'd been chasing this little bastard all over the territories. He went with me to Cheyenne, where we reported this information to Luke Voorhees.

"Luke immediately sought extradition papers from Governor John Hoyt, so he could bring McKimie back to Wyoming Territory. Luke wanted McKimie to stand trial for three stage robberies that he, Dunk Blackburn, James Wall, Webster, and Bill Bevins committed. From there, Luke would take McKimie to Dakota Territory and try him for the murder of Johnny Slaughter.

"Anyway—to make a long story short—local law officers arrested and held Robert McKimie. Seth tried, without success, to extradite him in a proper legal manner. The governor of Ohio, Richard Bishop, signed the papers and then rescinded them. Everyone seemed to believe it was because McKimie's wife's well-to-do family had lots of political connections.

"By the end of January of this year, Luke and Seth saw that the extradition was not going to happen, and they returned to the territories. Shortly thereafter, McKimie escaped from jail. We found out after he was recaptured that he had headed east, where he was joined by his wife. They remained in Richmond, Virginia, for a while and then went to Raleigh, North Carolina, where they stayed for a month. They traveled on to Charleston, South Carolina, and stayed another month there. Then they moved on to Savannah, Georgia, for two months, when Mrs. McKimie feared Robert would be recaptured.

"Apparently they had studied extradition laws and felt they'd be safe in Nassau. But they ran out of money, so Robert left his wife in Nassau and came back to New York. Then he moved on to Ohio, where he went back to his trade as a robber and thief until he was arrested by Detective John Norris. After his arrest, his wife returned to Chillicothe, Ohio, to be near him. A couple of weeks back, he attempted another jailbreak. That's when Seth Bullock left for Ohio to try to extradite him to Wyoming Territory. I just heard this from Luke Voorhees the day before yesterday, when I stopped off in Cheyenne on my way back from Ogallala."

Nottage said, "Interesting, Millard. Good to know." Turning to Boswell, he said, "I hate to see you go to Cheyenne on Christmas Day, but that's your call, Boz."

"Gentlemen, it's Christmas Eve. Let's go spend some time with our families. I hope you all have a very merry Christmas. I'll see you bright and early, Thursday morning."

As he removed his heavy jacket from the coat tree, Boswell said, "Ed, Millard…I'll walk with you back to the depot. I want to stop at Western Union and send Sheriff Lawry and Sheriff-elect-Rankin an update. I think I'm going to make their day."

Footnotes:
1. Property taken from dead deputies was listed in the *Laramie Sentinel* August 28, 1878.

Chapter 7

No Rest for Lawmen

Christmas Day, Wednesday, December 25, 1878: Sheriff-elect Boswell arrived at the Union Pacific Train Station in Cheyenne on the early morning eastbound train. Sheriff Thomas Jefferson Carr and Sheriff-elect George W. Draper met him. US Marshal Gustav Schnitger couldn't make it because he had gone to Fort Fetterman. Boswell greeted his associates, "It's good to see you. Merry Christmas!"

"It's good to see you, too, Boz. Merry Christmas! I'd like to introduce you to George Draper."

"I already know George. We met back in 1876 when he was freighting from Medicine Bow up to Fort Fetterman. I wasn't sure what happened to you after that, George."

"Well, Boz, I came down to Cheyenne and got into the hardware business. Then some friends talked me into running for sheriff, and—lo and behold—I got elected."

"What say we go over and get some breakfast? I'll bring you up to date on what we've found out so far from that bunch we arrested northeast of Rock Creek Station. By the time we're done interviewing this gang of outlaws, we'll be able to shed some light on the Elk Mountain murders. I think we'll also solve quite a few of the robberies in Albany County, Carbon County, and Laramie County, too."

Sheriff Carr gestured, "Come on. Let's head over to the Inter-Ocean Hotel for breakfast. Then we can walk over to the jail, get Irwin, and take him back to the depot in the jail wagon."

The law officers walked to the corner of 16th and Hill Streets, snow crunching under foot. The temperature had risen to about five degrees below zero, and a slight wind was blowing out of the northwest. Over breakfast, Boswell brought them up to date on the interviews with the outlaws. Then he asked Sheriff Carr, "You know that stage robbery when Boone and Johnny shot it out with the outlaws? Boone said he shot one of them and believed he might have killed him."

"Sure, I remember."

24: Thomas J. Carr, Sheriff, Laramie County, Wyoming Territory.

"Well, it's true. He did kill one of them. Even more important, the man he killed was Frank Towle, and Frank Towle was one of the murderers of Deputies Widdowfield and Vincents on Elk Mountain. John Irwin was part of the gang that was robbing that stagecoach when Towle was killed. With what I plan to get out of him, plus what we already have, I hope to pinpoint where they buried Towle. If I can find out the location, I'll get that information to Boone so he can go dig for him. Doesn't Laramie County still have that two-hundred-dollar reward for the killing or capture of road agents?"

25: Union Pacific Hotel and Depot, Cheyenne, Wyoming Territory

"They sure do."

"Well, old Boone can collect that reward and then go right on to Rawlins Springs and put in for that two-thousand-dollar reward they have on the head of each outlaw. Carbon County and the Union Pacific Railroad kicked in a thousand dollars each for every outlaw. They're figuring on paying up to twenty thousand, total. We can identify eight outlaws, for sure. The one named 'Joe Minuse'…we're still on the fence about him. But he would make it nine."

After breakfast, Sheriff Carr gestured, "Let's walk over to the city jail. You can get with Marshal McDonald and fill out the transfer papers. I know he'll be glad to get rid of Irwin. He always has a full house and needs the room. With the subordination of charges, it looks like he'll be going to territorial prison rather than coming back here. Anyway, after you get your prisoner, we'll get you on the next westbound passenger train or in the caboose of the next freight train, whichever will get you back to Laramie the quickest. You'll be able to spend the rest of Christmas Day with your family. We'll telegraph your office so a deputy can meet whatever train we put you on."

"Thanks. I'd really appreciate that," replied said Boswell.

The lawmen walked over to the city jail, which was located behind city hall and just across 17th Street from the hook-and-ladder company. Boswell brought Town Marshal McDonald up to date on the investigation, telling him it might not solve many Cheyenne crimes but could help solve some crimes committed in Laramie County. Marshal McDonald reported that he hadn't told Irwin he would be transferred to Albany County, thinking that the element of surprise might help the interrogation.

"Good thinking," Boswell said. "Well, it's good to see everyone. Wish I could stay a while and visit, but I need to get Irwin back over the hill to the Laramie jail. I'd like to have a little bit of Christmas Day with my family."

"I'll have the jailer get Irwin. Let's get you on your way."

By nine-thirty, everything was ready for the transfer. John Irwin was, indeed, surprised to learn he was being transferred to Laramie, where more serious charges would be filed against him. At a minimum, he would be charged with stealing and interfering with the US Mail. He eyed the lawmen nervously, no longer the ruffian he'd been when arrested. "What the hell is going on here? I already told you I'd pay for the damage to the theater. You can't ship me off to Laramie. I haven't done anything in Laramie. I haven't been to Laramie in over a year!"

Marshal McDonald told him, "Shut your damned mouth and sit down, or I'll set you down."

Boswell stepped in. "I'm Albany County Sheriff Nathaniel Boswell, and I'll be escorting you to Laramie on the next westbound train. You can go to Laramie the easy way or the hard way. Doesn't matter to me, but to Laramie you will go. There are serious charges waiting for you there—much more serious than shooting up the McDaniel Theater. I'll say this one time. Shut your mouth, and keep it shut. You'll have plenty of time to talk tomorrow. You'll speak only when I direct you to do so. You best understand me now; I won't stand for any rude behavior. And when you answer me, it will be, 'Yes, sir' and 'No, sir.' Do I make myself clear?"

Irwin hung his head. "Yes, sir."

The jailer came into the room with a floursack filled with Irwin's personal effects. "Sheriff, his pistol, holster, and cartridge belt—minus the cartridges, of course—are in the sack. We'll keep his horse, saddle, and bedroll at the county stable for the time being. The money he had in his possession will be turned over to the Court, and they can deal with the damages to McDaniel Theater. By the way, Sheriff Boswell, Boone May is waiting for you out front. He said he's going to Laramie City with you."

"Great! I was hoping he was here in Cheyenne. My telegram must have reached him. It'll be great to have a chance to talk to him. Boone always has new adventures to share."

"Tomorrow, we should have a chance to check the stolen livestock list against the horse Irwin had in his possession. Since Mr. Irwin doesn't have a bill of sale on that animal, I suspect it's stolen. We'll let you know what we find out."

"Thanks. Appreciate that."

The jailer reached into the sack and retrieved a heavy coat for Irwin to wear. "Sheriff, just sign the release form, and Mr. Irwin is yours."

Reaching into his coat pocket, Boswell pulled out a set of handcuffs and said, "I brought my own cuffs."

"What about leg irons? Do you want to put him in leg irons?"

"I don't think that'll be necessary for this trip. Do you, Mr. Irwin?"

"No, sir, Sheriff. I don't want to end up dead on Christmas Day."

Daniel Boone May was waiting in the outer office. He stuck out his hand and said, "It's good to see you, Boz. I got your telegram. I'm damn well ready to go identify my coat."

"Good to see you, Boone. I'm pleased you were in town and can make the trip to Laramie City with me and Mr. Irwin here."

Boone looked at John Irwin and said, "Is this little piss ant one of them that tried to shoot me?"

"He sure is."

John Irwin turned his full attention to Boone. When he realized this was the man that had killed Frank Towle, he became visibly shaken.

"Don't worry, you back-shooting little bastard. I'm not going to hurt you. I'll let the law take care of you."

Farewells said, the lawmen, Boone May, and John Irwin went out the door and headed toward the waiting jail wagon, which would take them to the railroad depot. No one said much. The men entered the yard office.

The yardmaster was expecting them. "Well, gentlemen, your timing is just about perfect. We have a westbound freight over on South 4 that is scheduled to depart at ten forty-five. Conductor Davis left here about twenty minutes ago. I told him he'd probably have several guests in his caboose for the trip to Laramie. He and the brakeman are walking the train now and should be back to the caboose about the time you get there.

"You'll have one siding stop to let an eastbound go by and one other twenty-minute stop at the Sherman Station. You should arrive in Laramie City about three p.m. We'll telegraph your office so they can send someone down to the railroad yard to pick you up, Sheriff."

"Thanks so much, and Merry Christmas to you."

"Merry Christmas to all of you. Now, you'd better get going."

Sheriff Carr and Marshal McDonald accompanied Sheriff Boswell, Boone May, and John Irwin to the caboose and waited until they were aboard. The men then parted company.

The return trip to Laramie was without incident. The train arrived on time, and a jail wagon was waiting for them. Shortly after three-thirty, John Irwin was booked into the Albany County Jail. The jailer was instructed to keep Irwin separated from the rest of the Rock Creek outlaws.

"I will deal with Mr. Irwin in the morning. Now, Mr. May and I will go home and spend the rest of Christmas Day with Martha and my daughter, Minnie."

On their way home, Boone turned to Boswell. "Thank you, Boz, for inviting me to your home for Christmas dinner."

"My old friend, it's my pleasure to have you join my family this evening."

Thursday, December 26, 1878, 8:30 a.m.: Sheriff Nottage and his deputies were already on duty when Boone May arrived. Boswell came in a little later and greeted them. "Good morning, gentlemen. I overslept this morning. When I finally got out of bed, Martha had breakfast waiting for me, and I sure couldn't pass that up."

Nottage said, "Good morning, Boz. I think you deserve a little extra sleep this morning."

Boswell asked, "Do you all know Boone?"

Deputy Donahue chimed in, "Everybody knows Boone! Boz, how about a cup of hot coffee?"

"Thanks. I'll just help myself. Boone, have you had a chance to look at the coat?"

"Yes, Boz. No question about it—it's mine. Do you see that small tear that has been mended at the edge of the left pocket? That repair is damn sure my handiwork. It's dirty and a little worse for wear, but it's my coat."

Boswell took a few sips of his coffee. "Is Tom Dayton coming over this morning?"

"I haven't heard from him. I talked to Dickinson this morning at the Union Pacific Eating House; he said he was going to send Special Agent Leach over about eight-thirty a.m. He had some reports to get out, so he said to go ahead and get started without him. He should be over between ten and ten-thirty, when he gets finished."

"I think we should resume our interviews with Fred Robie, and then John Irwin. We should save Dutch Charley for last, so we can use everything we've learned to try to get him to confess. Truthfully, I don't think we'll get much out of him."

Sheriff Nottage asked, "What do you want to do with Otto Olsen?"

"Let's just hang onto him for a few more days and see if we can sweat anything else out of him. The most we've got on him now is that he furnished information that could have been obtained through legitimate sources. At best, we could charge him with being an accomplice before the fact. The robbery was planned, but we stopped it before they could pull it off. Even if the judge gave him thirty days in jail, it would just be thirty days of feeding the sorry bastard at public expense.

"Of course, he was selling whiskey out of that shithole he calls his 'whiskey house.' But I think the best we can do is try scaring him back onto the straight and narrow. Unless, of course, the railroad or government find anything of value at that shack of his. Then it may justify the cost of a trial."

"I think you're right. If we don't come up with something else, we would be money ahead to turn him loose the first part of next week. We don't need any more worthless bastards using the county jail to receive two hots and a cot while they wait for spring."

The door opened, and Leach walked in. "Good morning, gentlemen." Looking around the room, his attention focused on May. "Boone May—I can't believe it. I don't see you for months, and then I suddenly keep running into you everywhere I go. Did they run your ass out of Deadwood again?"

"Well, Agent Leach…fancy meeting you here. I thought you'd be back over around Ogallala, chasing tramps."

"Naw, I ran all the tramps out of town. And I didn't lose my coat. By the way, did you get a chance to look at—"

"Yes, I did. Like I told Boz, there's absolutely no question about it…that's my coat. The Sheriff told me that these bastards confirmed I killed one of their group—Frank Towle. If we can get good directions to the place they disposed of his body, I'll try to find it next time I go by there. Hopefully, the snow isn't deep enough to cover the rocks they placed on his grave. The sooner I can find him, the easier it will be to identify him. God only knows what kind of shape that head is in already. We've had a lot of warm days since I killed the bastard. They buried him in sand, and probably not too deep, so I think I can dig him up. I hope I don't have to wait until spring, when the frost starts to come out of the ground. I may as well see if I can get the reward that's on his head. Of course, if I do, I'll split it with Johnny Zimmerman."

Nottage asked "How long are you going to stay here?"

"I'm going to sit in on the interviews today and go back to Cheyenne tomorrow."

Boswell said, "If everyone's ready, let's bring in Mr. Robie."

Thursday, December 26, 1878, 9:35 a.m.: The jailer escorted Fred Robie to a chair across from Boswell. Boswell took his time asking the first question, "What's your full name?"

"Frederic C. Robie. But most people just call me Fred."

The same questioning technique was used on Fred Robie as was used on Hank Harrington. Robie was singing like a coal mine canary by the time Superintendent Dickinson came into the room and sat down by Special Agent Leach. Robie gave a full confession, swearing he would plead guilty to the judge, and offering to testify against the others. He said that he had no intention of being tried for murders he had nothing to do with. About noon, the group finished with Fred Robie and sent him back to his cell.

Sheriff Nottage said, "Let's take a break and go get something to eat. We'll meet back here about one-thirty to continue."

In the afternoon, Tom Dayton rejoined the group. They brought him up to date, while the jailer went to get John Irwin. Irwin entered the room wearing handcuffs and shackles. He was ordered to sit in the chair directly across from Boswell.

Boswell began, "Gentlemen, this is John Irwin. Mr. Irwin's profession is robbing stagecoaches and ranches and shooting up theaters in Cheyenne. He is the missing member of the gang that we brought in on Tuesday. Mr. Irwin was not at Rock Creek when we captured the rest of the gang because he was sent to Cheyenne to get supplies. But instead of picking up the supplies, Mr. Irwin got all liquored up. When he was done chasing whores, he decided to shoot up the Gold Room at the McDaniel Theater.

"Gentlemen, the most important thing you need to know about Mr. Irwin is that he's one of the murderers of Deputies Widdowfield and Vincents on Elk Mountain. You may rest assured, after giving up most of Christmas Day to retrieve him, I do not have much use for Mr. Irwin. With that in mind,

I hope Mr. Irwin does not try my patience during this interview. So, we shall proceed. What is your name?"

"John Irwin."

"How old are you?"

"Twenty-eight."

For the prisoner's benefit, Boswell stopped the questioning and turned to Sheriff Nottage and Superintendent Dickinson, "Did you emphasize to all your deputies, jailers, and Union Pacific employees how important it is to keep this information to ourselves? If Doc Hayford, the editor of the *Sentinel*, gets wind that we have the deputies' murderers in our jail, he'll print it. All the other newspapers in the Territory will pick up on it, and if that happens, we won't stand a snowball's chance in hell of getting Irwin here and the rest of his gang to Rawlins Springs alive so Lawry or Rankin can hang the bastards."

Sheriff Nottage said, "We've done everything we can to keep this quiet. We've even told everyone they'll be fired if they leak this information. So far, the only thing that's leaked is that these outlaws are Deadwood Stage robbers and that they were planning to rob Thayer's enterprises, the Union Pacific Railroad, and the government warehouse payrolls at Rock Creek."

"Well, I'm hoping the last train robbery near Fort Steele will keep their attention for a while…at least until we have a chance to control the release of this information."

Dayton jumped in, "My sources tell me word is already on the street, and some vigilantes are keeping an eye on the courthouse, as we speak."

Boswell looked at Nottage. "You're still sheriff for a few more days. I think you should let the deputies know that if the vigilantes come for these bastards, they should just open the cells and let them do what they want. These lowlife sons of bitches are as worthless as the teats on a boar, and they certainly aren't worth getting any deputies hurt or killed trying to protect them."

"I full well agree. I'll give the order now. No extraordinary force or efforts are to be used if vigilantes come." Nottage left the room.

Boswell turned back to Irwin and asked, "Did you shoot Deputy Widdowfield in the face before, or after, you shot Deputy Vincents in the back?"

Irwin looked shaken. "Shooting a deputy in the face? What the hell are you talking about? I never shot anybody, let alone one of those deputies. I had nothing to do with that!"

As if on cue, Deputy Donahue jumped to his feet and repeated the performance he had given in the prior interrogations. Tom Dayton jumped up and grabbed the deputy's gun hand, pushing it away from Irwin's face. Boswell yelled at the deputy, "Put that damn gun away, and get out of here. I'm not going to let you shoot this son of a bitch in cold blood. He's going to be hanged soon enough, one way or the other. Now, get out of here, and go cool down!"

Boone May and Detective Leach refrained from showing their amusement as the deputy reluctantly put his revolver back in its holster. Looking enraged, he stormed out, slamming the door behind him. Sheriff Nottage returned to the room. "What's all the yelling about? What's going on in here?"

"Everything's all right, Sheriff. We were about a half-second away from having another prisoner escape and disappear."

"My term is up in a few days, and I damn sure don't need to answer any inquiries about escaped prisoners. Some of these young deputies are wound up tighter than the spring on a two-dollar watch."

John Irwin was clearly taken back. Once again, the performance had done the trick.

When everyone was seated, Sheriff Boswell resumed his inquiries. "For the last goddamned time, tell me about shooting those deputies on Elk Mountain."

Irwin squirmed as he confessed to some of his lesser crimes, declaring his innocence in the case of the murdered deputies. He said he'd pay the price for what he'd done…that he'd turn Territorial Evidence on everyone else, if necessary. It was clear he wanted no part of the blame for that crime.

By four o'clock, Irwin had finished his statement and was on his way back to his cell. Boswell said, "Let's take a fifteen-minute break and then bring in Mr. Dutch Charley."

"Sounds good to me," said Nottage.

Dayton told them, "I'll say one thing—I admire how quick these skunk bastards turn on each other, when the right pressure is brought to bear."

At four-fifteen, the jailer brought in Dutch Charley, wearing shackles and handcuffs. The lawmen watched him survey the room until he locked stares with Boswell.

"What's your name, young man?"

Sullenly, the prisoner replied, "Charles. Charles Randall."

"Do you go by the nickname 'Dutch Charley?'"

"I do."

"Why are you called 'Dutch Charley?'"

"When I was young, I had an uncle that said I sounded like a little Dutchman. He'd ask me to say certain words, and then he'd make fun of the way I said them. The nickname stuck. Now I kinda like it."

"When you were brought in, you gave your name as 'Charles Bates.' Which is it—'Bates' or 'Randall?' Or would it really be 'Clarke?' Maybe you're 'One-Winged Charley.'"

"Don't matter. One name's good as the next."

"That's true, I suppose. I notice you don't change your first name or your nickname."

"Never saw a reason to."

"But you have a reason to keep changing your last name?"

"Like I said, it doesn't matter anyway."

"All right, we'll let that go for now. Do you know why I had the jailer take your boots yesterday and give you that old, used pair you're wearing?"

"No idea. Guess he wanted them for himself. Wasn't much I could do to stop him."

"I find it strange, Dutch Charley, that you haven't raised any objections to being jailed in Laramie, and you haven't professed your innocence either. Why is that?"

"Didn't see any need to ask. Figured you'd tell me when you were good and ready."

"Well, you figured right. You know, Dutch Charley…I must be superstitious, because I know that I'd be mighty bothered about wearing a dead man's boots. Especially a man I'd killed. Myself, I'd worry that something bad might come from such an evil act."

"What the hell you are talking about? I bought those boots new. They damn sure never belonged to no dead man!"

"That will be enough of your bullshit Mister Dutch Charley. You had in your possession a murdered deputy's rifle, and you were wearing his boots. Your friend, Joe Minuse, is quite willing to testify against you and Big Nose George, McKinney, Sim Waun, Jack Campbell, Sandy Wells, Tim Reed—and your old, dead friend that shot Deputy Widdowfield in the mouth... Frank Towle. Did I miss anyone?"

"Are those names supposed to mean something to me? The only one I know is Joe Minuse, and I just barely know him."

Boswell glared. "Now don't bullshit me, Charley. I damn well know all those names mean something to you. And I'll tell you something…the papers will be ready tomorrow to send you to Rawlins Springs to be tried for murder and hung. Look around the room. We're all ready to testify at your trial. And I promise you, we'll be available to witness your hanging."

Boswell crossed his arms and leaned back in the chair, watching Dutch Charley's reaction. Dutch Charley clenched his teeth and fixed his stare on the wall. The room was absolutely quiet.

Finally, Boswell said, "We're gonna send you back to your cell now so you can await your trip to Rawlins Springs."

Charley started to rise from his chair, but then he sat back down. "Wait a minute, Sheriff. It sounds like you think Joe Minuse wasn't there."

"Joe said he wasn't there. He said he was in Brown's Park and that you told him about the killings when he returned. He even went so far as to confess that he was there to help steal horses. Joe said he'd rather go to prison for stealing horses than be hung for a murder you committed."

Dutch Charley said, "That lying son of a bitch! I'll tell you everything. We were all there, and I'm the only one that didn't fire a shot. I was totally surprised when Frank Towle shot that deputy in the face. When the other deputy tried to ride up the canyon, Joe and all the rest of them jumped out of the brush and started shooting at him. For a while, I thought he was going to get away. But then he fell off his horse. When he tried to get up and raise his pistol to shoot back, they just kept shooting him until he fell over dead.

"That goddamned Joe was shooting just as much as the rest of them. I never fired a shot. You've got to believe me. You want to try me for murder, and I'm the only one that didn't fire a shot! You're going to have that lying son of a bitch Joe testify against me? He's the one—he and the others—that shot the deputy over and over again."

"Well then, why don't you tell us your version of the story, starting at the beginning? Maybe we'll try Joe after all."

Dutch Charley told basically the same story they had heard before, adding Joe Minuse to the gang who shot the deputies. He closed by proclaiming, "I never took that dead man's boots. That was Jack Campbell."

The lawmen sat in silence, mulling over what they had heard. Finally Boswell asked, "Gentlemen, do any of you have questions for Charley?"

Nottage was the first to respond. "I have several questions." Turning to Charley, he asked, "When you all came down from the Powder River country to your camp near Medicine Bow, why was it that you and Sim Waun went down to Rock Creek to get information from Otto?"

"We both knew that country and could travel without being noticed. We both were known in these parts, so we had to be careful not to be seen. Sim said he didn't dare get caught anywhere near Carbon because some folks there would like to stretch his neck."

"Why would they want to do that?"

"Don't know. Never asked. Figured that was his business."

"Do you believe McKinney is Frank James, or just someone riding on his coattails to bask in his notoriety?"

"Oh, I think Mack is Frank James. Sim Waun is very close to him…probably an old family friend or relative."

"Why do you think Mack is Frank James?"

"Well, it was his idea to derail the train. He was always talking about how much he hated railroads and how much money we could get robbing an express car. Mack said, 'If all else fails, we can rob the passengers.' He told us how—back in Iowa—they derailed a train a few years back. The best I can remember, he said it was about fifty miles east of Council Bluffs, Iowa, on the Chicago, Rock Island, and Pacific Railroad. They chose a curve just before a cut or ravine as the best place to put the engine on the ground and into the ravine. Mack said they derailed the train by pulling the spikes. They left the rail in place with telegraph wire attached to it. Then they just waited out of sight, ready to pull the rail out of place when the engine was too close to stop.

"He said the best place to set up a derailment was just in front of a trestle or curve. That way, when the engine dropped to the ground, it would go into the ravine and stop with such force that the people inside would go flying. All the would-be heroes would be busted up enough that they couldn't fight back. He talked a lot about when he and Jesse rode with William Quantrill and Bloody Bill Anderson. He said his mother and stepfather were so taken with Quantrill that they gave that name to his younger sister as a middle name."

"Well, Charley, that surely does take a cold-blooded son of a bitch to come up with a plan like that. I guess that anyone who rode with William Quantrill's Raiders and Bloody Bill Anderson wouldn't be bothered by maiming and killing innocent passengers on a train. I doubt I'll get the honor of hanging those sons of bitches, but I damn sure would enjoy it if I did. Do any of you gentlemen have any more questions for Charley?"

No more questions were offered, so the jailer took Dutch Charley back to his cell.

"Well, Boz, what do you think, after hearing Charley's story?"

"I don't think it much matters now. The course is pretty well set. Although he's trying his best to exonerate himself and implicate Joe Minuse, there's part of me that still believes Joe's story."

"Are you really going to ship Charley out of here tomorrow?"

"No. I just said that to keep the pressure on him. I don't think we'll be ready to transfer him up to Carbon County for at least a week.

"Let's see, tomorrow is Friday. It'll take us several days to finish processing evidence and preparing letters to Sheriff Lawry and Sheriff-elect Rankin. That most likely will take until Tuesday of next week, and that's New Year's Eve. By the time we're ready to make the transfer, Sheriff Rankin will have taken office.

"I want to try to keep a lid on what we have here, if possible, but it's probably already too late for that. Daniel, do you still have a good supply of letter wax and that old seal around here?"

"Sure do. It's in the desk drawer."

"I'll seal the letters to Sheriffs Lawry and Rankin. Ed, can you arrange to have them hand-carried by the train conductors? We'll telegraph Sheriffs Lawry and Rankin to meet the train and pick up the hand-carried letters."

"Consider it done, Sheriff. I'll notify all the yardmasters. They'll make it happen."

"Sheriff Nottage, would you please double-check that we have a solid charge against each prisoner to make sure we can continue to hold them?"

"I took care of that yesterday, while you were in Cheyenne. One other thing before we leave…Doc Hayford, the editor for the *Laramie Sentinel,* was in the office, looking for more information on the men connected to the Elk Mountain murders. I told him you were in full charge of the investigations, and he'd need to talk to you. He'll be back in the morning for a story."

Boswell said, "Well, so much for keeping this quiet. All right, then. Here's what I want to happen. Sheriff Nottage, would you go ahead and meet with Hayford in the morning and give him a story? Do your best to find out what he knows, and try not to give him much more than he already has. If he presses you for more, just tell him he'll have to get everything else from me. Tell him you weren't there when the arrests were made, and that I'm still investigating. As soon as I'm finished, I'll meet with him.

"The story in the *Sentinel* on the twenty-third wasn't too bad, though it only listed six prisoners, counting Otto Olsen, and omitting Dutch Charley. Even the *Cheyenne Leader* did a better job getting information. They knew we arrested seven men, and they had all the names, except Charley's. I'm damned well not going to correct either one of those papers and let them know they missed the most important prisoner we have."

Nottage said, "They already know that Harrington had Widdowfield's horse and saddle. If the names of the Elk Mountain murderers get out, and if any of the rest of that gang is still around, they'll hightail it out of this part of the country. They may even try to break their friends out of jail or have them silenced.

"The only chance we have to break the Widdowfield-Vincents murder case is through our guests downstairs. We don't even know what any of the others look like. Any one of them could walk into the courthouse and bid us good morning, and we wouldn't know who the hell they were."

Boswell said, "Once this story hits the street, it'll go to every newspaper up and down the track. I've got to telegraph Sheriffs Lawry and Rankin and let them know we have a couple of men they will be very interested in talking to and tell them to expect a hand-carried letter with names and details, Tuesday evening."

"You're right, Boz. I'll meet Editor Hayford when he comes over in the morning and give him the basic story of the Elk Mountain murders. No names. I'll tell him if he gets names from any other sources, he shouldn't use them because it could put this case in jeopardy. I'll warn him that he'll have a hard time getting information from us in the future if that happens. I don't believe he'd want to risk that."

It was six-thirty when Sheriff Boswell sent everyone home.

Friday, December 27, 1878, 6:00 a.m.: Sheriff Boswell met Superintendent Dickinson, Special Agent Leach, and Boone May for breakfast at the Union Pacific Hotel Restaurant. Boswell asked, "Boone, do you think you can find Towle's body based on the directions the prisoners gave us?"

"Yeah, I think I can. We were searching pretty close to that area when we were looking before."

"If you find the grave and need confirmation of the confessions of these bastards for the Laramie County Commissioners, let me know. I'll get you one."

Boone said, "Thanks, I'd appreciate it."

"By the way," Boswell said, "Did I mention to you that I'm hiring Richard Butler as one of my deputies? He'll be joining me as soon as I'm sworn in. I really look forward to having my old and trusted friend with me. Don't know if any of you know…Richard and I are brothers-in-law. Richard's wife, Annette, and my wife, Martha, are sisters. They were both Salisburys."

Dickinson spoke saying, "Good. You will need all the loyal support you can find."

"There is a lot to do to get ready to be sheriff again," In the mood for more conversation, Boswell continued, "Boone, didn't you tell me you were in Deadwood when they brought Johnny Slaughter's body in?"

"Yes, I was. I didn't personally go look, but I was told thirteen buckshot formed a perfect circle just above his heart. I attended his funeral the following Tuesday, at the Grand Central Hotel. Reverend Norcross conducted the service. Must have been ninety people there. Some folks couldn't get into the building and just stood outside the front door."

"What a loss. Everyone really liked Johnny. I think he was only twenty-five years old. The next day, I had to go back on the road, but I'm sure they had a coroner's inquest before the body was taken to Cheyenne for burial. Marshal Slaughter went up to Fort Laramie to take his son's body back to Cheyenne."

"Boz, did you go to Cheyenne for his funeral service?"

"I did. Thomas Carr picked me up at the train, and we went to Peter Hamma's home, where Johnny's body lay in state until the service at the Congregational Church. Peter is married to Johnny's sister. Luke Voorhees furnished six beautifully-matched white horses to pull the hearse. There were nearly fifty carriages in the funeral procession that went out to Lake View Cemetery. Largest funeral ever held in Cheyenne. Very sad.

"And…" Boone sighed, "it only got worse for Old John Slaughter."

"How so?" Leach asked. "What could be worse than losing a son?"

"Less than a month later," Boz said. "Mrs. Slaughter, Johnny's mother, just leans back in her chair and takes her last breath."

"My God," said Dickinson.

Boz nodded. "Only fifty-four years old."

"Everyone said she died of a broken heart," Boone said.

"They laid her to rest next to her son," Boz said.

Leach shook his head. "Marshal Slaughter has certainly had his cross to bear."

Boz stood up. He reminded Boone that he would provide a sworn statement detailing the killing and identification of Frank Towle so Boone could collect the reward. "Thanks again for coming over and identifying your coat."

Boone grinned broadly. "Well, Sheriff...I just really liked that coat."

"Seriously, Boone—it was a big help in moving this case forward. Would you like to come back over to the sheriff's office for a while?"

"No thanks, Sheriff. I'm going to stay here at the depot and wait for Number 4 to take me back to Cheyenne. Gives Leach and me a chance to catch up on old times."

Shortly after that, Sheriff Nottage met with *Laramie Daily Sentinel* Editor Hayford. With the agreement that no names would be used, Nottage briefed Hayford on the information that had been provided by Joe Minuse. After Doc Hayford left, Sheriff Nottage and Sheriff-elect Boswell spent the rest of the day preparing the necessary reports and letters. On their way home that evening, a little after six, both men stopped to pick up newspapers. The article that appeared in the *Sentinel* was written with the normal newsman's flair for intrigue, but overall, it was acceptable.

Boswell spent the weekend preparing for the changeover at the Office of Albany County Sheriff, and finishing up paperwork on the Rock Creek arrest. He spent Monday and Tuesday mornings much the same way. By one-thirty Tuesday afternoon, the letter to Sheriff Lawry and Sheriff-elect Rankin was signed, sealed, and delivered to the yardmaster, who would give it to the conductor of the next train out of Laramie City.

Boswell decided to go home early and spend New Year's Eve with Martha, his wife, and their daughter, Minnie. Turning to Sheriff Nottage, he asked, "Daniel, can you believe that 1878 is gone already? Where does the time go?"

"Don't know, Boz. God willing, I'll see you next year."

Wednesday, New Year's Day, January 1, 1879, 8:30 a.m.: Sheriff Boswell received a telegram from Carbon County Sheriff James Rankin, informing him that a response letter had left Rawlins about two o'clock that morning and was being hand-carried to him. Now that he knew the train it would arrive on, he decided to go over to the yard office and pick up the letter personally. He figured he'd stop in and have a cup of coffee with Superintendent Dickinson while he was waiting.

By the time he got to the yard office, the conductor had already dropped off the sealed message with the yardmaster. It was a thick letter, so Boswell put it into his coat pocket and walked back to his office to read it. Sitting at his desk, Boswell broke the embossed seal and opened the letter.

In it, Sheriff Rankin praised the quick and decisive actions of the Albany County lawmen. He also recognized the pressure the sheriff's office was under from the public, who were demanding that something be done to bring the murderers in. Rankin said he'd informed Carbon County Attorney George C. Smith of the situation and was receiving legal advice to make sure the case would be trial-ready.

Rankin discussed the need to get the prisoners to Carbon County, as well as the risk of moving them, with gang members still on the loose who might try to break them out, and citizens' committees anxious for justice. He agreed that Dutch Charley should be brought up to Rawlins first, followed by Joe Minuse. This would give Sheriff Boswell more time to squeeze Minuse about other crimes he may be privy to. Sheriff Rankin noted his concerns about getting the prisoner through the town of Carbon. Even after he arrived at Rawlins Springs, Rankin would have to get him safely from the train to the jail.

Rankin recommended that the transfer be made on Sunday evening, January 5. Dutch Charley could be secreted in the express car on Number 3, which would have to stop in Carbon for water and coal. This would put Number 3 in Carbon about ten-thirty on Sunday evening. Hopefully, the citizens would be home in bed. Rankin requested that an Albany County deputy accompany Dutch Charley, since he had so many deputies out sick.

The word on the street was that one, or more, of the Elk Mountain murderers would soon be brought up to Rawlins Springs. The citizens would be watching for the Carbon County sheriff or deputies to go to Laramie City to pick up one or more of the murderers.

Sheriff Boswell wrote back to Rankin, agreeing to the plan. He wrote that he'd send Deputy Ed Kerns, who would also be carrying the transfer papers.

When the letter was finished and sealed, Boswell walked back to the Union Pacific Depot. There, he briefed Superintendent Dickinson on the prisoner transfer plan and gave the yardmaster the letter for Sheriff Rankin. He specified that he wanted the letter hand-carried by the conductor of the next westbound train.

Boswell planned to have a county buckboard outside the jail and ready to go, just as soon as they heard Number 3 coming into the south end of the yard on the day of the transfer. Under the cover of darkness, he—along with Deputies Kerns and Butler—would escort Dutch Charley down to the depot. The buckboard could be driven to within twelve feet of the express car. Boswell would help Deputy Kerns walk the prisoner over to the express car, and then he'd wait with Deputy Kerns and Dutch Charley until just before the train pulled out. Deputy Butler and the buckboard would be waiting for him across the street. After the train was gone, he would join Deputy Butler, and they would take the buckboard back to the county stable.

Sheriff Boswell wished the yardmaster and Superintendent Dickinson a happy New Year. To him, it still felt like 1878.

Chapter 8

Dutch Charley

Sunday, January 5, 1879: Just after sundown, Deputy Richard Butler stationed himself outside the courthouse, listening for Number 3 to arrive. Finally—off in the distance—he could hear the train coming into the south end of the railroad yard. He stepped back into the courthouse, where newly-sworn Sheriff Boswell, Deputy Ed Kerns, and Dutch Charley were waiting. "Looks like old Number 3 is about fifteen minutes late. Is everyone ready?"

Boswell said, "We're ready. Let's go."

They left the building and went down to the waiting buckboard. The three lawmen helped the manacled Dutch Charley into the back. Butler drove, with Boswell beside him. Kerns and Dutch Charley rode in back. Within ten minutes, they were alongside the express car and ready to board. A few citizens acknowledged them with waves, but for the most part, it seemed they were unnoticed. Boswell and Kerns helped Dutch Charley out of the buckboard, walked him across the open area to the west side of the depot, and then escorted him up the steps of the adjoining passenger car.

Conductor Charles A. Houston greeted them as he unlocked the express car door. "The yardmaster filled me in on what we have here, Sheriff." He checked his pocket watch. "It's five-twenty-five. We'll be pulling out in exactly twenty-eight minutes, so you'll want to get off just before then. Addressing Kerns, he added, "I'll come back just as soon as we clear the north end of the yard and see if you need anything."

Fletcher Campbell, the mail piler, was already busily sorting mail in the other end of the car. "Sheriff, I'm locking you in now. Fletcher will let you out and lock the door when you're ready to leave. Fletcher's kerosene lamps should give you plenty of light to watch your prisoner."

"Thank you, Charles. By the way, who is the hoghead tonight?"

"Engineer A.O. Rose. He's as good as they get. Ed and his prisoner will think they're back home in an easy chair. It's going to be a cold one tonight. Well, I'd better finish walking the train. I'll bid you good-bye for now."

The sheriff, his deputy, and Dutch Charley stood in the end of the car until some luggage was removed and the outbound luggage put on. As soon as the dockside door slid shut, they escorted Charley just past the center of the car and directed him to sit down on a trunk.

Deputy Kerns pulled a trunk over to the opposite side of the car to sit on, giving him a good view of his prisoner.

Boswell said, "Ed, if Charley makes one wrong move, you shoot the son of a bitch. Do you understand me?"

"Damned right, I do. If Charley gets foolish—Charley gets dead."

"I'm leaving now, so you stay alert. See you tomorrow. I'll have someone pick you up."

"Don't worry, Boz. I don't plan on letting this one out of my sight."

Boswell left the car and walked across Front Street to where Deputy Butler was waiting. From their vantage point, the giant black machine was barely visible in the cold dark night. They heard the conductor call, "All aboard." Within minutes, they saw the conductor's lantern signaling that all was clear to go. The engine inched forward. In the dark, they listened to the faint click of the links and pins as the slack was pulled out of the drawbars, and the sound of the steam pistons as they delivered power to the drivers. With each turn, the train picked up speed.

"God…I love that sound," Boswell sighed. "If I were a younger man, I think I'd want to be an engineer."

The engine's kerosene headlamp created a halo of light that silhouetted the engine, and the kerosene lamps on each side of the caboose glowed red. The two men watched the train until it had completely cleared the depot and was approaching the north end of the Laramie Railroad Yard.

"It sure does get dark quick when the sun goes down behind the Snowy Range."

"Yes, and the temperature drops right along with it."

Boswell confided to his brother-in-law and trusted friend, Deputy Butler, "I'm very pleased you've joined me." With that, they headed back to the courthouse.

The railroad tracks left Laramie, ran straight north about five miles, then zigzagged, following the Big Laramie River to Look-Out Station. From there, they continued about forty-five miles to Rock Creek Station. For the next twenty miles, they curved gradually toward the west, into Medicine Bow Station. From Medicine Bow, the tracks curved southwest for twenty miles, into the town of Carbon. They continued to curve southwest through Percy Station and then Saint Mary Station, until just before they got to Fort Steele. At that point, they turned west, through Benton, and on into Rawlins Springs.

Though he couldn't see out of the express car, Deputy Ed Kerns had made this trip enough times that he could guess where they were by the mail stops the train was making. The closer they came to Carbon, the more apprehensive he became. He would be relieved when he had Dutch Charley safely deposited in the Carbon County Jail in Rawlins Springs.

He turned to Dutch Charley, "Even with that little heating stove, it's cold in this car. It must be well below zero outside."

Dutch Charley gave an indifferent grunt.

Kerns surmised they were stopped at Medicine Bow Station. The train should pull out at about nine-fifty, and they would be at Carbon about ten-thirty. They'd stay in Carbon for at least thirty minutes to take on water and fill the coal tender.

With a gentle jerk, Number 3 started moving forward. Soon, the train was back up to speed; and the next thirty-five minutes went by in no time at all. The train began slowing again.

"We're coming into Carbon now," Kerns told Charley. "One of the deputies you murdered was from here. I want you to get over to the backside of those trunks and sit on the floor so I can stack these trunks up around you. I suggest that you keep quiet until we're well away from here. This is just a precaution. I sincerely hope your being on this train hasn't been leaked. I damn sure don't want any trouble with a citizens' committee."

For the first time, Dutch Charley looked anxious.

"Most likely nothing'll happen. It's late, it's dark, and it's cold out there. Probably twenty-five degrees below zero. But let's not take any chances. Just get over there."

Kerns' fears weren't unfounded. Some eighty to a hundred men had gathered, waiting for this train. Several masked men surrounded the train and began to board. There was no yelling and very little talking. They went about their business with precision, as if it had been rehearsed many times. They knew what they were after and where to find it. Two masked men climbed aboard the engine before it had come to a complete stop, pointing their guns at Engineer Rose and his fireman.

"Don't even think about moving this train! Our quarrel is not with you. Just do as you're told, and you'll not be harmed."

Quietly, fifteen masked men boarded the passenger car just behind the express car. Four other masked men located Conductor Houston two cars back, pushed him into a seat, and took his key. Two men stayed to guard him, and the other two headed to the express car.

Deputy Kerns didn't hear them unlock the door. For a moment, when the door opened, he thought Conductor Houston had returned. In the time it took to gather his senses, there were ten masked men in the car with their pistols drawn.

The leader said, "Nobody make a move, and you won't get hurt."

Two men grabbed and held Kerns's arms, while a third disarmed him. The mail piler, Campbell, stayed where he was, raising his hands in the air. The masked men ordered Kerns and Campbell to sit down on the floor of the car, and two men guarded them.

Deputy Kerns warned, "If you do this, it makes you no better than he is."

Several masked men moved through the car, searching every nook and cranny, looking for Dutch Charley. The leader hissed, "We're going to have a talk with your prisoner. You just sit there, shut your mouth, and you won't be harmed."

Some of the men moved the trunks. "We found him!"

More masked men joined them. They looked down at the prisoner, sitting on the floor with his knees pulled to his chest, trying to make himself as small as possible. They jerked Dutch Charley to his feet.

One vigilante stepped forward and slipped the noose end of a hemp rope around his neck. "You're coming with us!"

Dutch Charley tried to resist. "Good God, don't let them do this to me!"

He strained, trying to pull back toward the side of the car, when one of the masked men sneered, "Isn't it just like a cowardly, back-shooting son of a bitch to evoke the name of God when called upon to answer for what he's done?"

He bashed the prisoner on the right side of his forehead with the barrel of his pistol. "You're coming with us. Now, you have a choice - you can walk like a man, or we'll drag you out of here with this rope."

With a jerk on the rope, his captor began leading Dutch Charley out of the express car, accompanied by an entourage of masked men. The leader addressed the two men guarding Deputy Kerns, "Stay with him until we're off the train. Then come join us. Unload the deputy's gun and leave it with the conductor on your way out." Turning to Kerns, he added, "No one is to leave this train. Do you understand me, Deputy?"

"I understand."

"No heroics. This bastard isn't worth dying for."

As the group moved through the lighted passenger car, one of the masked men pointed at the prisoner, "Jesus Christ! Look at this. The sorry son of a bitch just pissed himself!"

At the end of the car, two men helped Charley navigate the steps in his shackles. As soon as he was solidly on the bottom step, one of the men on the ground gave a hard jerk on the rope. Losing his balance, Dutch Charley hopped off the step, landing on his feet. Then he fell forward, face first, into the crusted snow. As Charley moaned, two men pulled him to his feet. The group moved forward.

The mob parted as the vigilantes dragged the prisoner a short distance down the track, to an old corral. Near it was a telegraph pole. The passengers on the train and the railroad personnel were trying their best to see what was happening. Some were standing on the car steps. Some remained seated, raising the window shades and scraping the frost that had collected on the car windows. Curiosity had also brought several station employees out of the depot and onto the platform.

There was just enough moon to cast a little light on the snow. It was nearly thirty degrees below zero, and the frozen breaths of all the men joined into one mass. In the center of the mob was Dutch Charley, leaning against the corral, trying to steady himself, as his legs would no longer hold him up.

Fear and cold had his whole body trembling uncontrollably. One end of the rope was around his neck, and the other—which had been thrown up over the cross arm of the telegraph pole—was being held by one of the masked men.

The vigilantes waited. Within minutes, the crowd parted to make room for a woman, who was holding onto the arm of a man. Deputy Widdowfield's mother, Ann, and his brother, Joseph, stopped about eight feet away from Dutch Charley. Mrs. Widdowfield stood there, a heavy wool blanket around her shoulders and a dark shawl pulled up over her head so that just her face showed.

The men nodded to her, with respect.

Then the leader looked Dutch Charley square in the eye: "Start out by telling us your name."

The outlaw's voice broke as he replied, "Charles Randall. They call me 'Dutch Charley.'"

"Now, Dutch Charles Randall…where're you from?"

"Missouri. But I have no family there now. I have no family."

"We don't care about your family. What we want to know is exactly what took place up on Elk Mountain. And God help you if you try to lie about it."

Since he'd already confessed to Sheriff Boswell, Dutch Charley had nothing to lose by confessing again. Though he was terrified, he thought that if he cooperated, he might be sent on to Rawlins Springs to stand trial.

His voice shaking, he gave a quick description of the aborted train robbery. Then he began to tell them about ambushing the two deputies. At this point, the mob spokesman demanded to know who all was there. Without hesitation, Dutch Charley named all the members of the gang, including Joe Minuse. He told them that Frank Towle was the first to shoot one of the deputies, who had kneeled down to check the firepit. All the others—except him—had then begun shooting at the other deputy when he tried to ride up the canyon. Dutch Charley described how the injured man fell, tried to get up and shoot back, and then—after being shot several more times—finally fell dead. He confessed that they had robbed the dead men, taking clothes, boots, guns, horses, saddles, and other personal items.

The mob leader turned to the fallen deputy's mother, "Mrs. Widdowfield, have you heard enough?"

Tears streaming down her cold cheeks, she replied, "Yes, I've heard enough. My dead son cries out from his grave for justice."

With that, Ann Widdowfield and her son, Joseph, turned and made their way back through the crowd. When they were gone, the mob leader nodded his head to someone back by the coral, who immediately started rolling an empty kerosene barrel toward the telegraph pole.

When Dutch Charley heard that rolling barrel on the crusted snow, he knew what was about to happen. Again, he proclaimed his innocence, shouting that he hadn't killed anyone. The barrel was rolled into place next to the pole. Dutch Charley begged the mob, trying to bargain for his life in exchange for leading them to the men responsible for the shooting.

The mob leader addressed the prisoner, "I think you're a lying son of a bitch. Whether or not you shot those men doesn't matter. You were there. You were part of the gang. So now you pay the price."

Motioning his men on either side of Dutch Charley, they pulled the prisoner to the barrel and began lifting him. A third man grabbed him from behind. In one quick movement, they had him on the barrel. The man holding the rope pulled it taut. Dutch Charley sobbed and begged for his life.

One of the vigilantes growled, "Stand up straight like a man, you sniveling bastard."

Accepting his fate, Dutch Charley begged, "Please just shoot me! Please don't hang me—just shoot me!"

One man kept the slack pulled out of the rope, while another tied the rope in a pipe hitch around the telegraph pole, keeping the loose end taut. The mob leader nodded to someone behind Dutch Charley. In an instant, the barrel was kicked out from under him. He was still begging, "Please don't…"

The fall was too short to break his neck, so he hung there, strangling. In a last attempt to save himself, Charley threw his cuffed hands up above his head and grabbed the rope, but he was unsuccessful in holding on. The crowd watched silently as his fingers and the tips of his boots convulsed in the final throes of death. His body swung back and forth on the rope, eyes bulging, tongue protruding from his mouth.

When it was done, the crowd disappeared into the darkness. In five minutes, no one remained.

Deputy Ed Kerns stepped down off the train. With several passengers and most of the train crew, he walked over to look at Dutch Charley, twisting on the rope.

"Oh, my God!" he said. "How could I have let this happen? This wasn't supposed to happen."

Conductor Houston and Fletcher Campbell both reassured the deputy.

"There was nothing you could do against a mob like that," Houston told him, "except maybe get yourself killed."

"It wouldn't have mattered if you had ten more deputies with you," Campbell said. "They were intent on hanging him, and that's just what they did."

"Do you want to cut him down, Ed?"

"No, it's a crime scene now. And this is Carbon County, so we've got to leave everything as it is until Sheriff Rankin and the Carbon County officials have a chance to review what's happened."

"You hear that?" Houston called out to the onlookers, who had begun drawing closer to Dutch Charley's corpse. "Nobody touches anything."

Deputy Kerns said, "I need to walk back to the depot and telegraph Sheriff Rankin and Sheriff Boswell and let them know what happened. Then we need to get on our way to Rawlins. How long before we can pull out of here?"

"About another twenty minutes to finish taking on coal and water."

Even with this interruption, Union Pacific's Number 3 Passenger Train was less than a half hour behind schedule when it pulled out of Carbon.

At 12:40 Monday morning, Sheriff James Rankin was waiting at the Rawlins Springs Station to meet Number 3 and get the whole story from Deputy Kerns. The deputy, Houston, and Campbell came into the depot and walked toward the waiting sheriff.

Deputy Kerns began, "Sheriff Rankin, I can't tell you how upset I am at what happened to my prisoner. They were on me so fast, there was nothing I could do."

Both Houston and Campbell vouched for the stealth and speed of the mob. Sheriff Rankin wrote down the names of the conductor and express man, and after he jotted down a few facts they shared, he allowed them to return to their duties.

The two lawmen left the depot and walked to the sheriff's office, where several other deputies were awaiting their arrival. The coffee was hot, and a grateful Ed Kerns sipped his coffee for several minutes before he was ready to tell the story of the lynching.

When he was finished, Sheriff Rankin asked, "Ed, it's two-thirty in the morning. Would you like to go over to the Union Pacific Hotel and try to get some sleep?"

"No thanks, Sheriff. I wouldn't be able to sleep. If it's all right, I'll just stay here catch Number 4 back to Laramie in the morning."

"You won't be ready to go home on Number 4. County Attorney George Smith, who would've handled the prosecution, will want to meet with you. I'll have him with me in the morning. When we're done, we'll get you out of here on the earliest freight train available. It might be a little closer to noon."

"That's fine."

"I'm going to go on home now. I'll be back in the morning about six. Maybe we can have breakfast."

"Sounds good to me. I'll see you in the morning."

"Ed, try not to feel too bad about this. There wasn't anything you could've done."

"Thank you, Sheriff. No one aboard that train will ever forget last night."

Monday, January 6, 1879: Deputy Kerns met with Sheriff Rankin, County Attorney George C. Smith, and two different Carbon County deputies, giving them a thorough account of the events of the previous night. Then Rankin and Kerns walked to the Union Pacific Depot. They made arrangements with the yardmaster for the deputy to ride back to Laramie City in the caboose of the next eastbound freight.

26: Union Pacific Roundhouse, Rawlins, Wyoming Territory

27: Union Pacific Depot, Rawlins, Wyoming Territory

Chapter 9

Grand Jury Acts

Monday, April 7, 1879, 5:30 p.m.: Carbon County Prosecuting Attorney George C. Smith walked into the Carbon County Sheriff's Office and announced to Rankin, "The work of the Second Judicial District Grand Jury is complete. The Jury Foreman, J.F. Crawford, just brought in the findings. They found just cause to indict all nine men for murder: John Minuse, alias Joe Minuse; George Parott, alias Big Nosed George; Frank James, alias McKinney; John Wells, alias Sandy; Sim Waun; Jack Campbell; Tim Reed; Frank Tool, alias Frank Towle; and Charles Bates, alias Dutch Charlie. Frank Towle and Dutch Charley are now deceased, and Minuse is in jail, but we don't know what any of the other six look like."

Rankin said, "We need to put together a list of the various spellings of names, aliases, and descriptions for wanted posters. Maybe we can get a wanted poster from Missouri for Frank James. This isn't going to be easy. If these men were standing across the street, we couldn't identify them, except maybe Big Nose George."

Smith said, "At least we have their names, and two of the bastards are dead! Just seven more to go. It didn't take the Grand Jury long to deliberate after Frank Howard's testimony. Dickinson, Joseph B. Adams, John W. Vassor, and Joseph Bellamy outlined the details of the search, culminating in the location of the deputies' bodies. They had Joe Minuse's and Dutch Charley's confessions from Sheriff Boswell, and the anonymous eyewitness report of the lynching of Dutch Charley that was sent up from Carbon. The confessions and the Carbon eyewitness report tracked real close, until they got to the place where Joe Minuse claimed he was not there—that he only knew what Big Nose George, Jack Campbell, and Sandy Wells told him when they had met up on the Green River."

28: Frank James

Rankin responded, "In Dutch Charley's confession, he claimed he hadn't done any of the shooting—that Joe Minuse and the others had done it. I don't suppose an eyewitness would ever come forward, given the pressure Judge Blair applied trying to learn the identity of the lynch-mob members. And I'll say it again, if it hadn't been for Frank Howard, we may have never found out who killed Tip and Bob. That took courage."

Smith replied, "I agree with you on that. I felt sure the Grand Jury would find exactly as they did. So, I think Mr. Minuse has been resting long enough under the watchful eye of Sheriff Boswell. When do you plan on bringing him here?"

"I'd like to get him safely into our jail as soon as I can. It'll be impossible to keep the findings of the Grand Jury secret very long."

"Can you send someone to Laramie in the morning?"

"I'm going myself. I want to collect that son of a bitch personally," Sheriff Rankin replied. "We damn sure don't want a repeat of what happened to Dutch Charley."

"You're a damn good lawman, Jim."

"I'll go down on Number 4 in the morning, with Superintendent Dickinson and Frank Howard, and I'll return on Number 3 tomorrow evening, with the prisoner."

"Were you aware that Ed Dickinson has had Frank Howard staying at the Union Pacific Hotel in Laramie? He's on the Union Pacific's payroll—I think as a special agent."

"Yes, I'd heard that. It sounds like a good deal all around. It rewards him for what he did and keeps him fed, housed, and close at hand as a witness, while he waits to receive his part of the reward. I'll let them know I'm going to Laramie with them to bring back Joe Minuse. I'll also telegraph Sheriff Boswell and tell him that the Grand Jury has met and that I'll be in town tomorrow for a visit. He'll understand the message and have Minuse ready for transfer. I sure would like to have Minuse up here before the citizens of Carbon find out he's being moved."

Tuesday, April 8, 1879, 4:15 a.m.: Sheriff Rankin and Deputy Sheriff Howard L. Bair had about a half an hour to talk before "All aboard!" was called.

Looking at his pocket watch, Rankin said, "Not too bad. Number 4 is only about fifteen minutes late. She'll be moving by five. I guess I'd better get aboard now. Ed and Frank are already aboard."

Before Rankin boarded, Bair cautioned, "Jim, I know I don't need to tell you this, but I'm going to, anyway. Be very careful when you come back through Carbon tonight."

"Sure will, Deputy. Thank you for your concern."

Deputy Bair stood and watched the train pull out of the Rawlins Springs yard before returning to the sheriff's office.

The trip down to Laramie was uneventful. Union Pacific Number 4, an eastbound passenger train, stopped alongside the Laramie Depot at 10:50 a.m. The three men stepped down off the train, stood on the platform, and talked for a few minutes. Finally Dickinson said, "Would you like to get something to eat before going over to the courthouse?"

"Thank you, Ed, but I think the less people that see me, the better. I'll get something to eat at the jail."

Rankin said good-bye and started walking the five blocks to the Albany County Courthouse to meet Sheriff Boswell, who was waiting for him.

Boswell greeted him, "I heard Number 4 arrive a little while ago; so I knew you'd be along shortly. How're you doing, Jim?"

Rankin replied, "Doing very well, thanks. How about you, Sheriff? Are you pretty much settled back into the old routine?"

"Yes, I am. It didn't take long. Since the last time I was sheriff, I've served as town marshal, and I've spent a good deal of time working for the Rocky Mountain Detective Agency. I never got very far away from law enforcement, so it seems like I never left. Rumor has it that when you decided to run for sheriff, it strained your relationship with Sheriff Lawry."

Rankin said, "Yes, unfortunately it did."

"Why'd you do it?"

"Some members of the Republican Committee approached me about running for sheriff. I guess I'd thought about it from time to time. But I didn't mind working for Sheriff Lawry. I think he could have won a second term if he'd really wanted it. But he was thinking of getting married, and he couldn't make up his mind what he was going to do. And he said he wasn't sure if the Republican Committee would back him for a second term. It didn't seem like he could make a decision.

"I finally had to take a serious look at the others who were considering throwing their hats into the ring. If I were going to run, I needed some time to campaign. So I decided I'd run, just to keep from ending up working for some asshole."

"I can understand that. I always heard you were as loyal as an old hound dog."

"I do feel bad for Ike Lawry, but I guess it's all water under the bridge now. I've been told he feels that I stabbed him in the back. When I decided to run for sheriff, I wrote my younger brother, Bob, who was working as a jailer in Buffalo, Wyoming. I asked him if he would be interested in working as my jailer if I were elected sheriff. I told him the job would pay sixty dollars a month, and if his wife, Rosa—well, Rosanna—would cook for the prisoners, there would be extra pay for her. He wrote back and said he and Rosa would accept the jobs, as there's no way they could make that kind of money in Buffalo or back home in Pennsylvania. He said our sister, Mary Elizabeth—Lizzie—would come with them, to help with their three children. So when I got elected, they came out. I think that also stuck in Ike's craw. I heard he was complaining that I was turning the sheriff's office and jail into a family enterprise."

"Well hell Jim, when you pin on that badge, everyone wants to take a poke. Basically you just need to ignore as much as you can. So let me bring you up to date with what's going on. The word is already on the street that you're here to take Minuse back to Rawlins. Doc Hayford, editor of the *Laramie Daily Sentinel*, came in late yesterday afternoon and was asking all kinds of questions about moving Minuse. He said he and old Judge Peace, the editor of the *Laramie Times*, would be ready to go up to Carbon whatever day Minuse is moved. Can you believe those goddamned vultures? They intend to be there to report on the lynching of Minuse first hand.

29: James H. "Doc" Hayford, Editor, *Laramie Daily Sentinel*

"Doc and I go way back to when he first arrived in Cheyenne to be the editor of the *Rocky Mountain Morning Star* in the spring of 1867. I like to banter with him, but I'll be damned if I'll volunteer information to him on a situation like this."

"Boz, I'm curious. Where did he get the nickname 'Doc?'"

"He's a fascinating old fart. He's a medical doctor… graduated from University of Michigan Medical School. And that's not all. He also studied law in a lawyer's office in Fon du Lac, Wisconsin. He was admitted to the bar and practiced law for three years before the Civil War. He's a highly intelligent man and a very humorous writer."

"Interesting. I didn't know all that, but I do know he can be humorous."

"Anyway…if you don't mind, Jim, I'd like to ride back up with you, just in case the citizens of Carbon try to help Mr. Minuse join his friend, Dutch Charley. Ed Kerns still feels terrible about what happened under his watch."

"I know. Well, I'd welcome your company, Boz. Judge Blair subpoenaed twelve citizens of Carbon to come up to Rawlins Springs to testify in front of the Grand Jury. If they happen to be back in Carbon when we go through, I hope they'll be gunshy enough to keep their heads down and let us pass unmolested."

"I guess we'll know when we get there."

"Sometimes we don't give enough thanks for the efforts of others. But I want you to know that every living soul in Carbon County is grateful to you and your men for all you've done. If it weren't for you, we may have never been able to break this case."

"I appreciate you saying that. I'll pass it along to all those who were with me when we captured the bastards, and of course, Frank Howard."

"I met Frank when he and Dickinson came to Rawlins and testified to the Grand Jury. Then I rode with them back here today. I was glad to get a chance to thank him. I'm quite sure he'll be one of those subpoenaed when we try Minuse for murder. Sheriff, what's your gut feeling about Minuse?"

"Well, Jim, there's no question that he was part of the gang—he'll admit that. He swears he wasn't there when the killings took place. I guess about 75 percent of me thinks he's guilty as hell, and about 25 percent of me believes he's telling the truth about being over on the Green River, moving some horses up out of the Brown's Park area. He's admitted stealing horses and cattle while he was over on the Green River. He said he'd rather go to prison for stealing horses than be hung for murders he didn't commit. He says that—given a chance—he could prove his innocence. After Dutch Charley found out Minuse had given him up, that the evil little bastard implicated Minuse and claimed his own innocence. He made that statement when we were interviewing him. I was watching his every move, and there was something about his demeanor as he implicated Minuse that gave me doubts. It made me think Charley wanted revenge on Minuse for giving him up.

"Anyway, Minuse is our last shot at bringing in any of the rest of them. Judge Blair is absolutely furious about the lynching of Dutch Charley. He had us go down to Carbon several times to attempt to get names of the vigilantes that hung him. Of course, no one knows anything—none of them would give up a neighbor. E.E. Calvin, the telegraph operator at the Carbon Station, wrote up a detailed description of what he could see from the platform and what he could hear Dutch Charley saying just before they lynched him. He telegraphed it up to me in Rawlins Springs. Of course, he swears he couldn't see anyone's face and had no idea who any of the mob members were.

"Jim, have you had anything to eat since you left Rawlins Springs?"

"No, I haven't, Sheriff."

"Well, let's eat here at the jail before we leave. I've arranged for a buckboard to pick us up and haul us down to the train. I have all the transfer papers ready for you to sign before we leave. I also have all Minuse's personal belongings stashed there by the door. We're holding him on a Federal Arrest Warrant for interference with, and theft of, the United States Mail. They will subordinate their charges as long as he is going to be tried for murder or other serious crimes committed in the Territory."

"Good! He'll be formally charged with first-degree murder, just as soon as we get him to Rawlins."

Checking his beloved Hamilton pocket watch, Sheriff Boswell said, "I've requested that the two of us and the prisoner be fed at four-thirty, so we can be at the station by about five-fifteen."

Rankin said, "Deputy Jens Hansen, of Carbon, will be at the depot just in case we run into trouble. If we can get Minuse to Rawlins Springs, we'll be met by an entourage to help escort him to jail. It's only been a couple or three days since the full moon, so it will be fairly bright out when we reach the Carbon Station. I'm not sure if that will help or hurt us, but we should be able to see if a mob is approaching the train."

While the two lawmen dined, they talked about recent events in Rawlins Springs, Laramie, and the Territory in general. Sheriff Boswell said, "In spite of the hell-on-wheels beginnings of all these towns, I do think that—someday—they'll become totally respectable. I guess I had faith in this town, or I wouldn't have my wife and daughter here. I'll never forget how bad these end-of-the-track towns were ten years ago. There were six thousand men building the railroad. Then there were just about as many liars, thieves, con-men, whores, pimps, and sons of bitches here to beat them out of their money. Many of them have moved on, but we still have plenty of them here in Laramie City."

"We have plenty in Rawlins Springs, too. Most of the whorehouses and cribs are south of the tracks."

"I guess every track town is much the same. Many of the classier houses are not that far from the business district. Our church ladies are always after us to run the prostitutes out of town. In the old days, most of them were located in the area that used to be referred to as 'Tin Town,' south between here and Fort Sanders. As long as there's a demand, there will be a supply."

"As long as they aren't rolling these young dumb bastards, we pretty much leave them alone."

"We do the same. It's the armed outlaws robbing the trains, freight wagons, stagecoaches, and ranches that cause so many problems. You know, I think about every third stage out of Deadwood gets robbed."

"Yes, it's a shame. Well, the buckboard is outside. Let's get Joe Minuse and head over to the train. By the way, his given name is 'John,' but he said most people call him 'Joe.' So we've been calling him 'Joe.'"

"'Joe' or 'John'—the rope won't care."

The jailer brought Joe Minuse. "Here he is, Sheriff. Will there be anything else?"

"No, that's it for now. I'll see you tomorrow, when I get back from Rawlins Springs."

Boswell made the introductions. "Joe, this is Sheriff Jim Rankin from Carbon County." Minuse glanced at Rankin and nodded in acknowledgment.

Rankin said. "Mr. Minuse, Tip Vincents and Bob Widdowfield were good friends of mine. I thought you should know that. I'll do my duty and try to get you through Carbon alive so you can stand trial for the murder of my friends. It's not up to me to pass judgment on you; a jury in Rawlins Springs will do that. If they find you guilty, I'll hang you and consider it the best thirty dollars I ever earned. Enough said. It's time to go to the train."

Boswell reached down and picked up Minuse's meager belongings, and the trio headed toward the buckboard that Deputy Richard Butler had brought over from the county stable. Minuse was handcuffed and shackled with leg irons, consisting of two ankle irons connected by eight links of chain. Lawmen generally preferred this type of shackle because it allowed a prisoner to walk in short steps, but unable to run.

It took less than ten minutes for the buckboard to deliver them to the depot, where Minuse was helped down. Deputy Butler bid the two sheriffs good-bye and waited there until the train pulled out. With a lawman on each side, Minuse shuffled around the depot and down the passengers' platform to the steps of the first passenger car, in front of the Pullman car. The three men entered the car, the two sheriffs helping the prisoner up the steps. The car was less than half-full of passengers, and they were all at the other end of the car. The three men were barely seated when the two out-of-breath newspaper editors clambered aboard.

Doc Hayford of the *Laramie Daily Sentinel* and Judge Peace of the *Laramie Times* walked up to Sheriff Boswell. Hayford said, "You could have saved us a lot of last-minute running by just telling me yesterday what train John Minuse was going up on."

"You didn't ask me. Besides, I could see no reason to volunteer that information, as you have such a great grapevine. I didn't think anything escaped your notice."

"Your being so tight-lipped about Dutch Charley made me look a little inept to my readers, but I did hold back on the information you asked me not to print."

"I thank you for that. I'm sorry you looked bad to your readers. Now that you brought up the subject of Dutch Charley, you know you were wrong when you printed that he was captured at Green River."

"My information source said Green River, when he meant near Rock Creek Station. I should have put two and two together when he couldn't remember the name of one of the prisoners you had in the Albany County Jail. I was up against a deadline, and I hadn't seen you around to confirm the facts, so I just thought it made sense. Anyway, not many of my readers picked up on it, and I guess it really doesn't much matter now, anyway. Dutch Charley is dead."

Hayford went on to say "Sheriff, I'd like to interview Mr. Minuse."

"Goddamn it, how many times have I let you interview prisoners in my jail when an investigation is in process?"

"Well, now that you mention it…none."

"Then why in hell do you think I'm going to let you interview a prisoner just because we're on a damned train? Besides, he's no longer my prisoner. He's been transferred to Carbon County." Turning to his friend, Boswell asked, "Sheriff Rankin, are you willing to let these gentlemen interview Mr. Minuse?"

"Not on this train, and for sure not before he is booked into the Carbon County Jail. And then only if the prisoner agrees to be interviewed."

Hayford said, "No disrespect intended. We're just trying to give our readers an eyewitness account of what happens when this train pulls into Carbon Station. If a mob comes for Mr. Minuse like they did for Dutch Charley, or if you get into a gunfight with them, we want to report it just as it happened."

"So you think reporting on a lynching and maybe a shootout would help you sell a few more copies of that daily wipe you call a newspaper?"

"Now, Sheriff, I'm going to ignore that remark. I happen to know you read every issue."

"Only when you come down hard on the Democrats. Anyway, if a mob comes after the prisoner, we will protect him as best we can."

Sheriff Rankin looked at Minuse's face and observed, "Gentlemen, this talk is upsetting our prisoner. I'd appreciate it if you would move to the seats in the middle of the car."

The two newspapermen stood up, and Hayford replied, "We'll be right there if you need us."

The sheriffs exchanged glances, knowing they would not be needing any help from the two editors.

Number 3 pulled away from the Laramie depot seventeen minutes behind schedule. Unless they encountered unforeseen problems, they could make up most of that time before reaching Rawlins Springs. Sheriff Boswell motioned to the conductor to join them to discuss what might take place once they came to a stop at Carbon Station.

"When we stop at Medicine Bow Station, I want you to pull down all the window blinds and move the passengers into the adjoining Pullman car. Lock the doors, and keep them there until the train has departed Carbon Station. No exceptions for the women and children. If any men want to help us hold off attempts by the citizens' committee to remove Mr. Minuse from our custody, they'd be welcome."

By the time the train left Medicine Bow Station, the passenger car was empty except for the two lawmen and the prisoner.

Boswell looked at his fellow lawman, "Jim if you'll guard that door, I'll guard this one." Each sheriff took his position. The normal thirty-minute stop at Carbon seemed like hours, as the men waited anxiously. Finally, they heard the conductor call out, "All aboard!"

In another five minutes, the train lurched forward, the slack ran out of the draw bars, and the train began to move. The train got up to speed, and the two lawmen returned to their seats.

Boswell asked, "Well, what do you think of that?"

Rankin answered, "I guess Judge Blair's outrage and having certain Carbon citizens appear before the Grand Jury has caused them to keep their heads down and stay out of sight."

The passengers returned to their seats for the remainder of the trip. Number 3 was about twelve minutes behind schedule when it came to a stop alongside the depot in the Rawlins Springs yard. Two of Sheriff Rankin's deputies and two deputized posse members—each armed with pistols and shotguns—were on the platform, waiting to help escort Joe Minuse to the Carbon County Jail.

Wednesday, April 9, 1879, 1:00 a.m.: Robert Rankin, the jailer, secured Minuse in a cell. Then the lawmen had a chance to talk. They agreed that Sheriffs Rankin and Boswell would meet Prosecuting Attorney Smith at his office later in the morning for an in-depth discussion. After the meeting, Boswell could catch an afternoon freight train back to Laramie.

Before departing, Rankin said, "Boz, I want to say again—on behalf of my deputies, the citizens of Carbon County, and myself—how grateful we are for what you and your deputies have done to bring justice for our fallen comrades."

"Jim, don't forget that we have Frank Howard to thank for that. Our only regret is that we didn't capture all of them. In due time, I hope they'll all be brought to justice and hanged."

The lawmen bid each other goodnight. Sheriff Rankin went home, and Sheriff Boswell walked over to the Rawlins House and took a room there.

At ten a.m., Rankin and Boswell met Smith at his office. It was close to noon when the men completed their meeting, so they decided to go to the Union Pacific Restaurant for lunch. When the meal was over, the men parted company. Rankin and Attorney Smith went back to their offices, and Boswell caught a ride back to Laramie City in the caboose of a mid-afternoon freight train.

He settled into a window seat, rolled up his coat to use as a pillow, and wedged it between the seat and the window frame. He laid his head back and gazed out at the miles of endless prairie that streamed by his window. Boswell loved the wide open spaces and appreciated their rugged beauty.

As the train crossed the bridge over the North Platte River, at Fort Steele, the north end of Elk Mountain loomed large in the distance. The tracks turned south just past Medicine Bow Station, and the east side of the mountain would remain visible until they neared Rock Creek Station. Then the majestic Medicine Bow Peak would be the focal point of the scenery, while the Laramie Range would be in full view to the east.

Boswell welcomed the long trip back. It gave him time to reflect on the profession that—more or less—had been thrust upon him. He'd often thought about getting away from law enforcement… maybe he could operate his drug store instead of leasing it out. But he knew he could not abandon the law, as long as he was needed. In his heart, he loved the chase.

Chapter 10

The Minuse Trial

Thursday, April 10, 1879, 9:00 a.m.: Bench warrant in hand, Sheriff Rankin arrived at the jailhouse. He talked with his brother, Robert, before asking him to retrieve Joe Minuse. Robert brought the handcuffed Minuse into the parlor room, where he was formally arrested and charged with murder in accordance with the warrant. He then escorted Minuse across to the District Court for his arraignment. All of the other prisoners awaiting trial had been arraigned the previous Monday.

Rankin and Minuse arrived in the courtroom just before ten. Sheriff Rankin nodded to the clerk of the court, John W. Meldrum. Before they had a chance to sit, attorney Homer Merrill motioned for them to join him at the defense table. Holding out his hand, Merrill addressed Minuse. "John Minuse, as you are not presently represented by counsel, the Court has asked that I stand with you while you answer to the charges brought against you."

"Thank you, sir. I appreciate it."

"Sit down, and I will tell you what to expect when the Judge arrives. I have no idea if you are guilty or not. I just know what you are charged with. I recommend that you plead 'not guilty.'"

"Sir, I am not guilty."

> *Author's Note: Court-Appointed Counsel*
>
> *Though there was no national law requiring governments to provide an attorney for someone who could not afford one, the 1876 Compiled Laws of the Territory of Wyoming did require court-appointed counsel, at the request of a defendant who could not pay for one. In fact, it allowed for two attorneys. That law existed until 1975, when it was repealed.*

"Might I ask…as these proceedings go forward, will you obtain your own counsel?"

"I have no funds to pay an attorney."

"Then you have to make that clear to the Court, so an attorney will be appointed to represent you. It might even be me, depending on the rotation."

At 10:10 a.m., Clerk Meldrum stood and instructed, "All rise." Everyone in the courtroom immediately stopped talking and stood.

Judge Jacob B. Blair walked into the courtroom from his chambers and proceeded to the bench, where he sat. Looking around the courtroom, he declared, "Please be seated." Then turning to Clerk Meldrum, the Judge asked, "John, what is our first order of business?"

"It will be the arraignment of John Minuse on the charge of murder."

"Very well. This court is now in session."

Looking down at the case papers, Judge Blair said, "I see we have Case Number 265, Territory of Wyoming versus John Minuse, alias Joe Minuse. Mr. Minuse, please stand."

Minuse and his counsel, Homer Merrill, rose to their feet.

"Mr. Minuse, did your counsel explain the arraignment process?"

"Yes, sir, Your Honor. He did."

"Very well, then. Let us proceed."

Judge Blair began, "On April 7, 1879, the Grand Jury of Carbon County, Territory of Wyoming brought forth an indictment charging you, John Minuse—alias Joe Minuse—and others with willful murder of Robert Widdowfield and Henry H. 'Tip' Vincent, near Elk Mountain, in the County of Carbon, Territory of Wyoming, on or around the nineteenth of August 1878. You are being arraigned for the Murder in the First Degree of Henry H. 'Tip' Vincent. The Court now requires you to answer to the question. Are you guilty or not guilty of the things herein charged?"

30: Jacob B. Blair, Judge, Second Judicial District, Wyoming Territory

Minuse looked directly at Judge Blair, responding, "Not guilty."

"Very well. A plea of 'not guilty' has been entered for you into the Court record. Please be seated."

Merrill addressed the Court and said, "Your Honor, if it pleases the Court, I would like to address the matter of a future legal counsel for the defendant."

"Yes, Mr. Merrill. Please proceed."

"The defendant informs me that he is wholly without means and authority to obtain counsel or the witnesses necessary to create a proper defense."

Judge Blair asked, "Is this true, Mr. Minuse?"

"Yes, sir, it is true. I am without funds."

Glancing at Meldrum, Judge Blair instructed, "John, check the rotation of defense counselors on your roster, and see who is available."

Shuffling his papers, Meldrum said, "It appears that Merrill is next in line of rotation."

Turning back to Merrill, Judge Blair asked, "Is there any conflict that would prevent you from continuing on as Mr. Minuse's Counsel?"

"No, sir, there is none."

Judge Blair said, "We will recess for thirty minutes to give you time to talk with the defendant and prepare an affidavit declaring him indigent."

With this, Judge Blair rapped his gavel on its sound block and stood up to leave. Everyone in the room stood up as well.

At eleven a.m., the arraignment reconvened. Judge Blair asked, "Mr. Merrill, do you have Mr. Minuse's Declaration of Indigence prepared?"

"Yes, sir. I do, Your Honor."

"Then please bring it forward."

Judge Blair read the document aloud for the Court record:

(Note: words in italics are actual text)

Territory of Wyoming
County of Carbon

John Minuse, being first duly sworn, says I am the John Minuse indicted for the murder of Henry H. Vincent and Widdowfield. That I am wholly without

---

Author's Note: Minuse Declaration of Indigence

The original document was signed as follows:

Subscribed and swore to before me this 10th day of September A.D. 1879

J.W. Meldrum

Clerk Dist. Court

The date is a problem because the document was prepared in April–not September. My theory is that the clerk didn't sign the document until the end of the trial, which was in September.

means and without authority to obtain the witnesses necessary to make my defense; that I cause subpoenas to be issued for the following named witnesses:

W.A. Johnson
A. Hanson
A.G. Overholt
Charles Davis
A. McIntosh
Walter Frank

These witnesses are necessary to my defense
(Signed) John Minuse

When he finished reading the declaration, Judge Blair looked at the defendant and his Counsel and said, "Mr. Minuse, would the person you seek as a witness, W.A. Johnson, be the Sweetwater County Sheriff, William Adolphus Johnson?"

"Yes, sir, he is."

"It is hereby ordered that John Minuse be held over, without bail, for trial during the September session of District Court. It is further ordered that the court assigns Homer Merrill to represent the defendant."

With the rap of his gavel, Judge Blair stood. Everyone in the courtroom rose and watched him leave the room. Sheriff Rankin, who had been sitting directly behind Minuse, sat in an empty chair at the defense table to wait, while Merrill talked to the prisoner.

"John, we have a little over four months before the September session begins. I'll come over to the jail in about a week, and we can begin putting together the strategy for your defense."

"Thank you, Mr. Merrill. Most people call me Joe."

"Alright then, 'Joe' it will be. Well, for now, that about does it. I'll see you in about a week." With that, the two men shook hands.

31: William Adolphus Johnson, Sheriff, Sweetwater County, Wyoming Territory

Ten days later, Merrill met with his client. He took notes as they talked for about an hour and a half. They met several additional times in the jail parlor during the early summer. In August, the meetings became more frequent. They prepared the list of names that would be served witness subpoenas.

In all, nineteen witnesses from Albany, Carbon, and Sweetwater Counties would be subpoenaed by prosecuting attorneys James Francis, C.H. Hughes, and James Ross, and nine by Homer Merrill on behalf of the defendant. Witnesses received subpoenas in August, requiring their appearance in Rawlins September 8, 1879. The trial started the following morning.

September 9, 1879, Tuesday: By nine-fifty a.m., every seat in the courtroom was filled, and the attorneys for the prosecution were seated at their table. At the other table, Homer Merrill spoke in low tones to his client. Sheriff James Rankin sat directly behind Minuse.

At few minutes after ten a.m., Court Clerk Meldrum instructed, "All rise." Judge Blair walked into the courtroom from his chambers and proceeded to the bench.

"The Wyoming Territory, County of Carbon, Second Judicial District, Case Number 265, Territory of Wyoming versus John Minuse, alias Joe Minuse, is now in session. The Honorable Judge Jacob B. Blair presiding."

Judge Blair addressed the courtroom, "Please be seated. If the prosecution and defense are ready, let us proceed with the selection of the jury."

Jury selection took most of the morning, but in the end, produced twelve jurors:

1. William Braner
2. J.E. Pollock
3. Thomas Durant
4. John S. Jones
5. William Bragg
6. Charles Bush
7. William Slater
8. W.O. Prince
9. C.E. Blydinburg
10. John Cannon
11. Thomas Barnes
12. William Mayhall

After jury selection, the judge called a recess for lunch. After lunch, the judge considered several pre-trial motions, granting one that allowed Sweetwater County Sheriff William Adolphus Johnson to submit his testimony to be read and recorded, rather than appear in person.

Sheriff Johnson confirmed that livestock had been rustled in Sweetwater County, as Joe Minuse had confessed. He requested that Minuse be held over to be tried for theft if he were not convicted for the murder of Widdowfield and Vincents.

The counsels for the prosecution and the defense made their opening statements. The witnesses for the prosecution were sworn, examined, and cross-examined. The attorneys covered the attempted train derailment, the murders, and the search for the missing deputies. Union Pacific Superintendent Ed Dickinson and Special Agents Millard Leach and Frank Howard were questioned about Joe Minuse's arrest with the gang near Rock Creek. Noting the late hour, Judge Blair continued the trial to the next morning.

Wednesday, September 10, 1879: After the Court was called back into session, the counsel for the defendant, Mr. Merrill, mounted an excellent defense. He called four witnesses; A.C. Hanson, A.G. Overholt, Charles Davis, and Walter Frank, who testified that Minuse was, indeed, in the Green River area at the time the murders took place.

Witness Subpoenaed for the Prosecution:
E. Dickinson
J.B. Adams
M.F. Leach
William Dailey
William McCarty
John W. Vassor
Frank Howard
John LaFevor
Jesse Wallace

Witness Subpoenaed for Defense:
A.G. Overholt
Walter Frank
A.C. (Ariel) Hanson
Charles Davis
Thomas "Tom" Davenport
Thomas Gault
Jas Warran (Joseph Warrant)
Mrs. Jas Warran (Mrs. J. Warrant)
H. McIntosh
Sheriff William A. Johnson

The defense's final witness was Joe Minuse, himself. Minuse's statement was simple and straightforward. He admitted to being a member of the gang that had killed the two deputies, but he said he was not there when the deputies were murdered. He maintained that he was in the Green River area, helping friends move horses up from Browns Park, as his witnesses had testified.

Minuse stated that he intended to rejoin the gang near Medicine Bow, but the temptation for easy money around Green River had kept him there. He admitted that he'd stolen some horses around the Green River area, and he confessed that, on September 8, 1878, he'd stolen fourteen horses belonging to Al Noble, from his ranch near South Pass City.

Minuse testified he met George Parott, John Wells, and Jack Campbell on a Wednesday or Thursday (August 21 or 22) in 1878, and they'd spent several days with him before heading up to Jackson Hole. They had told him what had taken place on Elk Mountain, and none of them seemed to be much bothered by the murders. They wanted him to go with them, but he wanted to spend the winter around Fort Fetterman or in Cheyenne.

The prosecution asked several questions for clarification before stating that they had no further questions for the witness. Defense Attorney Merrill asked to have Sheriff William Adolphus Johnson's testimony read again. The counsel for the defense rested his case, and the prosecution did likewise.

At three-fifteen, Judge Blair gave the jury procedural instructions on their deliberations, and they were escorted to a private room.

September 10, 1879, Wednesday: At four forty-five, after deliberating an hour and a half, the jury sent word to Judge Blair that they had reached a verdict. Sheriff Rankin and Deputy Sheriff Cook returned the defendant to the courtroom for the reading. Within minutes, the attorneys, most of the witnesses, newsman John Friend, and several of the citizens had returned to the courtroom. People seemed surprised that the jury had already reached a verdict.

The jury members came in and were seated. The court clerk instructed everyone to rise, and Judge Blair entered from his chambers. After everyone was seated, the Judge called the court into session. Then he asked, "Has the jury reached a verdict?"

Jury Foreman William Braner stood up and said, "Yes, Your Honor, we have." He handed the written verdict to Judge Blair, who read it.

"Will the defendant please stand?" Merrill helped the shackled, handcuffed John Minuse to his feet. "Mr. Foreman, would you please state to the court the jury's verdict?"

"We find the defendant, John Minuse, innocent."

"Is this finding unanimous?"

"Yes, sir."

"So say ye all?" Each jury member answered "yes," in turn.

"John Minuse, you have been tried and judged by a jury of your peers. Of this charge you have been found innocent. However, there are Federal charges pending against you, and Sheriff Adolphus Johnson has also requested you be held in custody to answer for crimes committed in Sweetwater County, Wyoming Territory. Therefore, Sheriff Rankin, the court orders you to remand John Minuse into custody, awaiting transfer to Sweetwater County."

Sheriff Rankin answered, "Yes, Your Honor." He and Deputy Cook stepped forward—one on each side of the prisoner. "The Court wishes to thank the jury for your service in the performance of your duty. You are now dismissed. In Docketed Case Number 265, The Territory of Wyoming versus John Minuse…this case is now closed."

As soon as the Judge rapped his gavel on the sound block, Clerk Meldrum said, "All rise." Everyone stood while the Judge walked out of the courtroom. Minuse turned to Merrill and thanked him for the great job he had done.

Finally Sheriff Rankin said, "Come along, Joe. It's time to return to the jail."

As the trio walked back to the jail, Sheriff Rankin turned to Minuse, "Well, Joe, you proved yourself innocent of murder. I'll send a telegram to Sheriff Johnson asking him to come as soon as possible and take you to Green River to answer for stealing horses. Since you've already confessed to stealing horses, before and during your trial for murder, I'd think the court will sentence you as soon as possible."

Minuse smiled and nodded his head, just thankful for the verdict in the murder trial.

"Guess it doesn't look like I'll get to hang you after all, Minuse. But if you continue with your old ways, I may get that chance in the future."

After the prisoner was back in his cell, Rankin sent telegrams to fellow law enforcement officers, knowing full well that the newspaper people had already sent the results out on the wire. After he finished, he walked over to the Union Pacific Rawlins House to say good-bye to Dickinson, Leach, and Howard.

Rankin found the three men at a table in the restaurant.

"Sit down and join us, Sheriff. How about something to eat or at least some coffee?"

"Thanks. I'll join you for coffee. Gentlemen, what do you think of that verdict?"

Dickinson replied, "I guess I'm not entirely surprised. Minuse certainly had persuasive witnesses, all attesting to the fact that he was in the Green River area at the time the murders were committed."

Rankin said, "I've ordered extra deputies to be on duty, just in case we have some citizens' committee members who don't agree with the verdict. I want them to think twice before taking the law into their own hands. I telegraphed Sheriffs Johnson and Boswell about the outcome of the trial before I came over here. I'd appreciate it if you could stop by Sheriff Boswell's office and give him a good eyewitness report of the trial. Also, let him know that we'll interrogate Minuse on other matters until Sheriff Johnson comes to take him to Green River. Who knows? Maybe he'll give information on the whereabouts of the other killers."

Shortly afterward, the men parted company.

The following week, Joe Minuse was taken to Green River, where he was arraigned. He pleaded guilty to stealing horses and was sentenced to serve two years and six months in prison for that crime.

On November 28, 1879, he was taken to the Wyoming Territorial Prison in Laramie City, where he was booked as Prisoner Number Seventy-seven. He remained there until he was transferred to Nebraska State Prison on December 8, 1879. He was released in December of 1881.

Author's Note: Reciprocal Agreements

States and territories often had reciprocal agreements to house prisoners when one state's/territory's prisons were over-crowded.

With Frank Towle and Dutch Charley both dead and Joe Minuse found innocent of murder, the trail of the murderers of Deputies Widdowfield and Vincents again grew cold.

32: Wyoming Territorial Prison at Laramie

Chapter 11

Big Nose George Captured and Returned to Wyoming

December 22, 1879: Winter had officially started. In two days it would be one full year since Sheriff Boswell and his Albany County posse captured the gang of outlaws near the Rock Creek Station. Coal bins were full, and firewood was stacked high, as Wyoming settled into another long, cold winter.

With the ever-present wind and temperatures continuing to ratchet down, winter wore on without mercy. The spring of 1880 came and went, and summer was well underway. Ten long and frustrating months had passed since the jury in Rawlins Springs had found Joe Minuse innocent. Soon, it would be two years since Deputies Widdowfield and Vincents had been murdered on Elk Mountain.

Monday, July 12, 1880: All leads had been exhausted when Sheriff Rankin received a telegram from Deputy US Marshal Tom Irvine in Miles City, Custer County, Montana Territory. It said that a man fitting the description of George "Big Nose George" Parott had been arrested and was being held on suspicion of horse stealing. A second man, who gave his name as "Bill Carey," was also arrested. Irvine speculated that he could be one of the other outlaws involved in the Elk Mountain gang, most likely Jack Campbell. The telegram said that George Parott—who was going under the alias, "George Dixon"—had been in a local saloon drinking heavily and bragging about killing, or knowing who had killed, two deputies in Wyoming Territory, back in 1878. The telegram closed: "Please advise if you are interested in these individuals. The other men are most likely nearby, and we will arrest the lot of them if they can be located."

After Sheriff Rankin read the telegram, he called Deputy Lewis T. 'Tom' Cook to come into his office and handed him the telegram. The deputy scanned it and said, "I'll be damned. What do you think of this?"

Rankin and Cook agreed they needed to act as soon as possible. "Tom, would you please go to the County Attorney's office and ask George to join us, so we can decide how to proceed?"

Cook headed for the door, "I'll be right back."

Within twenty minutes, George Smith, Deputy Cook, and Sheriff Rankin were making plans. Smith said, "I'll need to send a telegram to Governor John Hoyt immediately to inform him of the arrest and request fugitive warrants. We also need to find out if the paperwork can be wired or mailed, or if it needs to be hand-carried to Governor Benjamin Potts in Helena."

Rankin said, "I need to find out the best way to get to Miles City. No matter what, it'll be a long, hot trip. When we go down to the Western Union Office to send this telegram, I'll have the Union Pacific agent at the depot put together an itinerary."

"Yes, it's imperative that you leave as soon as possible."

The travel plans would depend on whether or not Montana's governor would accept a telegram and allow extradition papers to be sent later. If Potts would, then the arrest warrants could be hand-carried to Officer Tom Irvine in Miles City to expedite picking up the prisoners. Rankin would leave just as soon as he received the signed fugitive warrants from Governor Hoyt. Traveling west to Ogden would offer the most miles by rail. *No matter which way I go,* Rankin realized, *it'll take six or seven days, each direction—maybe more.*

Sheriff Rankin sent a telegram to Tom Irvine listing the names that would be on the arrest warrant. George Parott, Jack Campbell, and John Wells were thought to be together. It was possible that other gang members had joined them. Rankin requested that Irvine arrest any of the gang members he could find and hold them on suspicion of murder in Wyoming Territory.

Thursday, July 22, 1880, 10:00 a.m.: Sheriff Rankin received a telegram from Deputy US Marshal David Boerum of Helena, Montana. Boerum and Officer Irvine had determined that one of the individuals being held in Miles City Jail was, indeed, Bill Carey. The citizens of Sun River country were offering a $1,000 reward for Carey's arrest and conviction for stealing horses.

Boerum recommended that Rankin meet with him and Under-sheriff Hathaway in Helena, and they could then proceed to Miles City together to take charge of Bill Carey and Big Nose George Parott, a.k.a. "George Dixon." That would give them three armed men to guard the two prisoners. Boerum and Rankin could discuss the safest way for Rankin to return to Rawlins Springs with the prisoner, once he got there.

Following protocol, the telegram from Boerum dictated that Governor Hoyt send the extradition papers and arrest warrants from Cheyenne to Rawlins Springs in a special courier pouch. It would be on the express car of Number 3 Passenger Train on Friday, July 23, 1880.

Rankin, with extradition documents in hand, would travel west to Ogden, Utah on the Union Pacific. At Ogden he would switch to the Utah & Northern to Red Rock, Montana Territory. From Red Rock, he would board a stagecoach to Helena. There, he could personally deliver the papers to Governor Potts.

Sunday, July 25, 1880: A little past midnight, Sheriff Rankin boarded Union Pacific Railroad Passenger Train Number 3 and began his long journey to bring the outlaws to justice. As westbound Number 3 approached the station at Green River City, he found himself staring out of the window, lost in his thoughts. He was concerned about getting his prisoner back to Rawlins safely. At least Prosecutor Smith had eased his anxiety about passing through Carbon. Smith told him that the citizens' committee seemed to be lying low, to avoid being identified by Judge Blair. Smith offered to travel back with Rankin from Cheyenne and suggested that Sheriff Boswell and some of his deputies could accompany them from Laramie to Rawlins Springs.

Number 3 pulled into Ogden, Utah Territory, in the late afternoon. Sheriff Rankin checked into the Union Pacific Depot Hotel to spend the night, before heading north the next day on the Utah & Northern Railroad. M.H. Beardaley, proprietor of the hotel, joined Rankin for coffee after his dinner, and the two talked about Rankin's journey. Beardaley told him that the Utah & Northern Railroad had been purchased at auction by S.H.H. Clark for the Union Pacific Railroad for $100,000 two years earlier, on April 4, 1878, and the Union Pacific had been dumping money and resources into the line ever since. That bode well for the next part of Rankin's trip.

Monday, July 26, 1880: Sheriff Rankin walked across the street to the Utah & Northern Depot, where his train was ready for boarding. He had reserved a Pullman in advance, as tonight would be the last good night's sleep he'd get before reaching Helena. The train pulled out of the station on time. He would arrive at the terminus, Red Rock Station, Montana Territory, before daylight on Tuesday, July 27, 1880.

Tuesday, July 27, 1880: At dawn, Rankin disembarked and had breakfast before boarding a stagecoach for Helena. He would get there at dusk. After procuring a room for the night at the Overland Hotel on Lower Main Street, he washed off some of the road dust before going down for his evening meal.

> *Author's Note: Rankin's Itinerary*
>
> One of the most interesting aspects of researching this story was documenting Sheriff Rankin's journey to pick up the Big Nose George and bring him back to Rawlins for trial. Other researchers have presented variations of his return route that have the lawman going as far east as Bismarck, Dakota Territory. But as far as I know, no one has shown the St. Paul, Minnesota leg of his journey. In his book, **Reminiscences of the Frontier Days**, published in 1935, Wilson Rankin wrote, "...the prisoner was moved by livery conveyance one hundred and seventy-five miles east to the terminus of the Northern Pacific Railroad at Medora, Dakota; thence by Sioux City and the Union Pacific to Rawlins..."
>
> When I uncovered an article in St. Paul's **The Pioneer Press** naming the hotel and room where he stayed, as well as the time he left for Omaha, it was a real find. Now we know that he traveled much farther east before heading southwest.
>
> Most of Rankin's return route, depicted on **Map 2**, has been documented in newspaper clippings and other references cite that he was in
>
> - Helena
> - Miles City
> - Fort Buford and Bismarck, Dakota Territory (by steamboat)
> - St. Paul, Minnesota
> - Sioux City, Iowa
> - Omaha, Nebraska
> - Cheyenne, Laramie, and Rawlins, Wyoming (by railroad).
>
> He likely traveled from Rawlins via Ogden to Red Rock by train, Red Rock to Helena by stagecoach, Helena to Miles City by stagecoach.
>
> Here's the bottom line: it was a long, rough journey—1,109 miles to Miles City and 1,833 back to Rawlins with a prisoner in tow—for a total of 2,942 miles. That's about the same as driving across the United States, from the Atlantic to the Pacific. Rankin was one tough lawman.

Wednesday, July 28, 1880: Sheriff Rankin rose, had an early breakfast, and then went across the street to the offices of Gilmer, Salisbury, and Company, brokers for most of the stage and freight lines. He checked his reservation on the company-owned Idaho and Montana Stage Line.

Since he had a little time, Rankin visited a bit with Agent H.A. Iddings, who had been the agent in Cheyenne before resigning to come to Helena and manage the Gilmer, Salisbury, and Company's business.

Iddings said, "I remember a very skilled stockman by the name of Joseph Rankin who furnished many a matched team for the line. Would he, by chance, be a relative of yours?"

Rankin said, "He's my brother. Joe and I have several small businesses, including freighting. One day, we intend to add stagecoaches to our enterprises."

With his ticket purchased, Sheriff Rankin headed over to Governor Potts's office for his eight-thirty meeting. The Governor greeted him and asked for an update. Rankin recounted the facts of the two murdered deputies, describing the impact of the loss on their families, friends, and communities. He told the Governor about the circumstances of the failed robbery at Rock Creek and about Frank Howard's role. He credited Sheriff Boswell and his posse for bringing in the outlaws, and he provided details on the Minuse trial.

The Governor reached into his desk drawer, pulled out a heavy, brown, unsealed envelope, and handed it to Rankin. "We had this prepared and signed two days ago, when we were assured that you were on the way to pick it up."

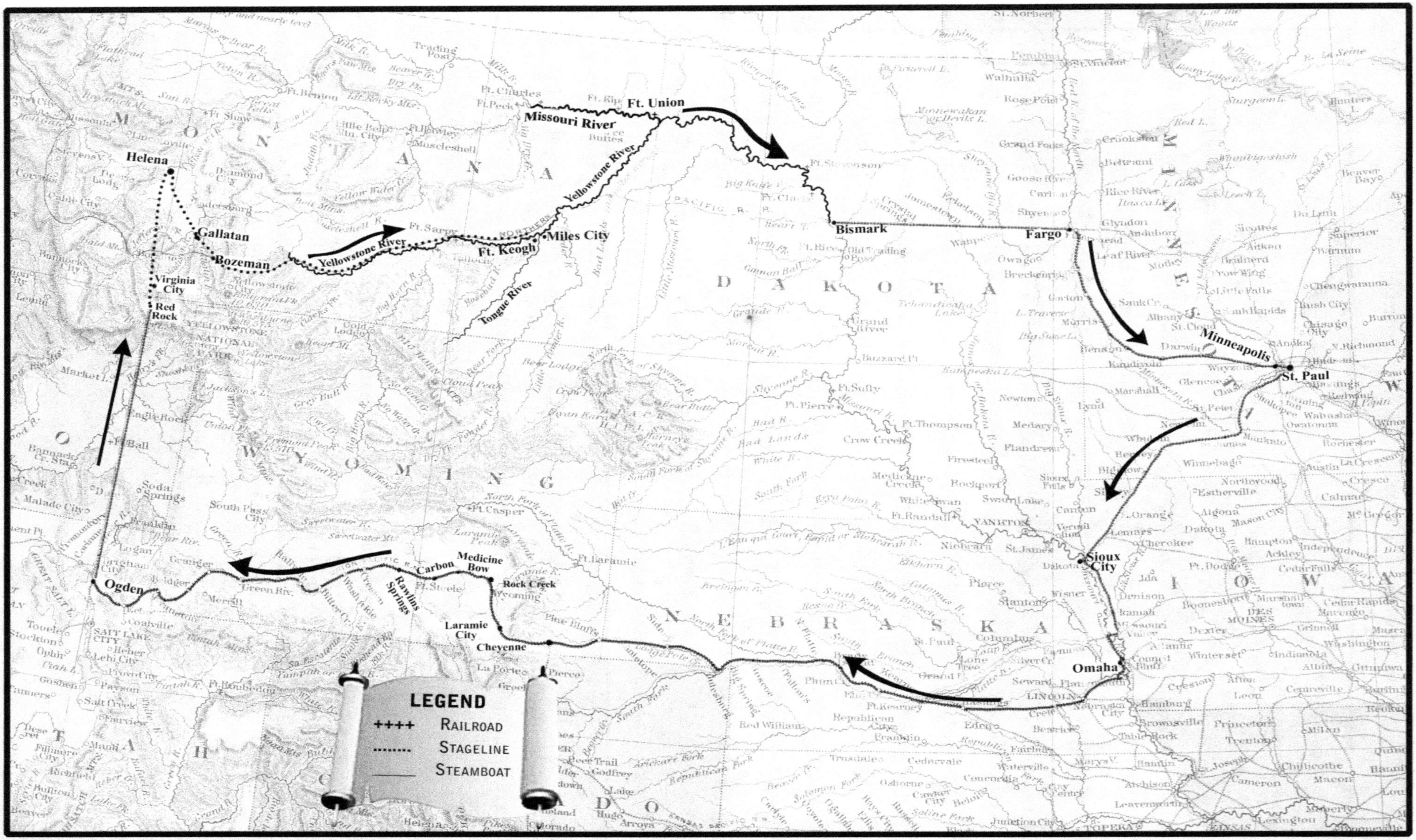

Map 2

LEGEND
++++ RAILROAD
····· STAGELINE
——— STEAMBOAT

Map: Courtesy David Rumsey Map Collection, www.davidrumsey.com.

33: Main Street, looking north from Bridge Street, Helena, Montana Territory

Author's Note: Stagecoaches

The stage line connecting the end of the railroad at Red Rock with Helena was owned by Gilmer, Salisbury, and Company. Jack T. Gilmer and Monroe Salisbury purchased the Wells Fargo Stage Line from Ogden, Utah, to Helena, Montana Territory, in 1869; it provided most of the service in Utah, Idaho, and Montana Territories.

Most of the stagecoaches that came with the purchase of Wells Fargo and Company were Concord coaches. The great Concord stagecoaches—made by the Abbot and Downing Company in Concord, New Hampshire—were brightly painted, with yellow running gear and coach bodies of a rich red. A skilled artisan, J. Burgham of the Abbot and Downing Company, painted a different ornamental landscape scene on the doors and other body parts of each coach.

When they bought the Cheyenne-to-Deadwood line from Yates and Company, Gilmer, Salisbury and Company bought six hundred horses. All the harnesses were bought from James R. Hill and Company of Concord, New Hampshire. With all the new business in the territories, it appeared they would have standing orders for new coaches for many years to come.

Sheriff Rankin opened the envelope and removed the document with the Great Seal of the Territory of Montana in the left-hand corner. He read the order granting the return of Jack Campbell and George Parott, alias "Big Nose George," to the Territory of Wyoming to face the charge of murder. The document was signed by Governor Potts, as well as the secretary of Montana Territory, on July 26, 1880. He slid the document back into the envelope.

"Governor Potts, it is possible that another member of the gang, John Wells—who goes by the nickname 'Sandy'—may also be in Montana Territory. They came up with sufficient proof that Bill Carey is not 'Jack Campbell.' However, I hope they will have arrested the real Campbell before I get to Miles City."

The Governor said, "I'm aware of that. I also understand that Deputy US Marshal Boerum and Under-sheriff Hathaway will accompany you to Miles City, where they will pick up Carey and bring him back to Helena to stand trial. The good folks of the Sun River country have put up a $1,000 reward for the arrest and conviction of Mr. Carey for horse stealing.

"I will write Governor Hoyt and advise him that I will accept arrest warrants and extradition papers by US Mail. That would save you a lot of days and hard miles. Unless, of course, the arrest has been made on this end of the territory. Then I'd welcome another visit from you."

Now that the transfer of the legal papers was completed, the Governor said, "Now that the Northern Pacific Railroad has taken care of its money problems and is building again, I expect the Northern Pacific to reach Miles City before winter of 1881 and Helena by 1883. But unfortunately, Sheriff, for now, the fastest way to get to Miles City is by stagecoach. You'll see some of the most spectacular country in the world, but every rut, bump, and stone in the road will help you remember your trip."

"Riding stagecoaches certainly does make a person appreciate a good passenger train."

"I don't envy your trip, but I wish you Godspeed. And I thank you, Sheriff, for removing these outlaws from the territory. We sincerely hope justice can be served."

As Rankin rose to leave, the Governor bid him farewell.

At eleven o'clock, extradition documents in hand, Rankin headed to the Idaho and Montana Stage Company Station. As he approached the stage station, he noticed two men standing near the coach. Though neither man was displaying a badge, he guessed that they were officers of the law. Rankin walked up to them and asked, "Would you gentlemen be Mr. Boerum and Mr. Hathaway?"

"Yes, sir. We are."

The stage driver put their carpet bags and satchels in the boot, and within fifteen minutes, they were ready to go. The driver and armed shotgun messenger were on the seat, and the passengers were inside. The stage station agent stepped up, closed the coach's door, thumped it with his fist, and said, "Gentlemen, have a good trip."

The driver released the brakes, whipped his reins, and yelled, "Yaaaw!" A beautiful six-horse hitch of powerful coach horses pulled against the traces and moved forward in unison. The wheelers—the two horses closest to the coach—were the largest, and chestnut in color. The swingers—the middle pair of horses—were slightly smaller, and also chestnut in color. The two leaders—a black and a white—were slightly smaller yet. As the coach moved forward, it rocked gently on the multi-layered leather thorough braces.

In all, there were twelve people on the coach. The driver and shotgun messenger were on the box of the front boot (the driver's seat). There were eight passengers in the coach, and a couple of

34: US Deputy Marshal John X. Beidler,
Known as "Terror of Evil Doers"

short-trippers were on the exterior China seat (top rear of the stagecoach). The two men on the China seat of the coach got off at the third stage stop. Three more of the men got off at the fifth stage stop. The two other Miles City passengers decided to try the China seat for a while to enjoy the fresh air. Now that the three lawmen had the coach to themselves, they could talk freely. Sheriff Rankin briefed his colleagues on the murder of the deputies.

Officer Boerum observed, "Officer John Xavier Beidler—folks call him 'X'—was tracking this same bunch of horse thieves for stealing horses from the Indians on the reservation.[1] When he heard about the capture of Big Nose George and Bill Carey, he traveled from Junction City to Miles City by steamboat to back up Deputy Marshal Irvine and Sheriff Bullard, just in case the gang tried to break them out of jail."

Rankin asked, "How did Officer Irvine and the others capture the outlaws?"

Boerum replied, "I'm not real sure, but we'll find out when we get there. I doubt that Officers Irvine and Beidler will go very far from the jail until we've left with the prisoners. Then I'll bet they'll be right after other members of the gang. I wish I could stay around and help, but we all need to get those prisoners safely out of Miles City to their rightful destinations.

Rankin noted, "From what we've learned, they were terrorizing Montana Territory before they killed the deputies, and several returned to Montana Territory afterward. We know that Frank Towle was robbing stagecoaches between Cheyenne and Deadwood when Boone May killed him. Big Nose George, Jack Campbell, and the one called 'Sandy' were all back up here working with Bill Carey. It's interesting to me that almost all these outlaws have been bullwhackers and freighters somewhere along the line, so they know the best areas to stop a stage or mail wagon."

35: Main Street, Miles City, Montana Territory

Officer Boerum said, "Old Hank Wormwood arrested the lot of them near Buffalo Rapids, just below Miles City, but he had no choice but to turn them loose. A notable individual perjured himself and swore they were in Canada when the victim, Morris Cahn, was robbed of fourteen thousand dollars between Fort Keogh and Fort Abraham Lincoln. Cahn was traveling with the Army paymaster's ambulance and had an armed escort, but they still managed to rob him.

"This gang is rumored to have committed at least fifty crimes. We'll never know for sure, but I'm guessing most of the stories are true."

Three more passengers joined the group along the way. For the next three nights, they stayed in the stage stations that dotted the three-hundred-and-fifteen-mile route to Miles City. They arrived at their destination on Saturday, July 31, 1880, at dusk. They checked into Mrs. Miller's freshly-remodeled, fifty-room Union Hotel, took hot baths, and ate their evening meals. Then the tired travelers bedded down for the night.

36: Montana manhunters—Billy Smith, Jack Hawkins, Tom Irvine, Louis King, and "Eph" Davis

Sunday, August 1, 1880: At half-past eight the next morning, Rankin, Boerum, and Hathaway met Deputy US Marshals Thomas H. Irvine and John X. Beidler, Sheriff Bullard, and Under-sheriff J.W. "Jack" Johnson in one of Mrs. Miller's small dining rooms.

Irvine said, "The way things are here in Miles City, secrecy is our best friend, but it's very hard to come by. Normally, Mrs. Miller puts the names of all her guests in the newspaper, but I've asked her not to submit your names. The fewer people who know you've been here, the better.

"I also spoke to my good friend, W.D. Knight, editor of the weekly *Yellowstone Journal*, and he has given me his word that nothing about the capture of Big Nose George and Bill Carey or your stay here will be leaked before the next issue, which will be Saturday, August seventh."

Rankin thanked him. "That was good thinking."

"The two men I deputized—Fred Schmalsle and Lem Wilson—will be here between eleven-thirty and noon to meet you gentlemen. They'll present witnessed affidavits pertaining to the capture, and get you to sign whatever they need to collect the reward money," Irvine said.

"That'll be our pleasure. We're looking forward to meeting them. We need to plan when we'll pick up the prisoners and decide the best way to leave here. Of course, we want to hear about the capture of these outlaws, too."

Boerum said, "I told Sheriff Rankin we think the best and most defensible way to travel is by steamboat. Tom, Jack—do you agree?"

Irvine thought for a moment and answered, "With layovers at Fort Buford and Fort Benton, it'll take you a lot longer to return by steamboat than it would to take a stagecoach back the same way you came. But if you return by stagecoach all the way, you'll be vulnerable to attack every mile of the trip, whether it's outlaw gangs trying to rob the stage or the prisoners' associates trying to rescue their friends, the result would be the same. Your prisoners would be set free."

Deputy Johnson said, "Last Monday, Cole, the driver of the Bismarck Stage, brought in mail that was stolen from an earlier stage by Indians. He also brought in the body of Dutchey, the driver. He was found near the mail sacks with a bullet hole in his head. Major Pope from Fort Keogh has sent troops out to find and punish the marauders."

Irvine continued, "You'd be more secure on a steamboat. The other advantage is that, on a steamboat, there are many places—including the boiler room—to secure the prisoners."

"Tom, I agree with you and Boerum. The best way to return is by steamboat," concluded Rankin. "Then I can take the Northern Pacific Railroad from Bismarck through St. Paul, Minnesota. It's a long route, but it's also the fastest way to get to Omaha."

Tom Irvine added, "The steamboat *Big Horn* will be off-loaded, reloaded, and ready to leave in the morning. When you're ready, I'll accompany you over to the ticket office to meet with the agent and book passage on her."

Boerum said, "Appreciate that. We should let the captain know we'll be bringing prisoners aboard, so he and his crew can back us up in case of trouble."

"Officer Beidler, you're welcome to come along, if you'd like."

Beidler said, "No, thanks. I have several things to attend to before returning those horses to their rightful owners. I'll meet you back here in the early afternoon so I can talk with Fred and Lem."

The men walked down to the ticket office and outlined their travel plans for the agent.

"Let me add this up..." the agent offered. "Looks like your return trip to Rawlins Springs will be about eighteen hundred miles. The way you came here from Rawlins Springs through Helena was eleven hundred miles. Although leaving here by steamboat and heading back through St. Paul is longer, it will be about the same amount of time, and a darn sight safer."

Boreum said, "A safer trip sounds good to me, not to mention no more dust and a more comfortable ride."

Showing his fondness for steamboats, the agent continued, "Gentlemen, the *Big Horn* is one fine boat, and a beautiful sight to behold! And this time of year, it's much cooler on the river."

Rankin said, "Let's book it."

"Very well. You'll travel together to Fort Buford. When you get there, Officer Boerum and Undersheriff Hathaway and their prisoner will transfer to the *Red Cloud*. You'll have about a two-day layover at Ft. Buford, waiting for the *Red Cloud*, but it'll be worth it. The *Red Cloud* will take you west to Fort Benton, and then you can take the stagecoach on into Helena.

"The *Red Cloud* left Fort Benton July twenty-third on her down-river trip to Bismarck. If anything would change her scheduling, they'll transfer you to *Eclipse*, *Far West*, *Rose Bud*, or one of the other Baker Company steamboats that'll still be running."

Boerum agreed, "That's fine with me. It'll be a nice change to ride something different, just as long as she doesn't kick up dust, smell like a horse, and draw flies."

Author's Note: The Steamboats

I found documentation that—on his return trip—Sheriff Rankin left Miles City on a steamboat. Two articles in **The Helena Daily Herald** *list the names of the steamboats as the* **Big Horn** *and the* **Red Cloud**.

The **Big Horn** *was considered to be the fastest boat on the river. She could carry 200,000 pounds of cargo and operate in water waist-deep to a man. She ran on the Yellowstone and Missouri Rivers and their tributaries between spring and fall. During the winter, the water level fell too low for safe travel.*

Captain John Todd helmed the **Big Horn** *when Jim Rankin made his journey. Todd had an excellent record in his more than fifty years on the river. His brother, Westly Todd, and R. Wesson were pilots on the boat. The clerk was Captain R.C. Mason, and he took very good care of the passengers.*

The **Big Horn** *was owned by the Coulson Line, which was managed by Captain D.W. Marrata. The main office was in Bismarck. Members of the crew were not allowed to smoke, drink, or swear.*

The **Red Cloud** *was a much larger boat. She could carry 324,000 pounds of cargo and operated only on the Missouri River, under the I.G. Baker and Company flag.*

Smiling, the agent said, "If you ever travel downriver on one of the steamboats carrying a dozen or so bales of buffalo, deer, and antelope hides, you'd think a horse's ass smelled like roses! But not to worry, most of the time a breeze takes care of that.

"Sheriff Rankin, you can stay right on the *Big Horn* to Bismarck, Dakota Territory."

Thinking about the prisoners they would be transporting, Irvine said, "The prisoners don't know you're in town. We wanted to make sure they wouldn't get word to their friends. So unless you have a reason to see them before you leave, I recommend that you stay away from the jail. We can take care of the paperwork here or at the sheriff's office. No need to tip our hand.

37: Steamboat *Red Cloud*

"We have them shackled together, and we'll have the blacksmith go over in the morning and separate the shackles just before you pick them up. We'll haul them down to the boat in the jail wagon at first light. Then we'll escort you down to the dock and stand guard until you're safely on your way. Does that meet your approval?"

All the lawmen agreed. After passage was secured, they walked across to the *Big Horn* and met with Capt. Jack Todd before returning to the small dining room at Mrs. Miller's Union Hotel. Rankin, Boerum, Hathaway, and Irvine were joined by Bullard and Johnson.

While they waited to be served, Rankin leaned back in his chair and asked Irvine, "Tom, when we were out and about, I heard several of the townspeople call you 'Marshal,' and just as many address you as, 'Sheriff.' You are a US Deputy Marshal, aren't you?"

"Yes, Jim, I'm a US Deputy Marshal."

Officer Boerum said, "I'm sorry, Jim. I never thought to explain his background. Now, Tom can tell you himself."

Irvine began, "Well, Jim…in 1878, I was nominated to run for sheriff and county assessor by the people's convention. I accepted the nomination, ran, and was elected. After I'd served for six months, it became apparent that the tax revenues and warrants couldn't sustain my position, so I approached the county commissioners and told them I didn't feel right about the financial burden this was causing the community. Helena has 3,600 citizens, and Butte has 3,300 citizens, but Miles City only has a population of 629 people, plus assorted woodcutters, herders, hide hunters, bone pickers, drifters, and tramps who—for the most part—don't own much taxable property.

"US Marshal Alexander C. Botkin of the District of Montana Territory had offered me a position as deputy US marshal, so I resigned my position as sheriff and county assessor and accepted the marshal job. This way, I'm in the area and involved with law enforcement, without being a financial burden to the community.

"After several lengthy discussions, the county commissioners said they would accept my resignation and appoint Mr. Bullard, here, to finish out my term of office. Mr. Bullard is a prosperous businessman and one of Miles City's favorite citizens. He offered to serve without salary for the remainder of my term, so the county would have an official sheriff and county assessor, but Under-sheriff Johnson and I handle the real law-and-order function.

"We do a pretty good business. Hell, we have fourteen lowlife bastards stacked like cordwood in that little jail, as we speak. With the drunks and less-violent ones, it's in the front door, sober them up, and out the back door. Then we can get ready for the next roundup. Revenues are a little more readily available, so the county commissioners are trying to decide whether to enlarge the current jail or build a new one."

Bullard laughed and said, "Tell them about taking the census."

"Of course, the US Marshal Service does have some odd little extra duties. I don't know if you know this, but one of the duties of the US Marshal Service is to take the census every ten years. I was taking the census on the reservation, and—of course—the Indians don't trust us. They thought we were there to do them harm. I'd go to the front door, and they'd be running out the back. I'd compare it to trying to count blowing leaves in a storm.

"Anyway, I do plan to run again. My official announcement will appear in the Saturday, August seventh, edition of the *Yellowstone Journal*. This time, I'll have a tough race on my hands. John W. Smith, the 'Old Frontiersman' who scouted for General Custer, has decided to run for the office on the Democrat Ticket. A.P. Flannagan, who is presently the county assessor, is running on the Reform Ticket. I'm running on the Peoples' Ticket. I'm not too worried about Flannagan, but Smith is very well-liked in these parts and may be hard to beat."

Just before noon, Fred Schmalsle and Lem Wilson came into Mrs. Miller's small dining room. Irvine stood and said, "Gentlemen, it is my pleasure to present the deputies that arrested Big Nose George and Bill Carey. Fred, Lem, let me introduce to you Sheriff Jim Rankin from Carbon County, Wyoming Territory, and US Deputy Marshal Boerum, and Under-sheriff Hathaway from Helena. I believe that you know everyone else."

Rankin, Boerum, and Hathaway shook hands with the heroes of the day. After they ordered dinner, Jack Johnson said, "Lem, Fred, these gentlemen are waiting for you to tell about the capture of Big Nose George and Bill Carey."

Schmalsle said, "I think Tom or Jack should start it; they both were involved before they brought us into it."

Irvine said, "All right, gentlemen. I'll start it, and each of you can jump in when your part comes around. During the past year, we've had Bill Carey, Jack Campbell, and John Wells—the one they referred to as 'Sandy'—in our jail for short stays. They were all in for minor charges...disorderly conduct, public intoxication, and such. We didn't realize who they really were or what they were wanted for.

"Sometime in early July, the man using the name 'George Dixon' and his friends had come to town and were trying to sell some horses. We were suspicious, so we began keeping an eye on them. They were staying in John Chinnick's cabin and had a number of horses in John's corral. Now, old John is a businessman and trader, and he's into many enterprises, such as freighting. He also has an interest in a ranch and owns a saloon and dance hall. We have reason to believe that he also has an interest in the sporting women that are using that old building down near the river for their cribs. John Chinnick walks close to the line, and we think he may cross over from time to time, but we just haven't been able to get enough evidence on him to arrest him. So, for now, he's nothing more than just a businessman. But when we saw Dixon and his friends with Chinnick, we paid attention.

"On the afternoon of Wednesday, July seventh, I telegraphed our boss, US Marshal Alexander C. Botkin, and told him my concerns about this group of men. I was curious how they came by the horses they had in their possession. Alex telegraphed us right back and instructed us to try to locate and arrest as many of the men as we could, on suspicion of stealing horses. He said he'd telegraph US Deputy Marshal John X. Beidler to come down from Junction City to see if he could identify any of the horses. Officer Beidler had been pursuing a gang that was stealing Indian and government horses, and he had good descriptions of some of the missing livestock.

"I took the telegram and met with Under-sheriff Johnson and Sheriff Bullard to formulate a plan. Since this gang knew all of us by sight, it wouldn't be easy to approach them. We decided it'd be best to use some of our trusted men to act like they were interested in buying horses and get the drop on them. We all agreed that the two best men to do this job would be Fred and Lem here. They're always available to help out.

"We deputized Lem and Fred and worked out the details of the plan. They agreed to start the deception on Friday, July ninth. We told them to take as much time as they needed to gain the confidence of the gang, so they could get close enough to make the arrest.

"On Thursday afternoon, July eighth, the suspect known as 'George Dixon' was drinking heavily in a local saloon. We later found out he was really George Parott or 'Big Nose George.' At any rate, he was well into his cups, and he began bragging about killing—or knowing who killed—two deputies in Wyoming Territory, back in eighteen-seventy-eight. One of the barkeeps slipped out and reported this information to me.

"I immediately went to Sheriff Bullard, and, together, we checked the old wanted sheets about the killing of those two deputies in Wyoming Territory. The description was a good enough match to Big Nose George, and the other descriptions would fit his companions.

"The wanted sheet listed a man called 'Jack Campbell' and, at the time, we thought he might be the fellow who gave his name as 'Bill Carey.' But as we reviewed our arrest records, we found that a man calling himself 'Jack Campbell' had been arrested for disorderly conduct and was jailed for a short time, several weeks earlier. He paid a small fine and was released. We also found that 'Bill Carey' had been arrested earlier on similar charges, had been held for several days, paid a small fine, and been released. With both names in our arrest records, we began to suspect that 'Carey' might really be John 'Sandy' Wells.

"Now that we believed we had at least one of the accomplices listed on the wanted sheets, we were pretty sure that George Dixon was, indeed, George Parott. We hoped to arrest the lot of them. If they were the gang that murdered the two Wyoming deputies, that raised the stakes, and it made our plans even riskier. These were dangerous men, and the last thing we'd want to happen was get one of our deputies killed. Of course, we didn't want to let them escape, either.

"We telegraphed US Marshal Botkins with the names of the suspects. He telegraphed back that 'Bill Carey' was wanted in the Sun River country and was thought to be part of the group pursued by Deputy X. Beidler. We were pretty confident that we were onto the Elk Mountain gang.

"We kept an eye on John Chinnick's shack and corral. We wanted to stay as close as possible without being noticed, so we could aid Fred and Lem, if needed."

Deputy Irvine paused for a moment and then asked, "Fred, Lem…which one of you would like to take it from here?"

Wilson nodded to Schmalsle, "Go ahead, Fred. You tell stories better than I do."

Schmalsle continued the tale, "During the meeting with Tom and Jack, we planned how Lem and I would approach John Chinnick's shack and start up a conversation about buying horses. We'd try to find out how many more horses they could provide, beyond those in Chinnick's corral. We all felt sure they had more horses in the vicinity and that the rest of the gang would be with them. If we could find the horses, we might be able to arrest the remainder of the gang.

"It was about two-thirty on the afternoon of Friday, July ninth, when three men came out of Chinnick's shack and sat down on the front porch. We already knew that John Chinnick was away on business and would not be back for several days, so we gave them a respectable amount of time to feel secure. Then Lem and I, dressed in our old workclothes, started walking straight across the patch of vacant ground toward the shack. We just acted as if we were looking for John to find out if any of the horses in his corral were for sale. While we were walking, one of the men got up and went inside, and we didn't see him again.

"The two men still on the porch just sat there and watched us every step of the way. We stopped about ten feet in front of them and bid them good afternoon. The one we suspected was Big Nose George asked what we wanted. The other man on the porch—who later was introduced as 'Bill'—said nothing.

"I told George we were there to talk to John about the horses there in the corral. George answered, 'Old Man Chinnick isn't here right now. What do you want to know about the horses?'

"I told him I have a small ranch near here, and I needed some good horses—already broke, if possible. I said I was looking for some that would make good cutting horses, and others that we could break and have ready for the fall roundup.

"George told me that Old John wouldn't be back for three or four more days—which, of course, we knew. Then he asked, 'What did you boys say your names were?'

"I introduced us, using our real names, and then he said, 'I'm George Dixon, and this is Bill Carey.'

"After that, we made some small talk about horses. We must have convinced them that our story was true, because George finally told us that the seven horses in the corral weren't John's—they belonged to them.

"Bill said, 'Come on. We'll walk over to the corral so you can have a good look at them.'

"There were seven fine-looking horses penned. Bill pointed his finger at three of the horses and said, 'Those three are our mounts and not for sale. The other four could be purchased for the right price.'

"I asked about the absence of brands on three of the horses. Bill said they'd bought them from an Indian on the reservation, and they had a bill of sale with his mark on it. Then he said he always provides a bill of sale for livestock he sells.

38: L.A. Huffman Studio, Miles City, Montana Territory

"We inspected the horses and discussed prices. Then I asked if they had any more horses for sale. George told us they may be getting more in the near future that we might be interested in looking at. We negotiated a bit more, and then Lem said, 'I think the prices seem fair. We'll get back to you in a couple of days—just as soon as finances can be arranged.' We said our farewells and left."

Schmalsle paused while the waiter served dinner. Then he began again, "On Saturday, July tenth, the four of us were taking turns watching Chinnick's cabin, hoping that other members of the gang might show up. About seven p.m., the two men left the cabin and walked toward the downtown area. About a block away from the Bella Union Theater, they stopped for a few minutes to look in the window of a store that had been closed for about a half hour. Then Bill walked up the street about a half block and went into Louis Bach's Brewery Saloon. George just sat down in the doorway of the store, as if he were planning to stay there for a while. Tom gave us the signal to go get George.

"At that very moment, Layton Alton Huffman—the photographer who has a studio next door to the Bella Union Theater—came out of his studio and locked up for the night.[2] Jack was across the street watching the saloon, and Lem and I—with our pistols hidden in our bib overalls—walked toward George. Tom stepped out of the Bella Union and summoned his good friend, Mr. Huffman, for a conversation. By keeping Mr. Huffman between George and him, Tom was partially-hidden from George's view. Tom told Mr. Huffman why he had stopped him and not to look around. Tom didn't tell Mr. Huffman, until later, that at least one of these men was wanted for killing two deputies.

"Lem and I were almost up to George before he spotted us. He looked a little surprised when we walked right up to him, pulled out our pistols, and said, 'Throw them up.' He put up his hands without resistance. We took his pistol and walked him around the corner to hand him off to Jack, who searched him for weapons before taking him to jail.

"Lem and I went back around the corner and headed toward the Brewery Saloon. Tom was still there, ready to back us up. When Lem and I went in, Bill Carey was at the bar, drinking. He never even looked around.

"We walked up behind him. I pulled out my self-cocker, put it to his head, and told him to throw up his hands. For a moment, I thought he might try to pull his gun, but he thought better of it when he saw that both Lem and I had our pistols trained on his head. While I kept him covered, Lem took his gun and handed it to Tom, who had joined us.

39: "Big Nose George" Parott, aka George Dixon

"I glanced at Mr. Huffman as we left the saloon. I swear, he was so excited, I thought he was going to jump out of his boots. We kept an eye out for the third man, but we never saw him again.

"We escorted Bill to jail and locked him up. The four of us then met in the office to discuss what to do to make sure our guests couldn't escape, even if some of their friends showed up. Jack suggested we send for the blacksmith and have their leg irons welded together, which we did. Neither George nor Bill could even go to the privy without the other, let alone make a run for it."

Sheriff Rankin said, "Gentlemen, it sounds like you've done very well. There's a two-thousand-dollar reward for Big Nose George, you know."

Officer Boerum, offered, "There will be a thousand-dollar reward on Bill Carey from the Sun River folks."

Rankin added, "There's a standing two thousand dollars per head for any of the other outlaws who took part in the Elk Mountain murders, as well."

Irvine said to Rankin, "Jack and I will come by the hotel at four-thirty tomorrow morning so we can go over to the jail together. That will give us six guns, counting Officer Beidler. If you think we need more, we can ask Fred and Lem to be available."

"I think six men should be enough. Plus, we should try to keep Fred's and Lem's identities a secret, just in case you need them again."

"I'll make sure we have the blacksmith there in the morning to cut the rivets securing the chain."

The men said goodnight and parted company.

Monday, August 2, 1880: The six men converged on the jail at approximately 4:45 a.m. The blacksmith arrived, bringing a small twelve-pound anvil, a four-pound hammer, and a very sharp cold chisel. The jailer brought out the two prisoners and their personal belongings, walking behind them as they shuffled side by side in the hallway. Both prisoners seemed surprised to see so many lawmen waiting for them.

Under-sheriff Jack Johnson addressed Carey first: "Bill Carey, this is Under-sheriff Hathaway and Deputy US Marshal Boerum. Of course, you know Officer X. Beidler…he interviewed you several days back. Officer Boerum and Sheriff Hathaway are here to take you back to Helena to stand trial for stealing horses."

Carey said nothing. Then Johnson turned to Parott. "George Dixon, this is Sheriff Jim Rankin. He is here to take you back to Rawlins Springs, in Wyoming Territory, to be tried for the murder of Deputies Widdowfield and Vincents."

Parott looked as if someone had kicked him in the guts.

Sheriff Rankin stepped in. "You have been indicted by the Grand Jury of Carbon County as 'George Parott, alias Big Nose George.' You have given your name here as 'George Dixon.' I don't really give a damn what you call yourself. The extradition papers have been served and approved by Governor Potts. It's not my job to judge you…just to take you back to stand trial."

Parott proclaimed his innocence. "My name is George Dixon, and I've never killed anyone, nor have I been in Wyoming Territory in the last five or six years! You're wasting your time taking me to Rawlins Springs. I've done nothing wrong, and I can prove that I'm innocent of whatever it is you are accusing me of doing. It's a miscarriage of justice to even take me there. They'll just have to turn me loose as soon as they see I'm not the man you are looking for."

Rankin replied, "Mr. Dixon, or whatever your name is…it would be in your best interest to just shut up and listen. I want you to understand something before we begin our trip to Rawlins, you low-life son of a bitch. The two deputies you murdered—Tip Vincents and Bob Widdowfield—were very close, personal friends of mine. So if you give me just the slightest provocation…as God is my witness, I'll kill you on the spot. Whether you arrive in Rawlins alive or dead is strictly up to you. And when you are tried and found guilty—and I do believe you will be found guilty—I'll take a certain amount of pleasure in hanging you."

Tom Irvine took charge. "First of all, we're going to separate the leg irons, so just lift them up on that small anvil."

With the leg irons on the anvil, the blacksmith put the cold chisel on top of the rivet and used the hammer in his right hand to strike the head of the chisel. On the fourteenth blow, the head of the rivet flew across the room. When the second rivet's head was cut off, the piece of chain fell to the floor, and the two prisoners were separated. The blacksmith picked up his tools and left.

Officer Boerum explained, "The jail wagon waiting outside will take us down to the boat dock. You'll be boarding the steamboat *Big Horn*."

Sheriff Rankin turned to the prisoners. "Just so we all understand each other…if you try to escape, I'll kill you where you stand. And if any of your outlaw friends tries to rescue you, I'll shoot you first, and then we'll kill them, too. From this point forward, you two will not communicate with each other.

If you do, I'll personally close your mouths. If we have an understanding here, then let's move on out to the wagon."

The two lawmen helped the shackled prisoners get up on the wagon bed, while Under-sheriff Jack Johnson climbed onto the seat and took the reins. The other five men positioned themselves, one at the rear and one at each corner of the wagon, looking out. As the wagon moved toward the boat dock, the officers walking alongside watched every alley and shadow, looking for potential ambush.

The prisoners went aboard and were handcuffed to a railing near the boiler room. The law officers stood guard, watching for any attempts at a rescue.

Monday, August 2, 1880, 6:00 a.m.: The *Big Horn* was poled away from the boat dock, and the big paddle wheel began moving the boat downstream on the Tongue River toward its junction with the Yellowstone. The three law officers on the boat and the three watching from the dock gave each other a final salute.

For the first two hours of the trip to Fort Buford, the three lawmen—one on each side and one back by the paddle wheel of the steamboat—watched the riverbanks for anything unusual. The prisoners, still shackled and holding their belongings, had been handcuffed to a bench. The further downriver they went, the less vulnerable to attack they would be. Barring problems, Rankin and his prisoner would arrive in Rawlins Springs by midnight, Saturday, August seventh .

Sheriff Rankin observed, "I can't believe how much hotter it is here than in Rawlins Springs. By noon, the temperature is stifling."

"If you think this is hot, wait until you get into Iowa and Nebraska," one of the pilots said.

40: Merchants Hotel, St. Paul, Minnesota

Tuesday, August 3, 1880: By eight the following morning, the steamboat *Big Horn* had traveled northeast on the Yellowstone River, entered the Missouri River, and tied up at the dock at Fort Buford. There would be a two- to three-hour layover while cargo was loaded and unloaded and a new supply of firewood taken aboard. Boerum and Hathaway got off with their prisoner, Bill Carey. They'd wait a day and a half for the steamboat *Red Cloud* to arrive from Bismarck on its run upstream on the Missouri River to Fort Benton. During the good-byes, the lawmen agreed to telegraph each other concerning the disposition of their prisoners.

By ten-thirty, the *Big Horn* was headed southeast down the Missouri River toward Bismarck, Dakota Territory. By midday Wednesday, August fourth, they arrived in Bismarck, and within three hours, Rankin and Parott were on an eastbound Northern Pacific Railroad passenger train, headed for Fargo, Dakota Territory. From Fargo they would travel southeast across Minnesota to St. Paul.

Thursday, August 5, 1880: The Northern Pacific Railroad passenger train arrived in St. Paul in the early hours of the morning. Sheriff Rankin, with his prisoner in tow, checked into the Merchants Hotel. They would stay in Room E until it was time to have a noon meal. They moved only when necessary because of the shackles on Big Nose George's legs. After they ate, they headed to the St. Paul and Sioux City depot, attracting curious stares from townspeople.

The trip to Omaha would require travel on both the St. Paul and Sioux City Railroad and the Sioux City and Pacific Railroad. The train was scheduled to leave at 2:30 p.m., and the trip would take eighteen hours. They would travel through Sioux City and Council Bluffs, Iowa, cross the Missouri River, and arrive at the Union Pacific Depot in Omaha, Nebraska at ten in the morning on Friday, August sixth.

Rankin telegraphed ahead to County Attorney Smith, in Rawlins, letting him know to meet him in Cheyenne. Then he telegraphed the Union Pacific Railroad Officials in Omaha to let them know he would be traveling through. He thought they might want to meet one of the suspects who had tried to derail their train and who had murdered two deputies. That done, Rankin chose a bench against the back wall of the waiting room, where he and his prisoner could sit.

They hadn't been seated long when a reporter from the *Saint Paul Pioneer Press* came in and asked for an interview. He said his editor had received a telegram from W.D. Knight, editor of the *Yellowstone Journal* in Miles City, tipping them off that Rankin and his prisoner would have a layover in St. Paul. Rankin granted him an interview.

The prisoner told the reporter that his name was "George Dixon," and, again, he professed his innocence. He protested his being taken to Wyoming Territory to stand trial.

The interview was brief, since they had to board the train for Omaha. The reporter stayed with them until the conductor called, "All aboard!" The conductors seated Rankin and his prisoner near the toilet, as far away from other passengers as possible, which was common practice.

Friday, August 6, 1880: At the stop in Sioux City, Conductor Watson boarded the train. He and Sheriff Rankin talked about the crime the prisoner had attempted and other railroad crimes.

Watson informed Rankin that John Rafferty, the engineer killed in the accident, had been a dear friend and neighbor. He shook his head and said, "The fireman and about twenty passengers were severely injured. Most of the cars remained upright, so the sons of bitches went through all the cars and robbed the passengers. For all that effort, we estimate those skunk bastards only got off with a few thousand dollars in money and jewelry."

In two hours, they were in Omaha, where they transferred to the Union Pacific Railroad. Rankin telegraphed ahead to notify Sheriff George W. Draper and City Marshal Andrew Ryan that he would be passing through Cheyenne early on Saturday with the prisoner. Sheriff Draper and some of his deputies wanted to talk to the prisoner, hoping he could help them clear up some of the unsolved robberies they still had on the books.

Rankin had barely finished the telegram when a special agent summoned him to a private room where several Union Pacific Officials were waiting, eager to get a look at the scoundrel accused of the attempted derailment of their train, as well as participating in the murder of the two dupities.

Finally, it was time to board Union Pacific Passenger Train Number 3. Sheriff Rankin helped his prisoner up the step, and they made their way to their seats. The heat in the car was stifling.

He said to a fellow passenger, "Damn, I don't know how people can stand to live around here, in this heat. I'll be so darned happy to get back to Rawlins Springs."

It would be dark soon, and Rankin was thankful that much of the trip from Omaha to Cheyenne would be at night, when they could open the windows wider in the passenger car and let some fresh air in.

Foot Notes:
1. John Xavier Beidler was known throughout the territories simply as "X" or "X Beidler." In 1860 and 1870, he probably participated in more citizen committees, miners court trials, and lynchings than any other person in the history of Montana Territory. "X" was absolutely fearless and had the reputation of "striking terror in hearts of evildoers" as noted in *The Yellowstone Journal*, July 24, 1880.
2. Layton Alton Huffman 1854–1931: Arrived in Miles City, Montana Territory, in December 1879, at the age of twenty-five, and served as the Fort Keogh photographer. Huffman is viewed as one of the great Western photographers of the period. Many of the photographs in this chapter are credited to him.

Chapter 12

Another Necktie Confession

Saturday, August 7, 1880: Number 3 arrived in Cheyenne at shortly after one p.m, and City Marshal Andrew Ryan, Laramie County Sheriff George W. Draper, and Deputy Martin were there to meet it. Although Parott sported a heavy beard, Ryan and Martin were positive they had seen him before. When they questioned him, Parott admitted to freighting between Cheyenne and the Black Hills, as well as Sydney and Deadwood. But he denied ever committing any crime.

Carbon County Attorney George C. Smith joined the group. He would accompany Rankin and the prisoner to Rawlins. Draper said he would telegraph Sheriff Boswell and let him know to meet Number 3 passenger train. Then he and Ryan said good-bye and left.

The train pulled out of Cheyenne and headed west through Borie, Granite, and Colorado Junction. It made its scheduled stop at Sherman Station and then headed down into Laramie City, where Sheriff Boswell and Deputy Butler would be waiting.

Saturday, August 7, 1880, just before 5:00 p.m.: Deputy Butler approached Sheriff Boswell. "Looks like old Number 3 is almost on time. Are you ready?"

"Let's go."

They left the courthouse and headed down A Street, toward the depot.[1]

Butler said, "Superintendent Dickinson made arrangements for all of us to meet in the small dining room, out of sight of those nosey Laramie loafers."

They entered the dining room, where Sheriff Rankin, Prosecutor Smith, Big Nose George, and Dickinson were already waiting. Sheriff Boswell addressed the prisoner, "So you're Big Nose George. I can damn well see why they call you that. I think I've seen you before…in Cheyenne a few years ago. Weren't you the asshole that was trying to beat one of Big Ass Mary's girls out of the brass chip you owed her? You didn't have a full beard then—just a mustache."

"Don't know what the hell you're talking about."

"Yeah, you do, you sorry son of a bitch. You wanted to take a free ride on that trolley. You're just lucky that Big Ass Mary didn't cut your gizzard out with that straight-edge razor she kept tucked in her garter. Dangerous business trying to cheat one of her sporting women."

"That wasn't me. I've never had a row with the whores in Cheyenne or any other place."

"Well, if that was you—and I still think it was—you didn't stick around long enough to try the hospitality of the Grey Stone Hotel."

Turning his head, Boswell asked, "So, Deputy Butler, have you seen George Parott before?"

"No, I don't believe I have. I think I'd have remembered him."

Superintendent Dickinson jumped in, addressing the prisoner. "I think I speak for everyone in this room…I'll be looking forward to the day we travel up to Rawlins and watch the Sheriff hang you."

Parott replied, "Hang me for what? I haven't done a goddamn thing!"

Rankin said, "Just shut up and eat, George. I'm sick and tired of hearing about your innocence. That's all I've heard since I picked him up in Miles City, and it's starting to chap my ass." Turning to the other lawmen, Rankin said, "We almost had *two* of these bastards on the way to the gallows."

"What happened?"

"We're pretty sure they had Campbell in jail in Miles City, under an alias. They held him overnight on a drunk-and-disorderly charge. But he paid the fine, and they turned him loose before they had any idea who he was or that he was wanted for murder."

Looking at his pocket watch, Dickinson said, "It's five forty-five. The train will be pulling out in about twenty minutes. You should start toward your car."

Sheriff Boswell said, "We'll walk with you, to make sure you get safely on your way."

As the three men boarded the passenger car, Boswell cautioned, "Stay alert, especially when you get to the town of Carbon."

"Don't worry, Boz. I don't plan on letting this one out of my sight."

Boswell and Butler left, and the conductor called, "All aboard!"

With a blast of steam, the driver pistons began moving the great iron driver wheels, and the powerful "four-four" steam engine moved forward. The click of the pin and link couplers echoed as the slack was pulled out of the draw bars, and the train picked up speed.

"God, I love that sound," Boswell smiled as the two men watched the train clear the depot and head toward the north end of the Laramie City railroad yard. "Come on…let's get some work done."

The closer Number 3 got to Carbon, the more apprehensive Sheriff Rankin became. Though he didn't really expect any problems, he would be relieved when he had Big Nose George safely deposited in the Carbon County Jail.

As the train came to a stop at Medicine Bow Station, Rankin checked his pocket watch and said, "This train should pull out at about nine-fifty, which will put us in Carbon about ten-thirty. We'll stop there for about thirty minutes to take on water and fill the coal tender."

The mailbag was loaded in the express car, and Number 3 jerked forward. Once the train was up to speed, time went by quickly. It wasn't long before the train slowed again, as it entered the coal town of Carbon.

Rankin turned to his prisoner, "We're coming into Carbon. This is where one of the deputies you murdered was from."

George sputtered, "I keep telling you, goddamn it…I didn't kill anyone."

"Shut up. I don't want to hear your bullshit."

Rankin unlocked one end of Parott's shackles and passed the chain through the cast-iron frame of the seat. Then he locked it again. He handed the key for the shackles and the key to the handcuffs to Smith and instructed, "Put the keys in your pocket, and then go sit on the other end of the car."

Turning back to Parott, he said, "This is just a precaution. I'm sure everyone in Carbon already knows you're on this train, and I don't want any trouble with any damned vigilantes that might want to hang you. Most likely, nothing'll happen. It's late, it's dark, and the conductor told me the mule-drivers are sponsoring a hop in town. I hope the good citizens are either in bed or at that dance. But I don't want to take any chances."

When the train stopped, they heard someone outside counting from one to fifteen. Alarmed, Sheriff Rankin yelled, "What the hell is that about?"

Fifteen masked men entered the car, surrounding the Sheriff and his prisoner. The entire group was very quiet. There was no yelling and very little talking. They went about their business with the same precision they had used with Dutch Charley. They knew who they were after and where they would find him.

Two masked men had climbed aboard the engine and yelled at the engineer and his fireman. "Don't you even think about moving this train. Our business is not with you. Just do as you're told, and you won't be harmed." Three other masked men had found the conductor in the next car, pushed him into a seat, and given him the same message.

When Sheriff Rankin saw the group enter the car, he drew his revolver and ordered them to stand back. Unfazed, the masked men pointed their pistols at Rankin's head and closed in around him. One of them ordered him to hand over his pistol and the key to unlock the chains securing the prisoner.

Rankin called out to other passengers, "I need help here to keep this damn mob away from my prisoner!"

Smith stood and moved toward the Sheriff, shouting his objections to the mob, but one of the vigilantes pointed a pistol at his head, pushed him down in his seat, and told him to shut up and stay put. After that, no one else offered to help Sheriff Rankin.

Several masked men grabbed the Sheriff from behind and took his pistol. They searched him, looking for the keys. When they couldn't find them, the mob leader ordered one of his men to go to the section gang's tool house and get a sledgehammer.

Parott took the opportunity to grab one man's pistol, but when he could not turn it in his cuffed hands, he was overpowered by members of the mob. The pistol's owner cursed, "That goddamned son of a bitch was trying to shoot me with my own gun."

Someone returned with a twelve-pound sledgehammer, and the vigilante leader told him where to strike the cast-iron seat member. After three blows, the cast-iron fastening broke enough to remove the chain.

Another man placed a rope around Big Nose George's neck, and two of the masked men jerked Big Nose George to his feet.

One said, "You're coming with us."

Parott resisted. "Good God! Don't do this. I was not in the crowd that killed those deputies. If I have to die, please just shoot me. I don't want to be hung!"

Tugging on the rope, the masked man sneered, "Come on, you cowardly, back-shooting bastard. You're going to answer for what you did."

Jerking the rope, the entourage made their way out of the passenger car.

Addressing the men guarding Sheriff Rankin, the vigilante leader instructed, "Stay with him until we're done with this son of a bitch. If he struggles, tie him up. No one's to leave this train. Do you all understand me?"

At the end of the car, two men helped Big Nose George navigate the steps in his shackles. Parott hopped off the bottom step and landed on his feet. The mob pushed him down the track to the old corral near the telegraph pole where Dutch Charley had been hanged. They shoved Parott under the massive horizontal beam that bridged the tops of the two vertical gateposts. Passengers and train personnel watched, some standing on the car steps and some still seated in the passenger car.

There was just enough moon to light the scene. Big Nose George leaned against the corral. The end of the rope had been thrown over the beam and was held by one of the masked men. The mob stood waiting.

In minutes, two figures emerged from the darkness: a woman escorted by a younger man. When she and her son reached the inner circle, Ann Widdowfield stood ten feet from Big Nose George. She said nothing, looking at the prisoner sadly.

The mob leader nodded to the Widdowfields and then turned back to Big Nose George. "Start out by telling us your name."

"I do not want to die with a lie in my mouth. I will tell the truth, so help me God, but give me a little time. I am so badly scared, I can hardly talk."

"You can have all the time you want. But I want to know now, what is your name?"

Slumping against the gate for support, he replied, "My name is George Francis Warden. Some people call me 'Big Nose George.'"

"Do you know why we removed you from the train?"

"Yes."

"Tell us what happened on Elk Mountain. And I'm warning you…tell the truth, and don't leave anything out."

Parott began, "I was in the party that murdered Widdowfield and Vincents."

"Who else was in this party?"

"Frank Towle, Mack…Frank James, Dutch Charley Clarke, Jack Campbell, Tom Reed, Sim Waun, Sandy, and me."

Big Nose George sputtered out a quick description of the aborted train robbery. Then he moved on to the ambush. "It wasn't 'til later I learned who the deputies were. I don't know for sure who killed the first man—Widdowfield. I think Frank Towle shot him through the mouth, when he got off his horse at our campfire. We saw him pick up the corks that had been cut off the horseshoeing we'd done…he said something about them being spikes. Then he knelt down by the campfire and put his hand in the ashes. We heard him say, 'It's hot as hell. We'll catch them before night.'

"That's when Frank—or someone—shot him in the mouth. Widdowfield fell forward into the firepit. His partner spurred his horse and took off up the canyon. That's when somebody in our crowd—I'm not sure who—shouted, 'Fire!' We all shot at him. We were so close to him, it was almost impossible for us to miss. We must have hit him at least twenty times.

"He fell off his horse. He tried to get up and shoot back, but he just fell over dead. Then some of our group robbed them—both of them. We took clothes, boots, guns, horses, saddle, and such. We got scared that others would come looking for these men, so we hid the bodies and covered them with brush. Sim Waun took charge of getting us out of there…he knew the country. We took their horses to dispose of later."

"So Dutch Charley was one of your group?"

"Yes."

"What was Dutch Charley's last name?"

"His name was Charles Clarke."

"What about Joe Minuse?"

"Joe Minuse wasn't there. He was supposed to be with us, but he never came back from the Green River country. I saw him there about five days after the killings.

"I've been a hard case, but I was partly led into that scrape."

One of the masked men interrupted, "I was riding a wild horse on the day those men were killed, and in the same direction, and would have passed your camp had my horse not thrown me. Would you have killed me if I chanced to pass that way?"

"I don't know."

One of the masked men asked, "Why did you kill those men?"

"We thought they were lawmen looking for us. Dead men tell no tales."

"Where are the rest of your gang?"

"Don't know. We separated that fall. I heard Dutch Charley was hung along the Union Pacific Railroad, and Frank Towle was killed in the Black Hills. Someone said Mack died of the fever up in the Yellowstone country, but I don't know about that. When we split up, he said he and Sim were going back to Missouri. Maybe he changed his mind. Jack and Sandy are still up in Montana Territory."

The leader of the vigilantes said, "This is the place where Dutch Charley was hung—right there on the cross arm of that telegraph pole."

Big Nose George fell to his knees.

The vigilante leader turned his head, "Mrs. Widdowfield, have you heard enough?"

"Yes, I have," she sighed. "He has confessed. Send him to Rawlins to stand trial. You don't need any more trouble with the judge. Maybe they can find out more about the rest of the gang, so they can be brought to justice, too."

At that, she and her son made their way back through the crowd. The mob leader looked down at the kneeling Parott, and spat out, "I'd just as soon hang you now, but we'll respect the widow's wishes. You swore to tell the truth, and you damn well better do just that when you get to Rawlins Springs." Turning to his men, he said, "Take him back to Sheriff Rankin."

Several of the masked men returned the prisoner to his seat on the train, leaving him sobbing. Rankin cursed them under his breath and then asked the station agent to telegraph his deputies in Rawlins about what had happened. Number 3 pulled out of Carbon twenty minutes late. The whole incident had lasted about thirty minutes.

Sheriff Rankin settled down, thankful that Big Nose George was on his way to Rawlins Springs to stand trial, instead of heading to Potters Field to join Dutch Charley.

Sunday, August 8, 1880, 12:35 a.m.: Passenger Train Number 3 came to a stop at the Rawlins Depot, thirty-eight minutes behind schedule. Deputy Sheriffs H.E. Flavin, J.W. Finley, L. Calvert, and Lewis Cook were waiting for the train. Initially, just two of them planned to meet the train, but after they heard about the incident in Carbon, they decided to bring along the other two deputies. All were armed to ensure that there were no similar problems in Rawlins Springs.

Smith and Rankin helped the shackled prisoner down to the ground. The trio quickly made their way toward the waiting lawmen. The deputies took note of the outlaw's looks. He appeared to be about thirty-five, 5'10" tall, about 160 pounds, dark complexion, black hair and beard. He had black eyes and a very prominent Roman nose. He was noticeably subdued from his brush with the vigilantes.

Turning to Rankin, Deputy Sheriff Flavin asked, "So you met up with some vigilantes?"

"Sure did. Those goddamned miners and mule skinners were on me before I could do anything. My neck and shoulders still hurt."

"Well, at least you made it back here with the prisoner. The telegram said someone would write up the prisoner's confession to the citizens' committee and send it up to us later today."

Rankin said, "Apparently he promised the vigilantes that he'd tell us the whole story, just the same as he told them."

Smith cautioned, "That confession was made under extreme duress. It would never be allowed in any court in this territory."

"It really doesn't matter. I believe we have enough evidence to find Mr. Parott guilty."

George Parott hung his head, "Sheriff, I've already made up my mind to tell you the whole thing."

A weary Rankin said, "For now, just get him locked up. We'll book him in later."

The jailer, Bob Rankin—Sheriff Jim Rankin's brother—was waiting to take custody of the prisoner. "I'm pleased to see you back, brother."

"Glad to be back. Can't wait to get into my own bed. It's been a long two weeks."

Deputies Cook and Calvert planned to stay at the jail for the remainder of the night, as backup in case the locals decided to pay a visit to Big Nose George.

Sheriff Rankin turned to Deputy Flavin, "Do something for me. Go back to the Western Union Telegraph Office, and wire Deputy Jens Hanson at Carbon. I'd like to know where in the hell he was when all this was going on."

Deputy Calvert said, "Go on home, Jim. We have everything under control. Juletta will be relieved to see you home safe. Get some rest."

"We'll plan on interviewing the prisoner as soon as we get a copy of George's confession to the vigilantes. Telegrapher E.E. Calvin was close enough to hear most of it. He'll write up his notes and telegraph them to me, later this morning. He said he couldn't recognize anyone, since they were all masked. But at least we'll have the confession.

"Glad that trip is over. Between you and me, I'm glad I didn't have to shoot one of those vigilantes to save that son of a bitch."

Footnotes:
1. "A" Street in Laramie was renamed "Thornburgh," after Major Thomas T. Thornburgh, who—with thirteen of his soldiers—was ambushed and killed south of Fort Steele during the Meeker Massacre. Later, the name would be changed to "Ivinson Avenue," in honor of businessman/banker Edward A. Ivinson.

Chapter 13

Arraignment

Sunday, August 8, 1880, 11:45 a.m.: George Parott was booked into the Carbon County Jail and charged with murder in the first degree. George Parott—a.k.a. Big Nose George, a.k.a. George Dixon, a.k.a. George Francis Warden—would be formally arraigned during the September session of Court.

Monday, August 9, 1880, 7:30 a.m.: At his office, Sheriff Rankin caught up on the arrests and bookings that had occurred during his absence. Deputy Sheriff Howard L. Bair arrived about eight o'clock and greeted him, "Good morning, Sheriff. You look rested."

"Morning, Howard. Well, it's hard to get any rest when you're transporting a prisoner. You have to sleep with one eye open. Let's get a cup of coffee and go into my office. I'll brief you on my trip, and you can bring me up to date on what's been going on here."

The two men talked until almost ten, when a trainman delivered a letter without a return address. Sheriff Rankin speculated, "I think this is what we've been waiting for."

He read the unsigned letter and passed it to Bair. "This is a more detailed version of what took place than what we got from the telegraph operator. I'd say this version of George's confession was extracted by the vigilantes.

"I notice that it tracks real close to the confession Sheriff Boswell got from Joe Minuse. Parott confirms that Minuse wasn't at Elk Mountain when the murders took place. Take it over and show it to County Attorney Smith when you're finished reading it. Ask him to come over this afternoon, before I talk to George."

Deputy Bair returned to the office shortly before noon and told Sheriff Rankin that Smith couldn't be there that afternoon. "He said you should let George read that vigilante letter, if he's literate. If he's not, then read it to him. Ask him if the letter describes his confession accurately. Then ask him if it's true. If it is, get him to sign it. If it's not, ask him to correct it."

Rankin headed home for lunch, saying that after two weeks of eating food on the road, it would be good to have his wife fuss over him a little. Around two o'clock, he went to the jail to meet with Parott. Big Nose George, wearing handcuffs and shackles, was brought into the jail parlor and directed to sit down across the table from the Sheriff.

"George, after the vigilantes got done with you, you said you'd tell me everything about the killings. I think you should know we got a letter describing what you told them. Would you like to read it?"

"Yes," George snapped.

"You know, you don't have to tell me anything, and you have the right to have an attorney present when we talk. You told me a few days back that you are indigent—that you don't have money to pay an attorney."

"That's right."

"The Court will appoint an attorney to represent you."

"I don't know that I need one. I plan on confessing everything I've done."

"The Court will provide you with an attorney, anyway. Do you want to talk to me before you get an attorney?"

"I'll talk to you now."

"OK, then take a look at this letter. Tell me if it's what you told the vigilantes. If it is, then sign the bottom. If it isn't, then write down what's different. And remember—you don't have to do this."

"I reckon this is going to cost me my life, but I'd rather be legally hanged by you, Sheriff, than lynched by a mob."

"You'll get a fair trial, Parott. We're not going to let a group of vigilantes drag you from this jail."

"You couldn't stop them from dragging me off the train. How are you going to keep them from coming into this rickety-ass jail after me?"

"It's just not going to happen."

The prisoner read the letter and nodded his head. "Yeah, it's what happened." He signed and dated the bottom and handed it back to the sheriff.

Later, Sheriff Rankin briefed Prosecutor Smith.

41: John Friend, Editor, *Carbon County Journal*, Rawlins, Wyoming Territory

Tuesday, August 10, 1880, 2:45 p.m.: Sheriff Rankin walked into his office. "Tom, I ran into Mr. Friend."

"Who?" asked Deputy Tom Cook.

"John C. Friend, the editor of the *Carbon County Journal*."

"What the hell does John want?"

"Permission to interview Big Nose George."

"What took him so long?"

"Don't know. I told him I'd have to ask the prisoner; it's his choice. So I stopped by the jail, and George agreed to the interview. I'll be there to make sure everything is handled properly. Could you stop by the *Journal* office on your way to work tomorrow and let them know we can do the interview in the afternoon? If the reporter gets any more out of George, I'll let Prosecutor Smith know right away."

Wednesday, August 11, 1880, afternoon: Sheriff Rankin escorted John Friend from the *Carbon County Journal* into the jail and introduced him to Big Nose George. Parott seemed pleased to have a new audience for his story. After the interview, Rankin walked over to brief County Attorney George Smith.

"So, Sheriff, did you learn anything new?"

"One thing. He told John Friend that his name is 'George Francis Warden.'"

"'George Francis Warden?' Where the hell did that come from? Have you heard that before?"

"As a matter of fact, I have. That's the same name he gave to the vigilantes in Carbon. Well, you know a lot of outlaws use aliases, mostly to keep from shaming their families if they get caught."

Smith acknowledged, "You're right. Anyway, as far as we're concerned, his name is 'George Parott.' That's what the indictment, arrest warrants, and extradition papers all say, and that's what his acquaintances all know him by."

Rankin continued, "Let's be sure to get Saturday's paper. They'll have the full story of the Carbon affair, as well as this interview with Big Nose George. Of course, those stories probably will be in all the other newspapers in the Territory, after they send them out."

Saturday, August 14, 1880: The *Carbon County Journal* ran extra copies of the paper, knowing that demand would be high. Sheriff Rankin got two copies hot off the press and headed to his office. He handed Deputy Cook one copy and then settled down at his desk to read the other.

CARBON COUNTY JOURNAL
August 14, 1880

THE ELK MOUNTAIN MURDER.

George F. Warden Gives the Whole Affair Away and Clears Up the Mystery

A JOURNAL reporter, in company with Sheriff Rankin, visited the jail Wednesday afternoon and interviewed Big Nose George, or George Francis Warden, as he gives his name. Warden, we should judge, is a man about 35 years old, five feet ten inches tall, rather spare built and will weigh about 160 pounds, dark complexion, black hair and beard, sharp, rather piercing black eyes and a very prominent Roman nose, and really not as bad a looking fellow as one would expect. He was arrested at Miles City, Montana, July the 15th, and arrived here Sunday morning.

Warden's story is as follows as near as we can give it from memory:

Our party pulled the spikes that held the rail, but the crowbar being a short one we could not pry out the rail. We laid in a gully nearby all day and watched the section men at work, they not discovering the rail had been tampered with until just as they were about to leave in the evening. Two of our party went into Medicine Bow station and purchased provisions. After the section men left in the evening, we again commenced work on the rail and were driven away by the approach of the passenger train from the East. When we left we proceeded direct to Elk Mountain.

The first we saw of Widdowfield and Vinson, they were about a mile off, and we took them to be loose horses, but shortly made out that they were men and were making direct for our camp. After a hurried consultation it was decided to hide our stock in the brush and conceal ourselves and let the men pass should they not be officers, and to kill them should they be such, as we expected they would say something to give us an idea as to who they were.

They rode up the trail to our camp fire, when the large man (Widdowfield) got off of his horse and stuck his hand into the fire, remarking, "It is hot as h–ll , they have been here and we will catch them before long."

One of our party had a lame horse for which he had been fixing a pair of shoes, and Widdowfield picked up the corks which had been cut off, saying they were heads of railroad spikes. Frank Toule, one of our party, then said, "Let's fire," and loud enough for all to hear, part of us shooting at the man on the ground and part at the man on the horse. I fired at the man on the horse.

After our volley the horses and rider run about fifty yards when the latter fell off his horse, and attempted to get up, holding his gun in his hands. Some twenty shots were fired at him and firing only ceased when we were certain he was dead. Jack Campbell took Widdowfields's boots and Dutch Charlie the best saddle.

After taking what valuables they had, we got scared and did not know what to do with the bodies but finally concluded to carry them down in the brush and cover them up which we did. We immediately broke camp, came down the canyon the same way we went up and started north. We crossed the railroad at Carbon and the Platte River about two miles above the mouth of the Muddy. Sim Wan was the leader of the party he being acquainted with the country. One of the party, called Mack, who was with us, claimed to be one of the James brothers. I left the party on Goose Creek where it broke up.

The foregoing is Warden's story as related to us. He seems to be very much frightened and depressed. Sheriff Rankin is taking every precaution for his safe keeping.

CARBON COUNTY JOURNAL
August 14, 1880

THE ARRIVAL OF BIG NOSE GEORGE

HE IS FORCIBLY TAKEN FROM THE TRAIN
Is Badly Scared and Wants a Little Time

Makes a full Confession

Carbon, Wyo. August 10, 1880
Editor Journal:

On Saturday evening last the fun loving public of this place were congregating for a hop to be given by the mule-drivers of Carbon.

No. 3 pulled in on time and to a few it was known that "Big Nose George," one of the Widdowfield-Vinson murderers, in charge of Sheriff Rankin, was on the train. As soon as the train stopped a shrill voice was heard, calling out numbers from one to about fifteen, and in response to the call about as many armed and masked men boarded the car in which the sheriff and his prisoner were seated. As soon as the sheriff saw the first of the mob enter the car he hastily drew his revolver and ordered them to stand back. They closed in and around him and ordered him to put up his hands and deliver over the key that unlocked the chain that the prisoner was secured to the car-seat with. The sheriff refused the key and called upon several in the car to help keep the mob away from the prisoner. The now impatient mob seized an axe and broke the fastening and at the same time a rope was dexterously thrown around the neck of Big Nose George, who up to this time appeared perfectly cool and collected, he was then quickly hustled out of the car and taken to a corral and placed under an ominous looking beam. Before leaving the car he said he was not in the crowd that killed Widdowfield and Vinson, but that if he had to die, and it looked like it, he would like to be shot and not hung.

As soon as he knew he was under the beam he weakened and said: "I do not want to die with a lie in my mouth, and I will tell the truth, so help me God; but, give me a little time, I am so badly scared I can hardly talk."

He was told he could have all the time he wanted and, as near as can be learned, he told the following:

"I was in the party who murdered Widdowfield and Vinson. The party consisted of Frank Toule, Mack, Dutch Charlie, Jack Campbell, Thomas Reed, Sim Wan and myself. My name is George Francis Warden.

I don't know who killed Widdowfield. When Widdowfield got off his horse to examine the place where our camp fire was and said: 'It's hot as h--l, we'll catch them before night,' somebody in our crowd said 'fire' and, our guns being in position, we fired almost simultaneously, I don't know who gave the command to fire. It was almost impossible for us to miss him; we were so close upon him, I think we all fired at Vinson. I saw Joe Manuse five days after on Green river. I have been a hard case, but I was partly led into that scrape. The horses that belonged to the dead men we took along, they were killed and other wise disposed of."

One of the masked men then said, "I was riding a wild horse on the day those men were killed, and in the same direction, and would have passed your camp had my horse not thrown me. Would you have killed me if I chanced to pass that way?

A: "I don't know."

Q: "Why did you kill those men?"
A: "On the principle that dead men tell no tales."

Q: "Do you know where the balance of the party is that were with you on the day of the murder?"
A; 'I do not. We separated the same fall I heard that Dutch Charlie was hung on the U.P.R.R. Frank Toule was killed in the Hills, and Mack died of the fever in the Yellowstone country."

The prisoner was then told that this was the place where Dutch Charlie was hung and he almost broke down.
The leader of the mob then ordered them back and turned the prisoner over to the sheriff, and Big Nose George breathed freer.
When he was seated in the car he slid down between the seats and burst into a hysterical fit of weeping.
No. 3 pulled out, the whole performance occupying about 30 minutes, and everybody took in the dance after a slight intermission.
Several parties here feel better satisfied since learning for a fact that Dutch Charlie was not hung innocently.
The only wonder is that Big Nose George did not climb the golden stair via the route.
Ignoramus.

Sheriff Rankin finished reading the articles and commented, "Everytime I think about the way those sons of bitches murdered my friends, I get so damn mad. I'll do everything humanly possible to bring all those murderers to justice."

Friday, August 20, 1880: Sheriff Rankin received copies of two Extradition Warrants issued to the Territory of Montana from Wyoming Governor Hoyt, signed and dated the eighteenth day of August, 1880. The first was for Jack Campbell and George Parott, alias Big Nose George, and the second was for John Wells, alias Sandy.

Tuesday, August 24, 1880, 1:30 p.m.: Sheriff Rankin and County Attorney Smith met to discuss the arraignments and trials that would take place in the upcoming session of court. Rankin brought a copy of the *Cheyenne Daily Leader* that one of his deputies got from a trainman friend, and they took a few minutes to discuss the article about the Elk Mountain murders. Then they turned their attention to the list of witnesses.

Most of the witness subpoenas had already been issued, but a few were still pending. They agreed that finding Frank Howard for the George Parott trial might be a problem. Smith said, "I doubt we'll need Howard's testimony, since Big Nose George has confessed his guilt, but you'd better know where he is, just in case we do."

Rankin replied, "Can't blame him for not trusting the law. That was an ugly misunderstanding last June, and I feel bad about my part of it."

Howard had been arrested for fraud when William J. Smith claimed that Howard had defrauded him of sixty-eight dollars. Howard had borrowed the money from Smith, giving him a voucher to present to the Union Pacific Railroad, who owed him the money. When Smith presented the voucher to the railroad, the paymaster, Joslyn, said that Howard had no payment coming to him. When Joslyn turned Smith away, Smith went to Rankin, claiming fraud. Rankin telegraphed the Sheriff in Salt Lake City, asking them to find and hold Howard, which they did. Rankin brought Howard back to Rawlins, and he appeared in Justice Court on June twenty-fifth. When pay records were introduced into evidence, he was exonerated of all charges. Despite everyone's apologies and the fact that the county bought him a ticket back to Salt Lake City, Howard was understandably unhappy.

"Well, I'll drop by the depot and see if any of the railroaders can shed light on where Frank might be," Rankin continued. "He talked like he was going to stay in Salt Lake City. I'll wire Ed Dickinson in Laramie City and see what he knows about Frank's whereabouts."

Monday, September 13, 1880, 8:30 a.m.: Sheriff Rankin arrived at the jail early enough to have coffee with his brother Robert before escorting the prisoner to Court for his arraignment.

"Morning, Bob. Is the prisoner about ready to go?"

"Ready when you are."

"I want to get him to the court by nine-thirty."

"He didn't eat very well this morning. Seems anxious about the court proceedings."

"I guess I'd be, too, if I were him."

"His Court-appointed attorneys—Samuel T. Lewis and his assistant from Laramie City, Charles W. Bramel—spent several hours with him on Friday."

The Rankin brothers enjoyed their coffee and conversation. At 9:15, Sheriff Rankin asked his brother to get the prisoner. "I'd better get going. Judge Blair doesn't like to be kept waiting."

Bob Rankin brought Big Nose George out, shackled and cuffed. Parott had been allowed to shave and trim his moustache once a week, and his hair had been cut.

"I'm ready to go, Sheriff. I just wanna get it over with."

The two men crossed the street to the first floor of the Masonic Temple, which was being used to house county offices and the District Court until the new courthouse building could be completed. When they entered the courtroom, they saw that it was standing room only. As they made their way to the defense table, Parott kept his head down.

All the spectators had known one or both of the dead deputies. They scrutinized the prisoner closely.

A man in the back of the room commented, "Parott should never have been allowed to leave Carbon alive."

His companion replied, "Yeah, but then we would've missed seeing them hang the son of a bitch here in Rawlins Springs."

The defense attorneys were already seated and deep in discussion with Prosecuting Attorney Smith, who stood beside them.

Smith said, "There's no goddamned way my office will accept a plea of 'Murder in the Second Degree.' No plea bargaining. We'll prove our case. He's already admitted to Murder in the First Degree to everyone who would listen to him." Smith returned to the prosecution's table.

Defense Attorney Bramel said, "George, sit next to me. Sheriff, you can sit just behind George."

Arraignment

Clerk of Court John W. Meldrum entered the courtroom and walked to the small table next to the judge's bench that he would share with J.C. Richardson, the official stenographer for the Territory of Wyoming. The table was just beside the judge's bench, which faced the prosecution and defense attorneys' tables. The spectators' gallery was behind these tables, and the jury chairs were on the side, behind a heavy oak railing. At the judge's left was the witness chair.

At 10:10 a.m., Meldrum stood and announced, "All rise."

Judge Blair walked into the courtroom and sat at his bench. He directed the spectators to be seated.

Meldrum remained standing while he announced, "Territory of Wyoming, County of Carbon, Second Judicial District Court is now in session. The Honorable Judge Jacob B. Blair presiding. Our first order of business is the arraignment of George Parott, Case Number 265, Territory of Wyoming versus George Parott. Please stand."

George Parott and his two attorneys rose to their feet. Judge Blair addressed the defendant, "On April seventh, eighteen-seventy-nine, the Grand Jury of Carbon County brought forth an indictment charging you, George Parott, alias Big Nose George, and others did willfully murder Robert Widdowfield and Henry H. 'Tip' Vincents, near Elk Mountain, in the County of Carbon, Territory of Wyoming, on or around the nineteenth of August, eighteen-seventy-eight. At this time, you are being arraigned for Murder in the First Degree of Henry H. "Tip" Vincents. The Court now requires you to answer to the question: are you guilty or not guilty of the things herein charged?"

Cautiously, Parott answered, "Guilty of Murder in the Second Degree."

Prosecutor Smith rose to his feet. "I object to such a plea, Your Honor. On behalf of the people, I object to a plea to a charge other than that which was set forth in the indictment."

"Mr. Smith, Mr. Lewis, Mr. Bramel, please approach the bench."

To the three attorneys before him, Judge Blair asked, "Gentlemen, just what is going on here?"

Smith said first, "Your Honor, the defense counsel approached me with this proposition less than fifteen minutes ago. I informed them that the prosecution could see no reason to allow such a plea bargain. At this time, the Territory is prepared to prove Murder in the First Degree in the murder of Henry H. Vincents."

"Is this correct, gentlemen?"

"Yes, Your Honor."

"I'm going to recess this arraignment until later this afternoon. Now, gentlemen, step back."

Judge Blair turned to Parott, who was standing with his counsel. "George Parott, at this time, I will not accept your plea. I'm going to recess this arraignment and continue it to later this afternoon. I now order you to return to your jail cell and meet with your counsel. They will explain to you the consequences of whichever plea you choose to make this afternoon."

Judge Blair addressed the two defense attorneys. "Gentlemen, make certain the defendant understands that the charge brought forth in the indictment is that of Murder in the First Degree. He must answer to that charge, 'guilty' or 'not guilty.' Are we clear on this matter, gentlemen?"

"Yes, Your Honor."

"This arraignment proceeding is recessed. I expect you to be back in Court at two this afternoon. You are now free to leave. Mr. Meldrum, let us proceed with the next item of business before this Court."

Monday, September 13, 1880, 2:00 p.m.: Clerk Meldrum entered the courtroom. The attorneys, George Parott, Sheriff Rankin, and Bailiff Thomas Durant were in their respective places. The spectators' gallery, again, was standing room only.

At 2:05, Judge Blair declared, "This Court is back in session. The Court will now continue the arraignment of George Parott, Case Number 265, Territory of Wyoming versus George Parott.

"George Parott, at this morning's session, I could not accept your plea. I ordered you to meet with your counsel to ensure you had a full understanding of the arraignment process. Did you meet with your counsel?"

"Yes, Your Honor."

"Very well, then. Let us proceed."

The judge read the indictment again and then addressed the defendant, "The Court now requires you to answer to the question, are you guilty or not guilty of the things herein charged?"

Parott looked at the Judge and answered, "Guilty."

Judge Blair paused and then continued, "Before accepting your plea, I deem it my duty to explain to you the consequences of your plea. Although your attorneys have no doubt explained this to you, this is a serious matter, and we should leave no room for doubt or misunderstandings.

"According to the law of this Territory, the penalty for Murder in the First Degree is death by hanging by the neck. That will be the consequence of the plea you seek to make. In view of these facts, I ask you, again, George Parott; are you guilty or not guilty of the crimes therein charged?"

He answered, "I am guilty."

Tears ran down the bandit's cheeks as Parott took his seat. Everyone in the courtroom sat silently.

The Judge addressed Prosecuting Attorney Smith, "I will expect you to produce evidence in Court that Vincents and Widdowfield really were murdered before I formally accept his plea and pass sentence on the prisoner. When you are ready to proceed, notify Mr. Meldrum, and he'll calendar the day and time to present. Once you have satisfied this Court, Mr. Parott will be sentenced. If possible, I'd like this matter resolved before we adjourn, and not continued into November."

Sheriff Rankin and Millard Leach escorted Big Nose George from the courtroom. Leach had requested an interview with Parott, which the sheriff and the prisoner granted.

Meanwhile, Judge Blair called Clerk Meldrum to the bench. "John, when we are through with Court today, I want you to go the jail and interview George Parott to ascertain whether or not he is competent."

"Yes, Your Honor. I'll do all I can to determine the man's competence."

Meldrum went to the jail about 7:15. He was taken to the prisoner, who was sitting on the edge of his bunk with his head in his hands.

Bob Rankin said, "George, John Meldrum, the clerk of the court, is here and would like to speak with you."

Parott looked up at Meldrum and asked, "What do you want?"

"Mr. Parott, Judge Blair asked me to come over and visit with you."

"Why?"

"Well, most prisoners charged with first-degree murder would have pleaded 'not guilty,' knowing that conviction on that charge would mean hanging. You have the right to plead any way you choose, but we want to make sure your plea is fully your choice. The Judge wants to make sure you don't feel threatened or under duress. I want you to understand that, if your plea was 'not guilty,' the Court would protect you during the trial."

Parott rocked back and forth for a minute, before responding. "Well, I've made up my mind that if this thing is going to cost me my life, I'd rather be hung by the Sheriff than by a mob. The way I figure, if I entered a plea of 'not guilty,' a mob would take me from the Sheriff and hang me."

"Let me assure you, again, that if you wish to change your plea to 'not guilty,' the Court will protect you."

After their talk, Meldrum reported his findings to Judge Blair. "Your Honor, I've just spent about an hour alone with the prisoner. At first he didn't really want to talk to me, but after I assured him the Court would protect him, regardless of what his plea was, he became more talkative. He told me pretty much the same things we've read in the papers. He says he is guilty, and he knows he'll have to pay with his life."

"What could you ascertain about his mental state?"

"Your Honor, my opinion is that he is competent to stand trial. He's terrified that he might end up in the hands of a lynch mob."

"Very well. Thank you, John."

Friday, September 17, 1880, 9:00 a.m.: The defense counsel notified Clerk Meldrum that George Parott wished to change his plea to "not guilty." Judge Blair asked Meldrum to notify all parties to be back in Court at five o'clock, so the defendant could change his plea.

Sheriff Rankin escorted George Parott back to Court a little before five.

At five p.m., the Court reconvened. Judge Blair announced, "This arraignment is back in session. It is my understanding that Mr. Parott wishes to change the plea he entered on Monday, September 13, 1880."

Defense Counsel Lewis replied, "Yes, Your Honor, he does."

"The Court will now continue the arraignment of George Parott, Case Number 265, Territory of Wyoming versus George Parott. Please stand."

Parott and his attorneys rose to their feet.

"George Parott, at the morning session of this Court, Monday last, I could not accept your plea and ordered you to meet with defense counsel to ensure your full understanding of the arraignment process. You did meet with your counsel, and in the afternoon session of Court, you entered the plea of 'guilty.' Is that correct, Mr. Parott?"

"Yes, Your Honor."

"And now you wish to change your plea."

"Yes, Your Honor."

"Very well, then. Let's proceed."

After the judge again read the indictment, he asked, "Are you guilty or not guilty of the things herein charged?"

Parott answered, "Not guilty."

"This Court accepts your plea of 'not guilty;' and as soon as the clerk has a chance, he'll calendar it for trial in November. This arraignment is now closed."

The judge rapped his gavel, and everyone in the room stood as Judge Blair left the courtroom.

About 5:45, Sheriff Rankin returned George Parott to the jail. Bob Rankin locked the prisoner in his cell and returned to the jail parlor, where his wife Rosa had brought coffee for the two brothers.

Sheriff Rankin turned to Bob, "Well, he changed his plea to 'not guilty.'"

"Well, as many times as I saw his attorneys here this week, I figured something like that was about to happen. How did Judge Blair react?"

"He took it in stride. Nothing ruffles his feathers. He just accepted the change and informed everyone that they'd be notified just as soon as Meldrum has the calendar set for November."

"Well, that's done, then."

"Guess so."

"So," Bob Rankin asked, "how is your campaigning for sheriff going?"

"I don't know. It's damn hard to get out to campaign when Court is in session. George Dustin is giving me a run for my money. He seems to be my biggest competitor for the Republican nomination. I hope the party comes through for me, but when it comes to politics, who the hell knows? All I can say is, there's an ass to fit every saddle."

"Who do you think the Democrats are going to nominate?"

"Personally, I think it'll be Ike Miller. He's well-known and well-liked around town. Last time I was in his Alhambra Billiard Hall, funning with him about those Rawlins Springs loafers that hang around his place, I asked him if he was giving away shots of whiskey and a free game of billiards in exchange for votes. That tight old Dane told me he'd start giving away whiskey the first Wednesday after hell freezes over. He's a good man. You can't help but like him."

George Smith stopped by the jail and joined the brothers for coffee. The political discussion continued.

"George, I wish you'd change your mind and run again."

"I appreciate you saying so, but I've had enough. I want to do something different for a while. Being county attorney does tend to tie you down."

"Who do you think will get the nomination?"

"I think Sam Lewis will get the nomination for the Democrats, and probably Homer Merrill for the Republicans. You'd better take ol' Ike Miller seriously, Jim. He's already talking about an ordinance that would force everyone to check their firearms when they come to town. That sounds real good to a lot of folks who would like to see Carbon County settle down. You'd better glad-hand everyone you see and kiss babies until your lips are chapped."

"Well, George, you may be right. But I don't have much patience for that bullshit. I just believe in getting the job done as best as I can."

Monday, September 20, 1880: In early afternoon, Prosecutor Smith stopped by the sheriff's office. "Sheriff, I just had a visit from Sam Lewis. Do you know what he told me?"

"With Sam, God only knows."

"He said he was on his way to send a telegram to Judge Blair on behalf of Big Nose George, who now wants to change his plea back to 'guilty.' George wants the Judge to come up from Laramie City on Saturday and sentence him."

"Well, one thing's for sure…Big Nose George gives the newspaper plenty to write about."

"The Judge will probably respond to both Sam and me. As soon as I get word, I'll let you know. Well, I'd better be on my way."

"Thanks for letting me know."

Thursday, September 23, 1880: Prosecutor Smith updated Rankin on the Parott case. "Jim, I received a telegram this morning from Judge Blair saying he'd come up on Saturday to pass sentence on George. Due to the press of business, I couldn't get away and come over to let you know. Turns out, that was just as well.

"I just received a second telegram from the Judge. Now he says he will *not* be up on Saturday to sentence George. After more thought, he now believes that—because the Court has adjourned until November eighth—any sentence handed down during this period would not be legal. He said he'll sentence George when Court is once again in session in November."

Chapter 14

Changes

After an early frost during the second week of September, the weather became mild—"Indian summer," according to the old-timers. The beautiful weather lasted well into October. For the most part, life returned to normal, or as normal as things could be during an election year. Both political parties held conventions in September, and with just a little more than six weeks to garner the support of the voting populace, everyone was campaigning for their candidates.

The *Carbon County Journal* ran articles heralding the virtues of "Our Candidates," meaning the Democrat candidates. The two most-watched races were for sheriff and county attorney. Incumbent Sheriff James G. Rankin was the Republican candidate, and businessman Isaac Carson Miller was the Democrat candidate. For county attorney, Prosecuting Attorney Homer Merrill was the Republican candidate, and Samuel T. Lewis was the Democrat candidate. All the candidates were civil to one another because they liked each other.

Saturday, October 30, 1880, 11:30 a.m.: Sheriff Rankin walked into the county jail to have coffee with his brother, an issue of the morning's *Carbon County Journal* tucked neatly under his arm.

"G'morning, Bob. Did you get a copy of that son-of-a-bitch John Friend's daily wipe?"

"Yeah. I read it. That bastard is coming at you with both barrels blazing."

"That letter of endorsement he published is dated October twenty-sixth, Golden, Colorado, but I think he's been sitting on it since the convention. He just wanted to print it closer to the election."

Jailer Rankin replied, "I know our former boss, Ike Lawry, is behind this. He wanted George Dustin to be drafted as the Republican candidate. When that didn't happen, he and that bunch of turncoats he associates with threw their support behind a Democrat, Ike Miller! Just look at who signed this letter: 'Captain Lano, Thomas O'Leary, J.S. Hickey, W.V. Doolittle, I.M. Lawry, H.E. Flavin, R. Patterson, and Frank Higley.' Course, we don't know if they *really* signed the letter that was published, but it sure does look bad."

"The one that surprises me most is Flavin. He spent all that time with us, and when he left, I wasn't aware that he had a problem with me. I promise you this—I'll ask him to his face, next time I see him."

The jailer said, "I thought when they all got gold fever and went prospecting around Leadville, Colorado, I'd seen the last of them for a while. Then this letter."

"Well, several of these men have been back in town for a couple of weeks. I've seen them. I figured they were back to winter here. You know, looking at the style of writing, I'm thinking John Friend himself may have written it for them."

"Jim, the part that really makes me angry is the way they imply you can't handle the job when things get rough. Like when they say, 'We all want to see a man for sheriff have a little sand and judgment, and we know Miller has both. We know of what we speak—we have seen Miller in tight places, and he did not skip or flinch.' Hell, the only time Ike Miller's ever in a tight place is when he's throwing some drunk out of his saloon! Don't get me wrong: I like Ike Miller, but these bastards have gone too far when they try to make you out to be a coward, compared to him."

> **Author's Note: Frank Murray**
>
> *Government teamster Frank Murray and Charles Chapman were in Richard Dailey's saloon playing cards and drinking. Murray got loud, became threatening, and fought with Dailey, who threw him out.*
>
> *Murray went to his wagon and got a rifle and six-shooter and went looking for Chapman. He wanted to get back ten dollars he'd lost to Chapman in the card game. When he caught up with Chapman and demanded his money back, Chapman gave him the money and a twenty-dollar gold piece. Murray took the money and then shot Chapman in the head.*
>
> *Murray started up Cedar Street, cursing and threatening to shoot anybody that tried to get close to him. Sheriff Rankin went out to subdue him, and Murray started shooting at him. Rankin deputized Harry Errett, Bill McCarty, Private Anthony Hobert with the Third Cavalry at Fort Steele, and several other men. Eventually, the Sheriff and Private Hobert caught up to Murray, who'd gone between the wagons behind the jail.*
>
> *Murray started shooting at them, and they had no choice but to shoot back before innocent people were hurt. Both Hobert and Sheriff Rankin shot simultaneously, and Murray fell dead.*
>
> *John Friend wrote a glowing report about this incident in his* **Carbon County Journal.**

"What I don't understand is why John Friend has changed his tune about me. He hadn't run the *Journal* more than a week when he wrote that piece about how I brought down Frank Murray last year. Treated me like a hero. Now, he's changed his tune.

"Last Saturday, he wrote that character assassination about me, saying I didn't know what to do to stop that mob that tried to get at that murdering son-of-a-bitch Fernando Fierce that you have locked up in back. Made me look like an addle-brained dullard. 'Course it was good that Dr. Maghee and some other good citizens got them stopped in front of Fred Wolf's Saloon. But I wouldn't have let them lynch anybody."

"Don't worry, brother. If you get reelected, John Friend will be kissing your ass again to get a story."

Tuesday, November 2, 1880: Election Day: There was a good turnout for the election. The voters of Carbon County trickled into the polling stations throughout the day. By early afternoon Wednesday, the ballots had been tallied. The official verification and announcement would come later. Most of the incumbents held onto their positions. However, in the race for sheriff, Isaac C. Miller defeated Jim Rankin, 693 votes to 650. In the race for County Attorney, Homer Merrell received 760 votes to Samuel T. Lewis's 584.

Monday, November 8, 1880, 10:00 a.m.: The November session of District Court convened, with Judge Blair presiding. In late October, the Court had ordered a special grand jury, and that jury was sworn in on that first day of Court. Isaac Carson Miller—the newly-elected sheriff—was appointed foreman. He would have ample time to serve on the grand jury before being sworn in as sheriff in January.

Sam T. Lewis and Charles W. Bramel—counsel for George Parott—filed a Motion for Change of Venue. The motion was accompanied by a supporting affidavit, sworn and subscribed by George Parott on November 8, 1880, before Judge of Probate M.E. Hocker.[1]

Judge Blair addressed the clerk of court, "John, I'll need to rule on this motion today. Please notify the defendant and his counsel and the prosecutor to be here at two this afternoon to receive my ruling."

At two o'clock, all parties were seated at their respective tables awaiting Judge Blair. Nearly every seat in the gallery was filled with spectators. Soon thereafter, Judge Blair walked into the courtroom, and convened the session.

"Gentlemen, in reference to Case Number 265, The Territory of Wyoming versus George Parott, the Court has a motion and supporting affidavit filed on behalf of the defendant, George Parott, seeking a change of venue. Before ruling on the motion, I will read same for the record."

Territory of Wyoming)
County of Carbon) to wit:

<u>*In the District Court of the Second Judicial District*</u>
Territory of Wyoming)
vs.   ) Motion for
George Parrott   ) Change
*   of Venue*

Now comes the defendant George Parott in his own proper person and by his Counsel S.T. Lewis and C.W. Bramel and moves the Court now here for a Change of Venue in this cause for the following reason, to wit: that the Judge before whom this cause is now pending is prejudiced against the defendant and that defendant cannot obtain a fair and impartial trial before said Judge. In support of which said Motion and Affidavit of the defendant is herewith filed.

Lewis and Bramel
Attys. for defendant

Then the judge read Parott's affidavit requesting change of venue.

"After careful consideration, the Court grants the defendant's Motion for Change of Venue, and notice is hereby given that the Honorable William Ware Peck, Associate of the Supreme Court, will be the Presiding Judge. Case Number 265 is hereby set to continue at ten a.m., Monday, November fifteenth, eighteen-eighty. Court is adjourned."

42. Photocopy of George Parott's affidavit requesting change of venue, showing Big Nose George's signature (with the correct spelling of his name).

Monday, November 15, 1880, 12:27 a.m.: The Hon. William Ware Peck arrived from Cheyenne on Union Pacific Passinger Train Number 3. He looked forward to getting a few hours of sleep at the Union Pacific Railroad Hotel before going over to the courthouse at nine a.m. He wanted ample time to talk to Judge Blair and Clerk John Meldrum.

After breakfast at the Union Pacific Restaurant, Judge Peck walked to the courthouse. He had dressed for the weather. It had snowed again, and the temperature was twenty degrees below zero.

Judge Blair had already spotted him when Judge Peck walked in the front door of the courthouse. "God almighty, Bill. Did you bring this weather up from Cheyenne with you?"

"No, Jacob, I did not. But it sure makes me realize how much I was enjoying the beautiful Indian summer we had."

43: William Ware Peck, Judge, Third Judicial District Court, Wyoming Territory

"It's been snowing for the last four days. Appears this'll be as bad a storm as that four-day storm last March. You probably couldn't see much coming in on Number 3 in the dark, but the cuts are trying to drift shut. It was thirty below zero last night, and for the rest of the week, they're expecting it to drop every night…could get as low as forty-five to fifty below zero. The ranchers are expecting to lose a lot of their cattle and sheep.

"But anyway, it's good to see you, my friend. Come on into my chambers. I'll have John bring in the files so you can familiarize yourself with the case."

Meldrum brought several large files to the Judge's chambers.

"The prosecution issued subpoenas for their witnesses back on the eighteenth of August, requiring them to appear September thirteenth. Then they were all notified to appear on November eighth. Of course, with the change of venue, they were sent home and told to report back tomorrow, the sixteenth. We have thirty-six potential jurors called for the Petit Jury. They should be able to come up with twelve that are acceptable."

"Jacob, you mentioned that George Parott's counsel contacted you after adjournment in September… said he wanted to change his plea back to 'guilty.'"

> **Author's Note: Sagebrushing**
>
> *Judge William Peck was so disliked in Uinta and Sweetwater Counties that the Wyoming legislators passed a redistricting bill (which was known as the "Sagebrushing Act") which placed those two counties into Judicial District Two. Judge Peck was transferred to District Three, made up of two unorganized and lightly populated counties, Peace and Crook. This exile through redistricting was known as "sagebrushing."*
>
> *President Hayes, a good friend of Judge Peck's, was so displeased that Territorial Governor Thayer had not vetoed the redistricting act, he did not extend Thayer's appointment for a second term.*

Judge Blair said, "I told the defendant and his counsel that I didn't think a plea accepted when Court was adjourned would be legal. I told them they'd need to pursue that on November eighth. But instead of pursuing the plea change, they filed a Motion for Change of Venue and requested you by name. I think they came up with this new strategy when they found out that Prosecuting Attorney Smith was bringing William Wellington Corlett from Cheyenne to take over this case."

"You're right, Jacob. I think that's exactly what they're counting on. And if they insist on using Corlett, I'd have no choice but to recuse myself. But if they think my feelings for Mr. Corlett would cloud my judgment in any way, they don't really know me.

"It's true that I don't much like Mr. Corlett and his Southern States Rights cronies. They did a pretty good job of sagebrushing me. I guess they thought I was too much of a threat. Of course, since I don't have much to do in my new third district, I've had a lot of time to write most of the Supreme Court opinions. So they didn't render me completely impotent.

"But you can rest assured, Jacob, I'm here to see that the defendant gets a fair trial. I'd never allow anyone—including that conniving lawyer—to cloud my judgment. So let the matter proceed to trial."

Meldrum told him, "We've calendared the trial to begin November sixteenth at eleven a.m., so you'll have ample time to review. A Special Grand Jury was summoned and began their work last Monday. They finished all their work and were discharged Saturday. They issued three indictments. The Grand Jury Foreman was Isaac C. Miller, who has been elected sheriff and will take office in January. Do you know him?"

"I've met him. Isn't he the one that has that billiard hall and whiskey shop?"

"That's the one."

"He struck me as a real personable man. What do you think Sheriff Rankin will do now?"

Meldrum said, "I don't know. He and his brothers have several businesses…horses, livery stable, freighting, mining, and who knows what else. He's one tough character, and he'll always land on his feet. I've heard on the grapevine that Bill Daley will become Sheriff Miller's under-sheriff."

Judge Blair added, "I think Robert Rankin will stay on as jailer. It's a good job and—most of the time—not too demanding. He has a local delivery service and short-distance freighting operation that he runs on the side.

"Well, it's time for Court."

44: Rankin Brothers' Stage Line

November 16, 1880, Tuesday, 11:00 a.m.: Everyone was seated, awaiting Judge Peck. As before, nearly every seat in the gallery was filled. Shortly thereafter, Clerk of the Court John W. Meldrum called the Court to order. Judge William Ware Peck began proceedings.

Judge Peck announced, "Our first order of business this morning will be jury selection for Case Number 265, Territory of Wyoming versus George Parott . On April seventh, eighteen-hundred-and-seventy-nine, the Grand Jury of Carbon County brought forth an indictment charging you, George Parott—alias Big Nose George—and others with murder. Specifically, the indictment says you unlawfully, willfully, purposely, maliciously, feloniously, deliberately, premeditatedly, and with malice of forethought murdered Robert Widdowfield and Henry H. Vincents near Elk Mountain, in the County of Carbon, Territory of Wyoming, on or around the ninteenth of August, eighteen-seventy-eight. You were charged and arraigned for the Murder in the First Degree of Henry H. Vincents. Are the defense attorneys ready to proceed?"

"We are, Your Honor," responded Samuel Lewis.

"I see here the triers for the prosecution will be Mandeville E. Hocker, William L. Ash, and Nelson L. Andrews." Addressing Prosecutor Smith, Peck said, "Mr. Smith, I see here that Homer Merrill has withdrawn from this case, and William W. Corlett is to take charge as soon as he arrives."

"Yes, Your Honor. Due to a conflict in scheduling, Mr. Merrill is involved with another case before the Court. When that case concludes, he'll be available to assist where needed."

"Very well, gentlemen. As Mr. Corlett has not graced us with his presence, and I see before me two very capable prosecutors, I see no reason to delay further. Let us proceed."

Most of the day was consumed by jury selection. Finally, about four-thirty p.m., the process was complete. Twelve men had been selected: Thomas Creighton, O.A. Hamilton, George Birmingham, A.W. Eaton, A.W. Reynolds, E.J. Bowen, Walter French, Charles Kesterton, W.W. Chapman, L.W. Kling, E.L. Swazey, and C.E. Rand.

Prosecutor Smith addressed the bench, "Your Honor, now that the jury has been selected and sworn, and since neither Mr. Corlett nor Ed Dickinson—one of the prosecution's key witnesses—has arrived, the prosecution requests the Court for continuance until tomorrow."

Defense Attorney Lewis quickly responded, "I object! Your Honor, the prosecution is stalling for time because they know they don't have a proper case against the defendant. The defense is ready to proceed with its opening statement. The prosecution has had since last August to prepare their case. Because it's obvious they don't have a case, the defense moves that all charges be dropped against the defendant, without prejudice."

Judge Peck barked, "Motion denied!"

"Your Honor, before you grant the prosecution's Motion for Continuance, the defense requests that the prosecution submit a proper affidavit listing the reasons for the request."

"Agreed. Request granted." Judge Peck looked at his gold pocket watch and continued, "It's after five. I'm going to recess the Court and allow everyone time to have supper. I'll expect you back at seven this evening. Mr. Smith, I suggest you use this time to prepare an affidavit to support your motion. Be prepared to submit it to me when we come back."

"Yes, sir."

Smith was back in the courtroom at quarter of seven, motion and affidavit in hand. As soon as Meldrum returned, the prosecutor filed them with the Court. At seven, the courtroom was about three-quarters full. John Meldrum declared that Court was in session and handed the Judge the prosecutor's motion and supporting affidavit to review.

"The first order of business this evening is to read and rule upon the prosecution's Motion for Continuance." Judge Peck began to read aloud:

Territory of Wyoming   )
County of Carbon) SS

In the District Court of the 2nd Judicial District

Territory of Wyoming   )
*   vs.   ) Motion*
George Parrott Et al   )

Comes now G.C. Smith Prosecuting Attorney on behalf of the Territory of Wyoming and moves the Court now hereto continue the further proceedings in this cause until tomorrow Morning (November 17th 1880) for the reasons set forth in the affidavit hereto annexed.

G/C. Smith
Prosecuting Attorney

"And now I will read the affidavit in support of Motion for Continuance."

Territory of Wyoming)
County of Carbon) SS

G.C. Smith being duly sworn says he cannot now safely proceed to trial in this cause wherein The Territory of Wyoming is Plaintiff and George Parrott Defendant for the following reasons: Because of the absence of E. Dickinson who is a material witness on behalf of the Prosecution and without who's testimony the Prosecution cannot safely proceed to trial. That the evidence of Mr. Dickinson is material for the Prosecution in this cause. That the same facts cannot be proven by any other witness who can be as readily obtained. That Mr. Dickinson was subpoenaed to be here at this time as deponent is informed by the Sheriff and last night informed the Sheriff that we should let him know when he was wanted and he would be here. That deponent ordered the subpoena issued for him to be here on Monday the 15th which was yesterday. That he is not now absent with the consent of deponent or by his conveyance. That deponent had reason to expect said witness to be here and did expect him to be here at this time. Deponent further says that he was taken by surprise in this case in that up to this morning when the case was called deponent expected that Honorable W.W. Corlett would take charge of and manage the case. That Mr. Corlett was engaged in this case and that deponent had arranged with Mr. Corlett to manage this case and take charge of the trial and that deponent relied on that arrangement up to this morning. That when the case was before the Court in September last Mr. Corlett was in the case as Counsel for the Prosecution and that then and since that time deponent consulted with Mr. Corlett and from that understanding deponent relied on Mr. Corlett to manage the case and that deponent is therefore not prepared to proceed and do justice to the Territory. That last week when His Honor Judge Blair set this case down for trial he said to deponent that he desired to sit the case so as suit the convenience of Mr. Corlett, as well as his Honor Judge Peck and from which deponent inferred that Mr. Corlett would certainly be at this time. Deponent says that he is informed that there has been an accident on the Union Pacific Railroad today or last night and that Mr. Dickinson, who is Division Superintendent on said Railroad, has gone to said accident or wreck and will certainly be here by tomorrow morning. Deponent further says that he will be ready to proceed with this case tomorrow and that in his opinion there will be no time lost by these continuances for the reason that Mr. Dickinson is familiar with the evidence in the case and will be of great assistance in the management of the case. That as deponent did not expect to manage the case he is not as familiar with the case as he desires to be and should be to manage the same and therefore asks the indulgence of the Court until tomorrow morning in order that he may converse with the witnesses and become familiar with the case and also that Mr. Dickinson may be here to assist him.

G.C. Smith
Prosecuting Attorney

Subscribed and sworn before me this 16th day of November A.D. 1880

W.W. Meldrum
Clerk of District Court
2nd District of Wyoming Territory 2

"Mr. Smith, I am aware that Mr. Corlett, the Wyoming Territories' delegate to Congress, is in Cheyenne undergoing close scrutiny to determine his fitness for an appointment to the Supreme Court. You should have anticipated that this process would take a good deal of time and had another of your triers primed and ready to manage this case.

"After reviewing your motion for continuance and supporting affidavit, and in view of the late hour, I hereby grant your motion. However, gentlemen, there is time this evening for you to give your opening statements before we recess for the evening. Tomorrow, I'll expect either you or one of your able assistants to be in this Courtroom ready to proceed, Mr. Smith. Are you ready to present your opening statement?"

"Yes, Your Honor."

Smith walked over to the jury. "Gentlemen of the Jury…during these proceedings, we will prove to you beyond a shadow of a doubt that premeditated, First-Degree Murder was committed on, or about, August ninteenth in the year of our Lord eighteen-seventy-eight, at a location known as 'Rattlesnake Canyon' on Elk Mountain."

Smith pointed at the defendant, "George Parott—alias Big Nose George, and others did willfully—with malice of forethought—secret themselves is such a way as to ambush and murder Robert Widdowfield and Henry H. Vincents. We will introduce many witnesses who helped locate and bring the two murdered men down off Elk Mountain so they could receive a Christian burial. These same men also collected what evidence the outlaws left at the place where the cold-blooded murders took place. You will hear witnesses describe the type of wounds inflicted on the deceased by the murderers. You will also hear from several witnesses to whom George Parott confessed his crime of murder. Gentlemen, I have no doubt that after the evidence has been presented, you will find George Parott guilty of Capital Murder in the First Degree."

Smith walked back to his table and sat down. Judge Peck addressed the defendant's table, "The defense may now proceed with your statement."

Counsel Lewis stood. "Thank you, Your Honor." He began, "Gentlemen of the Jury…the prosecution would like you to believe that the defendant, George Parott, is a cold-blooded murderer that has confessed his crimes to anyone who would listen to him. Yes, it's true that George Parott has confessed to participating in these tragic killings. But, did the prosecutor mention that this confession stems from an incident that took place in the town of Carbon late on the evening of Saturday, August seven, eighteen-eighty? No, of course not!"

Lewis paced in front of the jury as he continued, "When you learn all the facts about this alleged confession and the extreme circumstances that led to it, you will have no choice but to find the defendant 'not guilty.'

"When Sheriff Rankin testifies, you will learn that he was overpowered by the members of a vigilante committee. You'll hear how the defendant, George Parott, was forcibly dragged from the train and taken to the exact spot where an acquaintance of his had been lynched by this same vigilante mob, two years earlier. You will hear how the defendant was pulled up in the air by the rope around his neck, until he agreed to confess. Under those circumstances, the defendant would have confessed to killing President Lincoln, if that's what the mob wanted to hear! Of course he told them what they wanted to hear…he wanted to save his life.

"I believe that such abject fear would cause any one of us to confess to anything, to avoid being hung by such a cruel mob. And yes, gentlemen, George Parott has repeated that confession for one simple reason: he feared that if he stated he was not guilty, the mob would come here, pull him from the jail, and lynch him.

"The defendant has good reason to fear vigilantes. Barely three weeks past, a mob or vigilante committee right here in Rawlins Springs kicked in both doors of the jail and removed Fernando Fierce, fully intending to lynch him. If it weren't for the efforts of Dr. Maghee and some other trusted citizens standing up to the mob, Fernando Fierce would not be alive today, and the Grand Jury wouldn't have been able to indict him for the murder of Joseph Hornbeck, as they did yesterday.

"It's been very difficult to convince the defendant, George Parott, that the law would protect him from that mob, if he were to correctly plead 'not guilty.' Gentlemen, a confession given under such extreme duress cannot be viewed as credible. After you have reviewed all the alleged evidence, I'm confident that you will do the right thing and return a verdict of 'not guilty.'"

With that, Lewis returned to his seat.

Judge Peck pronounced, "We will adjourn until ten a.m. I want to remind the jury not to discuss the case with each other or anyone else. I wish to meet now with all counsel for the prosecution and defense in my chambers."

Judge Peck rapped his gavel and left the room. He was sitting at his desk when the counsel came into chambers. "Gentlemen, please be seated. I will make this as short as I can. I'm not sure if one or all of you are trying to set back this trial, and it really doesn't matter. I'm sure that everyone here is familiar with the difficulties between Mr. Corlett and me. Rest assured that if Mr. Corlett appears in the morning, and if the prosecution still wishes to have Mr. Corlett manage this trial, I'll recuse myself. This trial will not advance until Judge Blair has ample time to appoint a Judge pro tem to act in my stead. With that said, gentlemen, we shall see what tomorrow brings."

Footnotes:
1. In the motion for change of venue and the defendant's affidavit, Big Nose George signed his name in his own hand and spelled his name "Parott." Up to this point, newspapers and Court documents used various spellings: "Parrott," "Parrot," and "Parott." The defendant's spelling—"Parott'—was used in later Court documents, but still not exclusively.
2. The original handwritten cursive document was submitted to the court, containing many stricken words, insertions, abbreviations, and misspellings. For ease of reading, most of the corrections G.C. Smith made to these documents are included in this chapter.

Chapter 15

The Trial

NOTE: The sections of this chapter in italics were taken directly from the transcript of the original trial. [1]

November 17, 1880, Wednesday: At the Judge's request, the clerk of the court, John Meldrum, made arrangements with the bailiff, Thomas Durant, to add another row of chairs against the back wall of the courtroom. He also left orders that everyone in the courtroom must be seated, to minimize the noise caused by the shuffling of feet. All the chairs in the courtroom were occupied before nine-thirty a.m. The defendant and the sheriff, as well as the attorneys for both sides, arrived just before ten.

At ten a.m. sharp, Judge William Ware Peck walked into the courtroom and sat down at the bench. He declared, "Please be seated."

John Meldrum announced, "Territory of Wyoming, County of Carbon, Second Judicial District Court, Case # 265. Territory of Wyoming versus George Parott alias Big Nose George. The Honorable Judge William Ware Peck presiding."

Judge Peck asked, "Mr. Smith, are you still managing the case for the prosecution?"

"Yes, sir. I will be managing the case until early afternoon, when Homer Merrill will take charge of the case."

"Very well, then, Mr. Smith, please proceed with the direct examination of your witnesses."

"The first witness for the prosecution is Sheriff James G. Rankin. Sheriff, please come forward and be sworn."

Rankin approached the witness stand. The clerk instructed, "Sheriff Rankin, please raise your right hand. Do you swear to tell the truth, the whole truth, and nothing but the truth, so help you God?"

Rankin said, "I do."

Judge Peck said, "Sheriff Rankin, please be seated. Mr. Smith, you may begin."

Prosecutor Smith looked at his notes for a few seconds before beginning his direct examination of the witness:

Q: "For the record, would you please state your name?"
A: "James G. Rankin."

Q: *"You may state your official position in this county."*
A: *"Sheriff of Carbon County."*

Q: *"State if you resided in this county about August, 1878."*
A: *"I did."*

Q: *"State if you filled any official position at the time? If so what was it?"*
A: *"I was deputy sheriff, then."*

Q: *"State where you were about the 17th of August, 1878."*
A: *"I disremember dates, but it was the 16th or 17th–it might have been the 16th or 17th–I was on my way from Laramie to here on the passenger train—to the best of my belief."*

Q: *"State what train were you on."*
A: *"What is called 'Number 3 passenger train.'"*

Q: *"State if you came on through to Rawlins that night or not."*
A: *"No, sir. At Rock Creek Station, I received a message from Sheriff Lawry stating that there had been a rail taken up between Como and Medicine Bow stating that there had been some foul play or other and asking me to go to the Express Car, which I did. When I came to Medicine Bow there was another message asking me to step off and go with Mr. Adams back to the bridge where the rail had been taken up, the next morning and investigate the matter."*

Q: *"Now, Sheriff, just go on and state everything you know about that and what you did from that right on."*

Defense Counsel Lewis jumped up, "Your Honor, I must object on the grounds that question calls for a narrative answer."

"Sustained. Mr. Smith, rephrase your question, and try to limit the scope."

"Yes, sir."

Q: *"This message was the one you received when you reached Medicine Bow in the express car?*
A: *"I got another message asking me to step off there that night and go the next day and investigate the matter of that rail that had been taken off.*

Judge Peck addressed Sheriff Rankin,

Q: "Sheriff, the Court needs to be perfectly clear about these messages. *This other message was the one you received when you reached Medicine Bow in the express car?"*
A: *"No—received one at Rock Creek, instructing me to go in the express car, and then when I came to Medicine Bow, I received the second message."*

Q: *"The other message was the second, was it?"*
A: *"Yes, sir."*

Q: *"The first message was received at Rock Creek?"*
A: *"Yes, sir."*

Q: *"I am not alluding to that. The second message was received at Medicine Bow, which place you reached in the express car?"*
A: *"Yes, sir.*

Smith said, "Your Honor, if it would please the Court, may I give my understanding as to the order in which these events took place?"

"Please proceed, Mr. Smith. Enlighten the Court."

"It is my understanding that information in the message received by Sheriff Rankin at Medicine Bow requested that he meet up with Mr. Adams in the morning and investigate an attempted derailing of a train. *A party of several beings, including the defendant as named in the indictment, had removed the fish plates from two contiguous rails of the Union Pacific Railroad Company between Medicine Bow and Como in this County of Carbon. And that this same party had placed upon the contiguous parts of the rail a wire attachment for the purpose of displacing the track, with thus inference to the passage of the passenger and express cars of the train, so as to wreck the train. That having so disturbed or interfered with the track, the party fled that locale. Vincent, named in the indictment, pursued them; and that while in the pursuit and near to them, he was fired upon from the party and killed. Which is the killing charged in the indictment. And that the defendant, George Parrott was one of the party from which the firing came."*

Q: "Sheriff Rankin, did I accurately state the events as set forth in the message you received at Medicine Bow Station?"

A: "Yes, sir. As to the best of my recollection, you stated the events accurately."

"Objection! Your Honor, the prosecution has gone beyond leading this witness and has given a statement on behalf of the witness. Now, by means of a question, he further proposes it be introduced as a statement of fact."
"Objection overruled, and exception noted."

Q: "Sheriff Rankin, would you please state in your own words how you complied with the instructions in the message to meet Mr. Adams at Medicine Bow?"
A: *"The next morning,* Joseph *Adams and I started out on horseback to the bridge where this rail should've been taken up. We found some other parties there,* the Albany County *Sheriff from Laramie and one or two other parties. We differed somewhat in opinion* as to jurisdiction. We finally came to the conclusion that the area in question was indeed in Carbon County and not in Albany County. An eastbound *freight train come along,* and the section foreman flagged it down. Sheriff Nottage and the other two men went on her back to Laramie. Before leaving, Nottage said, 'If you find that these outlaws doubled back into Albany County, wire us, and we will come back up and pursue them.' After we said our good-byes, *I says to Adams, 'It is a pretty fine morning; let us take a ride.' We struck due south–went up a mile and a half…two miles–where we struck a fresh trail of horses all shod. It had rained the night before for four or five hours. This made it easy to find their trail. We followed the trail a ways—probably two miles—without ever speaking a word. Finally, I says to Adams, says I: 'What do you think of this?' He said, 'Somebody is driving stock.' I told him, says I: 'If this is driving stock—'"*

"Objection. Your Honor, defense fails to see the relevance as to whether or not the gentleman that accompanied the sheriff on this ride knows the difference between shod horses and stock?"
    "Sustained." Judge Peck then asked,

Q: *"Who was this man?"*
A: "Joseph B. *Adams,* Your Honor."

"Mr. Smith, please continue."

Q: *"Sheriff, now please state what you did* after you struck, or located the fresh trail made by the shod horses."
A: *"We followed that trail for about five miles. We then left the trail, came back to Medicine Bow Station, got an engine there and ran to Carbon. We got fresh horses there and struck south in the direction of Elk Mountain. Finding the trail fresh again five and a half miles from Carbon, or there about, we followed the trail from there, probably two or two and a half miles up on top of a mountain—a low mountain or high hill. There came on a severe hail storm and blinded the trail— the trail had scattered. We struck out from there to within about two miles of Foote's Ranch—at Elk Mountain. Struck the road leading from Percy to Foote's Ranch, then followed the road to Percy—getting in there about sundown. In the meantime, we put some men on a hand car and*

run them to the top of Medicine Hill to see if any trail had crossed the railroad. They reported no trail had crossed. We was then satisfied that they were south of the railroad. We stayed there at the Percy Station that night. At one o'clock—between twelve and one—Mr. Dickinson came back down to Percy Station. Special Agent Tip Vincents was with Mr. Dickinson. I heard him telling Mr. Vincen what to do the next day when Deputy Sheriff Widdowfield came down from Carbon. As Sheriff Lawry was short-handed, I came back to Rawlins that night. Eight days after that, I went with a party to search for their bodies. We went up in what is called Rattle Snake Cañon in Elk Mountain. The first day's search, we accomplished nothing. We came back the second day. We found the bodies lying in the brush. Then we came back to Percy Station to make arrangements to bring the bodies down out of Rattle Snake Cañon to the railroad."

Q: *"Who do you mean when you say 'Mr. Tip Vincen?'"*
A: *"This Henry H. Vincent."*

Q: *"The person mentioned in the indictment?"*
A: *"Yes, sir."*

Q: *"You may state if you were acquainted with Henry H. Vincent in this lifetime."*
A: *"I was."*

Q: *"If so, then how long had you been acquainted with him?"*
A: *"I had been acquainted with him for four or five years."*

Q: *"You may state when you last saw Henry H. Vincent alive."*
A: *"At Percy Station."*

Q: *"You may state if you know whether Henry H. Vincent is living."*
A: *"He is not, to the best of my knowledge."*

Q: *"You may state how you know he is not living."*
A: *"Well I never have saw him living since that night."*

Q: *"State if you have seen his dead body."*
A: *"I cannot say that I saw his dead body. The first man we found there was Bob Widdowfield—some other members of the party went on up the cañon and found the other body. The two bodies were laying some fifty yards apart. Widdowfield's body was laying in some very thick underbrush. I rode up to where I could just see the body. I was not anxious to see it. I could not say that it was Vincents' body that was lying there because of the putrefying condition. I saw a body lying there, but I could not say it was Vincent body."*

Smith said, "I have no further questions for the witness at this time. However, I will need to recall him later when we discuss the capture and extradition of George Parott from Montana."

"Very well, the defense may now cross-examine the witness."

Defense Counsel Lewis said, "We have no questions of this witness at this time, Your Honor."

"Sheriff Rankin, you may step down. Mr. Smith, you may call your next witness."

"At this time, Your Honor, the prosecution would like to call Mr. John Foote. John Foote, would you please come forward and be sworn?"

After Foote was sworn and seated, Judge Peck said, "Mr. Smith, please continue."

Q: *"Would you please state your name?"*
A: *"John F. Foote."*

The Trial

Q: "Mr. Foote, *where do you reside?*"
A: "I reside in *Rawlins, Wyoming,* and at my ranch at Elk Mountain."

Q: *"Carbon County?"*
A: *"Carbon County."*

Q: *"How long have you resided in Rawlins?"*
A: *"Something over twelve years."*

Q: *"You may state if you were acquainted with Henry H. Vincent in his lifetime."*
A: *"Yes, sir, I was acquainted with such a man."*

Q: *"You may state what you know, if anything, concerning his death."*
A: *"I could not tell you much about his death. All I know about it, he was found dead about two years ago."*

Q: *"State what you know of it."*
A: *"I think it was two years ago last August, somewhere about the 20th of August—somewhere near that time that the body was found in what is called 'Rattle Snake Pass,' near Elk Mountain."*

Judge Peck asked,

Q: *"In the pass, or near it?"*
A: *"In the pass."*

Prosecutor Smith again took over the questioning of the witness:

Q: *"You may state if you were present when the body was found."*
A: *"I was, Sir."*

Q: *"Now,* Mr. Foote, *state fully and particularly everything connected to, or with the finding of, the body, such as its overall condition and positioning."*
A: *"Well, sir, we found the body—it had been hidden in the brush—a few sticks throwed over it. He was lying on his back—I think pretty square on his back."*

Q: *"Do you remember anything in particular about his clothing? Was there anything special about his clothing—boots or hat?"*
A: *"He had no boots or hat on—he was barefoot at the time. He had on a pair of pantaloons. I think he had a coat on—yes, I am pretty sure he had a coat on."*

Q: *"State what marks of violence, if any, were on his body?"*
A: *"There were several holes in the man. I should judge he had been shot by the looks of him."*

Q: *"In what portion of the body* were these holes?"
A: *"One in the breast here. And one, if not two, in the leg."*

Q: *"Which breast, if you remember?"*
A: *"It was his left breast."*

Q: *"Any other wounds on the body?"*
A: *"I didn't notice any more—didn't pay much attention to the wounds."*

Judge Peck asked the witness,

Q: *"You say there was one in the breast and one or two in the…one in the left breast?*
A: *"I think it was in the left breast."*

Judge Peck continued,

Q: *"And one or two more holes—where?"*
A: *"In his leg."*

Q: *"Which leg?"*
A: *"I could not tell you."*

Prosecutor Smith again took over the questioning.

Q: "Mr. Foote, *you may describe the wound in the breast with reference to its size, etc."*
A: *"I do not know as I could. A wound a little larger than my finger I should think. Something of the size of that. I did not pay much attention to them."*

Q: *"Would you state again where this body was found?"*
A: *"It was in Rattle Snake Pass."*

Q: *"What County and Territory?"*
A: *"Carbon County, Wyoming Territory."*

Q: *"I think you stated it was found about the 20th of August?"*
A: *"Somewhere about the 20th of August two years ago."*

Judge Peck asked the witness,

Q: "Was the body found *at the head of the Pass?"*
A: *"Pretty near the head of Rattle Snake Creek—head of the pass."*

Prosecutor Smith told the witness,

Q: "Mr. Foote, *state if you know whether the wound was such a one as would be caused by a gunshot?"*
A: "Yes, sir, *I should judge it was, by the looks of it."*

Smith said, "Your Honor, I have no further questions for this witness."
"Very well, the defense may now cross-examine the witness."

Defense Counsel Lewis said, "Thank you, Your Honor. I do have some questions for this witness."
"You may proceed."

Q: *"Mr. Foote, what condition was the body when you found it, specifically referencing the state of decay?"*
A: *"It did not appear to have decayed any. However, it was swollen considerably."*

Q: *"How could you tell whether or not these wounds that you have described were gunshot wounds?"*
A: *"They looked a good deal like it. When I see a dead deer, I can generally tell whether it was shot or had a sharp snag ran through it."*

Q: *"Did you remove the clothing in order to ascertain he had been shot?"*
A: *"Yes, sir, on his breast."*

Judge Peck asked the witness,

Q: *You said that the wound in the breast was about the size of the finger?"*
A: *"I should think it was."*

Q: *"What I want to get at is this: Do you mean to say that the orifice or opening of the wound at the surface was about the size of the end of your finger?"*
A: *"Yes, sir."*

"Thank you Mr. Foote. Please proceed, counselor."

Q: *"Did you observe any trail there, or near there?"*
A: *"Yes, sir."*

Q: *"State what you did observe."*
A: *"We saw a horse trail before we found the bodies. The trail that we saw was* the one we had first noticed, *somewhere near about three quarters of a mile from where we found the bodies."*

Q: *"You stated that the trail was a horse trail. Would you please describe this trail so that the jury can know whether it showed tracks of one horse or of several horses?"*
A: *"I should judge that there was eight to twelve head of horses."*

Q: *"How far from this trail was the body that you found in the brush and under the sticks—Vincents' body?"*
A: *"That* trail *was near*by. Another trail *was about three quarters of a mile away, and another trail was close by. The country is all tracked up around there so you could not distinguish one trail from another—it is tracked up so."*

Q: *"You remarked that there was one trail right close to the body. How close to the body?"*
A: *"Probably four hundred yards."*

Q: *"That was not the trail that you saw three-quarters of a mile from where you found the body?"*
A: *"I would judge it was part of it."*

"That is all the questions I have for this witness at this time."
"Very well, Mr. Lewis. Mr. Smith, do you have any re-direct examination for this witness?"
"Yes, sir. I do."
"Please proceed."

Q: "Mr. Foote, did you see *any evidence of a camp there—fire pit or anything of that kind?"*
A: *"Yes, sir. There had been a camp fire there. Looked as though there had been persons that made their bed around close by the fire—that is, a short distance from the fire."*

Q: *"State if there was anything found about the fire or about the camp."*
A: *"There was nothing found very close to the camp. There was a gun and an old saddle, I believe."*

Q: *"Where was that found?"*
A: *"It was found probably seventy-five yards from the camp fire."*

Q: *"In which direction?"*
A: *"It was east of the camp."*

Q: *"Would you please describe this cañon to the jury?"*
A: *"I do not know as I can do that."*

Q: *"Describe it the best you can—how it's situated?"*

A: *"It is a cañon or pass. The kind of cañon that run up between two mountains. Bushes and brush in the bottom of it."*

"That is all I have for this witness."
"Very well, Mr. Smith. Mr. Lewis, do you want to re-cross this witness?"
"Yes, sir, I do."

Q: *"Mr. Foote, at the season of the year which you described as having discovered a dead body, would you say it was anything unusual to find trails of horses or cattle through that country?"*
A: *"No, sir. Very often see trails, of course."*

Q: *"I will ask if it is anything unusual for men to camp out in this country anywheres, usually where night overtakes them?"*
A: *"I have camped out a good many times myself and have seen a good many men camping out here."*

Judge Peck asked the witness,

Q: *"What was done with the body of Vincents, if you know?"*
A: *"Yes, sir. It was put into a coffin and brought into Rawlins."*

Q: *"And buried?"*
A: *"Yes, sir."*

"You may continue, Mr. Lewis."
  "I have no further questions for this witness, Your Honor."
  "Very well. Thank you, Mr. Foote. You may step down."
Judge Peck looked at his watch, "It is now five minutes after the noon hour. We will recess until two o'clock. If you wish to get something to eat, please do so. Gentlemen of the jury, do not discuss the case with each other or anyone else."

Judge Peck rapped his gavel and stood. Everyone in the courtroom rose to their feet and stood quietly as Judge Peck left the room.

When Court reconvened at two, Prosecutor Smith remained standing and addressed Judge Peck, "Your Honor, due to the press of other Court business, I will be turning the management of this case over to the newly elected county attorney, Homer Merrill. I will be back to assist Prosecutor Merrill, as time permits."

"Very well, gentlemen. Prosecutor Merrill, please proceed."

"At this time, Your Honor, the prosecution would like to call Mr. William Daley. William Daley, please come forward and be sworn."

After the witness was sworn and seated, Judge Peck instructed, "Mr. Merrill, please continue."

45: Homer Merrill, Prosecuting Attorney, Carbon County Wyoming Territory

Q: *"Would you state your full name?"*
A: *"William Dailey."*

Q: *"Mr. Dailey, where is your place of residence?"*
A: *"Rawlins, Wyoming."*

Q: *"Carbon County?"*
A: *"Carbon County."*

Q: *"How long have you resided in Rawlins, Carbon County?"*
A: *"Made this my home since 1869."*

Q: *"State if you were acquainted with Henry H. Vincent in this lifetime."*
A: *"I have seen him several times."*

Q: *"State whether or not you were well acquainted with him."*
A: *"Yes, sir, I was."*

Q: *"You may state if you were present when his body was found."*
A: *"Yes, sir, I was."*

Q: *"State when and where it was."*
A: *"It was about the 26th or 27th of August, 1878, at the head of Rattle Snake Cañon—about the head of it—near Elk Mountain."*

Q: *"State if you were present when the body was discovered."*
A: *"I was within hailing distance of it. I was looking for the body."*

Q: *"You may state if you examined the body after it was found."*
A: *"I did, to a certain extent."*

Q: *"State what marks of violence, if any, were on the body. How far did you examine the body?"*
A: *"I did not remove any of the clothing that was on the body but stooped down and turned the coat back a little this way [gesturing with his hand] and noticed a large wound there about the right breast."*

Q: *"In the right breast?"*
A: *"Yes, sir, It appeared to me that the ball had entered behind. He was lying on his back, and it looked to me from the appearance of it that the bullet had left the body in that place—that it entered at some other place. That was the largest wound I noticed."*

Q: *"State if you noticed any other marks?"*
A: *"I think there were two lower down and one higher up."*

Q: *"Same portion of the breast?"*
A: *"Rather to the right."*

Q: *"Of the same breast?"*
A: *"Yes, sir, that was my recollection."*

Q: *"You may state who all was present at the time, as far as you remember."*
A: *"I think Jesse Wallace was present and William Ike and George Swassor."*

Q: *"State, if you know, what was the condition of his wearing apparel—his clothing?"*
A: *"Well, I do not know as I noticed anything very singular about him."*

Q: *"Particularly about his boots—cap?"*
A: *"His boots were gone—had no boots—feet was bare. I do not believe there was any cap there. I do not recollect of a cap being on the body."*

Judge Peck asked,

Q: *"Was there any hat?"*
A: *"No, sir."*

Prosecutor Merrill continued:

Q: "Were there *any straps about the person?*"
A: "There was a strap—a strap or belt, I think it was…an old cartridge belt around his leg, either just above or just below his knee. Somewhere close to his knee."

Judge Peck asked the witness,

Q: "*Which leg?*"
A: "I think it was the right leg."

Merrill continued his examination of the witness.

Q: "*State whether or not John F. Foote was one of the parties present at the time the bodies were found.*"
A: "Yes, sir. He was in the party."

Q: "*Describe to the jury the spot in which you found the body of Vincent.*"
A: "We found him in the timber—small timber—pine. A few quaking asp mixed with the pine. Some of the pine had been cut and were laying over the body."

Q: "*Describe the ground in that vicinity—the face of the country.*"
A: "It was rather smooth. The ground was on a little incline."

Q: "*Have an appearances of a recent camp?*"
A: "Not close to Vincents' body—not nearer than two hundred yards that I noticed."

Q: "*What was there?*"
A: "It appeared there had been quite a large camp at that place."

Q: "*Notice any fire—remains of a fire?*"
A: "Yes, sir. I think there had been three fires close together, and some little distance from there was where another one had been."

Q: "*State if there was any property found near the body or near the camp.*"
A: "Near the camp I found a rifle. An army gun—one of those Springfield, I believe…used in the army…fifty caliber."

Judge Peck asked,

Q: "It was a *Springfield rifle?*"
A: "I think it was a Springfield. I have got the rifle in my possession."

Merrill continued.

Q: "Mr. Daley, did you notice if *there was any shelter near or about the camp or cañon?*"
A: "Yes, sir. There was considerable brush *and large weeds* that appeared to have been used for shelter."

Q: "*State if there were any tree bough shelters or anything of that character, at any point in the cañon.*"
A: "Yes, about half a mile from that camp I spoke of, there was one."

Q: "*In what direction?*"
A: "Down the cañon."

Q: *"Describe it."*
A: *"It was some willow brush cut and bent over—what the Indians call a wickiup."*

Q: *"State what was the position of this wickiup, having reference to the height or the bottom of the cañon."*
A: *"Well, it was some distance up on the side of the hill...little ways from the trail—an old trail—running up the cañon."*

Q: *"In a position to command a view of the entrance of the cañon?"*
A: *"Yes, sir, I think it was."*

Q: *"State if the wounds described on the body of Vincent were such as would be received from a gunshot."*
A: *"Yes, sir."*

Q: *"Have you seen many gunshot wounds?"*
A: *"I have—quite a number."*

Judge Peck asked,

Q: *"Then you are familiar with gunshot wounds?"*
A: *"To a certain extent, yes, sir."*

Q: *"That is very indefinite. If you never saw but one wound, of course you would be familiar to a certain extent. Have you seen them frequently?"*
A: *"Yes, sir. I saw, I believe, eighty-two bodies at one time in this country, and all those bodies were shot more or less."*

Prosecutor Merrill resumed the questioning.

Q: *"You are familiar with the use of a gun, are you not?"*
A: *"Yes, sir. Somewhat."*

Q: *"Mr. Daley, what was the size of the wound opening in the body? The wound that you spoke of first—the one in the right breast."*
A: *"I think I could turn any finger in it."*

Q: *"Large enough to turn your finger?"*
A: *"Yes, sir. I think it was."*

Q: *"What was the size of each of the other wounds that you saw, further out on the same breast?"*
A: *"I believe the wounds were further in—in the breast. It was my intention to say so."*

Q: *"I thought you meant between that and the shoulder blade."*
A: *"No, sir—between that wound and the other side."*

Q: *"Between that wound and the center of the body?"*
A: *"Yes, sir."*

Q: *"Now, what if anything—did you notice about the opening of each of the other wounds or 'the orifice,' as we call it?"*
A: *"They were smaller apparently."*

Q: *"About how much?"*
A: *"One fourth smaller."*

Q: "I understand you, you turned down the clothing so as to see the breast where these wounds were."
A: "We turned the clothing back a little bit."

Q: "Could you look in toward the breast to the flesh?"
A: "Under the outer shirt—there was a blue shirt on the body similar to what I am wearing."

Q: "These holes that you say were holes in the shirt?"
A: "Yes, sir. They showed through to the flesh."

Q: "This large hole showed plainly through to the flesh so you could see the flesh through it?"
A: "Yes, sir."

Q: "Did you see the flesh at the opening of the main wound?"
A: "Yes, sir."

Q: "Mr. Daley, what made you conclude that the shots entered the body from behind—the shots that produced these wounds?"
A: "I did not suppose that any but the one I spoke of—the large wound—entered from behind. My experience of a bullet wound has been that where it passes out of the body of a man or animal it makes a bigger hole or wound than where it enters. That is why I drew my conclusion."

Q: "What sort of a missile from a firearm produced, according to your observation, this larger wound? A wound such as the one you observed the flesh at the opening."
A: "I think a forty-four or forty-five or fifty caliber firearm would produce that wound."

Q: "Would it call for the bullet to make a wound like that?"
A: "I presume it would, yes, sir."

Q: "Judging from the shape, was it a bullet hole or a shot wound?"
A: "I should think it was a bullet."

Q: "What was done with Vincent?"
A: "The body was left there at the time."

Q: "How long?"
A: "I understood it was left there until the next day. The next I saw the body was here at Rawlins."

Q: "What caused you to be out there searching for Vincent body?"
A: "I went from here with a party searching for it and Widdowfield, together."

Q: "Did you find another body there?"
A: "Yes, sir."

Q: "Whose body was it?"
A: "Bob Widdowfield's."

Q: "How far from Vincent?"
A: "About two-hundred or two-hundred and fifty yards. Somewhere about that distance."

Q: "Did it show any wounds upon it?"
A: "Yes, sir."

Q: "Gunshot wounds?"
A: "Yes, sir."

Q: *"Describe these wounds for the Jury."*
A: *"The body of Widdowfield was in a more putrefied state than that of Vincent, and the only wound that I observed was one here in the side of the head."* Pointing with his finger he said, *"I think it was about here—side or back of the head."*

Q: *"In the neck?"*
A: *"Yes."*

Q: *"How large?"*
A: *"Pretty large wound."*

Q: *"Describe it—you have described the size of the Vincent wound."*
A: *"It would be very hard to tell how large a wound it had been."*

Q: *"Because of the state of purification?"*
A: *"Yes, sir."*

Q: *"Is that the only wound you saw on him?"*
A: *"I believe that is the only wound that I saw on Widdowfield."*

Q: *"Did you say how far his body lay from Vincent?"*
A: *"About two hundred and fifty yards."*

"Your Honor, the defense moves to strike those portions of the testimony that relates to Widdowfield."

"Sustained. The defense's motion to strike is granted. The jury will disregard any mention of Widdowfield. You may continue with your direct examination, Mr. Merrill."

"I have no further questions for this witness, Your Honor."

"Mr. Lewis, the defense may cross-examine the witness."

"I have no questions for this witness, Your Honor."

"Very well. Thank you, Mr. Daley. You may step down."

Judge Peck looked at his watch. "It is now 2:50 p.m. We will recess until 3:15 p.m. Gentlemen of the Jury, do not discuss the case with each other or anyone else."

When Court reconvened at 3:15 p.m., Judge Peck began, "Mr. Merrill, you may proceed with your next witness."

"At this time, Your Honor, the prosecution would like to call Mr. Jesse Wallace."

Q: "Please state *your* full *name*."
A: *"Jesse Wallace."*

Q: *"Where do you reside?"*
A: *"Rawlins, Carbon County, Wyoming Territory."*

Q: *"How long have you resided there?"*
A: *"About eight years."*

Q: *"State if you were acquainted with Henry H. Vincent in his lifetime."*
A: *"I was."*

Q: *"State if you were present when his body, dead body was found."*
A: *"Yes, sir."*

Q: *"State where, and under what circumstances, it was found."*
A: *"It was found in Rattle Snake Cañon. He was dead."*

Q: *"Where* is Rattle Snake Cañon?"
A: "On *Elk Mountain.*"

Q: *"In what county* is Elk Mountain?"
A: *"Carbon, Wyoming* Territory."

Q: "State when you and the others found this body."
A: *"It was two years ago, last August."*

Q: "You may state how you came to be there."
A: *"These men were missing, and a party of us—went over there to look for them, to see if they could be found."*

Q: "State how well acquainted you were with Mr. Vincent in his lifetime."
A: *"I was as well acquainted with him, as I am with any people who live around here."*

Q: "You may state the condition of the body of Mr. Vincent when he was found, with reference to marks of violence."
A: "Well there were several bullet holes in his breast. I suppose they were made by bullets."

Q: "Which breast, if you remember?"
A: "On both sides."

Q: "State what examination you made of the body."
A: *"I stood by it and looked at it pretty close. That is about all—went close to it."*

Q: "Was the breast bare when you were looking at it?"
A: *"Yes, sir. I believe it was."*

Judge Peck asked the witness,

Q: "Please state, again, when *you* first *saw bullet marks.*"
A: *"Yes, sir. At the time we were there."*

Merrill resumed his examination of the witness:

Q: "Please *state the size of those wounds—the openings."*
A: *"Probably near half-inch."*

Judge Peck asked the witness,

Q: *"In diameter?"*
A: *"Yes, sir."*

Merrill continued,

Q: "You may describe his clothing, boots, shoes, hat."
A: *"He didn't have any boots on."*

Q: "What was the condition of his feet?"
A: *"I could not say."*

Q: "Did he have a *hat?"*
A: *"I do not think I seen any hat."*

The Trial

Q: *"State if there were any straps about his person."*
A: *"He had a cartridge belt around his left leg."*

Q: *"How was it fastened?"*
A: *"It was bound around his leg. It had a buckle that was fastened."*

Q: *"Now state when this was—day, month, year."*
A: *"It was on the 27th day of August, 1878, we found those persons."*

Q: *"You may describe the condition of the countryside where the bodies were found, having reference to its being woody or otherwise."*
A: *"There was a lot of brush around there and trees—some open places amoungst them."*

Q: *"Where was Vincent body, and in what position was it when found?"*
A: *"He was lying on his back and had been dragged into the brush and covered over with brush and sticks."*

Q: *"You may state if the body was found near what would seem to indicate there had been a camp."*
A: *"Yes, sir."*

Q: *"Describe that."*
A: *"The body was found, as near as I can judge, about two-hundred yards from the place where there had been a camp—couple of campfires. That was the highest camp up the cañon. Had been a camp below—a little one."*

Q: *"Any property found near the camp, or at the camp?"*
A: *"Yes, sir. There was an old gun."*

Q: *"What else?"*
A: *"Some straps—old stirrup straps and a saddle girth—that had been cut off and throwed away."*

Q: *"Anything else?"*
A: *"Old boots—been thrown away."*

Q: *"Mr. Wallace, state if you are familiar with firearms and are in the habit of handling them."*
A: *"Yes. I handled them some."*

Q: *"How much?"*
A: *"Considerably."*

Q: *"You are familiar, then, with fire arms?"*
A: *"Yes, sir."*

Q: *"State if you are familiar with gunshot wounds."*
A: *"Yes, sir. I have seen a good many."*

Q: *"State, from your knowledge, what caused the wounds upon the person of Vincents."*
A: *"I should say they were gunshot wounds."*

Q: *"Any doubt in your mind about it?"*
A: *"Not a bit."*

Q: *"State if you found, in any portion of the cañon, what is termed in this country as a wickiup?"*
A: *"Yes, sir."*

Q: *"Where was that?"*
A: *"That was below this camp I am speaking of."*

Judge Peck asked,

Q: "*How* far below*?*"
A: "About a half mile."

Merrill continued.

Q: "Please tell the Court how this *camp was situated with reference to its height—above or below the trail, if there was a trail.*"
A: "It was a little above. That is, on the side of the hill."

Q: "State whether or not it was so situated as to command a view of the entrance to the cañon or pass."
A: "Yes, sir. It was—that is for the greater part of the cañon."

Q: "From below?"
A: "From below—further down the cañon."

Judge Peck interjected,

Q: "We are speaking now of Rattle Snake Pass, I take it?"
A: "Yes, sir."

Merrill continued.

Q: "You may state to the jury now, Mr. Wallace, how you came to go to this Rattle Snake Pass."
A: "The sheriff got up a party here to go there and search for these men."

Q: "Did you proceed upon information obtained elsewhere—anything of that sort?"
A: "No, sir. I did not."

Q: "No information of firing occurring there at some previous time?"
A: Before we left Rawlins, do you mean?"

Q: "No. After you got out in the country."
A: "Yes, sir."

Q: "State that."
A: "We obtained some information when we got there about some shooting being done up there."

Q: "State what that information was."

Lewis intervened, "Your Honor, I must object. I know of no place in this country by the name of 'there.' This kind of answer can only tend to confuse the Jury."
Judge Peck sustained the objection. Then he asked the witness,

Q: "What do you mean by 'there?'"
A: "Your Honor, we met a man near the mouth of the cañon there—that is near the entrance of Rattle Snake Cañon. That is where we first noticed him—saw this man I am speaking of."

Q: "You say you saw this man at the mouth of the cañon. What purpose took you there?"
A: "We were on our way to look for these men."

Q: "The two men that you have mentioned?"
A: "Yes, sir."

Q: *"Widdowfield and Vincent? Under the direction of the sheriff of the county?"*
A: *"Yes, sir."*

Q: *"Did you on this occasion go up the cañon and find the body of Vincent as you have described?"*
A: *"Yes, sir. Found it the next day."*

Q: *"Was it in consequence to the information you received from this man you met? The man you met when you arrived at the mouth or foot of the cañon. Did you go up the cañon, in consequence of information that you got at that spot, namely, at the entrance of the cañon?"*
A: *"Well, sir. We were going to go up the cañon anyway. This man guided us up to where the spot, as near as he could tell, where the shooting took place."*

Q: *"You were going up the cañon anyway?"*
A: *"Yes, sir. I suppose so. That was the intention."*

Merrill continued.

Q: *"What did you want the information for, if you were going up anyway."*

"Objection: The prosecutor is—"
   "Prosecution withdraws the question, Your Honor."
   "Very well. Please continue, Mr. Merrill."

Q: "Mr. Wallace, *state if you know what became of the body of Vincent.*"
A: *"I never saw it afterwards. It is said to be buried up here in the graveyard."*

Q: *"He was dead?"*
A: *"Yes, sir. He was dead there too."*

Judge Peck asked,

Q: *"The body—Mr. Vincents's body—was not brought back by your party?"*
A: *"No, sir. It was left up there in the pass. Another party—I believe the next day—went back up and brought it back to Rawlins."*

"Prosecutor Merrill, please continue."
   "Your Honor, the prosecution has no further questions for this witness."
   "Very well, Mr. Lewis, the defense may cross-examine the witness." Lewis stood and as he walked toward the witness said, "Thank you, Your Honor."

Q: "Mr. Wallace, I would like you to clarify a few of your answers for the Court."
A: "Certainly—glad to do it for you."

Q: *"You say that the camp you speak of was the highest camp up the cañon? Did you go up the cañon any further?"*
A: *"Yes, went clear over the divide, through this pass."*

Q: *"What do you mean when you say 'divide?'"*
A: *"The Continental Divide."*

Q: *"I understand you to say that you saw the breast of this dead man?"*
A: *"Yes, sir."*

Q: "Saw the wound?"
A: "Yes, sir."

Q: "Uncovered the body?"
A: "Some other person threw the shirt aside. I don't know who it was."

Judge Peck asked,

Q: "You saw the naked breast?"
A: "Yes, sir."

Q: "Was it in the naked part that you saw these several wounds that you previously described?"
A: "Yes, sir."

Q: "And you could see them through the shirt too?"
A: "Saw them through the shirt."

Q: "Did these holes you saw in the shirt correspond with the holes in the breast?"
A: "Yes, sir."

"Mr. Lewis, you may continue questioning Mr. Wallace."
  "Thank you, Your Honor. The defense has no further questions for this witness."
  "Mr. Merrill, would the prosecution like to re-examine this witness?"
  "No, sir. We have no further questions for this witness"
  "Very well. Mr. Wallace, you may step down."
  "At this time, Your Honor, the prosecution would like to call Mr. Taylor Pannock to the stand."
  After Pannock was sworn and seated, Judge Peck instructed Mr. Merrill to begin his examination of the witness.

Q: "Give your name and residence."
A: "Taylor Pannock, Warm Springs, Carbon County, Wyoming."

Q: "How long have you resided at Warm Springs?"
A: "Something over ten years."

Q: "State if you were acquainted with Henry H. Vincent in his lifetime."
A: "I was."

Q: "You may state if you saw his dead body and—if yes—where."
A: "I did."

Q: "Under what circumstances?"
A: "Very bad."

Q: "Where?"
A: "In Rattle Snake Cañon—the head of it."

Q: "When was that?"
A: "Along the last of August."

Q: "What year?"
A: "1878—near the last of August."

Q: "You may state if you know—if you know what became of the body of Vincent."
A: "The body was brought into Fort Steele."

The Trial

Q: *"Did you assist in bringing it in?"*
A: *"I did."*

"Thank you, Mr. Pannock. The prosecution has no further questions for this witness."

Judge Peck turned to the defense attorney, "Mr. Lewis, you may proceed with your cross-examination of this witness."

"The defense has no questions for this witness."

"Very well. Mr. Pannock, you may step down."

At 5:15 p.m., Judge Peck stopped the proceeding. "This is a good time to break for supper. We will recess until 7:00 p.m. Gentlemen of the jury, do not discuss the case with each other or anyone else."

Court reconvened at 7:05 p.m. Judge Peck began, "Prosecutor Merrill, you may proceed with your next witness."

"At this time, Your Honor, the prosecution would like to call Mr. Millard F. Leach."

Q: *"You may state your name."*
A: *"M. F. Leech."*

Q: *"State your occupation."*
A: *"Engaged in mining, at present."*

Q: *"State what your occupation was in August, 1878."*
A: *"I was—the first part of the month—I was keeping a little store at Julesberg, Colorado. I was employed by the U.P. (Union Pacific Railroad) at the latter end of the month."*

Q: *"In what capacity did the U.P. employ you?"*
A: *"Detective."*

Q: *"State if you are acquainted with the defendant George Parrott."*
A: *"I am acquainted with him since September of this year."*

Q: *"You may state if you had any conversation with him."*
A: *"Yes, sir."*

Q: *"Please tell the Court under what circumstances the conversation with Mr. Parrott occurred."*
A: *"I was here with a witness during the last term of Court in September, the day that he was arraigned and pleaded guilty. After he pleaded guilty, I went over to the jail and asked for an interview with him—in the parlor there—the Sheriff's parlor."*

Q: *"Who was present?"*
A: *"The Sheriff was present part of the time."*

Q: *"Sheriff Rankin?"*
A: *"Yes, sir. Dr. Maghee and two other men that I do not know."*

Q: *"State if you held out any inducements for Mr. Parott to talk."*
A: *"No, sir. I was very particular to tell him that it was beyond my power to do anything for him."*

Q: *"Did you make any threats?"*
A: *"No, sir."*

Q: *"Any offers of reward?"*
A: *"No, sir."*

Q: *"Now you may state what that conversation was."*

(Counsel for the defendant here objects; which objection, however, is withdrawn for the present.)
Judge Peck directed, "Mr. Merrill, please proceed with your examination."

Q: "Mr. Leach, *at whose solicitation did you go to the jail and have an interview with this defendant?*"
A: "No one's, sir."

Q: "Went on your own volition?"
A: "Yes, sir."

Q: "*What was your objective* in going to the jail and speaking with the defendant?"
A: "*Well, I had a great many ideas about* the attempted train derailing and murders. There were many questions I had and was never fully satisfied with in regard to this crime. *I wanted to see whether he would confirm them.*"

Q: "When you had ideas with reference to which you say you were dissatisfied about, was it not when you was in the employ of the Union Pacific Railroad Company as a detective?"

Lewis said, "Objection. Your Honor, the prosecution is leading the witness."
"Denied. Please continue, Mr. Leach."

A: "*I had formed some* very strong opinions at that *time in regard to* this crime *and have been* following *the case ever since, and I was continually getting some new ideas about it by hearing the different stories from these different men in regard to the matter. At the time I spoke to George Parrott, I was not in the employ of the* Union Pacific Railroad Company."

Q: "Still, you were not a disinterested party to this conversation."
A: "Yes, I might say that I was disinterested. I was simply asking for my own information. I supposed, of course, that anything he might say to me that day would not help him in any way nor be of any disadvantage to him because I supposed that he would be sentenced that evening or the next morning. I went away that evening never expecting to see him again. These other gentlemen that were present came in while I was there. They didn't go there at my solicitation."

Judge Peck broke in,

Q: "*Have you named the other gentlemen?*"
A: "*I named two of them. The others I do not know.*"

Q: "Go on and describe these men—the other two men. Who were these other two men?"
A: "Sheriff Rankin and Doctor Maghee were the only two I know."

Q: "Were there any others?"
A: "There were two others there."

"Please continue, Counselor."

Q: "Now, I will ask you if the conversation to which you have alluded as having had with this defendant was made in the presence of all of these men that were there."
A: "Well, Sheriff Rankin left sometime during the conversation. The other three men were there during the whole of the conversation."

Q: "This defendant was in prison at the time of this conversation, was he not?"
A: "He was in the Sheriff's parlor. It is in the—I suppose it is in the—jail. It was not in the cell."

Q: *"Was he in the parlor when you first met there?"*
A: *"Yes, sir."*

Q: *"Where did they take him after the conversation?"*
A: *"I could not... Yes, they took him back to the cells. I remember going as far as the door with him."*

Q: *"Did the other parties go with him as far as the door?"*
A: *"I think not. I think I went there to bid him good-bye and left him a few minutes afterwards."*

Q: *"Was George Parrott aware, at the time of this conversation, that you were not an officer?"*
A: *"I could not say as to that. I could not say that he was or that he was not."*

Q: *"Was it pre-concerted on the part of the parties that you have described as having heard this conversation that you should all meet there at once?"*
A: *"No. It was not on my part. I simply asked Sheriff Rankin if I could have an interview with him, and whether he told anybody else about it, I do not know. I went over—followed him over there to the jail."*

Q: *"Sheriff Rankin?"*
A: *"Yes, sir. When he took the prisoner from here over."*

Q: *"Was the defendant shackled at the time of the conversation?"*
A: *"I think he was, but I would not be positive about that."*

Q: *"Who commenced the conversation?"*
A: *"I did."*

Lewis quickly responded, "Your Honor, I object on the ground that the question calls for speculation in reference to the alleged conversation between this witness and the defendant. If such a conversation did indeed take place, it undoubtedly would have been under extreme duress and must be disallowed by the Court."

Merrill countered, "Your Honor, testimony of a witness yet to be called, namely Dr. Maghee, will verify the accuracy of the conversation in question."

Judge Peck ruled, "The defense's objection is denied."

Then Judge Peck proceeded to question the witness.

Q: *"Mr. Leach, did you go back with the sheriff at the time he took the defendant direct from the Court to the jail?"*
A: *"I ask him here in the courtroom if I could have an interview with him, and he said I could. Probably half a minute after that, he started out of the door, I followed."*

Q: *"After he started with the prisoner?"*
A: *"Yes, sir."*

Q: *"To take him to the jail?"*
A: *"Yes, sir."*

Q: *"Did he tell you where you might have the interview?"*
A: *"Yes, he said to come over with him."*

Q: *"And you went accordingly?"*
A: *"Yes, sir."*

Q: *"Now, when he reached the jail building, into what room did he first take Parrott?"*
A: *"He started towards the cells, then afterwards turned around and came back. He said there were some ladies in the parlor. He then invited them out and asked me to go in there."*

Q: *"Did you go in there?"*
A: *"Yes, sir."*

Q: *"Where was Parrott?"*
A: *"He was standing in the hall at the time."*

Q: *"What was done with him?"*
A: *"I went in there, and they brought him into the parlor. And these other three men followed in. The same ones that had followed me in from the street."*

Q: *"And you stated that you—why did you think he would be sentenced that evening or in the morning?"*
A: *"I asked somebody here in the courtroom, I believe. They answered that the prisoners would all be sentenced together when the Court was over, and they were through with the other prisoners."*

Q: *"Why did you think, when you asked the sheriff for the interview and started to the jail, that he would be sentenced at all?"*
A: *"He had pleaded guilty—and I supposed the next thing was sentencing him."*

Q: *"Well, now, what was it that you asked of the sheriff to which he told you that you could have the interview?"*
A: *"I explained to him that there was some points about which I had been at fault on, and I believed if George would talk, I could satisfy myself about them and asked if he had any objections, and he said, 'no.'"*

Q: *"That is the sheriff said that?"*
A: *"Yes."*

Q: *"What I am at is: what was the subject upon which you wanted to talk with George Parrott? Anything to do with the death of Vincent?"*
A: *"It was partly in connection with the man that I had suspected of being there with them, but was not positive as to whether he was or not."*

Q: *"Being where with them?"*
A: *"At the time Vincent and Widdowfield were killed—at the time the rail was taken up."*

Q: *"After you got into the parlor, the ladies went out? And that's when Sheriff Rankin brought in the prisoner, Parrott, did he?"*
A: *"Yes."*

Q: *"And the sheriff, you, the prisoner—who was the other man?"*
A: *"Dr. Maghee."*

Q: *"And the other two men were present were they—at the conversation?"*
A: *"Yes, sir."*

Q: *"I understood you to say that the sheriff went out while the conversation was going on."*
A: *"Yes, sir."*

Q: *"The ladies were not in the room?"*
A: *"No, sir."*

Q: *"Parrott was shackled?"*
A: *"I could not be positive now about that. I am inclined, however, to think that he was not. I think the sheriff took the handcuffs off while they were in the hall. Still, I would not swear to that because I am not positive on that point."*

The Trial

Q: *"Repeat the remark that you made earlier, in answer to the examination by Mr. Merrill, as to what you said to Parrott about his not expecting any favor from you—repeat that remark as nearly as you can—as you recollect."*

A: *"I told George that it was beyond my power to be of any help to him. But as I thought that he and his party had done an irreparable injury, that he might, by telling me all he knew about it, could probably be helpful in case some of the balance of them were arrested. What he might tell, if I should be sworn as a witness, might help in the matter. And the other thing was that a great many of us had thought that Joe Manuse was engaged in this crime with them. I wanted to be satisfied on that point."*

Q: *"Was this the subject of the disturbance or the displacement of the rail and the death of Vincent and Widdowfield?"*

A: *"Yes, sir."*

Q: *"That you wanted him to tell you about?"*

A: *"Yes, sir."*

Q: *"Did anybody else, on that occasion, make any promise of favor or help to him, provided he would tell?*

A: *"No one said anything to him except Dr. Maghee. He first spoke to me, and his excuse to me for wanting to talk to George was this—there was a man named Dutch Charlie that was hung at Carbon. Dr. Maghee knew a Dutch Charlie, and he wanted to satisfy himself whether the Dutch Charlie that he knew was the same one that was hung at Carbon. We, of course, had a description of the one that was hung at Carbon; so he asked George to describe this one that he knew, that was with them at Elk Mountain—and George described the man to the Doctor, and the Doctor says it is the same one that I know."*

Q: *"I asked if the Doctor, before George began to talk, made any threat or promise."*

A: *"No, sir."*

"Your Honor, the defense objects to this line of questioning as it appears that you are interviewing the witness for the prosecution."

"Your objection is noted. However, I must deny it. It is of paramount importance that the Court be satisfied that the defendant spoke freely and willingly, without the influence of threat or promise of favor. So, Mr. Merrill, let us continue."

Q: *"You have stated that, on this occasion, nobody made any promise of benefit to George Parrott if he would speak."*

A: *"No."*

Q: *"On this occasion, did anybody make a threat to him or an intimation of threat or injury or prejudice the prosecution in which he had pled guilty, if he did not speak?"*

A: *"No, sir. I started the conversation with him by asking him if he had any objections to telling me about this."*

Q: *"What did he say to that?"*

A: *"He said, no—he was glad to have the opportunity."*

Q: *"Did anybody there make any threat or intimation of threat to that it would be better for him if he did tell about the Vincent matter and the Widdowfield matter?"*

A: *"No, sir."*

Q: *"Or it would be worse for him if he did not? Did anybody make any threat or intimation of threat to him, on that occasion, that it would be worse for him if he did not speak about the Widdowfield and Vincent matter, than if he did?"*
A: *"No, sir."*

"Your Honor, again the defense must object to this line of questioning, as it still appears that you are interviewing the witness for the prosecution."

"Mr. Lewis, again your objection is noted. However, I must again deny it for the same reason as before. It is of paramount importance that the Court be satisfied that the defendant spoke freely and willingly, without the influence of threat or promise of favor.

"Mr. Leach, I have one more question at this time."

Q: *"On that occasion, did anybody of the company which was there—I mean the sheriff, yourself, Dr. Maghee, or either of those two strangers—did anyone make any promise or threat to George Parrott?"*
A: *"No, sir."*

"Very well. The Court is satisfied to this point. By reviewing the list of witnesses you intend to call, it would appear that Mr. Leach's testimony will be further substantiated. You may continue, Mr. Merrill."

"Thank you, Your Honor. To further support the confession of the defendant pertaining to the murder of Henry H. Vincent, Dr. Thomas Maghee will be interviewed tomorrow. John C. Friend, the editor of the *Carbon County Journal*, has also been subpoenaed to appear with a copy of the article he wrote, which appeared August 14, 1880. He will bear witness that the information and confession he received from the defendant was freely given."

"Your Honor, I object upon the grounds that the preliminary examination made of the witness to the Court showed the testimony is incomplete and self-serving. And at the time John C. Friend interviewed the defendant, he was still in a state of terror caused by his near lynching at the hands of a vigilantes in the town of Carbon."

"Objection overruled. Mr. Merrill, you may continue."

Q: *"Mr. Leech, commence at the beginning of that conversation at the jail, if it began there, and narrate fully and particularly all the conversation that occurred, making it complete and giving it in the language of the parties or in the language that it occurred, as near as possible."*
A: *"Before I said anything to the prisoner, Dr. Maghee asked me if I had any objection to his being present. He had some points in regard to this man, Dutch Charlie, that he would like to have settled in his own mind. I told him that there was none on my part. The sheriff made no objection, and he came into the room. Two other men followed us in. I do not know who they were. I suppose they were citizens of this town. I stated to George distinctly that I was not in a position to help him in any way, or to do anything against him—that there was some points in that case that I had never been fully satisfied on."*

Q: *"In what case?"*
A: *"In the Widdowfield and Vincent case—being killed and the taking up of the rail. I went on then to state that one reason that I had always had a theory in regards to the train that they intended to capture...it was this: I could not understand why they undertook to ditch a westbound passenger train that was supposed to have no money, except what the passengers might have. The other was, I knew that Joe Manuse had left that country at the same time that they had—or about that time. I knew positively that he had come in this direction the same as they had—that he was seen in Elk Mountain a few days after this rail was taken up and these men—Widdowfield and Vincent—were murdered. But still, on his trial he proved an alibi. I said to him that Joe Manuse had proved on his trial an alibi. That is, he had proved that he was in Brown's Park the day that this rail was taken up and the day before the*

The Trial

murder at Elk Mountain in which Vincent and Widdowfield were killed. I told him those were points I would like to have settled. I would like to know why it was they undertook to ditch a westbound passenger train and whether Joe Manuse was with them, or was not with them. Well, he says, 'I will be glad to tell you all I can about it.' He says, 'Ever since that murder, every time I shut my eyes nearly, I see those murdered men, and anything that I can do to bring the balance of them to justice,' he says, 'I will be glad to do it.' I told him the points I wanted to settle were these I have just stated and says, 'I wish you would commence from the time you left up north and tell me about your trip from the time you left there till you got back.' He went on then to tell me that when they left up there..."

Q: "Where? Up north?"
A: "Somewhere on the head of Powder River or one of the branches of it—that their party consisted of Jack Campbell, Charlie Clark—known as 'Dutch Charlie,' Sim Wan, Tom Reed, a man they called 'Sandy,' and another they called 'Mac' or 'McKinney'—supposed to be Frank James, Frank Tole, and himself. He says...he went on then and described their trip down, I believe."

Q: "State, as near as you can, everything he said."
A: "He told me...I have forgotten the number of days he said they were coming to the Platte River."

Q: "From where?"
A: "Powder River. They got to Medicine Bow Station, finally, sometime during the night. Some of their party went to the tool house and got out some tools: a claw hammer, I believe a sledgehammer... tools for drawing spikes out of the railroad ties. He says, 'We went to a point three or four miles east of Medicine Bow Station early in the morning and started to take up a rail.' He says, 'While we were engaged in this, I was myself there standing on the bridge—the eastbound passenger train came along, the engine almost hitting me and knocking me off the bridge before I could get out of the way.' I says then, 'That is something that we didn't know before. We didn't know before that your party had tried to ditch the morning train.' 'Yes,' he says. 'We did.' He says, 'We tried to ditch the eastbound passenger train. We went over the hill a short distance and stayed there during the day until toward evening. We came back and loosened the rails, took some telegraph wire and tied to the rails, and laid in wait for the next train, which we understood was the train going west—passenger train. While we were laying there, section men came along on the car, discovered this rail had been tampered with, and stopped and commenced to repair it. Our leader, McKinney, wanted us to fire into these section men and kill them,' but he says Frank Tole and himself objected to it. 'We didn't come here to kill section men' and says they let the section men go then, and after they had repaired this rail and left, he says, "We left and went to Elk Mountain. 'After they repaired this rail and left, we left and went in the direction of Elk Mountain.' He says, 'We got to Elk Mountain and camped in a cañon there intending to rest up,' and now I am not clear on one point here as to the object of waiting. He told me, but I have forgotten what it was. Whether it was waiting for Joe Manuse to rejoin them or resting their horses—I could not be positive what he said in regards to that matter."

Q: "Waiting where?"
A: "In Elk Mountain—that they camped there and waited there. He says, 'We put out a guard—kept out a guard—so that we would not be surprised by any parties that might follow us.' He says, 'We got into Elk Mountain Sunday afternoon, following the time that we took this rail up—the rail was taken up Saturday evening. Monday morning the man that we had out on guard seen, what he supposed at first was, two head of loose stock, but after watching them for a while, he discovered that they were two men on horseback. He took up—he had a little fire where he was stationed.' He says, 'this man had cut some brush and put in the ground—shelter blind—at this point where he was on guard. When he discovered that these objects were men, he took up the branches that were in the fire and threw them into the creek so as to put out the fire and then came up and reported to us

what he had seen.' He says, 'We put out our fire and got in a brush right behind the fire, about ten or twenty feet from the fire. In the course of time, these two men came along on horseback.' And he says, 'we made up our minds that if they were herders that we would let them go through. That is, if they rode right on past us, we would not molest them. But…' he says, 'they came up there and the tallest man of the two noticed where their camp fire had been, got off his horse. He comes to this camp fire, puts hand into the ashes, and made some remark about it being very hot, and we must be very close to them.' He says, 'at that moment, Frank Tole fired, shooting this man, in the face. The man fell dead in the ashes.' He says, 'the balance of us fired at the other man; but I believed—at the time—we missed him because he kept on riding up the cañon. We all run out and fired a second time after him, when he fell from his horse. After he fell from the horse, he got up partly on his knees and tried to raise up his gun—had the gun in his hands when he fell.' He said, 'we fired the third time, and this man fell dead.'

He says, 'we went out—some of the party went then to robbing these men. One of them pulled off the boots of one man and took his gun.' And then they put a strap around one of the men's legs—one or both. I would not be positive how he stated that—put a strap around his leg and dragged him off into the brush and buried him up with old dead brush. He said, 'We stayed there a short time after that.' While right there I asked him…I says, 'did you do any of the shooting?' He says, 'Yes, sir, I done as much shooting as any of them—as any of the party that was with me.' He says, 'we stayed there a little while afterwards and then went on…left there—went a short distance, and my party divided up and took separate routes back to Powder River.' Then I asked him what he knew about Frank Tole. He said that Frank Tole had left their party a short time after this Elk Mountain affair and that he heard Frank Tole had been killed on the Black Hill Stage Line while trying to rob the stage there and that they had some trouble amongst them in regards to the matter. And when they got up north on Goose Creek—or somewhere in that neighborhood—that they kind of divided up, part of them going off by themselves, and him and one or two others making a crowd of their own. He says, 'after I got up there, I thought I would go back—I would leave the crowd—and that I would go back to Utah where I used to work teaming.' And told me the point on the Central Pacific Railroad *where he was going and says, 'if I had went there, I would have been safe. I never would have been here.' I think that was about all the conversation I had with him that day."*

Q: "Mr. Leach, what did you ask George *about* Joe *Manuse?*"
A: "I had ask him if Manuse was with them, and he said not. That Manuse had either left Powder River just ahead of them, or just behind, to go to Brown's Park after some horses and after a man there. And, as I understood him to say—or at least I understood it that way from his conversation in regard to the matter, that they had expected Joe to join them. But Joe hadn't got here in time."

Q: "State if there was anything said in regard to leaving property at the camp of any character."
A: "He said that Dutch Charlie took a Sharps rifle, I believe it was, belonging to one of these murdered men and had throwed away his own carbine."

Q: "Anything else?"
A: "Nothing that I can recollect of now."

"Your Honor, the prosecution has no further questions for this witness."
"Very well. Mr. Lewis, the defense may cross-examine the witness."
Q: "Mr. Leach *did George tell you anything about how he happened to join this party—how it came about?*"
A: "There was a good deal of preliminary talk in regard to the matter that I have forgotten now. Because I was not…as I have stated before…I was not there expecting to make any use of what he might tell

me, one way or the other, and I only paid strict attention to what he said in regard to the men that was with him and the train they tried to rob and whether Joe Manuse was with them or not."

Q: "I want to tax your memory in regard to that. It is very important to the defendant whether he told you how he came to join this party or not…whether he told you anything about that."
A: "I do not recollect what he said in regard to that. I know he said something about…I know he told me how they got the party up, but I was not very much interested in that and did not pay much attention."

Q: "Did he tell you where it was made up?"
A: "Yes, it was made up somewhere on Powder River, or some of the branches of the Powder River."

Q: "Did he tell you what he was doing at the time—what his occupation was?
A: "No, sir. He did not."

Q: "Did he tell you…do you remember whether or not he told that he was working on a ranch up on Powder River at the time this party was gotten together?"
A: "No, sir. He didn't say anything about a ranch."

Q: "Did he tell you whether or not he was forced to join the party?"
A: "No, sir. He didn't say anything about that…didn't say that he was forced, that I know of."

Q: "I want to call your attention now to the time. The conversation about pulling the rail…did he tell you anything about pulling a gun on one of the men at that time?"
A: "Yes, he said when one of them spoke about killing these section men…he said that…at the time that the leader spoke about killing these section men and that he did pull his gun, him and Frank Towle, I believe, and made some remark about them—that they didn't come there to kill section men. They came there to rob a train."

Q: "George said that they would have to kill him first?"
A: "Yes."

Judge Peck interrupted, "I understand that George Parrott said that he and another man drew their guns when the leader—who you said was McKinney—wanted them to fire on the section men, saying that they didn't come there to kill section men. And I understood you to say that you said that George also told you that they would have to kill him first."

A: "Yes, sir. He said that."

Judge Peck instructed Lewis to continue.

Q: "During this conversation with Parrott, did he or did he not tell you that in the first instance of joining this party, whose names you have mentioned, that he was compelled to do it by threats and intimidation from them?"
A: "No, sir. I do not think he did. I have no recollection."

Q: "Do you swear he did not do it?"
A: "Yes, I am willing to swear that he did not; because if he had said so, I think it would have struck my attention particularly."

Q: "I will ask you another question with reference to these section men. How many rails did he tell you that his party had displaced, or undertook to displace?"
A: "I do not think that he named the number of rails. He spoke of rails—plural—all the time."

Q: "Did he during the conversation say that the section men fixed more than one rail?"
A: "No, sir. I think not."

Q: "Was that after the passenger train going east had passed over the rail?"
A: "Yes, sir. The passenger train, he said, passed them there early in the morning and that this was late in the evening at the time the section men discovered the tampered with rail. They hadn't succeeded, he said, in getting that rail loose in time for the eastbound passenger train, but during the afternoon, they had loosened these rails, expecting to get the next train coming."

Q: "And you are sure that he told you that he and Frank Tole prevented McKinney and others from killing the section men by drawing their guns on them?"
A: "Yes, sir."

Q: "Now did he, or did he not, in that conversation, state to you that, after this transaction, they abandoned the road, and the party on whom he had pulled his gun threatened his life and called him a coward and demeaned him."
A: "He said that the occasion, or that occasion, had caused bad feeling amongst their party, and after this Elk Mountain affair had taken place that they separated and never worked together afterwards. That there was bad blood between them."

Q: "I would like to know if he didn't say that, after this transaction there—the taking up the rail, they were starting off together…if he didn't say that they threatened his life. They compelled him to go with them until they got out of the country."
A: "I would not be clear on that point. I know that he told me they had a quarrel. As I stated before, there was a great deal of what he told me that I didn't pay a great deal of attention to."

Q: "How is it that you are so clear with reference to these men taking up the rail, the conversation concerning the taking up the necessary implements for that business, and the matter, as narrated, concerning the killing of these men, but fail to remember any conversation connected with the exculpability of the defendant?"
A: "In the first place, I was considerably surprised that they had went there and undertook to take a rail up early in the morning, when we always believed that the first tampering with the rail was in the *evening*. And I listened very particularly to that part of it. When he spoke of this having a quarrel…I had heard that before from Joe Manuse when he was interviewed by Sheriff Boswell down in Laramie City. Joe got it from Frank Tole as Frank's excuse for leaving that party, and I didn't pay very much attention to what he told me about that part of it, because I had heard it before."

Q: "How many shots did the defendant tell you he fired?"
A: "He says, 'we fired about twenty shots.'"

Q: "'We' did?"
A: "Yes."

Q: "Didn't he tell you that he only fired one shot?"
A: "No, sir. He did not. I asked him that question…about that. I says, 'did you do any shooting?' He says, 'I done just as much shooting as anybody. I do not know whether I hit anybody, but I did just as much shooting as the balance of them, and I am just as guilty as they are.'"

Q: "Have you stated the time the section men fixed this rail or the time the passenger train came along and this defendant told you he was standing on the bridge and came near being knocked off there?"
A: "Yes, sir."

Q: *"He told you that, did he?"*
A: *"Yes, sir."*

Q: *"Do you remember his telling you during the conversation that he was off—away from the bridge?"*
A: *"No, sir."*

Q: *"To the right of the track?"*
A: *"No, sir. I understood him to say that he was on the bridge and that the engine came near hitting him. I says, 'didn't the engineer notice you?' He says, 'yes, but I suppose he took us for section men.'"*

Q: *"How far from the bridge was it said that this rail was taken up?"*
A: *"I never was right at that spot myself."*

Q: *"How far from the bridge did he say?"*
A: *"He said they started to take up the rail at the west end of the bridge."*

Q: *"What is your feelings towards the defendant. Are you prejudiced against him?"*
A: *"I do not know that I am particularly against him. I have always said—and always felt—if he was guilty of that, that he ought to be hung. And said that more than a hundred times."*

Q: *"You feel that way now, while testifying as a witness, do you?"*
A: *"I am here just simply as a witness."*

Q: *"You feel that way?"*
A: *"I have not changed my mind. No, sir."*

Judge Peck asked,

Q: *"Did he state—I am referring to the same conversation in the jail parlor and what George Parrott said to you—did he state where this bridge was at the west end which they endeavored to tamper with the rails?"*
A: *"Three or four miles east or west of Medicine Bow—I do not know which he said...three or four miles. I never was at that exact point myself."*

Q: *"Did he describe what bridge it was?"*
A: *"No, sir. He said, 'three or four miles from Medicine Bow.' That is the way he stated it."*

Q: *"You do not recollect that he said either 'east' or 'west?'"*
A: *"No, sir."*

Q: *"Did he state what year or month it was?"*
A: *"No. I think he didn't mention the dates. Only he spoke about it being Saturday...being Saturday morning."*

Q: Did he talk of the time—season—whether winter, fall, spring, or summer?
A: No, sir. Nothing said about that either.

Judge Peck turned to the defense attorney and said, "Mr. Lewis, you may continue."
"Your Honor, the defense has no further questions for this witness at this time."
"Very well. Mr. Merrill, does the prosecution wish to re-direct examine the witness?"
"Yes, sir. The prosecution does have a few more questions."

Q: "Mr. Leach, please *state if you know whether or not there has been any other attempt, except this one mentioned by you, to pull the rail in the vicinity of Medicine Bow, before or since? Has there been more than one attempt to pull a rail?"*
A: *"No, sir. Not to my knowledge."*

Q: *"Has there been more than one murder at Elk Mountain?"*
A: *"Not since I have been in the country, which has been since 1872. I have never heard of one."*

"I have no further questions for this witness, Your Honor."

"Mr. Lewis, do you wish to re-cross-examine the witness?"

"No sir, Your Honor. The defense has no further questions for this witness."

"Very well. Thank you, Mr. Leach. You may step down."

Judge Peck looked at his watch and then at the jury. "Gentlemen, it is now nine-forty p.m. We will adjourn until ten in the morning. I want to remind the jury not to discuss the case with each other or anyone else." The Judge rapped his gavel and left the room. Everyone in the courtroom rose to their feet and stood quietly until he was gone.

Footnotes:
1. The original handwritten transcript of the trial is in the State of Wyoming Archives in Cheyenne, Wyoming. A copy of the transcript is in the Carbon County Museum in Rawlins, Wyoming. The original is faded and very difficult to read. In developing this chapter, the transcript of the witness's testimony was followed as closely as possible. However, it was necessary to reconstruct the trial process, protocols, and some of the dialogue for clarity.

Spellings in transcript are in italics.

Cañon for canyon
Daily for Daley
Leech for Leach
Manuse for Minuse

Parrott for Parott
Tole for Towle
Vincen, Vincent for Vincents

A discussion of names is available in *Author's Notes.* Also see the *Sources by Chapter*.

Note that this transcript was finalized by J. C. Richardson on March 18, 1881, and approved by Judge Peck on April 4, 1881. The original trial took place in November 1880.

Chapter 16

Big Nose George Changes His Plea

Thursday, November 18, 1880, 10:00 a.m.: Judge Peck proceeded to the bench, asked the spectators to be seated, and convened the session.

Defense Counsel Bramel stood up. "Your Honor, may I address the Court?"

Judge Peck said, "Yes, Mr. Bramel. Please proceed."

"Your Honor, at this time, the defendant, George Parott, desires to withdraw his plea of 'not guilty' and enter a plea of 'guilty,' or such other plea as the Court would receive."

The courtroom buzzed at this turn of events. Judge Peck rapped his gavel three times and demanded, "Order in the Court!"

The courtroom quieted.

Judge Peck warned the spectators, "One more outbreak like that, and I'll clear this courtroom!" Then Peck turned to the defendant, "George Parott, please stand."

Parott stood with Bramel on one side and Defense Counsel Lewis on the other.

"George Parott, is it your desire to change your plea from 'not guilty' to 'guilty'?"

"Yes, Your Honor."

Judge Peck pronounced, "This Court will recess until three p.m. to allow the defendant time to confer with his counsel. Gentlemen, I instruct you to fully inform the defendant what the consequence will be, should he elect to abandon his defense. Gentlemen of the jury, do not discuss the case with each other or anyone else." With that, the Judge left the courtroom.

At three o'clock that afternoon, the court reconvened. Judge Peck addressed the defendant's counsel, "Gentlemen, have you conferred with the defendant as you were instructed?"

Bramel answered, "Yes, Your Honor, we have conferred with the defendant and fully explained to him the law and the penalties. And it is still the wish of the defendant to withdraw his plea of 'not guilty' and enter a plea of 'guilty,' or such other plea as the Court would receive."

Judge Peck turned to the defendant. "George Parott, please stand for the reading of the indictment.

"On April seven, eighteen seventy-nine, the Grand Jury of Carbon County brought forth an indictment charging you, George Parott, alias 'Big Nose George,' and others with willful murder of Robert Widdowfield and Henry H. 'Tip' Vincents, near Elk Mountain, in the County of Carbon, Territory of Wyoming, on or around the nineteenth of August, eighteen-hundred-and-seventy-eight. You have been charged specifically with the murder of Henry H. 'Tip' Vincents. The Court now requires you to answer the question: are you guilty or not guilty of the murder of Henry H. Vincents, as charged?"

Parott responded softly, "Guilty."

Judge Peck continued, "Very well, George Parott. The Court hereby accepts your plea of 'guilty' for the crime herein charged. As your plea of guilty has been entered and accepted by this Court, at this time, the Court discharges this Petit Jury. Gentlemen of the jury, the Court wishes to thank you for your service. You are free to go. However, you may remain seated in the jurors' seats as spectators until this session is closed, if you choose to stay."

Prosecutor Merrill stood. "Your Honor, now that the defendant has changed his plea to 'Guilty of Murder in the First Degree,' as charged, and the Court has accepted the plea, the Territory of Wyoming hereby moves that sentence be pronounced."

Bramel stood quickly. "Your Honor, the defense objects to the prosecutor's motion. The defendant and counsel understood that pleading guilty to the indictment might be for either Murder in the First or Second Degree. However, after carefully examining the indictment and consulting with a number of authorities on the question, all are of the opinion that the indictment would only support a plea of Murder in the Second Degree.

"Your Honor, the defense requests adequate time in which to prepare and present our position as to the question of first-degree or second-degree murder. To this end, the defense requests the Court recess until this evening or tomorrow morning."

Judge Peck said, "The Court will take the prosecution's motion and the defense's objection under consideration and will rule on both after the next break. The defense's request for time to prepare your position is hereby granted. I presume, Mr. Bramel, that the authorities which you reference, and others, are busily preparing your position?"

"Yes, Your Honor."

Judge Peck looked at his watch and said, "Gentlemen, it is now three-forty p.m. We will recess until eight this evening." Peck rapped his gavel and left the room.

Well before eight p.m., the courtroom was full. Although the jury had been dismissed, all the members had returned to the jury seats as spectators.

At eight o'clock, Court reconvened. Judge Peck spoke, "Gentlemen, prior to the Court's recess this afternoon, Mr. Merrill made a motion that the Court pass sentence on Mr. Parott, inasmuch as he has changed his plea from 'not guilty' to 'guilty' of the charges as indicted. Mr. Bramel, for the defense, objected to Mr. Merrill's motion on grounds that the indictment charged the defendant with the crime of First-Degree Murder when it would only support Second-Degree Murder. Does this pretty well sum it up, gentlemen?"

Both Prosecutor Merrill and Defense Counsel Bramel responded, "Yes, Your Honor."

"Very well then. Mr. Merrill, would you please restate your motion for immediate sentencing of the defendant and why you think such sentencing should take place now?"

"Yes, Your Honor. It is deemed by the prosecution, on behalf of the people of the Territory of Wyoming, that under the circumstances where the defendant has pleaded guilty to First-Degree Murder, as charged in the indictment, that sentence should be passed immediately."

"Thank you, Mr. Merrill."

"Mr. Bramel, would you please state your argument as to why you believe this Court should not proceed as Mr. Merrill has requested?"

"Your Honor, as I stated earlier, we believe—and so do a number of authorities—that the indictment was for Second-Degree Murder, and to this end, we move that the Court does not entertain any sentence other than one for Second-Degree Murder. Due to the lack of time, we were unable to finish our brief and submit it to the Court. We hereby request additional time in which to finish and submit our brief."

"Gentlemen, sentencing will not take place this evening. Mr. Bramel, you have until four p.m. tomorrow to submit a brief that supports your position. The Court will take your arguments under advisement and will rule upon them prior to sentencing. Mr. Meldrum, would you please check your calendar for a sentencing date?"

Meldrum replied, "It can be docketed on Wednesday, December fifteenth, at twelve noon, if it pleases Your Honor."

"The fifteenth will do. If there is no other business before the Court, we will adjourn until December fifteenth." The Judge and the clerk left the room, and Sheriff Rankin escorted the prisoner and counsel out the side door. The spectators in the gallery remained, debating whether or not Big Nose George might spend the rest of his life in prison, rather than being hanged.

Wednesday, December 15, 1880: Albany County Sheriff Boswell had traveled to Fort Hall, Idaho, to pick up William Fitzpatrick and A. Marion. The two outlaws had robbed the quartermaster's safe and would be turned over to the post commander at Fort Sanders to await trial. He had planned his trip to coincide with the sentencing of Big Nose George, as he wanted to be in attendance at Court. Early that morning, he and his two prisoners arrived on eastbound Number 4 Passenger Train. At five o'clock, he dropped the two men off with Bob Rankin at the Carbon County Jail for safekeeping.

Sheriff Boswell met Sheriff Rankin for breakfast. He looked forward to hearing how the trial had gone.

46: Nathaniel K. Boswell, Sheriff, Albany County, Wyoming Territory

"Boz, it's like we're having a reunion, with all the people who've come to town for the sentencing of Big Nose George. I've seen Governor Thayer, Millard Leach, John Lafever, Ed Dickinson, Joe Widdowfield, and several others from Carbon. They all arrived yesterday. And now you're here. I don't know who all we'll see before the day is out. Attorney Merrill has done well for himself, since he moved his law practice up here from Laramie. And now he's been elected as Carbon County Attorney."

After breakfast, the two sheriffs walked back to the jail to escort George Parott to Court for sentencing. Sheriff Rankin greeted his brother. "Good morning, Bob. Is the prisoner about ready to go?"

"He's ready when you are. Do you have time for a cup of coffee?"

"Sure do. We just have to get George to Court by eleven-thirty."

"Attorney Bramel came up from Laramie Monday, on Number 3. Both court-appointed attorneys were here yesterday and spent the better part of two hours with him."

Enjoying his cup of coffee, Sheriff Boswell mused, "Charles Bramel is a real political crusader. In 1875, he bought that little newspaper, *The Laramie Independent*, from T. J. Webster, and changed the name to the *Laramie Daily Chronicle*. He moved the *Chronicle* to the upstairs rooms in Ivinson's bank building.

"The *Chronicle* was like your *Carbon County Journal* in its Democrat Party leanings. Of course, his intent was to counter the Republican leanings of Doc Hayford's *Laramie Sentinel*. From day one, the jabs and political bantering were fierce, and Bramel soon learned firsthand what most said about Doc Hayford…that he could throw more dirt with a teaspoon than any other man could throw with a scoop shovel.

"In fact, I think it might have been Doc Hayford who drove Charles back into law. One fine spring day, while crossing a muddy street in Laramie back in 1876, Charles got into a verbal altercation with that fire-and-brimstone preacher, Edmondson, and ended up pushing him down in the mud. Doc Hayford would reference the mud incident on a regular basis just to irritate Charles. It wasn't too many months later that Charles gave up his newspaper and turned his full attention back to his law practice. Every once in a while, I chide him a little about his method of taming wild-eyed preachers."

The storytelling went on. Rankin said, "I heard the Judge almost didn't make it up on Number 3 last night."

"What happened?"

"I don't have all the particulars, but it seems he arrived late at the station in Cheyenne, and Number 3 had already left. So Judge Peck—being the resourceful man that he is—contacted the Cheyenne yardmaster and convinced him of how important it was for him to be here this morning to sentence Big

Nose George. Well, the Cheyenne yardmaster dispatched an engine and tender with Judge Peck aboard to catch Number 3. He wired ahead and had Number 3 held at Colorado Junction. Sure enough, the special engine and its passenger caught up to the waiting train at Colorado Junction, where the good Judge boarded and proceeded on to Rawlins."

About ten-fifteen a.m., Rankin said, "Well, Bob, I'd better get the prisoner and head for the Court. Judge Peck doesn't like being kept waiting."

Jailer Rankin got up and went down the hall to the jail cells. In a few minutes, he returned with George Parott, shackled and cuffed.

"Mr. Parott, I'm here to escort you to Court for sentencing. Are you ready to go?"

"I'm ready to go, Sheriff. I just want to get it over with."

"Bob, why don't you join us at Court? I doubt it'll take very long."

"Sure, let me get my coat. It's damn cold out there."

By the time the four arrived at the courtroom, it was packed. As they made their way toward the defense table, Big Nose George looked at the crowd out of the corner of his eyes. The mood was solemn.

The defense attorneys were already seated and were having a private discussion with Prosecutors Smith and Merrill, who were standing next to them.

Smith was shaking his head as he addressed Bramel, "I hope Judge Peck denies your motion of Murder in the Second Degree."

Sheriffs Rankin and Boswell, Jailer Bob Rankin, and Big Nose George approached the table. The attorneys acknowledged their arrival.

Boswell asked Smith, "May I sit in that vacant chair behind you?"

"You sure can, Sheriff."

Defense Attorney Bramel directed, "George, you sit in this chair next to me. Sheriff, you and your brother can sit in those chairs behind George."

Meldrum entered the courtroom at eleven-forty and a few minutes after noon announced the arrival of Judge Peck. As he instructed those in the courtroom to be seated, the Judge spotted his good friend, former-governor Thayer, among the spectators. He motioned for the governor to sit at his right hand.

With a rap of his gavel, Judge Peck declared, "This Court is now in session. Let it be noted that the prosecution, defense counsel, and defendant are all present. The first order of business is to rule on the motions that are before the Court.

"The first item at hand is the prosecution's motion for Sentence of Death and Judgment. The second is the defense counsel's brief requesting Arrest of Judgment, on grounds of the indictment being irregular and defective, which was brought forth in opposition to the prosecution's motion for Sentence of Death and Judgment upon George Parott. These actions were filed on the eighteenth and nineteenth days of November in a correct and timely manner.

"The defense motion for Arrest of Judgment sets forth the argument for precluding the sentence of Murder in the First Degree on the grounds that the indictment supports only Murder in the Second Degree. These are their three reasons:

1. That the Grand Jury which found this indictment was not legally constituted by law as required to inquire into the offense charged.
2. That the facts stated in the indictment do not constitute an offense punishable under the law of this Territory with death.
3. That said indictment is vague, indefinite, and uncertain, and that the defendant is not fully informed as to the crime with which he is charged, and for which he is required to answer.

Again, I have thoroughly reviewed the indictment and find no weight to justify the granting of this motion. Therefore, this motion is denied. It is further ordered by the Court that the prosecution's motion for Sentence of Death and Judgment upon the said George Parott, filed herein on the said eighteenth day of November, AD, eighteen-hundred and eighty, is hereby granted and allowed."

Judge Peck addressed the defendant. "George Parott, stand up."

Parott stood with his counsels, Lewis and Bramel.

"George Parott, do you have anything to say as to why the sentence of the law should not be passed upon you? If you do, you are under no restraint whatever and may do so without fear or hindrance."

Parott's voice cracked as he replied, "I have not, Your Honor."

Judge Peck read the indictment and the plea. Then he continued, "I have been, and am still, of the opinion that you entered this plea from an honest conviction of conscience. Judge Blair gave you to understand the serious consequences in making such a plea and asked you to change it, no doubt, on account of the weightiness of this matter. Even with your continued insistence of your guilt, the Court did not accept your plea, at first. A full half day intervened after you were warned of the consequences attached to your plea so that you could meet with your counsel and have time to reflect on your action. You, afterward, withdrew this plea and entered a plea of 'not guilty,' and this case was set for trial. In the interim, you telegraphed Judge Blair, who had returned to Laramie City, and requested he come back to Rawlins Springs, as you wished to change your plea back to 'guilty.' Judge Blair refused to allow you to change your plea while this Court was not in session.

"Then your counsel, on your behalf, filed a motion for Change of Venue, as it had become your belief that Judge Blair was prejudiced against you. At the beginning of the November session, Judge Blair granted the motion, and I was brought in to hear this case. You continued with your plea of 'not guilty,' until all the evidence was heard. Then you announced to the Court that you wished to, again, change your plea to 'guilty.' Your plea of 'guilty' was accepted by the Court. This change of plea, I am convinced, you did from an honest conviction of conscience.

"As an act of kindness, I deem it my duty to tell you that there is not a shadow of a chance that this sentence won't be carried out or that there will be any postponement. Although there can be no mercy expected from this earthly judge, you may seek and obtain mercy and pardon from the Heavenly Judge, before whom you are soon to appear. Although you have led a life of crime, you may die a Christian man.

"I now come to the most painful duty that devolves upon an earthly judge. The members of the bar, the officers of the Court, and the spectators will now rise. The sentence of this Court is that you, George Parott, on the second day of April in the year of our Lord, eighteen-hundred and eighty-one, between the hours of ten o'clock in the forenoon and four o'clock in the afternoon, in the place and manner prescribed by law for that purpose, in the County of Carbon, Territory of Wyoming, and by proper officers, be hanged by the neck until you are dead.

"It is also ordered by this Court that the appropriate officer of the Court have a transcript of the testimony made by the stenographer and filed with the clerk of Court, to be paid for by the County Treasurer."

Judge Peck rapped his gavel. "This case is closed."

Judge Peck exited to his chambers with former-governor Thayer. The spectators remained standing. Sobbing, the prisoner required the assistance of the Rankin brothers as they moved toward the door.

Sheriff Boswell pulled Rankin aside briefly. "I'm going to stay here for a little while to talk to some old friends. I'll meet you back at the jail later this afternoon. I'd be pleased if you could join me for supper at the hotel this evening. Then if it's all right with Bob, I'll take a nap in the parlor until about three a.m. My two prisoners and I will head to Laramie on Number 4."

The Rankin brothers left the courthouse with their prisoner.

Chapter 17

Attempted Escape

The latter part of December 1880 was as cold as the first part. The smell of wood and coal fires permeated the air as smoke rose from chimneys and bent with the prevailing northwest wind. Christmas would come and go, and then it was 1881.

Monday, January 3, 1881: The winners of the hard-fought election were sworn in and took over their respective offices. The new sheriff of Carbon County, Wyoming Territory, was Isaac Carson Miller.

Thursday, January 6, 1881: During the regular meeting of the Carbon County Commissioners, the commissioners approved payment of a $2,000 reward for the capture of Big Nose George: $1,000 to William T. (Fred) Schmaisle and $1,000 to William H. Irvine of Miles City, Montana Territory. With the $2,000 paid to John Lafever and Frank Howard for the capture of Dutch Charley Clarke and $2,000 paid to D. Boone May for killing and bringing in the head of Frank Towle, the total reward paid out to date for bringing to justice the perpetrators of the Elk Mountain ambush was $6,000.

Friday, February 18, 1881: A few minutes after nine a.m., Sheriff Miller walked into the parlor of the county jail to meet with Jailer Rankin. The two men sat down at a small table and discussed jail rations, expenses, and other items of business. Then Sheriff Miller asked, "How is George Parott's mood?"

"Overall, he's been in better spirits ever since he was sentenced. I believe it's lessened his fear of being lynched by a mob of vigilantes."

47: Isaac Miller, Sheriff of Carbon County

Author's Note: Isaac Miller

Isaac Miller migrated from Denmark to the United States and had been in Wyoming Territory for ten years before he was elected sheriff. During his decade in the Territory, Miller had tried his hand at mining gold, raising sheep and cattle, and working in the saloon business. He owned the Alhambra Saloon, which he would sell.

Although he would always have a Danish accent, Sheriff Miller continually worked on his English. Through the years, he became a well-spoken man.

The ever-present violence in the Territory and his experience owning and running a saloon helped form his core beliefs. One of his beliefs—that firearms should not be allowed in town—helped get him elected sheriff, an office he would hold for two terms.

In 1884, he would be elected mayor of Rawlins, and James G. Rankin would, again, be elected sheriff of Carbon County.

Miller was married to Ida Kerk.

"Hanging George Parott will be my first execution, and I want to make sure I do it according to the letter of the law. I'm meeting next Monday with County Attorney Merrill to go over the territorial law pertaining to hangings.

"I don't look forward to hanging a man, but it's part of the job that I've sworn to do, and I'll do it. I'm thinking of having that portion of the law printed in the *Journal* so that everyone will know that what I do is correct. That also would give us as many copies of the law as we might need…better than having a secretary transcribe it and having only two or three carbon copies."

"Ike, that's a good idea."

"I was talking to Jim, and he told me that he and your brother, Joe, are going to Cheyenne next week to negotiate the purchase of a livery stable there."

"Yes, that's their intent. They've been talking with Russell Thorp. He told Jim and Joe that it was his goal to buy out the Cheyenne–Black Hills Stage Line from Gilmer, Salisbury, and Company in the next year or two. He's very serious, and, by God, he just might get the job done."

"Well, I certainly wish them well in the venture. I don't think anyone knows horses better than your brother Joe."

"Speaking of Cheyenne, last week George Parott got a letter from Reverend Dr. Claxton. He wanted to come and pray with George. I told George it was strictly up to him if he wanted to meet with Reverend Claxton. I was a little surprised when he said he'd be looking forward to praying with the good Reverend, as it might help ease his mind.

"He's not been eating very much, and he can't sleep. A while back, he pulled a hunger strike and didn't eat for several days. Maybe he thought it'd be better to starve to death than to be hanged. But he gave in when he caught the smell of Rosa's biscuits and sausage gravy drifting down the corridor.

"At any rate, the Reverend arrived here on Number 3 on Wednesday and has been coming over to pray with George several times a day. I expect him to be here within the hour. From what he said, he plans on leaving tonight on the Number 3 to complete his journey to Salt Lake.

"On another topic, have you had a chance to meet Dr. Maghee's new associate, Dr. Osborne?"

Sheriff Miller replied, "Yes, I met him yesterday. He said he'd just arrived a little after midnight on Number 3 Passenger Train. John E. Osborne from Bristol, Vermont. Said he just recently became a doctor."

"Hope he has better luck than Doc Maghee did when he first moved here. Do you think his wife will ever come back to Rawlins?"

"I just don't know. Poor man. Guess he and the missus had a difference of opinion about staying here."

"Well, Sheriff, personally, I think they split the sheet, and she won't be coming back."

Miller got up to leave. "Well, I'd better go make my rounds."

"You have a good day, Sheriff."

Tuesday, March 22, 1881, 7:30 p.m.: The cold wind, with its razor edge, had blown hard all day, but it subsided a bit by sundown. It was a typical long, cold Wyoming winter. Whenever the temperature crept up above ten degrees, the locals called it a "heat wave." Soon, spring blizzards would hit the territory and exact a heavy toll on newborn animals, both wild and domestic. The mighty Union Pacific Railroad would grind to a halt, if not for snow fences and train sheds built in the cuts to prevent them from drifting shut.

The prisoners had their evening meal, and now it was time to lock down the cells. Robert Rankin left the iron-grated door open as he entered the jail corridor to close the cells and lock the prisoners in for the night. What he did not know was that, during the afternoon, Big Nose George had somehow gotten his shackles off and secreted himself in the watercloset. When Rankin entered the cell area, George attacked him from behind, using the shackles—which weighed seven or eight pounds—as weapons. He hit Rankin over the head three times. The shackles cut through the scalp, making three ugly wounds—one near the back and top of his head and one on each side, at the front of his head in his hairline.

After striking the third blow, Parott stepped back, thinking he had done the job. This gave Rankin the opportunity to strike a powerful blow with his fist, knocking Parott back against the corridor wall. Rankin escaped from the cell area and into the corridor, with Parott trying to grab him from behind.

Rosa Rankin, hearing the conflict, pulled the iron-grated door to the corridor closed, locking her husband in with the prisoner and preventing Parott's escape. Rankin's sister, "Lizzie" (Mary Elizabeth)—who happened to be there—ran into the street screaming, "Help! Jailbreak!! He's killing my brother! Help, help! Jailbreak!"

Mrs. Rankin, now armed with a pistol, screamed at Big Nose George, "Get away from my husband, or I'll kill you where you stand."

Bob Rankin, who was now in the corridor, hurried toward the iron-grated door, and Rosa let him out. Realizing he had no chance to escape, George Parott slunk back into the watercloset.

Rankin's head, neck, and shoulders were soaked with blood. His wife grabbed a tea towel, folded it in quarters, and put it on her husband's head wounds. Rankin held it in place with his left hand, while holding the pistol in his right hand. He yelled into the dark cell area, commanding one of the other prisoners to come out of his cell and light a lamp. At that point, Parott came out of the watercloset and returned quietly to his cell. He sat on the edge of his bunk, his head in his hands.

In minutes, the first armed men arrived. The crowd grew, until no one else could get into the jail. Many stood outside in the cold, waiting to hear reports from those who were inside.

After a quick assessment, one of the men yelled, "Someone go get a doctor, Sheriff Miller, and an off-duty jailer to relieve Bob."

In less than twenty minutes, Dr. Osborne was there, tending the wounds on Bob Rankin's head. Under-sheriff Bill Daley arrived, reporting that Sheriff Miller was in the Medicine Bow area on some tax-collecting business. Two off-duty jailers, William Simms and John Landon, showed up to relieve Rankin.

Once it appeared that Rankin's condition was stable, Daley, Simms, and Landon asked him what had happened. Because it had been dark, Rankin did not know what he had been hit with…only that it was heavy. His wife and sister were at his side, and neither could add much to his account.

48: Rosa Rankin, Wife of Robert Rankin, Carbon County Jailer

49: Dr. John E. Osborne, Rawlins, Wyoming Territory

Daley, Simms, and Landon went to search the cells for Parott's weapon. They were well-armed, and they were backed up by enough armed men to start a small war. As they moved toward the corridor's grated door, Rankin—still wearing his bloody shirt—joined them. A remorseful George Parott was forced to come out and sit on a bench in the corridor. They discovered that he was not wearing his shackles. Simms stood guard on Parott, while Landon searched the watercloset. Rankin and Daley searched his cell.

The shackles, a boy's single-bladed hawkbill knife, and a piece of sandstone were found in Parott's cell. The knife evidently had been used to cut the rivets off the shackles. The sandstone was worn, indicating that it had been used to sharpen the knife.

Since the incident seemed to be over, and the crowd had quieted down, J. C. Sumner, the blacksmith, put new rivets into the shackles that, once again, were placed on Big Nose George's ankles. Parott was returned to his cell, and Daley turned to the crowd. "I thank you for your support in helping to prevent a jailbreak. Now, I ask you to all go home. I'll make sure Sheriff Miller knows about your support."

Rankin was sitting at the table, with his fresh bandages. Dr. Osborne instructed Jailer Rankin and his wife and sister to send for him if the wounds started bleeding again. A short time later, Daley left.

Chapter 18

Another Lynching

Tuesday, March 22, 1881, 9:50 p.m.: With the jail under control, it seemed Rawlins Springs would settle down for the night. But small groups of men were gathering along the streets and corners. By ten o'clock, these groups began heading toward the jail.

At ten-twenty, Jailer Rankin was lying on a lounge in his room when the guard, Mr. Simms, heard a rap on the door. A man commanded, "Open the door."

Simms inquired, "Who's there?"

The voice answered, "Friends."

Simms replied, "Come back tomorrow."

The door burst open, and several masked men pointed pistols at Simms. It happened so quickly, all he could do was throw up his hands and take a seat.

Some of the men entered the room where Rankin was resting. They covered him with a pistol, while one of the masked men took the keys from his pocket. By this time, the corridor was filled with masked men.

The men moved to the cell block. When they had difficulty unlocking Big Nose George's cell, someone came forward with an axe. With a few heavy blows to the door, the lock and staples were broken. Several men entered his cell, pulled the prisoner to his feet, and dragged him out. One of the men tied Parott's hands with a short piece of soft rope, about the length of a piggin string. Then they dragged him down the corridor, out the jail door, into the street. The mob, with George Parott in tow, moved southeast toward the railroad tracks.

John Landon, a special guard, confronted the men, but one of the masked men told him to take a walk. Later, Landon would say he did not resist the masked man's order, as it was backed up with a pistol. He just turned around and walked away.

Big Nose George walked as fast as his shackles would allow. When he stumbled, the men at his side caught him under the arms and dragged him. George Parott, whose greatest fear was being lynched by a mob, now knew his fate. Sobbing, he pleaded, "For God's sake, don't do this! Let the hangman do it, or just shoot me. Please don't do this!"

The mob continued to grow. Word had spread quickly, and many townspeople were curious to witness this mob justice. More than a hundred spectators had gathered, including many of the town's best law-abiding citizens.

The group stopped by a telegraph pole across from the J.W. Hugus and Company Store. Not a lawman was to be seen, and no one attempted to stop the spectacle that was unfolding. Several masked men went to the office of Doctors Maghee and Osborne. Dr. Osborne had returned to restock his medical bag after tending to Rankin. The men demanded that Osborne accompany them to the hanging so he could verify George's death.

John C. Friend, editor of the *Carbon County Journal,* along with Prosecutor Samuel T. Lewis, were standing within twenty feet of the prisoner. Dr. Osborne stopped just west of the telegraph pole, where he stood quietly and watched the proceedings. It was an eerie sight.

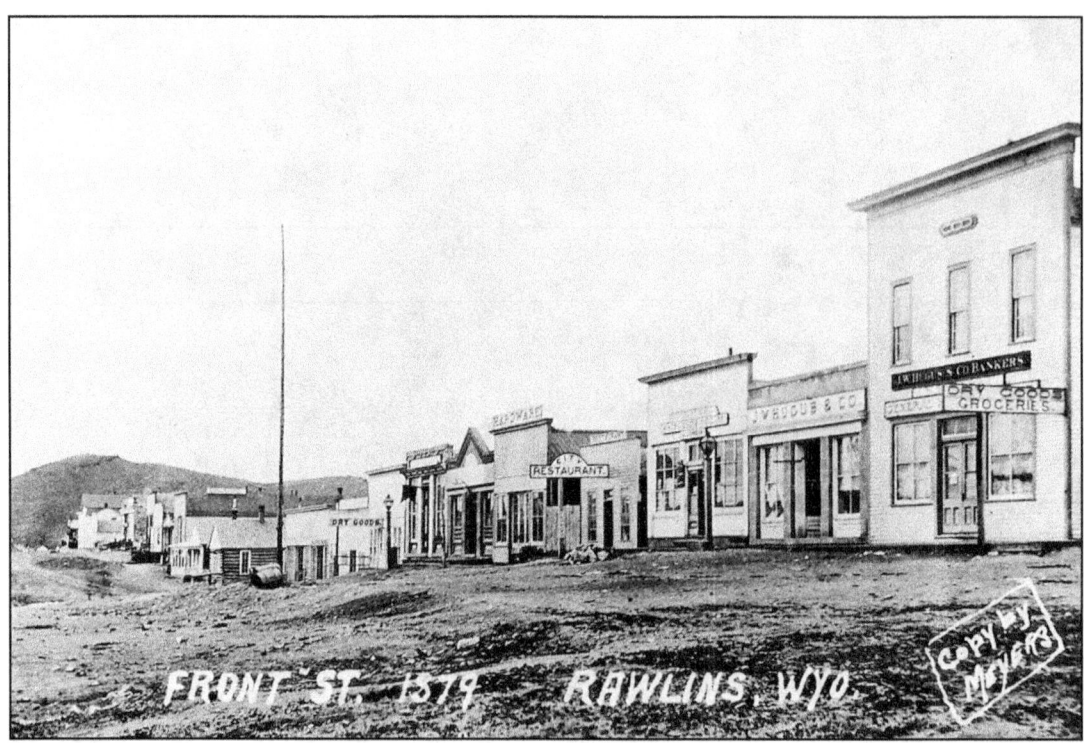

50: Front Street, Rawlins, Wyoming Territory

The spectators' frozen breaths rose in the air on the bitterly cold night. Everyone was quiet…they did not want to miss anything.

A man in a white mask threw a rope up and over the cross arm of the telegraph pole. He began making the seven wraps of a hangman's noose. Another member of the vigilantes located a barrel and rolled it next to the telegraph pole. The man in the white mask motioned the two men on either side of Parott to lift him up on the barrel.

Big Nose George was begging for his life. The slack was pulled out of the rope, and the loose end was tied into a pipe hitch around the pole.

Quickly, someone kicked the barrel out from under Parott, and he dropped. The rope had enough stretch and slack so that he was standing on tiptoe, gasping for air.

One of the masked men yelled, "Hang him over again, and make a good job of it this time."

The leader cursed under his breath. Then he instructed two of the vigilantes to go find something taller. In minutes, the two men were back with a ladder. They propped it against the pole. The man in the white mask adjusted the rope around Parott's neck.

Big Nose George pleaded with the leader, "It's a shame to take a man's life this way!" His voice breaking, he begged, "Give me time, and I'll climb the ladder myself. When I get high enough, I'll jump off and break my neck."

Two men helped Parott mount the ladder, steadying him on the lower rungs. It was a slow process because his hands were tied behind his back. As he climbed higher, the slack was pulled out of the rope. When he reached a height of about seven feet, the leader signaled for one of the men to secure the rope's end to the pole.

Someone pulled the ladder out from under Big Nose George, but Parott managed to free his tied hands and grasp the telegraph pole. Hanging onto the pole with both hands, he climbed about six or seven feet above the ground. Looking at the crowd, he cried, "For God's sake…someone shoot me! Don't let me choke to death!"

He slipped several feet, but he climbed up again, staying there until his arms could no longer hold his weight. Sobbing, he slid down the pole until the rope cut off his sounds. His body jerked back and forth, the full weight of his body bearing on the rope around his neck. His arms were wrapped around the pole for some time. His ear had rubbed off completely on the telegraph pole, and blood trickled down his cheek and onto his shirt. At last, his arms fell to his side, and movement subsided.

John Friend touched Sam Lewis on the shoulder, urging, "Go see if he's dead yet."

Lewis felt Parott's chest for a heartbeat and couldn't find one, but Dr. Osborne checked the body and found a slight pulse.

Five minutes later, the doctor checked again. Finding no pulse, he said, "This man is now dead."

Tuesday, March 22, 1881, 11:10 p.m.: The body of Big Nose George Parott was left hanging from the telegraph pole. The crowd—now nearly two hundred—began to slip away as quietly and quickly as it had formed.

Coroner A.G. Edgerton and Under-sheriff William Daley cut down the body at about midnight and brought it to Daley's undertaking establishment. After removing the shackles from the body, they went home.

Wednesday, March 23, 1881: The next morning, Edgerton impaneled a Coroner's Jury consisting of foreman D.P. Hughes, P.L. Smith, Robert Galbraith, Frank Blake, Walker France, and S.M. Miller. At the direction of the foreman, the jury walked over to William Daley's undertaking shop, where they viewed George Parott's remains. The jury returned to the sheriff's office in the Masonic Hall to continue the inquest.

Six witnesses were sworn: Wm. Simms, Chas Scribner, A. Geer, J. C. Davis, Wm. Daley, and S.T. Lewis. Each gave testimony about the events of the evening of Tuesday, March 22, 1881.

The jury brought in a verdict as follows:

Territory of Wyoming)
County of Carbon) ss

At an inquisition holding at Rawlins, in Carbon County, on the 23rd day of March, A.D. 1881, before me, A.G. Edgerton, Coroner for said county, upon the body of George Parrott, alias Big Nose George, lying dead, by the jurors whose names are here-unto subscribed, the said jurors upon their oath do say that said Parrott, alias Big Nose George, was forcibly taken from the jail by a party of masked men, to us unknown, taken to a telegraph pole and there hung by the neck with a rope until he was dead.

In testimony whereof the said jurors have hereunto set their hands the day and year aforesaid.

JURORS. (Signed by)

D.P. Hughes,	*R.M. Galbraith*
Frank Blake,	*D.W. France*
P.L. Smith,	*S.M. Miller*

Attest: A.G. Edgerton, Coroner

Tuesday, April 5, 1881: Trial transcript filed.

Epilogue

Medical Studies and New Shoes for the Doctor

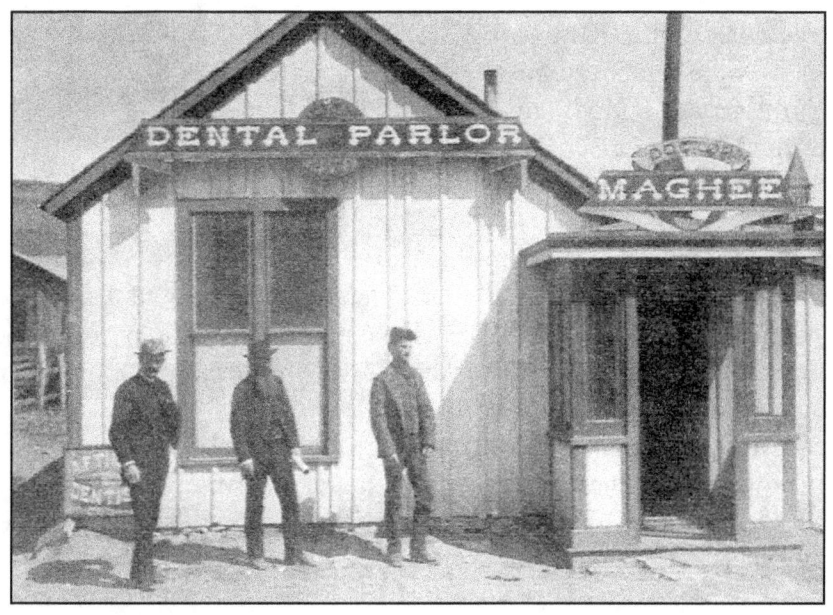

51: Dr. Maghee (middle) in front of his office

On the afternoon of March 23, 1881, Dr. Osborne went to Coroner E. G. Edgerton with a special request: he wanted to obtain the remains of George Parott for medical study.

Osborne had discussed the matter with Dr. Maghee, and they decided that if no one claimed the body, they would like to perform an autopsy. They wanted to study the criminal brain in comparison to a normal brain. Who better to study than Big Nose George Parott? Doctor Maghee also wanted to use the cadaver to teach his young student, Lillian Heath.

Edgerton had planned to have the local undertaker bury Parott in Potter's Field if no one claimed the body. But hearing Dr. Osborne's request, the coroner agreed to have the undertaker deliver the body to the doctor's office instead. He reminded the young doctor that, when they were finished with their study, it would be their responsibility to dispose of the remains at their own cost.

The next morning, George Parott's body—along with the shackles—was delivered to the doctors, as promised. They left his body in an unheated room with an open window so it would remain cool while they prepared a salt-brine tank. It was the middle of the afternoon before Doctor Osborne had a chance to remove Parott's clothing. Then he cast a death mask out of Plaster of Paris. Hanging had caused the body fluids to pool in his feet, and swelling and rigor mortis made it impossible to remove Parott's boots; they had to be cut from his feet.

The doctor removed the plaster mold midmorning the following day. The death mask would be used later to cast a bust of Parott. With the assistance of Dr. Osborne and Lillian Heath, Dr. Maghee began the autopsy. The scalp was cut at the hairline on the back of the head and then skinned forward to the eyebrows, where it was cut away. They sawed off the top of his skull so the brain could be removed, weighed, measured, and studied. The doctors gave Lillian Heath (who would become Dr. Lillian Heath Nelson) the skull cap as a memento. The skull was cleaned, measured, and studied. They used an old metal bath tub to soak the cadaver in salt brine, preventing decomposition.

Through the next several weeks, the doctors and their student removed the skin from Parott's chest, back, and thighs to expose and study musculoskeletal systems and major organs. During the process, they removed a bullet he had carried in his body for years. Eventually, most of what was left of Big Nose George—along with his clothes, boot soles, and a bottle of Lydia E. Pinkham's Vegetable Compound—were put in a whiskey barrel, taken out behind Dr. Maghee's office, and buried. This fulfilled their obligation to dispose of the body, and at no cost.

The barrel and its contents would be forgotten until its rediscovery on May 11, 1950.

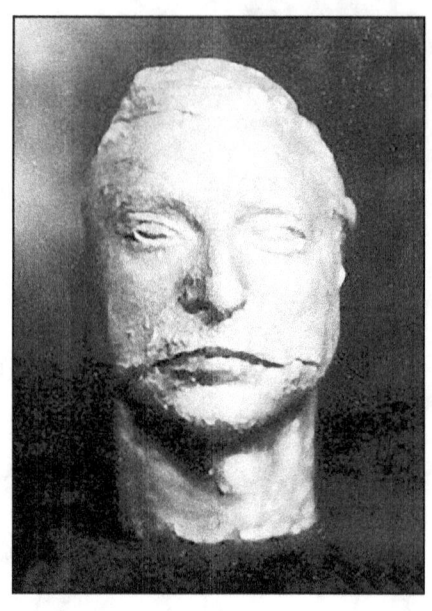

52: Parott's Death Mask

But there's one final, memorable twist to this story. Dr. Osborne, an aspiring politician, had the skin from Big Nose George's back, chest, and thighs tanned. Later, he sent the tanned skin to a master shoemaker in Denver, Colorado, who used it to make a pair of two-tone oxford shoes. In interviews, Dr. Osborne embellished the story, saying he asked the shoemaker to put a nipple on the toe of each shoe, but the shoemaker failed to do it.

Dr. John Osborne would become the third governor of the State of Wyoming. He wore those shoes while campaigning, proudly announcing that he was "tough on crime" and that he "walked on criminals." Some saw this as shocking. Others saw it as an appropriate end for a remorseless murderer who had killed two deputy sheriffs during an ambush on Elk Mountain.

Today, the plaster death mask of Big Nose George Parott, his skull, and the shoes made from his skin are on display at the Carbon County Museum. His skull cap and shackles are at the Union Pacific Railroad Museum in Council Bluffs, Iowa. Deputy Robert Widdowfield is buried in the Carbon Cemetery at the site of the old Town of Carbon, and Deputy Henry H. "Tip" Vincents is buried in the Rawlins, Wyoming Cemetery.

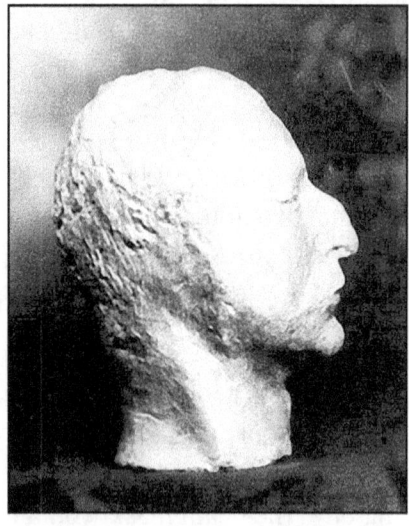

53: Parott's Death Mask

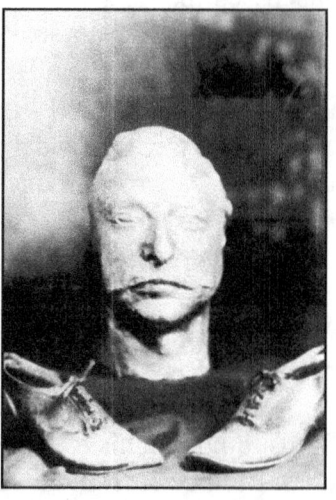

54: George Parott's Death Mask and the infamous Shoes

Medical Studies and New Shoes for the Doctor

55: Parott's Shackles

Author's Notes

The Outlaws

Nine outlaws were indicted for the murders of the deputies on Elk Mountain. One was found innocent (Minuse), two were lynched by vigilantes (Dutch Charley and Big Nose George), and one was killed during a stagecoach robbery (Towle). The remainder of the gang were never apprehended and brought to justice. Who were these outlaws? Some of their identities may never be known with certainty, but here are some additional facts and thoughts that add to the story.

Frank and Jesse James

Frank James likely was the leader of the Elk Mountain gang during the planning and attempt to derail the Union Pacific passenger train near Medicine Bow Station, in August 1878. The James' gang had used this same method on July 21, 1873, near the small community of Adair, Iowa, on the Chicago Rock Island and Pacific Railroad. John Rafferty—the engineer of the train—had been killed, and many passengers were severely injured, according to the *Leavenworth Times*, July 23 and 29, 1873.

He was indicted by the Carbon County grand jury both by name— "Frank James"—and by his aliases, "Mack" or "McKinney."

Various authors have speculated that Jesse James may have been a member of the Elk Mountain gang as well, although, based on my research, I believe he was probably in Tennessee at the time of the deputies' murder.

Both James brothers ventured into the Wyoming Territories on different occasions. In his diary, O.P. Hanna wrote that the James boys and their gang were already there when he arrived in 1878. *"Jesse James and his gang had a hideout in the Little Goose Creek Valley, not far from the new Fort McKinney, about forty miles North..."* This may be where Frank James adopted the alias "McKinney" or "Mack."

According to Agnes Wright Spring in her book, *The Cheyenne and Black Hills Stage and Express Routes*, Sheriff N.K. Boswell arrested Jesse James in Laramie City, but the sheriff had been forced to turn James loose for lack of evidence and because he could not get a positive identification.

Jesse and his older brother Frank James honed their skills riding with William Clarke Quantrill— of "Quantrill's Raiders"—and William "Bloody Bill" Anderson. Jesse loved the limelight, while Frank went out of his way to stay in the shadows. John N. Edwards, editor of the *Kansas City Times*, was their friend. It is said he was smitten with the James brothers. He seems to be most responsible for creating the myth that Frank and Jesse James were Robin Hoods of the Old West. The reality is that the James brothers were cold-blooded killers, influenced by hard times and the Civil War.

According to his obituary in the *New York Times*, "Frank surrendered in Jefferson City, MO in 1882. After his surrender James, was taken to Independence, MO, where he was held in jail three weeks, and later to Gallatin, where he remained in jail a year awaiting trial. Finally James was acquitted and went to Oklamoma to live with his mother. He never was in the penitentiary and never was convicted of any of the charges against him." In the final thirty years of his life, he worked a variety of jobs. He died of natural causes, on his family farm in 1915 at the age of seventy-two.

Sim Wan/Charles James

In Big Nose George's confession, he said, "Sim Wan led the gang off of Elk Mountain and crossed near the Town of Carbon, as he was the most familiar with that part of the country. He also went out of his way to keep from being seen in the area to prevent anyone from recognizing him."

Sim Wan (aka "Sim Waun," "Wann" or "Wahn") may have been Charles James, alias "Sim" James. He probably was related to the James brothers. In *Atlas of Wyoming Outlaws at the Territorial Penitentiary*, author Elnora L. Frye wrote:

Charles James—alias "Sim" James—February 10, 1874—Held for safe-keeping with Carbon County guard, George Csoxford, awaiting trial on a charge of murder of Yardmaster J. A. McPherson on January 19, 1874, at Carbon, Wyoming. Remarks: The prisoner was a coal miner, and the killing resulted from a drunken and gambling quarrel between railroad men and coal miners. On February 6, 1874, James escaped from the Carbon County jail in the freezing weather and was recaptured by a hunter at Saint Mary's Station. He was brought to the penitentiary in shackles. Legend says he was a nephew of Jesse and Frank James of Missouri. Prisoner escaped on the evening of March 9, 1874, when he led in the attack on the night guard, James Mills, and beat him about the head and face with chains that were fastened to his wrist and the guard's own revolver. Never recaptured. Sources: **Laramie Daily Sentinel** *on these dates and* **Laramie Daily Boomerang** *of October 7, 1907.*

More than ten years later, in May 1885, Sheriff Rankin received word that Sim Wan had been captured in Miles City, Montana. This is the piece that was published in the *Carbon County Journal*, May 23, 1885:

"The reward for their apprehension having been withdrawn several years ago, the powers that be do not seem to be as anxious as they formerly were to bring these murders to justice. Deputy Ed Ordway was sent to identify him, and then Sam Foreman was dispatched with the requisition from the Governor, for Wan's extradition."

It is not clear how Deputy-sheriff Ordway knew Sim Wan, unless he had encountered him as "Sim James" in the incidents described above by Elnora Frye.

Sim Wan/James was not returned to Rawlins. They brought him as far as Laramie, where it was determined that he was the wrong man, and he was sent back to Miles City. It is possible that the night guard, James Mills—who had been attacked by Charles James and others associated with the prison where he had been held—would have been able to identify him.

It's also interesting to note that the *Journal* got it wrong about the status of the case in that May 23 article. There is no evidence that the reward was ever withdrawn, and—in fact—Indictment No. 265 remained in full force. The *Journal* must have realized its error, because an article published on August 1, 1885, states:

We hear some talk about the probability of Sim Wahn being lynched at Carbon or upon his arrival here. There are perhaps some persons who would like to see Wahn lynched that they might profit from the reward. Now we will just slowly whisper in the ear of these would-be lynchers that they had better let this matter out. Carbon County has had a sufficiency of strangling matches.

In a cursory review of Frank and Jesse James's family tree, the name "Charles" shows up quite a few times, sprinkled across generations. None appear to be close contemporaries of Frank and Jesse.

Frank and Jesse's mother, Zerelda Cole, was first married to John James. Upon his death, she married Benjamin Simms. And upon his death, she married Dr. Reuben Samuel. In the James family list of names, both "Simms" and "Sims" are listed, as well as the name "Wand." The name "Wand" caught my eye and made me wonder if that is where "Sim Wan" began.

I shall leave that up to the James brothers' aficionados to ponder.

Thomas Reed

Though the name in the Carbon County Indictment for Murder No. 265 was "Tim Reed," it is likely that this person was actually "Thomas Reed," who was held at the Territorial Penitentiary at Laramie. In Elnora L. Frye's, *Atlas of Wyoming Outlaws at the Territorial Penitentiary*, she noted:

Thomas Reed—January 9, 1879—held for safe keeping by US Marshal, until next term of court on a charge of Larceny of US Mails. Trial was held on February 5, 1879, and released from custody on February 20, 1879.

The confessions given to Sheriff-elect Boswell in December, 1878 named "Tim Reed," and that name was used until Big Nose George Parott identified the man as "Thomas Reed," in his statement of August 1880. After George Parott's confession, newspapers—including the *Carbon County Journal*, August 14, 1880—began using the name, "Thomas Reed," instead of "Tim Reed."

Thomas (Tim) Reed was identified as having ridden with several outlaw gangs in the Black Hills, including the gang headed up by Persimmon Bill.

Frank Towle

There was a reward for Frank Towle, either dead or alive, so D. Boone May located Towle's grave, retrieved his head, and claimed the reward. What happened to his head after that? There are several stories, including this, as the most likely one. After the head was positively identified as Towle's, it was disposed of at the Rawlins Springs town dump, where kids were later seen kicking it around like a football.

The sworn affidavit filed in the Carbon County Court House at Rawlins Springs reads:

Territory of Wyoming
Carbon County, Wyo. T.
To Boone May, Dr.

For reward of Frank Toll one of the Murders [sic] of Widdowfield and Vincent [sic]
Territory of Wyoming, County of Albany

Boon May being first duly sworn on oath says: That on the night of 13th of September A.D. 1878 he shot and killed Frank Toll one of the murders [sic] of Widdowfield and Vincent on the Old Womans fork on the Black Hills Stage road running from Cheyenne to Deadwood that the affiant has the head of the said Frank Toll in his possession sufficient to identify him and that affiant is prepared to prove that the man killed by him as above stated is the identical Frank Toll and the murderer of Widdowfield at Elk mountain in said Carbon County.

Boone May (signed)

Subscribed and sworn to before me this 29ty day of January A.D. 1879
(Seal) John D. Brockway, Notary Public

Dutch Charley Clarke

Though some reports claim he was captured at Green River, I believe Dutch Charley was the seventh man captured at Rock Creek Station.

Dutch Charley had a number of aliases—"Dutch Charlie Bates," "Dutch Charlie Randall," "Charles Bayles," and "One-Winged Charlie." In George Parott's interview with Millard Leach and Dr. McGhee, he identified Dutch Charley as "Charles Clark." The description he provided confirmed Dr. McGhee's belief that the man lynched at Carbon was the man he knew as "Dutch Charley Clarke."

The confusion regarding Dutch Charley's capture resulted from two articles that appeared in the *Laramie Dailey Sentinel*. The first article appeared on January 3, 1879, and reported, "Taken in by John Lafever at Green River, Dutch Charley a.k.a. Baylis a.k.a. Davis—Captured this week…" The second article appeared on January 10, 1879, under the headline, "RETRIBUTIVE JUSTICE—The hanging of Dutch Charley at Carbon." The second article states that Dutch Charley was captured two weeks earlier at Green River and credits Sheriff Boswell with the capture.

To make the arrest at Green River, Sheriff-elect Boswell of Albany County would have had to travel roundtrip from Laramie City to Green River City at the very time he was at Rock Creek Station capturing the other seven outlaws. The roundtrip to Green River was approximately 470 miles by rail, crossing Carbon County, and going well into Sweetwater County. Both Carbon and Sweetwater Counties had very capable sheriffs. Boswell could have asked the Sweetwater County sheriff to arrest Dutch Charley and hold him. Carbon County Sheriff Lawry could have picked him up and returned him to the Carbon County Jail, in Rawlins Springs, the seat of the county where the murders took place.

For the same reasons Sheriff Boswell could not have made the trip to Green River to capture Dutch Charley, John Lafever could not have done so, either. At that time, Lafever had not been hired by Boswell to be a deputy. I believe the *Sentinel* got some of the facts, people, and places mixed up.

In the December 23, 1878, *Laramie Daily Sentinel*, Editor James H. "Doc" Hayford listed the names of five of the outlaws associated with the Elk Mountain murders. He also named Otto Olsen, the owner of the Whiskey House, as the outlaws' spotter. The report did not name the seventh man. Either Hayford did not know the name, or Sheriff Boswell asked him not to divulge it. This story was picked up and carried by several other newspapers.

The headline of the *Cheyenne Daily Leader*, December 24, 1878, had it partly correct: "WE ARE SEVEN." The article, entitled "Capture of Band of Outlaws," gives a fairly accurate account of what took place during the capture. It lists names of six men captured, and—midway in the article—states, "The name of the seventh man our reporter failed to learn…"

On December 27, 1878, the *Laramie Daily Sentinel* reported, "THE MURDER OF VINCENT AND WIDDOWFIELD" and "Full Particulars by an Eye Witness…" The last paragraph states, "We could give a good deal more information on this matter, but just now an embargo is laid upon us. The foregoing is, however, absolutely correct and reliable, and subsequent proceedings will ere long be made public." Since this was portrayed as an eyewitness account, it must have come from Dutch Charley, as he was the only member of the gang available to give such an account.

Judge Blair certified and ordered the reward for Dutch Charley to be paid to Frank Howard and John Lafever. Carbon County paid each man $1,000. The *Cheyenne Daily Sun*, July 20, 1879, says the reward was specifically for capture of "Dutch Charley Clarke," for his part in the murders of Deputies Robert Widdowfield and Henry H. "Tip" Vincents. This article helps verify that the unnamed "seventh man" in the capture near Rock Creek was Dutch Charley. This fact was reaffirmed in the *Carbon County Journal*, January 10, 1880, and January 17, 1880, under "County Warrants Paid," showing "Frank Howard" and "John Laferve" [sic] having been paid $1,000 each for the capture of Dutch Charley.

Big Nose George Parott

- **What Was George's Real Name?**

Other names attributed to George Parott are "Parrot," "Parrott," "George Francis Warden" and "George Dixon." The August 20, 1881, edition of the *Cheyenne Daily Leader*, printed a type set copy of the handwritten request for a certificate of death submitted by the French Consulate on behalf of Parott's wife (see reprint below.) In the article, George's last name was spelled "Parrot." However, I believe the correct spelling is "Parott" because that's the way George signed his name on the November 8, 1880, Affidavit in Support of the Motion for Change of Venue.

Consulat-- General de France
a New York New York, Aug. 11, 1881

To the Honorable Governor of the Wyoming Territory, in Cheyenne City, Laramie Co., Wyo.
Sir: I have the honor to ask respectfully for a transcript or certificate of death relating to the late George Parrot, alias, George Au-Gros-Nez, who was lynched in the beginning of last March at Rawlins, Carbon County, Wyoming. The aforesaid certificate of death is required by the widow of this convict. Therefore I will be very much obliged to you if you have the kindness to give the necessary orders for sending this document to my office.
I remain, sir, Respectfully yours,
A. Lefaiore,
Consul General of France.

Of course this request makes us realize how very little we know about Parott's personal life. Obviously his wife must have been French. No mention is ever made that he spoke with an accent, so one can only ponder this relationship.

- **The Arrest**

Some newspaper accounts of Big Nose George's arrest identify two additional lawmen associated with the case, but I have not been able to verify that they had anything to do with the arrest.

An article about the arrest first appeared in the St. Paul and Minneapolis *Daily Pioneer Press* and was reprinted in Miles City's *The Yellowstone Journal*. It mentions an old frontiersman and detective named "Bill Langston." *The Yellowstone Journal* version also mentions "Detective Hines," who is said to have been with Sheriff Rankin when the heavily chained prisoners were escorted from the jail.

- **The Transcript of the Trial**

George Parott was to be hanged in Rawlins, Wyoming, on April 2, 1881. Instead, he was lynched by vigilantes on March 22, 1881. I have reviewed the transcript, and I believe that some portions of the testimony were omitted (for example, complete testimony of Pannock and Sheriff Rankin), probably because the clerk of the court rushed to finish the transcript after the unexpected lynching.

The Lawmen

Nathaniel Kimball Boswell, Sheriff of Albany County, Wyoming Territory.
Appointed May 25, 1869. Served May 1869 thru December 1870.
Elected November 1870. Served 1871 through 1872.
Elected November 1878. Served 1879 through 1880.

John R. Brophy, Sheriff of Albany County, Wyoming Territory.
Elected November 1874. Served 1875 through 1876.

Daniel Nottage, Sheriff of Albany County, Wyoming Territory.
Elected November 1876. Served 1877 through 1878

Isaac M. Lawry, Sheriff of Carbon County, Wyoming Territory.
Elected November 1876. Served 1877 through 1878.

James G. Rankin, Sheriff of Carbon County, Wyoming Territory.
Elected November 1878. Served 1879 through 1880.
Elected November 1884. Served 1885 through 1886.

Isaac Carson Miller, Sheriff of Carbon County, Wyoming Territory.
Elected November 1880. Served 1881 through 1882.
Elected November 1882. Served 1883 through 1884.

Joseph P. Rankin, US Marshal, District of Wyoming.
Appointed September 22, 1890. Served four-year term.

John W. Dykins, Sheriff of Sweetwater County, Wyoming Territory.
Elected November 1876. Served 1877 through 1878.

William Adolphus Johnson, Sheriff of Sweetwater County, Wyoming Territory.
Elected November 1878. Served 1879 through 1880.

Thomas H. Irvine
- Sheriff of Custer County, Montana Territory.
  Elected November 1878. Served six months in 1879 and resigned.
- Deputy US Marshal, District of Montana Territory.
  Appointed June 1879. Served July–December 1879 and all of 1880.
- Sheriff of Custer County, Montana Territory.
  Elected November 1880. Served 1881 through 1882.
  Elected 1882. Served 1883 through 1884.

Other Characters

Frank Howard

In 1893, Frank Howard's life took a deadly twist. He was sharing a house in Dixon, Wyoming, with Charles Horn. Both Howard and Horn were hard drinkers, and Horn was known to become mean after a few drinks. Most of the time, Horn carried a pistol stuck in the waistband of his trousers.

Howard got involved with Grace Bicktold, a woman of questionable reputation. Eventually, Bicktold shifted her affections to Horn, fueling a rivalry that became increasingly bitter. Horn boasted that he was going to move Howard out of the house—forcibly, if necessary. Howard had had enough.

On December 31, 1893, an inebriated Howard borrowed a Sharps rifle from one of his friends. He lured Horn from Bicktold's room, took aim, and shot him in the head. Then Howard panicked and fled for the hills on foot. An armed posse caught up with him about thirty miles from town.

Bicktold was in the darkened house with Horn, but she did not witness the shooting. Still, she was the most damaging witness at the Coroner's Jury held in Dixon, Wyoming, the Grand Jury, and the trial, which was held in Rawlins. She testified that she saw Howard through the window, leaving with a rifle in his hand. She went after her old lover with a vengeance.

Frank Howard's trial was held on June 5, 1894, Case File No. 339, Carbon County, District Court, Third Judicial District, State of Wyoming. He was found guilty of Murder in the First Degree and sentenced to hang on November 23, 1894. Howard had a lot of sympathizers in the Rawlins area. Many citizens knew him and remembered his heroism in the capture of the Elk Mountain murderers. He was also respected as a Union Pacific Special Agent. His friends signed a petition to Governor Osborne, requesting that his sentence be commuted to Life in Prison.

On November 20, 1894, Osborne granted a fourteen-day Stay of Execution, moving the execution date to December 7, 1894. Though the people of Rawlins made valiant efforts to get Howard a new trial and to get the sentence commuted to Life in Prison, they failed. Frank Howard was hanged on Friday, December 7, 1894, at 10:30 a.m. by Sheriff Jens Hansen and Deputy Sheriff Newton "Newt" T. Rankin.

It was a sad ending to the life of the man who was so instrumental in bringing justice for the murders at Elk Mountain. More than that, it's ironic that the man who could have saved Howard's life was none other than Governor Osborne, the former doctor and "tough on criminals" politician who'd benefitted from Howard's bravery by ultimately acquiring a new pair of shoes for his campaign.

Robert T. Rankin

Jailer Rankin, husband of Rosa Rankin and younger brother to James G. and Joseph P. Rankin, suffered the rest of his life from the severe head wounds he received when Big Nose George attacked and beat him with the shackles while attempting to escape from jail. Rankin's personality was so changed that he spent time in the mental hospital at Evanston, Wyoming, and he eventually lost his family.

56: Gold watch presented to Rosa Rankin

John Lafever

John Lafever (also spelled "Leferve," "Lafevre," and "Laferve") accepted Sheriff N.K. Boswell's offer to become Albany County deputy sheriff.

William Daley

William Daley, who owned a lumber company and a funeral parlor, also served as under-sheriff to Isaac Miller.

Rosanne Rankin

Carbon County Commissioners presented Rosa Rankin with a beautiful gold watch and key in a velvet-lined case for preventing Big Nose George's escape from the Carbon County Jail.

Widdowfield's Second Grave

Deputy Sheriffs Henry H. "Tip" Vincents and Robert Widdowfield both have gravestones in the Rawlins, Wyoming, cemetery. The headstone for Henry H. "Tip" Vincents is a tall, slender, white marble. The headstone for Robert Widdowfield is a rectangle-shaped piece of dark granite, inscribed: "Robert Widdowfield, Killed August 19, 1878 near Elk Mountain while in pursuit of train robbers."

57: Widdowfield's grave in Rawlins, Wyoming

The interesting thing is that Robert Widdowfield is not buried in that grave. He is buried in the Carbon Cemetery at the site of the old Town of Carbon. There, his headstone is identical to that of Tip Vincents's in Rawlins. Both stones were purchased by Carbon County.

The legend behind Widdowfield's gravestone in Rawlins is worth telling. In late 1878, a Rawlins citizen stopped by the cemetery to pay his respects to the two murdered deputies. He found the headstone for Henry H. Vincents, and he saw an unmarked grave a few feet from Vincents's grave that he assumed was Widdowfield's. Thinking it was a travesty that Widdowfield didn't have a nice headstone like Vincents', he took up a collection among the local merchants and bought a stone for Widdowfield. It was placed on that unmarked grave, where it stands today. The real occupant of that grave is a herder that froze to death the previous winter.

The Doctors

Doctor Thomas G. Maghee

Son of Joseph B. and Mary (Jacobs) Maghee, Thomas was born in Evansville, Indiana in 1842. The University of Wyoming Library's, *Wyoming Biography Data Base,* shows that Thomas Maghee married his first wife, Mollie Williams, in 1866. The 1880 United States Federal Census lists her name as "Mary E." The couple, with their four children, lived in Green River City, Sweetwater County, Wyoming Territory, prior to moving to Rawlins Springs. In 1885, Dr. Maghee married his second wife, Evelyn Baldwin.

Dr. Maghee had a long and interesting career. In his early days in the territories, Dr. Maghee served as a contract Army physician at several camps and forts in Nebraska and the Wyoming Territory. He served at Camp Brown (later renamed, "Fort Washakie") from September, 1873 through May, 1877. He established his medical practice and owned a drug store in Green River City. He also was a Union Pacific contract surgeon and traveled to Rawlins Springs to see patients at the Union Pacific Hotel.

In June, 1879 he moved his family to Rawlins Springs and set up his medical practice there. He still maintained his office and drug store in Green River City, and he went back there on a regular basis. His practice grew in Rawlins Springs, and in February, 1881, he brought in a recent graduate of the University of Vermont—physician John Eugene Osborne—to be his associate.

58: Dr. Thomas Maghee, Rawlins, Wyoming Territory

Dr. Maghee practiced medicine in Rawlins well into the twentieth century. He was a pioneer in reconstructive surgery. Remarkable photos of his work on a sheepherder that tried to commit suicide with a shotgun are on file at the State of Wyoming Archives.

After more than thirty years of service to the residents of Rawlins, Dr. Maghee and Evelyn relocated to Lander, Fremont County, Wyoming. He loved the beautiful country in that part of the state, and that is where they lived the rest of their lives.

Doctor John Eugene Osborne

Osborne was born June 19, 1858 in Westport, Essex County, New York. He was the son of John C. Osborne and Mary E. (Rail) Osborne. Dr. Osborne studied medicine at the University of Vermont, graduating in 1880. He moved from Bristol, Vermont, to Rawlins Springs, Wyoming Territory, arriving February 17, 1881, to serve as an associate of Dr. Thomas Maghee and a contract surgeon for the Union Pacific Railroad.

During his long and colorful life in Wyoming, Dr. Osborne was a physician, businessman, and politician. As a businessman, Dr. Osborne became the largest sheep owner in Wyoming. He amassed large real-estate holdings, including the Osborne Building in Rawlins, and he served as chairman of the board of the Rawlins National Bank.

As a physician, he treated Robert Rankin's head wounds on March 22, 1881. Later that same evening, he witnessed the lynching of Big Nose George and verified his death. His use of the villain's skin to make a pair of shoes to further his political career is the punchline of this book.

59: Dr. John E. Osborne, Third Governor, State of Wyoming

As a politician, Osborne served in the Wyoming Territorial Legislature from 1883 to 1885. He was elected mayor of Rawlins in 1888, and he was alternate delegate to the Democratic National Convention from Wyoming in 1892.

After Wyoming attained statehood, John E. Osborne was the second elected governor of Wyoming and the third to serve in that position. He was elected to complete Francis E. Warren's term of office. Because the election had been so bitter, he feared his opposition would try to block access to the building to prevent him from being sworn in. Being the resourceful man that he was, the night before the ceremony, he crawled along a ledge of the Capitol building and through a window to the governor's office. That's where he was waiting to be sworn in when the sun came up.

Governor Osborne's term of office was from January 2, 1893, through January 7, 1895. He was elected and served as a US Representative from the State of Wyoming from 1897 to 1899. He was a member of the Democrat National Convention from Wyoming from 1900–1920, and he ran for the US Senate in 1918.

Dr. Osborne married Salina Smith on November 3, 1907, and he lived in Rawlins, Wyoming, until his death April 24, 1943. He is buried at Cedar Hill Cemetery, in Princeton, Kentucky. Though he was not a native of the Wyoming Territory, his involvement in the story of Big Nose George assured him a place in Wyoming history.

Doctor Lillian Heath Nelson

60: Dr. Lillian Heath, Rawlins, Wyoming Territory

Dr. Lillian Heath was born December 29, 1865, in Burnett Junction, Wisconsin, to William A. and Calista Hunter Heath. Her father moved his family to Fond du Lac, Wisconsin, where they lived for a short time before moving to Aplington, Iowa. William Heath, like many other men of the time, had an overpowering desire to move west, and in 1873, the Heath family moved to Laramie City, Wyoming, Territory. J.H. Triggs,' *History and Directory of Laramie City, Wyoming Territory* shows: "HEATH, W.A., painter, residence: Front Street, between A and B." In 1877, the family moved to Rawlins Springs, Wyoming Territory, where William Heath was employed as a locomotive painter.

William Heath became friends with Dr. Thomas Maghee and assisted him in treating patients. Because of her father's involvement with the doctor, Lillian Heath became interested in medicine. At age sixteen, while she was attending Rawlins Springs High School, she began helping Dr. Maghee. At first, she helped with obstetric patients. In time, she began assisting with bullet wounds and amputations.

Lillian Heath studied with Dr. Maghee for seven years and then moved to Keokuk, Iowa, where she completed her education at the College of Physicians and Surgeons at Hughes College. In 1893, at the age of twenty-eight, she returned to Rawlins to practice medicine, becoming the first woman doctor in Wyoming. She married Lou Nelson when she was thirty-three.

Dr. Heath received Big Nose George Parott's skull cap from Dr. Maghee and Dr. Osborne, and she kept it as a memento through her adult life. Eventually, the skull cap, along with the leg shackles he wore when he was lynched, were donated to the Union Pacific Railroad Museum located in Council Bluffs, Iowa.

61: Author Max Atwell with the Big Nose George exhibit, 1968

Photographs and Maps

Photographs

1. Remains of George Parott found in 1950, Rawlins, Wyoming: Carbon County Museum, Rawlins, Wyoming
2. Dr. Lillian Heath Nelson with George Parott's skull cap: Carbon County Museum, Rawlins, Wyoming
3. Dr. Ben Sturgis, Carbon County coroner, and Lou Nelson: Carbon County Museum, Rawlins, Wyoming
4. Sturgis and Nelson with a perfect fit: Carbon County Museum, Rawlins, Wyoming
5. James G. Rankin, sheriff, Carbon County, Wyoming Territory. Carbon County Sheriff's Office, Rawlins, Wyoming
6. Isaac M. Lawry, sheriff, Carbon County, Wyoming Territory, Carbon County Sheriff's Office, Rawlins, Wyoming
7. Daniel Nottage, sheriff, Albany County, Wyoming Territory: Albany County Sheriff's Office, Laramie, Wyoming
8. Town of Carbon, Wyoming Territory: Union Pacific Railroad Museum Collection, Council Bluffs, Iowa
9. H.H. Vincents's gravestone, Rawlins, Wyoming Cemetery: Atwell Collection
10. H.H. Vincents's gravestone, Rawlins, Wyoming Cemetery: Atwell Collection
11. Robert Widdowfield's gravestone, Carbon, Wyoming Cemetery: Atwell Collection
12. Robert Widdowfield's gravestone, Carbon, Wyoming Cemetery: Atwell Collection
13. Reward poster: Carbon County Museum, Rawlins, Wyoming
14. Daniel Boone May: Wyoming State Archives and Historical Department, Cheyenne, Wyoming
15. John Milton Thayer, former governor, Wyoming Territory: University of Wyoming, American Heritage Center, Laramie, Wyoming
16. Rock Creek, Wyoming Territory: University of Wyoming, American Heritage Center, Laramie, Wyoming
17. Nathaniel K. Boswell, sheriff, Albany County, Wyoming Territory: University of Wyoming, American Heritage Center, Laramie, Wyoming
18. Thomas Jefferson Dayton, sheriff, Albany County, Wyoming Territory: University of Wyoming, American Heritage Center, Laramie, Wyoming
19. Union Pacific Depot, Laramie, Wyoming Territory: Union Pacific Railroad Museum Collection, Council Bluffs, Iowa
20. Albany County Courthouse, Laramie, Wyoming Territory: University of Wyoming, American Heritage Center, Laramie, Wyoming
21. Lynching in Laramie, Wyoming Territory: University of Wyoming, American Heritage Center, Laramie, Wyoming
22. Lynching in Laramie, Wyoming Territory: University of Wyoming, American Heritage Center, Laramie, Wyoming

23. Joe Minuse: Wyoming State Archives and Historical Department, Cheyenne, Wyoming
24. Thomas J. Carr, sheriff, Laramie County, Wyoming Territory: University of Wyoming, American Heritage Center, Laramie, Wyoming
25. Union Pacific Hotel and Depot, Cheyenne, Wyoming Territory: Union Pacific Railroad Museum Collection, Council Bluffs, Iowa
26. Union Pacific Roundhouse, Rawlins, Wyoming Territory: Union Pacific Railroad Museum Collection, Council Bluffs, Iowa
27. Union Pacific Depot, Rawlins, Wyoming Territory: Union Pacific Railroad Museum Collection, Council Bluffs, Iowa
28. Frank James: Missouri History Museum, St. Louis, Missouri
29. James H. "Doc" Hayford, editor, *Laramie Daily Sentinel*: University of Wyoming, American Heritage Center, Laramie, Wyoming
30. Jacob B. Blair, judge, Second Judicial District, Wyoming Territory: Wyoming State Archives and Historical Department, Cheyenne, Wyoming
31. William Adolphus Johnson, sheriff, Sweetwater County, Wyoming Territory: Sweetwater County Museum, Green River, Wyoming
32. Wyoming Territorial Prison at Laramie: *Wyoming Tales and Trails*
33. Main Street looking north from Bridge Street, Helena, Montana Territory, page 101: Montana Historical Society Research Center—Photograph Archives, Helena Montana
34. US Deputy-marshal John X. Beidler, page 102: Montana Historical Society Research Center—Photograph Archives, Helena, Montana
35. Main Street, Miles City, Montana Territory, page 103: Montana Historical Society Research Center—Photograph Archives, Helena, Montana
36. Montana Manhunters, L. to R.—Billy Smith, Jack Hawkins, Tom Irvine, Louis King, and "EPH" Davis, page 104: Montana Historical Society Research Center—Photograph Archives, Helena Montana
37. Steamboat *Red Cloud,* page 106: Montana Historical Society Research Center—Photograph Archives, Helena, Montana
38. Laton Alton Huffman Studio, in Miles City, Montana Territory, page 109: Montana Historical Society Research Center—Photograph Archives, Helena, Montana
39. "Big Nose George" Parott, a.k.a, George Dixon: Wyoming State Archives and Historical Department, Cheyenne, Wyoming
40. Merchants Hotel, St. Paul, Minnesota: Edward Bromley Collection, Published 1890
41. John Friend, editor, *Carbon County Journal*, Rawlins, Wyoming Territory: Carbon County Museum, Rawlins, Wyoming
42. Photocopy of George Parott's affidavit requesting change of venue, showing Big Nose George's signature (with the correct spelling of his name)
43. William Ware Peck, Judge, Third Judicial District Court, Wyoming Territory: Wyoming State Archives and Historical Department, Cheyenne, Wyoming
44. Rankin Brothers Stage line: *Wyoming Tales and Trails*
45. Homer Merrill, Prosecuting Attorney, Carbon County, Wyoming Territory: Carbon County Museum, Rawlins, Wyoming
46. Nathaniel K. Boswell, Albany County, Wyoming Territory : American Heritage Center, University of Wyoming
47. Isaac C. Miller, sheriff, Carbon County, Wyoming Territory: Carbon County Sheriff's Office, Rawlins , Wyoming
48. Rosa Rankin, Wife, Robert Rankin, Carbon Jailer: Carbon County Museum, Rawlins, Wyoming
49. Dr. John E. Osborne, Rawlins, Wyoming Territory: Carbon County Museum, Rawlins, Wyoming

50. Front Street, Rawlins, Wyoming Territory: Union Pacific Railroad Museum Collection, Council Bluffs, Iowa
51. Dr. Maghee (middle) in front of his office: Carbon County Museum, Rawlins, Wyoming
52. George Parott's Death Mask: Wyoming State Archives and Historical Department, Cheyenne, Wyoming
53. George Parott's Death Mask : Wyoming State Archives and Historical Department, Cheyenne, Wyoming
54. George Parott's Death mask and the infamous Shoes: Wyoming State Archives and Historical Department, Cheyenne, Wyoming
55. Parott's Shackles: Wyoming State Archives and Historical Department, Cheyenne, Wyoming
56. Gold watch presented to Rosa Rankin by the Carbon County Commissioners: Carbon County Museum, Rawlins, Wyoming
57. Robert Widdowfield's gravestone, Rawlins, Wyoming Cemetery: Atwell Collection
58. Dr. Thomas Maghee, Rawlins, Wyoming Territory: Carbon County Museum, Rawlins, Wyoming
59. Dr. John E. Osborne, Third Governor, State of Wyoming: Wyoming State Archives and Historical Department, Cheyenne, Wyoming
60. Dr. Lillian Heath, Rawlins, Wyoming Territory: Carbon County Museum, Rawlins, Wyoming
61. Max Atwell with the Big Nose George exhibit 1968: Atwell Collection
62. Author's Photo: Russell J. Harrison
63. Cover Photo: "Elk Mountain" © 2011 Milonica, used under a Creative Commons Attribution-Share Alike 3.0 Unported ((http://creativecommons.org/licenses/by-sa/3.0/deed.en) license.
64. Technical assistance: Donna Kamper, kamper@kamper.com, www.kamper.com

Maps

1. Wyoming Territory, page 4: David Rumsey Map Collection. www.davidrumsey.com
2. Sheriff Rankin's route of travel to pick up Big Nose George Parott, page 100: David Rumsey Map Collection. www.davidrumsey.com

Museums

CARBON COUNTY MUSEUM
904 Walnut St.
Rawlins, Wyoming 82301

CARBON COUNTY SHERIFF'S OFFICE
Carbon County Court House
Rawlins, Wyoming

UNIVERSITY OF WYOMING
American Heritage Center
1000 E. University Ave.
Laramie, Wyoming 82071

ALBANY COUNTY SHERIFF'S OFFICE
525 Grand Ave. Suite 101
Laramie, Wyoming

MONTANA HISTORICAL SOCIETY RESEARCH CENTER
PHOTOGRAPH ARCHIVES
225 N. Roberts
Helena, Montana 59620-1201

UNION PACIFIC RAILROAD MUSEUM
200 Pearl Street
Council Bluffs, Iowa 51503

WYOMING STATE ARCHIVES AND HISTORICAL DEPARTMENT
Barrett Building
2301 Central Avenue
Cheyenne Wyoming 82002

MISSOURI HISTORY MUSEUM
5700 Lindell Boulevard
St. Louis, Missouri 63112-0040

SWEETWATER COUNTY MUSEUM
3 East Flaming Gorge Way
Green River, Wyoming 82935

EDWARD BROMLEY COLLECTION
Published 1890
http//www.chuckstoysand.com

WYOMING TALES AND TRAILS
http//www.wyomingtalesandtrails.com

SOUTH DAKOTA STATE ARCHIVES
900 Governors Drive
Pierre, SD 57501

MINNESOTA HISTORICAL SOCIETY
345 W. Kellogg Blvd.
St. Paul, MN 55102

ATWELL COLLECTION
Max R. Atwell's private photo collection

Sources

In telling this story, I compiled information from many sources. For the most part, these sources are court records, newspaper articles, periodicals, books, and information gathered from the Internet. I used great diligence in finding, extrapolating, and threading together the bits of information that exist.

Where I found major inaccuracies and/or discrepancies, I have discussed them to clarify how and why conflicting sources were used or—in some cases—ignored.

This storyteller has read thousands of articles and partial accounts of the story of the Widdowfield and Vincents and Big Nose George. Following are the articles that I actually used in this book.

Prologue: Bones in a Whiskey Barrel

- *The Rawlins Daily Times,* "Big Nose George Turns Up—In Whiskey Barrel," May 12, 1950.
- *The Rawlins Daily Times,* "Skin Game in Wyoming," May 12, 1950.
- *The Rawlins Daily Times,* "Nose Nearly Hanged at Carbon, Also," May 13 1950.
- *The Rawlins Daily Times,* Jubilee Special, Reprint of "Lost Towns of Carbon County" Includes Song/Poem written by Jean Osborne, "The Lynching Of Big Nose George," January 13, 1965.
- *Rocky Mountain News,* "Big Nose George Parrott, Skull And Skin Are Grisly Reminders of Lynching; Rawlins Won't Forget Big Nose George," September 18, 1955.
- *The Denver Post,* "Skull of 'Big Nose' George," (New Museum—At Rawlins Displays), July 13, 1956.

Chapter 1: Investigation of Attempted Train Derailment

- *Laramie Daily Sentinel,* "Personal Mention," (Dickinson takes Thomas Edison and others hunting and fishing), August 19, 1878.
- *Laramie Daily Sentinel,* "Local Jottings," (Pay Car Arrives...), August 19, 1878.
- *Laramie Daily Sentinel,* "A Sensational Story," (Attempted Train Robbery—a rail was taken up near Medicine Bow...), August 24, 1878.
- *Cheyenne Daily Leader,* "Jaws Of Death," (Big Nose George Has a Thrilling Experience) August 11, 1880.
- *Cheyenne Daily Leader,* "Big Nose George," (He is arraigned for murder and pleads guilty... George interviewed by M.F. Leach...George Parrot is not yet 29 years of age...), September 15, 1880.
- *Cheyenne Daily Sun,* "Confession At Carbon," (Big Nose George Taken from the train and a Rope put around his Neck—He squeals upon the Whole Gang and is Returned to the Sheriff), August 10, 1880.
- *Cheyenne Daily Sun,* "Sprightly Incidents," (Pertaining to the Seizing of Big Nose George), August 11, 1880.
- *Cheyenne Daily Sun,* "George P. Warden gives the Whole Affair Away and Clears up the Mystery," August 17, 1880.

- *Carbon County Journal,* "The Arrival Of Big Nose George," (He Is Forceably Taken From The Train), August 14, 1880.
- Ibid. "Elk Mountain Murder," (George F. Warden Gives the Whole Affair Away and Clears Up the Mystery)
- Territory Of Wyoming, County of Carbon, District Court, Second Judicial District No. 265 Testimony in the Case of Territory of Wyoming v. George Parott, November 18, 1880, Testimony index James Rankin, Pages 1–9; John G. Foote, Pages 9–18; William Daily, Pages 18–31; Jesse Wallace, Pages 31–42; Taylor Pannock, Pages 42 and 43; and M.F. Leech, Pages 41–80.
- Gorzalka, Ann, *Wyoming Territorial Sheriffs*. 539 Cassa Road, Glendo, Wyoming 82213, High Plains Press, Copyright 1998.
- Larson, Taft Alfred, *History of Wyoming*. University Of Nebraska Press, Copyright 1965, 1978.

Internet References:

- Trains, Banks, Stagecoaches, (The Daring Exploits of this Band of Lawless Men, A List of robberies attributed to the James—Younger Gang,) http://www.islandnet.con/~the-gang/rob.htm
- Union Pacific Railroad at ALLExperts, Company Officers, President Sidney Dillon (1874–1884). http:/experts.about.com/e/u/un/Union_Pacific_Railroad.htm
- Ancestry.Com, 1880 United States Federal Census, James G. Rankin. http://ancestry.com
- Ancestry.Com, 1880 United States Federal Census, Millard F. Leech. http://ancestry.com
- Frank and Jesse James Family Outline. http:/rootsweb.com

Chapter 2: Passing the Evening at Percy Station

- *Laramie Daily Sentinel,* "The Train Robbery", (Full Detail of the Affair), June 1, 1878.
- Ibid. "From Rock Creek", "Singleton Returns From Fort Fetterman…"
- *Laramie Daily Sentinel,* "Trapped," (Rankin and His Party Capture Train Robbers,) June 3, 1878.
- *Laramie Daily Sentinel,* "The Capture," (Details of the Pursuit and Arrest of the Train Robbers), June 4, 1878.
- *Laramie Daily Sentinel,* "The Fort Fetterman Road," June 6, 1878.
- Ibid. A Hard Case, --We learn from L. Calvert, the companion robber…
- Frye, Elnora L. *Atlas of Wyoming Outlaws at the Territorial Penitentiary*: Printed by Pioneer Printing and Stationery, Cheyenne, Wyoming, Copyright 1990 by Elnora Frye
- Gorzalka, Ann. *Wyoming Territorial Sheriffs*: 539 Cassa Road, Glendo, Wyoming 82213. High Plains Press, Copyright 1998.

Internet References

- The Officer Down Memorial Page, Inc., Special Agent Robert Widdowfield. http://www.odmp.org
- The Officer Down Memorial Page, Inc., Special Agent Henry Vincent. http://www.odmp.org
- The Origins of the Posse Comitatus, Bonnie Baker, *Air & Space Power Journal—Chronicles Online.* http://www.airpower.maxwell.af.mil/airchronicles/cc/baker1.html
- Ancestry.Com, 1880 United States Federal Census, James G. Rankin. http://ancestry.com
- Ancestry.Com, 1880 United States Federal Census, Millard F. Leech. http://ancestry.com

Sources

Chapter 3: Ambush and Murder On Elk Mountain

- *Laramie Daily Sentinel,* "A Worthy Officer," (Omaha Confirming The Appointment Of Ed Dickinson As Laramie Division), July 12, 1878.
- *Laramie Daily Sentinel,* "A Man Murdered," July 16, 1878.
- *Laramie Daily Sentinel,* "Train Robbers," (Henry And Thomas), July 23, 1878.
- *Laramie Daily Sentinel,* "Local Jottings," (A Model House…Trabing Brothers New Store…), July 31, 1878.
- Ibid. *(*Sheriff Lawry of Carbon County Arrived This Morning To Pick Up Thomas And Return On Number Three)
- *Laramie Daily Sentinel,* "Personal Mention," (Dickinson Takes Thomas Edison and Others Hunting and Fishing), August 19, 1878.
- *Laramie Daily Sentinel,* "Local Jottings," (Pay Car Arrives…), August 19, 1878.
- *Laramie Daily Sentinel,* "A Sensational Story," (Attempted Train Robbery—a Rail Was Taken Up Near Medicine Bow…), August 24, 1878.
- *Laramie Daily Sentinel,* "Lawrence Fee City Marshal," August 26, 1878.
- *Laramie Daily Sentinel,* "Robbers," (…Widdowfield & Vincent Murdered…), August 27, 1878.
  Laramie Daily Sentinel, "Sequel To Robbers," (…Bodies Found…Description Of Horses And Other Property Taken Form Murdered Deputies…), August 28, 1878.
- *Laramie Daily Sentinel,* "Local Jottings," (…Reward offered…, and Latest From the Robbers; and After the Road Agents…), August 29, 1878.
- Ibid. *"After the Road Agents…"* (Sheriff Bullock, Boone May and Davis in pursuit…)
- *Laramie Daily Sentinel,* "Train Robbery-Green River," August 30, 1878.
- *Laramie Daily Sentinel,* "Another Tragedy, Marshal Fee," August 31, 1878.
- Ibid. (Deputy Donahue, Sheriff Nottage and Night Watchman Butler)
- *Laramie Daily Sentinel,* "Reward increased," September 2, 1878.
- *Laramie Daily Sentinel,* "The Train Wrecks," September 3, 1878.
- *Laramie Daily Sentinel,* "Black Hill Stage Stopped, --Robber Killed," (Frank Towle), September 16, 1878.
- *Laramie Daily Sentinel,* "Western News," (Money collected to buy Head Stones for Widdowfield and Vincents), September 16, 1878.
- *Laramie Daily Sentinel,* "Political Straw," (Sheriffs Race), September 18, 1878.
- *Laramie Daily Sentinel,* "Ed Dickinson Superintendent from Laramie City to Green River City," September 23, 1878.
- Ibid. "Soldiers and Civilian Posse riding trains with express cars trying to prevent robberies"
- *Cheyenne Daily Leader,* "Probably Murdered," August 28, 1878.
- *Cheyenne Daily Leader,* "That Double Murder," August 30, 1878.
- Territory Of Wyoming, County of Carbon, District Court, Second Judicial District No. 265, Testimony in the Case of Territory of Wyoming v. George Parott, November 18, 1880, Testimony index James Rankin, Pages 1–9; John G. Foote, Pages 9–18; William Daily, Pages 18–31; Jesse Wallace, Pages 31–42; Taylor Pannock, Pages 42 and 43; and M.F. Leech, Pages 41–80.
- Gorzalka, Ann, *Wyoming Territorial Sheriffs.* 539 Cassa Road, Glendo, Wyoming 82213, High Plains Press, Copyright 1998.

Internet References:

- *The Origins of the Posse Comitatus,* Bonnie Baker, *Air & Space Power Journal—Chronicles Online.* http://www.airpower.maxwell.af.mil/airchronicles/cc/baker1.html

Chapter 4: Robbery Plans Divulged

- *Laramie Daily Sentinel,* "Reward Increased," September 2, 1878.
- *Laramie Daily Sentinel,* "The Train Wrecks," September 3, 1878.
- *Laramie Daily Sentinel,* "Black Hill Stage Stopped," (Robber Killed, Frank Towle…), September 16, 1878.
- *Laramie Daily Sentinel,* "Western News," (Money collected to buy Head Stones for Widdowfield and Vincent), September 16, 1878.
- *Laramie Daily Sentinel,* "Political Straw," (Sheriffs Race), September 18, 1878.
- Ibid. "Soldiers and Civilian Posse riding trains with express cars trying to prevent robberies"
- *Laramie Daily Sentinel,* "Lawrence Fee will run for Albany County Constable," October 7, 1878.
- Ibid. "Boswell beat out Nottage at convention," (Boswell will run for Sheriff), October 7, 1878.
- *Laramie Daily Sentinel,* "Another Robbery," (Boone May and Taylor arrest Henry Borris-AKA-Charles Henry), October 9, 1878.
- Ibid. (Henry Borris claims he was in Deadwood and failed to join his friends at Canyon Springs)
- Ibid. (Detective Seth Bullock still in pursuit of robbers).
- *Laramie Daily Sentinel,* "Carbon County Republican Ticket," (J.G. Rankin beat out Sheriff Lawry at Convention), October 10, 1878.
- Ibid. "Republican Ticket," (J.G. Rankin for Sheriff and J.B. Adams for County Clerk)
- *Laramie Daily Sentinel,* "Our Ticket" (Tell of Boswell's reputation), October 11, 1878.
- *Laramie Daily Sentinel,* "Road Agents," (Trabing Brothers the latest victims,) October 14, 1878.
- *Laramie Daily Sentinel,* "Davis Dungsford Captured by Detective M.F. Leach near Ogallala," (Davis thought to leader of Vincent, Widdowfield killers), November 2, 1878.
- Ibid, "Boone May opinion about Davis Dungsford."
- *Laramie Daily Sentinel,* "J.R. Brophy ahead of Boswell. Still ballots to count," November 5, 1878.
- *Laramie Daily Sentinel,* "Albert Speers, Stage Robber Captured by Detective M.F. Leach and taken to Cheyenne," November 8, 1878.
- *Laramie Daily Sentinel,* "Carbon County Ticket," (List J.G. Rankin Sheriff, J.B. Adams County Clerk, etc.), November 11, 1878.
- *Laramie Daily Sentinel,* "Boswell wins over Brophy by 36 votes, and other," November 19, 1878.
- Ibid. "Albany County Election results," November 19, 1878.
- *Cheyenne Daily Leader,* "Probably Murdered," August 28, 1878.
- *Cheyenne Daily Leader,* "That Double Murder," August 30, 1878.
- *Cheyenne Daily Leader,* "Stage Robbers," October 16, 1878.
- *Cheyenne Daily Leader,* "Albert Spears Captured By Detective M.F. Leach," November 2, 1878.
- Gorzalka, Ann, *Wyoming Territorial Sheriffs.* 539 Cassa Road, Glendo, Wyoming 82213, High Plains Press, Copyright 1998.
- Triggs, J.H., *History And Directory Of Laramie City, Wyoming Territory.* Printed By *Laramie City Daily Sentinel Print*, 1875.

Internet References

- Ancestry.Com, 1870 United States Federal Census, John Lafever. http://ancestry.com
- Ancestry.Com, 1880 United States Federal Census, Millard F. Leach. http://ancestry.com

- Assistant Surgeon Thomas G. Maghee, The Medical History of Fort Washakie. http://www.windriverhistory.org/exhibits/jkmoore/medhistory.htm

Chapter 5: Outlaw Gang Captured

- *Laramie Daily Sentinel*, "Reward increased," September 2, 1878.
- *Laramie Daily Sentinel*, "The Train Wrecks," September 3, 1878.
- *Laramie Daily Sentinel,* "Black Hill Stage Stopped," (Robber Killed, Frank Towle…), September 16, 1878.
- *Laramie Daily Sentinel*, "Western News," (Money collected to buy Head Stones for Widdowfield and Vincent), September 16, 1878.
- *Laramie Daily Sentinel*, September 18, 1878, "Political Straw, Sheriffs Race."
- *Laramie Daily Sentinel*, "Ed Dickinson Superintendent from Laramie City to Green River City," September 23, 1878.
- Ibid. "Soldiers and Civilian Posse riding trains with express cars trying to prevent robberies,"
- *Laramie Daily Sentinel*, "Lawrence Fee will run for Albany County Constable," October 7, 1878.
- Ibid. "Boswell beat out Nottage at convention," (Boswell will run for Sheriff).
- *Laramie Daily Sentinel*, "Another Robbery," (Boone May and Taylor arrest Henry Borris-AKA-Charles Henry), October 9, 1878.
- Ibid. "Henry Borris claims he was in Deadwood and failed to join his friends at Canyon Springs"
- Ibid. "Detective Seth Bullock still in pursuit of robbers"
- *Laramie Daily Sentinel*, "Carbon County Republican Ticket," (J.G. Rankin beat out Sheriff Lawry at Convention), October 10, 1878.
- Ibid. "Republican Ticket," (J.G. Rankin for Sheriff and J.B. Adams for County Clerk)
- *Laramie Daily Sentinel*, "Our Ticket," (Tell of Boswell's reputation) October 11, 1878.
- *Laramie Daily Sentinel*, "Road Agents," (Trabing Brothers the latest victims.) October 14, 1878.
- *Laramie Daily Sentinel*, "Davis Dungsford Captured by Detective M.F. Leach near Ogallala," (Davis thought to be leader of Vincent, Widdowfield killers), November 2, 1878.
- Ibid. "Boone May opinion about Davis Dungsford"
- *Laramie Daily Sentinel*, "J.R. Brophy ahead of Boswell Still ballots to count," November 5, 1878.
- *Laramie Daily Sentinel*, "Albert Speers, Stage Robber Captured by Detective M.F. Leach and taken to Cheyenne," November 8, 1878.
- *Laramie Daily Sentinel*, "Carbon County Ticket," (List J.G. Rankin Sheriff, J.B. Adams County Clerk, etc.), November 11, 1878.
- *Laramie Daily Sentinel*, "Boswell Wins over Brophy by 36 votes, and other…," November 19, 1878.
- Ibid. "Albany County Election results"
- *Laramie Daily Sentinel*, "Detective M.F. Leach of Ogallala is in Laramie City," November 22, 1878.
- *Laramie Daily Sentinel*, "UP Ice house is almost ready for roof…," November 30, 1878.
- *Laramie Daily Sentinel*, "Sheriff Lawry is on a visit east," December 6, 1878.
- *Laramie Daily Sentinel*, "Capture of Outlaw," (The Whole Gang Taken In A Clean Sweep. Particulars by eye witness), December 23, 1878.
- *Laramie Daily Sentinel,* "Personal and Local News," (Boone May was in City Yesterday, Christmas Day), December 26, 1878.
- Ibid. "Another Train boarded by Robbers near Fort Steele"

- Ibid. "What they were after"
- *Laramie Weekly Sentinel,* "The Murder of Vincent and Widdowfield," (Full Particulars by an Eye Witness), December 27, 1878.
- *Laramie Daily Sentinel,* "Capture of Outlaws," (One Whole Gang Taken in a Clean Job, particulars by eye witness), December 28, 1878.
- *Cheyenne Daily Leader,* "We Are Seven," (Capture of Band of Outlaws), December 24, 1878.
- Ibid. "Personal," (Sheriff I.N. Lawry, of Carbon County, who was married in Chicago…), December 24, 1878.
- *Cheyenne Daily Leader,* "Irwin A Road Agent," December 28, 1878.
- Ibid. "Train Robbers"
- Ibid. "December Drifting," (Among the names of the brave men who captured road agents…)
- *Cheyenne Daily Leader,* "Rock Creek Robbers," (The Inside History of the Capture by Boswell's Band), January 2, 1879.
- *Carbon County Journal,* "Outlaw Albert Spears captured by Detective M.F. Leach," November 2, 1878.
- Territory Of Wyoming, County of Carbon, District Court, Second Judicial District No. 265 Testimony in the Case of Territory of Wyoming v. George Parott, November 18, 1880, Testimony index James Rankin, Pages 1–9; John G. Foote, Pages 9–18; William Daily, Pages 18–31; Jesse Wallace, Pages 31–42; Taylor Pannock, Pages 42–43; and M. F. Leech [sic] Pages 41–80.
- Triggs, J.H., *History And Directory Of Laramie City, Wyoming Territory*. Printed by *Laramie City Daily Sentinel* Print, 1875.

Internet References:

- Ancestry.Com, 1870 United States Federal Census, John Lafever. http://ancestry.com
- Ancestry.Com, 1880 United States Federal Census, Millard F. Leach. http://ancestry.com

Chapter 6: Confessions

- *Laramie Daily Sentinel*, "Sheriff Lawry is on a visit East," December 6, 1878.
- *Laramie Daily Sentinel*, "Capture of Outlaw," (The Whole Gang Taken In A Clean Sweep. Particulars by eye witness), December 23, 1878.
- *Laramie Daily Sentinel*, "Personal and Local News," (Boone May was in City Yesterday, Christmas Day), December 26, 1878.
- Ibid. "Another Train boarded by Robbers near Fort Steele"
- Ibid. "What they were after"
- *Laramie Weekly Sentinel,* "The Murder of Vincent and Widdowfield," (Full Particulars by an Eye Witness), December 27, 1878.
- *Laramie Daily Sentinel*, "Capture of Outlaws," (One Whole Gang Taken In A Clean Job, particulars by eye witness), December 28, 1878.
- Ibid. "Held for Trial"
- *Laramie Daily Sentinel*, "Mr. Boswell brought up from Cheyenne…,"
- *Laramie Daily Sentinel*, "*Sentinel* will be published every Friday Morning," December 31, 1878.
- *Laramie Weekly Sentinel*, "Held for Trial," January 3. 1879.
- *Cheyenne Daily Leader,* "Stage Robbers," October 16, 1878.
- *Cheyenne Daily Leader*, "Albert Spears captured by Detective M.F. Leach," November 2, 1878.

- *Cheyenne Daily Leader*, "We Are Seven," (Capture of Band of Outlaws), December 24, 1878.
- Ibid. "Personal," (Sheriff I.N. Lawry, of Carbon County, who was married in Chicago…), December 24, 1878.
- *Cheyenne Daily Leader*, "Irwin A Road Agent," December 28, 1878.
- Ibid. "Train Robbers"
- Ibid. "December Drifting," (Among the names of the brave men who captured road agents…), December 28, 1878.
- *Cheyenne Daily Leader*, "Rock Creek Robbers," (The Inside History of the Capture by Boswell's Band), January 2, 1879,
- Territory Of Wyoming, County of Carbon, District Court, Second Judicial District No. 265 Testimony in the Case of Territory of Wyoming v. George Parott, November 18, 1880, Testimony index James Rankin, Pages 1–9; John G. Foote, Pages 9–18; William Daily, Pages 18–31; Jesse Wallace, Pages 31–42; Taylor Pannock, Pages 42, 43; and M. F. Leech, Pages 41–80.
- Gorzalka, Ann, *Wyoming Territorial Sheriffs*. 539 Cassa Road, Glendo, Wyoming 82213. High Plains Press, Copyright 1998.
- Pence, Mary Lou, *Boswell, the Story of A Frontier Lawman*. Printed by Pioneer Printing and Stationer Co., Cheyenne, Wyoming, Copyright Mary Lou Pence, Laramie, Wyoming 1978.
- Triplett, Frank, *The Life, Times And Treacherous Death Of Jesse James*. Reprint of *The Long Suppressed*, 1882 Edition, Konecky & Konecky, 150 Fifth Ave., New York, NY 10010, Copyright 1970, by The Swallow Press, Inc.

Internet References:

- Ancestry.Com, 1880 United States Federal Census, Millard F. Leach. http://ancestry.com
- United States Marshals Service, United States Marshal Seth Bullock, Historical Perspective. http://www.usdoj.gov/marshals/history/loyal_community.html. Accessed April 23, 2006.

Chapter 7: No Rest for Lawmen

- *Laramie Daily Sentinel*, "Capture of Outlaw," (The Whole Gang Taken In A Clean Sweep. Particulars by eye witness), December 23, 1878.
- *Laramie Daily Sentinel*, "Personal and Local News," (Boone May was in City Yesterday, Christmas Day), December 26, 1878.
- Ibid. "Another Train boarded by Robbers near Fort Steele"
- Ibid. "What they were after"
- *Laramie Weekly Sentinel*, "The Murder of Vincent and Widdowfield," (Full Particulars by an Eye Witness), December 27, 1878.
- *Laramie Daily Sentinel*, "Capture of Outlaws," (One Whole Gang Taken In A Clean Job, particulars by eye witness), December 28, 1878.
- Ibid. "Held for Trial"
- *Laramie Daily Sentinel*, "Mr. Boswell brought up from Cheyenne…), December 30, 1878.
- *Laramie Daily Sentinel*, "*Sentinel* will be published every Friday Morning," December 31, 1878.
- *Laramie Weekly Sentinel*, "Held for Trial," January 3, 1879.
- *Cheyenne Daily Leader*, "Table of Distances," (Cheyenne to Deadwood Stage Stops), August 25, 1877.
- *Cheyenne Daily Leader*, "Road Robbers," March 27, 1877.

- Ibid. "Johnny Slaughter Murdered," (Stage Driver Murdered)
- Ibid. "John Slaughter Notified of his Son's Death," (City Marshal Notified of Son's Murder)
- Ibid. "City Marshal J.N. Slaughter," (Parents left to bring back body of Son)
- *Cheyenne Daily Leader,* "John Slaughter Funeral," April 5, 1877.
- *Cheyenne Daily Leader*, "Death of Mrs. John Slaughter the Town Marshal's wife," May 1, 1877.
- *Cheyenne Daily Leader,* "Article puts Mckimie in Denver in the years 1873 & 1874," February 22, 1878.
- *Cheyenne Daily Leader*, "Story of the murder of Johnny Slaughter…), March 27, 1878.
- *Cheyenne Daily Leader*, "Stage Robbers," October 16, 1878.
- *Cheyenne Daily Leader*, "Albert Spears captured by Detective M.F. Leach," November 2, 1878.
- *Cheyenne Daily Leader*, "WE ARE SEVEN," (Capture of Band of Outlaws), December 24, 1878.
- Ibid. "Personal," (Sheriff I.N. Lawry, of Carbon County, who was married in Chicago…), December 24, 1878.
- *Cheyenne Daily Leader*, "Irwin A Road Agent," December 28, 1878.
- Ibid. "Train Robbers"
- Ibid. "December Drifting" (Among the names of the brave men who captured road agents…)
- *Cheyenne Daily Leader*, "Rock Creek Robbers," (The Inside History of the Capture by Boswell's Band), January 2, 1879.
- Territory Of Wyoming, County of Carbon, District Court, Second Judicial District No. 265 Testimony in the Case of Territory of Wyoming v. George Parott, November 18, 1880, Testimony index James Rankin, Pages 1–9; John G. Foote, Pages 9–18; William Daily, Pages 18–31; Jesse Wallace, Pages 31–42; Taylor Pannock, Pages 42 and 43; and M.F. Leech, Pages 41–80.
- Chiefs of Police, Cheyenne, Wyoming, 1867–Present, Courtesy Cheyenne Police Department, Cheyenne Wyoming.
- Frazer, Robert W., *Forts of the West.* University Of Oklahoma Press, Publishing Norman, Publishing Division of the University. Copyright 1965, 1972.
- Gorzalka, Ann, *Wyoming Territorial Sheriffs*. 539 Cassa Road, Glendo, Wyoming 82213, High Plains Press, Copyright 1998.
- Frye, Elnora L., *Atlas of Wyoming Outlaws at the Territorial Penitentiary*. Printed by Pioneer Printing and Stationery, Cheyenne, Wyoming, Copyright 1990 by Elnora Frye.
- Bridwell, J.W., *The Life And Adventures Of Robert Mckimme, Alias "Litttle Reddy ," From Texas*. Printed and Published at the Hillsboro Gazette Office, Hillsboro, Ohio, December, 1878.
- Pence, Mary Lou, Boswell, *The Story Of A Frontier Lawman*. Printed by Pioneer Printing and Stationer Co., Cheyenne, Wyoming, Copyright Mary Lou Pence, Laramie, Wyoming 1978.
- Triggs , J.H., *History Of Cheyenne And Northern Wyoming*. Printed At The *Herald Steam And Job* Printing House, Omaha, Nebraska 1876, Copyright Secured 1876.
- Triggs , J.H., *History And Directory Of Laramie City, Wyoming Territory*. Printed By *Laramie City Daily Sentinel* Print, 1875.

Internet References

- William N. Hockett, Boone May—*Gunfighter of the Black Hills*. http://www.bar-w.com/boonemay.html
- Ancestry.Com, 1880 United States Federal Census, Millard F. Leach. http://ancestry.com

Sources

Chapter 8: Dutch Charley

- *Laramie Weekly Sentinel*, "Held for Trial," January 3, 1879.
- *Laramie Sentinel* (Daily), "Retributive Justice," (The Hanging of "Dutch Charlie" at Carbon), January 10, 1879.
- Ibid. "Dutch Charlie," (Taken up on Number 3 last Sunday…)
- *Laramie Daily Sentinel*, "Jail Breaking," January 31, 1879.
- *Laramie Daily Sentinel,* "The Vincent—Widdowfield Murders," April 11, 1879.
- *Laramie Weekly Sentinel*, "Blood Curdling Adventure," (Judge Pease and Doc. Hayford travel on train taking Joe Minuse to Rawlins), April 11, 1879.
- *Laramie Daily Sentinel,* "Manuse the Murder, Safely Landed in Rawlins," April 17, 1879.
- *Laramie Weekly Sentinel*, "Joe Manuse, Supposed to have been with Gang…," November 29, 1879.
- *Cheyenne Daily Leader*, "Strung Up," (Sudden Termination of the Murderous Career of Dutch Charlie), January 7, 1879.
- *Cheyenne Daily Leader*, "Laramie Laconics," (The Body of Dutch Charlie has been cut down…), January 10, 1879.
- *Cheyenne Daily Leader,* "Laramie Laconics," (Dutch Charlie's real name…), January 11, 1879.
- Ibid. "Leach the Detective is autographed…"
- *Cheyenne Daily Leader*, "Jail Breaking," (Deputies Butler & LaFerve…), January 31, 1879.

Internet References:

- The Officer Down Memorial Page, Inc., Special Agent Robert Widdowfield. http://www.odmp.org
- The Officer Down Memorial Page, Inc., Special Agent Henry Vincent. http://www.odmp.org
- Genealogy.com, Robert Widdowfield-1. http://familytreemaker.genealogy.com
- Genealogy.com, Robert Widdowfield-2. http://familytreemaker.genealogy.com
- Ancestry.Com, 1880 United States Federal Census, Millard F. Leach. http://ancestry.com

Chapter 9: Grand Jury Acts

- *Laramie Daily Sentinel*, "The Vincent-Widdowfield Murders," April 11, 1879.
- *Laramie Weekly Sentinel,* "Blood Curdling Adventure," (Judge Pease and Doc. Hayford travel on train taking Joe Minuse to Rawlins), April 11, 1879.
- *Laramie Daily Sentinel,* "Manuse the Murder," (Safely Landed in Rawlins), April 17, 1879.
- *Laramie Weekly Sentinel*, "Joe Manuse, Supposed to have been with Gang…," November 29, 1879.
- Territory Of Wyoming, County of Carbon, District Court, Second Judicial District No. 265 April 7, 1879: No, 265—Indictment—For Murder: John Minuse alias Joe Minuse, George Parott alias Big Nose George, Frank James alias McKinney, John Wells alias Sandy, Sim Waun, Jack Campbell, Tim Reed, Frank Tool, and Charles Bates alias Dutch Charley, on August 20, 1878 with force of arms did Murder Henry H. Vinsen
- April 9, 1879: Territory of Wyoming, Bench Warrant for Murder: John Minuse
- Territory Of Wyoming, County of Carbon, District Court, Second Judicial District No. 265, Declaration of Indigents By John Minuse and request the court to provide Service of Subpoenas for Defendant.

Internet References:

- http://www.usdoj.gov/marshals/history/index.html
- The Officer Down Memorial Page, Inc., Special Agent Robert Widdowfield. http://www.odmp.org
- The Officer Down Memorial Page, Inc., Special Agent Henry Vincent. http://www.odmp.org

Chapter 10: The Minuse Trial

- *Laramie Weekly Sentinel*, " Blood Curdling Adventure," (Judge Pease and Doc. Hayford travel on train taking Joe Minuse to Rawlins), April 11, 1879.
- *Laramie Weekly Sentinel*, "Joe Manuse, Supposed to have been with Gang…," November 29, 1879.
- *Cheyenne Daily Sun*, "John Lafarve and Frank Howard Collect Reward on Dutch Charlie," July 20, 1879.
- Territory Of Wyoming, County of Carbon, District Court, Second Judicial District April 7, 1879: No, 265—Indictment—For Murder: John Minuse alias Joe Minuse, George Parott alias Big Nose George, Frank James alias McKinney, John Wells alias Sandy, Sim Waun, Jack Campbell, Tim Reed, Frank Tool, and Charles Bates alias Dutch Charley, on August 20, 1878 with force of arms did Murder Henry H. Vinsen
- April 9, 1879: Territory of Wyoming, Bench Warrant for Murder: John Minuse
- Territory Of Wyoming, County of Carbon, District Court, Second Judicial District No. 265, Declaration of Indigents By John Minuse and request the court to provide Service of SUBPOENAS for Defendant.
- No. 265 Territory of Wyoming v. John Minuse, Subpoena to Appear on September 8, 1879: John Lafever–Overholt on behalf of Prosecution
- No. 265 Territory of Wyoming v. John Minuse, Subpoena to Appear on September 8, 1879: McCarty, Jesse Wallace and Wm. Daily on behalf of Prosecution
- No. 265 Territory of Wyoming v. John Minuse, Subpoena to Appear on September 8, 1879: Thomas Gault, Jos Warren, Mrs. Jos Warren, H. McIntosh, Chas Davis, W.A. Johnson, A.C, Hanson on behalf of Defendant
- No. 265 Territory of Wyoming v. John Minuse, Subpoena to Appear on September 8, 1879: Tom Davenport on behalf of Defendant
- No. 265 Territory of Wyoming v. John Manuse, Subpoena to Appear on September 8, 1879: Willis Frank on behalf of Defendant
- No. 265 List of Men called for September, 9, 1879 Jury Duty, Territory of Wyoming v. John Minuse
- No. 265 List of Men selected to serve on September 9, 1879 Jury, Territory of Wyoming v. John Minuse
- No. 265 List of Jury, Triers, Witness for Prosecution and Witness for Defendant September 9, 1879 Trial, Territory of Wyoming v. John Minuse
- No. 265 Jury Verdict of "Not Guilty" Delivered September 10, 1879 in the Case of Territory of Wyoming v. John Minuse

Internet References:

- William Wellington Corlett. http://politicalgraveyard.com. Accessed December 5, 2005.
- Jacob B. Blair. http://politicalgraveyard.com. Accessed May 6, 2007.

Sources

Chapter 11: Big Nose George Captured and Returned to Wyoming

- *Cheyenne Daily Leader*, "William Henry Harrison Llewellyn and D. Boone May Tried for murder of Curley Grimes," (Verdict innocent), February 29, 1880.
- *Cheyenne Daily Leader*, "Frank Howard, Alleged Detective Bagged for Criminal Act," June 22, 1880.
- *Cheyenne Daily Leader*, "Minor Mention Frank Howard," (Charges Discussed), June 29, 1880.
- *Cheyenne Daily Leader*, "Red Handed Rascals," (Captured of outlaws of the Elk Mountain Affair), July 20, 1880.
- *Cheyenne Daily Leader*, "Identifies Outlaws," July 20, 1880.
- *Cheyenne Daily Leader*, "The Blair Case," (...Judge Blair...), July 26, 1880.
- *Cheyenne Daily Leader*, "Big Nosed George," (En route to Rawlins—Will Pass Through To Day), August 7, 1880.
- *Cheyenne Daily Sun*, "John Lafarve and Frank Howard Collect Reward on Dutch Charlie," July 20, 1879.
- *Cheyenne Daily Sun*, "Big Nose George, Will Be Taken Thru Cheyenne to-day," August 7, 1880.
- *Cheyenne Daily Sun*, "Rankin's Prisoner." August 8, 1880.
- *The Yellowstone Journal*, "Boone May Accepts position Golden Terra," July 10, 1880.
- Ibid. "Detective Liewellyn,"
- Ibid. "US Deputy Marshal, Tom Irvine duty to take Indian Census."
- *The Yellowstone Journal*, "A Fast Boat,"
- Ibid. "Bismark Stage Robbed of Mail by Indians."
- Ibid. "Custer County Sheriff Bullard, Under Sheriff J.W. Johnson."
- Ibid. "X. Beadler Arrived Last Week From Junction City," (Will Stay Several Weeks).
- Ibid. "Freshly Remodeled Union Hotel," (50 Rooms).
- Ibid. "Advertisement for many Stage Lines."
- *The Yellowstone Journal*, "14 Prisoners in Jail," (No More Room for Tramps), July 31 1880.
- Ibid. "Thomas H. Irvine Announces Candidacy for Sheriff,"
- *The Yellowstone Journal*, "Thomas Irvine Formal Announcement to run for..." August 7, 1880.
- Ibid. "Corralled," (Story of Big Nose George and Bill Carey Arrest).
- Ibid. "Prisoners Shackles Welded Together."
- *The Yellowstone Journal*, "Political Announcements," August 7, 1880.
- Ibid. "Big Nose George & Bill Carry, welded chains."
- Ibid. "Big Nose George and gang rob...Morris Cahn in February 1979...,"
- *The Yellowstone Journal*, "Big Nose George," (reprint of interview with Pioneer Press in St. Paul, Minn.), August 14, 1880.
- Ibid. "Tom Irvine," (Is working with Will Liewellyn in Northern Wyoming).
- *The Yellowstone Journal*, "Census Returns," August 21, 1880.
- *The Yellowstone Journal*, "For Sheriff–Thomas H. Irvine," (Reform Party), October 23, 1880.
- Ibid. "Commission Accepts Resignation."
- *The Yellowstone Journal*, "JOHN W. SMITH FOR SHERIFF," October 30, 1880.
- *The Yellowstone Journal*, "Irvine 302 Votes," November 6, 1880.
- *The Yellowstone Journal*, "Our County Election," November 13, 1880.
- Ibid. "County Election Returns."
- *Helena Daily Herald*, July 1, 1880, "A Man."
- Ibid. 4 state railroad map
- *Helena Daily Herald*, "Rail Road Time Table—Omaha to St. Paul," July 2, 1880.

- Ibid. "Overland Hotel," (Stage Office Gilmer, Salisbury & Co.)
- *Helena Daily Herald*, "Capture of Noted Criminals," August, 16, 1880.
- Ibid. "Steamboat."
- *Black Hills Daily Times*, "Captured Outlaws," July 25, 1880.
- *Black Hills Daily Times*, "Another Brace of Them Rounded Up," July 27, 1880.
- Ibid. "James F. Towle."
- Ibid. "...Driving a Bull Team over the Cheyenne—Black Hills route...,"
- Ibid. "...joined a gang of horse—thieves and road agents of which Jack Campbell, Dutch Charlie, Frank Towle and Mckinney..."
- *Black Hills Daily Times*, "...Boone May carries Frank Towle's Head to Rawlins to claim reward..."
- *Black Hills Daily Times*, "Curley Grimes Death," (Boone May), August 14, 1880.
- *Black Hills Daily Times*, "Llewellyn," August 15, 1880.
- Ibid. "District Court," (Boone May And W.H. Liewellyn Charged with killing of Lee alias Curly Grimes)
- *Black Hills Daily Times*, "Albert Spears captured by Detective M. F. Leach," August 14, 1880.
- *Black Hills Journal*, "...Jack Campbell jailed and through miscalculation he was set free...," (before gang moved to Sun River Country), January 5, 1879.
- *Pioneer Press*, "Big Nose George," (Sheriff Rankin Interview), August 6, 1880.
- July 19, 1880, Requisition For Fugitive From Justice, Wyoming Territory, Issued by Governor John W. Hoyt,--To his Excellency the Governor of the Territory of Montana,... For Jack Campbell, George Parott alias Big Nose George...stands charged with the crime of Murder...
- July 19, 1880, Requisition For Fugitive From Justice, Wyoming Territory, Issued by Governor John W. Hoyt, ---To his Excellency the Governor of the Territory of Montana...for John Wells alias Sandy...stands charged with the crime of Murder...
- August 18, 1880, Territory Of Wyoming, Executive Department...Request for James G. Rankin to receive and secure the said Jack Campbell and George alias Big Nose George....stands charged with the crime of Murder in the Territory of Wyoming....and have taken refuge in The Territory of Montana......and bring them unmolested into this Territory....By The Governor: John W. Hoyt...
- August 18, 1880, Territory Of Wyoming , Executive Department,...Request for James G. Rankin to receive and secure the said John Wells alias Sandy......stands charged with the crime of Murder in the Territory of Wyoming....and have taken refuge in The Territory of Montana......and bring them unmolested into this Territory....By The Governor: John W. Hoyt...

Internet References:

- Benjamin Franklin Potts, Governor Montana Territory. http://politicalgraveyard.com
- Newspaper Items, Utah Northern (Utah & Northern). http://utahrails .net. Accessed December 22, 2005.
- Montana Governors. http://www.invista.com/society/government/leader/ustates/montna.htm
- Northern Pacific Railroad. http://members.aol.com/Gibson0817/npacific.htm
- The Officer Down Memorial Page, Inc., Special Agent Robert Widdowfield. http://www.odmp.org
- The Officer Down Memorial Page, Inc., Special Agent Henry Vincent. http://www.odmp.org
- United States Marshals Service, District Marshals—D/Montana, Historical Perspective. http://www.usdoj.gov/marshals/district/mt/general/history/.html

Sources

- United States Marshals Service, District Marshals—D/Nebraska, Historical Perspective. http://www.usdoj.gov/marshals/district/ne/general/history/.html
- United States Marshals Service, District Marshals—D/North Dakota, Historical Perspective. http://www.usdoj.gov/marshals/district/nd/general/history/.html
- United States Marshals Service, District Marshals—D/South Dakota, Historical Perspective. http://www.usdoj.gov/marshals/district/sd/general/history/.html
- United States Marshals Service, District Marshals—D/Wyoming, Historical Perspective. http://www.usdoj.gov/marshals/district/wy/general/history/.html
- Ancestry.Com, 1880 United States Federal Census, James G. Rankin. http://ancestry.com
- Ancestry.Com, 1880 United States Federal Census, Robert Rankin. http://ancestry.com
- *John Xavier Beidler Journal,* Edited by Helen Fitzgerald Sanders & William H. Bertsche, Jr., " X. Beidler, Vigilante." Copyright 1957 by the University of Oklahoma Press, Publishing Division. Composed and printed at Norman, Oklahoma, U.S.A., by the University of Oklahoma Press.

Chapter 12: Another Necktie Confession

- *Cheyenne Daily Leader*, "Jaws Of Death," (Big Nose George Has a Thrilling Experience), August 11, 1880.
- *Cheyenne Daily Sun*, "Rankin's Prisoner," August 8, 1880.
- *Cheyenne Daily Sun*, "Confession At Carbon," (Big Nose George Taken from the Train and a Rope put around his Neck, He squeals upon the Whole Gang and is Returned to the Sheriff.), August 10, 1880.
- *Cheyenne Daily Sun*, "Sprightly Incidents," (Pertaining to the Seizing of Big Nose George), August 11, 1880,
- *Carbon County Journal*, "The Arrival Of Big Nose George," (He Is Forcible Taken From The Train), August 14, 1880.
- *Laramie Weekly Sentinel*, "Big Nose George," (The Vincent—Widdowfield Murder,…is jailed In Rawlins Springs…), August 14, 1880.

Internet References:

- The Officer Down Memorial Page, Inc., Special Agent Robert Widdowfield. http://www.odmp.org
- The Officer Down Memorial Page, Inc., Special Agent Henry Vincent. http://www.odmp.org
- Ancestry.Com, 1880 United States Federal Census, James G. Rankin. http://ancestry.com
- Ancestry.Com, 1880 United States Federal Census, Robert Rankin. http://ancestry.com
- Genealogy.com, Robert Widdowfield -1. http://familytreemaker.genealogy.com
- Genealogy.com, Robert Widdowfield -2. http://familytreemaker.genealogy.com

Chapter 13: Arraignment

- *Cheyenne Daily Leader*, "Big Nose George," (He is arraigned for murder and pleads guilty), (…George interviewed by M.F. Leach,…George Parrot is not yet 29 years of age…), September 15, 1880.
- *Cheyenne Daily Leader*, "A Legal Halt," (BNG attempts to plead guilty to second degree murder to save his life.), September 18, 1880.
- *Cheyenne Daily Leader*, "Minor Mention," (BNG Withdraws plea of "Guilty"…), September 21, 1880.

217

- *Cheyenne Daily Sun*, "Sprightly Incidents," (Pertaining to the Seizing of Big Nose George), August 11, 1880.
- *Cheyenne Daily Sun*, "George P. Warden gives the Whole Affair Away and Clears Up the Mystery," August 17, 1880.
- *Carbon County Journal*, "Big Nose George Pleads Guilty," September 18, 1880.
- Ibid. "J.B. Adams tendered his resignation…"
- *Carbon County Journal*, "Big Nose George again changes mind…," September 25, 1880.
- Ibid. "Judge Blair did not come up last night…"
- *Laramie Weekly Sentinel*, "The Trial of Big Nose George," (Pleads guilty), November 20, 1880.
- Territory Of Wyoming, County of Carbon, District Court, Second Judicial District December 15, 1880, No, 265—Indictment—For Murder: Territory of Wyoming v. George Parrot alias Big Nose George, Frank James alias McKinney, Sim Waun, Et al
- No. 265 Territory of Wyoming v. George Parrott, Subpoena to Appear on September 13, 1880: J.B. Adams, Ed Dickinson, James Bellamy, J.G. Rankin, Frank Howard, and M.H. on behalf of Prosecution…

Internet References:

- Jacob B. Blair. http://politicalgraveyard.com. Accessed May 6, 2007.
- The Officer Down Memorial Page, Inc., Special Agent Robert Widdowfield. http://www.odmp.org
- The Officer Down Memorial Page, Inc., Special Agent Henry Vincent. http://www.odmp.org
- The Desperados, (Those who rode with the James—Younger Gang,) http://www.islandnet.con/~the-gang/bio.htm
- Genealogy.com, Robert Widdowfield -1. http://familytreemaker.genealogy.com
- Genealogy.com, Robert Widdowfield -2. http://familytreemaker.genealogy.com
- Ancestry.Com, 1880 United States Federal Census, Millard F. Leach. http://ancestry.com

Chapter 14: Changes

- *Cheyenne Daily Leader*, "Big Nose George," "He is arraigned for murder and pleads guilty" (…George interviewed by M.F. Leach…George Parrot is not yet 29 years of age…), September 15, 1880.
- *Cheyenne Daily Leader*, "A Legal Halt." (BNG attempts to plead guilty to second degree murder to save his life.) September 18, 1880.
- *Cheyenne Daily Leader*, "Minor Mention." (BNG Withdraws plea of "Guilty"…), September 21, 1880.
- *Cheyenne Daily Sun*, "Sprightly Incidents," (Pertaining to the Seizing of Big Nose George), August 11, 1880.
- *Cheyenne Daily Sun,* "George P. Warden gives the Whole Affair Away and Clears Up the Mystery," August 17, 1880.
- *Carbon County Journal*, "Big Nose George Pleads Guilty," September 18, 1880.
- Ibid. "J.B. Adams tendered his resignation…,"
- *Carbon County Journal*, "Big Nose George again changes mind…," September 25, 1880.
- Ibid. "Judge Blair did not come up last night…,"
- *Laramie Weekly Sentinel,* "The Trial of Big Nose George," (Pleads guilty), November 20, 1880.

- Territory Of Wyoming, County of Carbon, District Court, Second Judicial District December 15, 1880, No, 265—Indictment—For Murder: Territory of Wyoming v. George Parrot alias Big Nose George, Frank James alias McKinney, Sim Waun, Et al
- No. 265 Territory of Wyoming v. George Parrott, SUBPOENA to Appear on September 13, 1880: J.B. Adams, Ed Dickinson James Bellamy, J.G. Rankin, Frank Howard, and M.H. on behalf of Prosecution…

Internet References:

- William Wellington Corlett. http://politicalgraveyard.com. Accessed December 5, 2005.
- Jacob B. Blair. http://politicalgraveyard.com. Accessed May 6, 2007.
- The Officer Down Memorial Page, Inc., Special Agent Robert Widdowfield. http://www.odmp.org
- UW libraries—Wyoming Biography Database search results, Maghee, Thomas G., last updated October 20, 2004. http://www-lib.uwyo.edu/db/Bio/single.Asp?Key=4574
- Assistant Surgeon Thomas G. Maghee, The Medical History of Fort Washakie. http://www.windriverhistory.org/exhibits/jkmoore/medhistory.htm

Chapter 15: The Trial

- *Cheyenne Daily Leader*, "Minor Mention." (BNG Withdraws plea of "Guilty"…) September 21, 1880.
- *Cheyenne Daily Leader*, "Oakes Ames, Monument to be built at Sherman," September 29, 1880.
- *Cheyenne Daily Leader,* "Territorial Convicts," September 30, 1880.
- *Cheyenne Daily Leader,* "Special Train, Ames Monument," October 1, 1880.
- *Cheyenne Daily Leader*, " From Rawlins." (Big Snow Storm Out There–Big Nose George–trial is in progress), November 20, 1880.
- *Cheyenne Daily Sun*, "Big Nose George," (Says the *Journal*, again changes mind), September 28, 1880.
- *Carbon County Journal*, "Big Nose George Pleads Guilty," September 18, 1880.
- Ibid. "J.B. Adams tendered his resignation…"
- *Carbon County Journal*, "Big Nose George again changes mind," September 25, 1880.
- Ibid. "Judge Blair did not come up last night…"
- *Carbon County Journal*, "Coroner's Jury," (Joseph Horbeck), October 23, 1880.
- Ibid. "Shooting Affray, (Hornbeck murder…)
- Ibid. "Hornbeck Funeral…"
- Ibid. "Local Intelligence," (Rankin Bros sell teams to Perkins and Taylor).
- Ibid. "Our Candidates," (I.C. Miller for Sheriff).
- Ibid. "The Hanging Bee," (Dr. Maghee).
- *Carbon County Journal*, "Democratic Ticket & Republican Ticket," October 30, 1880.
- *Carbon County Journal*, "Old Timers." (I.M. Lawry and others indorse Miller for Sheriff), October 30, 1880.
- *Carbon County Journal*, "The Results & Election Day & Election Returns," (results of the election & numerical count by candidate), November 6, 1880.
- *Carbon County Journal*, "Doings of the District Court," (The trial of Big Nose George set for next Monday), November 13, 1880.
- Ibid. "Doings Of The District Court," (Fernando Fierce indicted for the murder of Joseph Hornbeck…)

- *Carbon County Journal*, November 20, 1880, Doings of The District Court, Tuesday, Court Convened (Territory v. Big Nose George),-Thursday, Big Nose George Changes Plea to Guilty…
- *Carbon County Journal*, "Hon W.W. Corlett," November 27, 1880.
- *Laramie Weekly Sentinel*, "The Trial of Big Nose George," (Pleads guilty), November 20, 1880.
- Territory Of Wyoming, County of Carbon, District Court, Second Judicial District No. 265 Territory of Wyoming v. George Parrott, Subpoena to Appear on September 13, 1880: J.B. Adams, Ed Dickinson James Bellamy, J.G. Rankin, Frank Howard, and M.H. on behalf of Prosecution…
- No. 265 Territory of Wyoming v. George Parrott, November 8 1880, Defense Motion for Change of Venue…
- No. 265 Territory of Wyoming v. George Parrott, November 8 1880, Defense Affidavit in Support of Motion for Change of Venue…
- No. 265 Territory of Wyoming v. George Parrott, Subpoena to Appear on November 15, 1880: J.G. Rankin, Wm. Daley, Jos. Bellamy, Wm. McCarty, E. Dickinson, M. F. Leach, J.C. Friend, and W.S. Cox on behalf of Prosecution…
- No. 265 Territory of Wyoming v. George Parrott, Subpoena to Appear on November 16 1880 at 7- O'Clock P.M.: Dr. T.G. Maghee, Taylor Pannock, John F. Foote, Jesse Wallace, Jos. Widdowfield on behalf of Prosecution…
- No. 265 Territory of Wyoming v. George Parrott, Subpoena to Appear on November 18, 1880: John C. Friend –Bring with you a copy of the *Carbon County Journal* containing interview with Big Nose George on behalf of Prosecution…
- No. 265 List of Men called for November 16, 1880 Jury Duty, and Triers, Territory of Wyoming v. George Parott…
- No. 265 List of Men selected to serve on November 16, 1880 Jury, and Witness for Prosecution, Territory of Wyoming v. George Parott…
- No. 265 Territory of Wyoming v. George Parott, November 17, 1880, Prosecution Motion for Continuance until Tomorrow…
- No. 265 Territory of Wyoming v. George Parott, November 17, 1880, Prosecution Affidavit in Support of Motion for Continuance until Tomorrow…
- No. 265 Territory of Wyoming v. George Parott, November 17, 1880, Defense Motion in Arrest of Judgment…
- No. 265 Territory of Wyoming v. George Parott, November 18, 1880, Prosecution Motion for Sentence…
- No. 265 Testimony in the Case of Territory of Wyoming v. George Parott, November 18, 1880, Testimony index James Rankin, Pages 1–9; John G. Foote, Pages 9–18; William Daily, Pages 18–31; Jesse Wallace, Pages 31–42; Taylor Pannock, Pages 42 and 43; and M.F. Leech, Pages 41–80.

Internet References:

- William Wellington Corlett. http://politicalgraveyard.com. Accessed December 5, 2005.
- Jacob B. Blair. http://politicalgraveyard.com. Accessed May 6, 2007.
- The Officer Down Memorial Page, Inc., Special Agent Robert Widdowfield. http://www.odmp.org
- The Officer Down Memorial Page, Inc., Special Agent Henry Vincent. http://www.odmp.org
- Genealogy.com, Robert Widdowfield -1. http://familytreemaker.genealogy.com
- Genealogy.com, Robert Widdowfield -2. http://familytreemaker.genealogy.com

Sources

- UW libraries—Wyoming Biography Database search results, Maghee, Thomas G., last updated October 20, 2004. http://www-lib.uwyo.edu/db/Bio/single. Asp?Key=4574
- Assistant Surgeon Thomas G. Maghee, The Medical History of Fort Washakie. http://www.windriverhistory.org/exhibits/jkmoore/medhistory.htm

Chapter 16: Big Nose George Changes His Plea

- *Cheyenne Daily Leader*, "From Rawlins." (Big Snow Storm Out There,–Big Nose George, trial is in progress), November 20, 1880.
- *Cheyenne Daily Leader,* "Big Nose George," (The Notorious Road Agent and Murder Sentenced to be Hanged), December 16, 1880.
- Ibid. "Minor Mention," (There remains but one more of the infamous gang…)
- *Cheyenne Daily Leader*, "Minor Mention," (Ex-Gov. Thayer was in Rawlins Court the day Big Nose George…), December 18, 1880.
- *Cheyenne Daily Sun*, "He Rode into the West," December 15, 1880.
- *Cheyenne Daily Sun*, "Sentence of Big Nose George," December 16, 1880.
- *Carbon County Journal,* "The Results & Election Day & Election Returns (election results & numerical count by candidate), November 6, 1880.
- *Carbon County Journal*, "Doings of the District Court," (The trial of Big Nose George set for next Monday), November 13, 1880
- Ibid. "Doings of the District Court," (Fernando Fierce indicted for the murder of Joseph Hornbeck)
- *Carbon County Journal*, "Doings of the District Court," (Tuesday, Court Convened), (Territory v. Big Nose George), (Thursday, Big Nose George Changes Plea to Guilty…), November 20, 1880.
- *Carbon County Journal*, "Hon W.W. Corlett," November 27, 1880.
- *Carbon County Journal*, "Court will meet Wednesday," (…Big Nose George Sentence of Defendant.), December 11, 1880.
- *Carbon County Journal*, "Cheyenne Sun says that Judge Peck got left at Cheyenne and had to hire Engine to overtake No. 3 at Colorado Junction…," December 18, 1880.
- Ibid. "Elk Mountain Murder," (George Parrot one of the Murders of Deputies Vinson and Widdowfield,–Has received His Sentence and will be hanged on April 2nd 1881)
- Ibid. "For Sale," (Mrs. Maghee offers to sell all her house hold goods as she will be visiting the states. Dr. Maghee will stay in Rawlins Springs…)
- Ibid. "Times Trills." (Mr. John Lafever Just in from North Park…)
- Territory Of Wyoming, County of Carbon, District Court, Second Judicial District December 15, 1880, No, 265—Indictment—For Murder: Territory of Wyoming v. George Parott alias Big Nose George, Frank James alias McKinney, Sim Waun, Et al
- No. 265 Territory of Wyoming v. George Parrott, Subpoena to Appear on September 13, 1880: J.B. Adams, Ed Dickinson James Bellamy, J.G. Rankin, Frank Howard, and M.H. on behalf of Prosecution…
- No. 265 Territory of Wyoming v. George Parott, November 8 1880, Defense Motion for Change of Venue…
- No. 265 Territory of Wyoming v. George Parott, November 8 1880, Defense Affidavit in Support of Motion for Change of Venue…
- No. 265 Territory of Wyoming v. George Parrott, Subpoena to Appear on November 15, 1880: J.G. Rankin, Wm. Daley, Jos. Bellamy, Wm. McCarty, E. Dickinson, M. F. Leach, J.C. Friend, and W.S. Cox on behalf of Prosecution…

- No. 265 Territory of Wyoming v. George Parrott, Subpoena to Appear on November 16 1880 at 7- o'clock P.M.: Dr. T.G. Maghee, Taylor Pannock, John F. Foote, Jesse Wallace, Jos. Widdowfield on behalf of Prosecution…
- No. 265 Territory of Wyoming v. George Parrott, Subpoena to Appear on November 18, 1880: John C. Friend –Bring with you a copy of the *Carbon County Journal* containing interview with Big Nose George on behalf of Prosecution…
- No. 265 List of Men called for November 16, 1880 Jury Duty, and Triers, Territory of Wyoming v. George Parott…
- No. 265 List of Men selected to serve on November 16, 1880 Jury, and Witness for Prosecution, Territory of Wyoming v. George Parott…
- No. 265 Territory of Wyoming v. George Parott, November 17, 1880, Prosecution Motion for Continuance until Tomorrow…
- No. 265 Territory of Wyoming v. George Parott, November 17, 1880, Prosecution Affidavit in Support of Motion for Continuance until Tomorrow…
- No. 265 Territory of Wyoming v. George Parott, November 17, 1880, Defense Motion in Arrest of Judgment…
- No. 265 Territory of Wyoming v. George Parott, November 18, 1880, Prosecution Motion for Sentence…
- No. 265 Testimony in the Case of Territory of Wyoming v. George Parott, November 18, 1880, Testimony index James Rankin, Pages 1–9; John G. Foote, Pages 9–18; William Daily, Pages 18–31; Jesse Wallace, Pages 31–42; Taylor Pannock, Pages 42 and 43; and M.F. Leech, Pages 41–80.
- No. 265 "Guilty Verdict" Delivered December 15, 1880 in the Case of Territory of Wyoming v. George Parott, George Parott Sentenced to be hanged on April 2, 1881…

Internet References:

- Jacob B. Blair. http://politicalgraveyard.com. Accessed May 6, 2007. http://www.usdoj.gov/marshals/district/sd/general/history/.html
- United States Marshals Service, District Marshals—D/Wyoming, Historical Perspective. http://www.usdoj.gov/marshals/district/wy/general/history/.html
- Ancestry.Com, 1870 United States Federal Census, John Lafever. http://ancestry.com
- Ancestry.Com, 1880 United States Federal Census, James G. Rankin. http://ancestry.com
- Ancestry.Com, 1880 United States Federal Census, Robert Rankin. http://ancestry.com
- Ancestry.Com, 1880 United States Federal Census, Thomas G. Maghee. http://ancestry.com
- Ancestry.Com, 1890 United States Federal Census, Thomas G. Maghee. http://ancestry.com
- Ancestry.Com, 1900 United States Federal Census, Thomas G. Maghee. http://ancestry.com
- Ancestry.Com, 1920 United States Federal Census, Thomas G. Maghee. http://ancestry.com
- Ancestry.Com, 1880 United States Federal Census, Millard F. Leach. http://ancestry.com
- Genealogy.com, Robert Widdowfield -1. http://familytreemaker.genealogy.com
- Genealogy.com, Robert Widdowfield -2. http://familytreemaker.genealogy.com
- Changing the Face of Medicine, Biography Dr. Lillian Heath Nelson,
- UW libraries—Wyoming Biography Database search results, Maghee, Thomas G.,last updated October 20, 2004. http://www-lib.uwyo.edu/db/Bio/single. Asp?Key=4574
- Assistant Surgeon Thomas G. Maghee, The Medical History of Fort Washakie. http://www.windriverhistory.org/exhibits/jkmoore/medhistory.htm

Sources

Chapter 17: Attempted Escape

- *Cheyenne Daily Leader*, "Big Nose George," (Attacks the Jailer & tries escape), March 23, 1881.
- *Carbon County Journal*, "Big Nose George fears of vigilantes subside," February 2, 1881.
- *Carbon County Journal*, "Big Nose George in better spirits…," February 12, 1881.
- *Carbon County Journal*, "OFFICIAL DIRECTORY," (Miller, Daley Edgerton etc.), February 19, 1881.
- Ibid. "Dr. John E. Osborne arrived in town Thursday,"
- *Carbon County Journal*, "The Rankin Bros purchased Thorp's Livery in Cheyenne," March 5, 1881.
- Ibid. "Ex-Sheriff Rankin visits Cheyenne,"
- *Carbon County Journal*, "Sheriff Miller publishes in newspaper Law relating to Executions Section 170 -173 Page 161," March 12, 1881.
- *Carbon County Journal*, "Reverend Dr. Claxton from Cheyenne visits Big Nose George to administer spiritual consultation," March 19, 1881.
- Ibid. "The *Laramie Boomerang* News Paper starts up in Laramie City,"
- *Carbon County Journal*, "Gone Up Higher," (The Penitent "Sick Man" Recovers and Attempts Life of Jailer, An Indignant People Assist Him on His Way up the Golden Stair.), March 24, 1881.
- *Laramie Weekly Sentinel*, "The Way of the Transgressor, George Parott, better known as Big Nose George was hanged…," March 26, 1881.

Internet References:

- John Eugene Osborne. http://politicalgraveyard.com. Accessed October 31, 2005.
- John Eugene Osborne. http://en.wikipedia.org/wiki/John_Eugene_Osborne. Accessed August 19, 2006.
- Ancestry.Com, 1880 United States Federal Census, James G. Rankin. http://ancestry.com
- Ancestry.Com, 1880 United States Federal Census, Robert Rankin. http://ancestry.com
- Ancestry.Com, 1880 United States Federal Census, Thomas G. Maghee. http://ancestry.com
- UW libraries—Wyoming Biography Database search results, Maghee, Thomas G., last updated October 20, 2004. http://www-lib.uwyo.edu/db/Bio/single. Asp?Key=4574
- Assistant Surgeon Thomas G. Maghee, The Medical History of Fort Washakie. http://www.windriverhistory.org/exhibits/jkmoore/medhistory.htm

Chapter 18: Another Lynching

- *Carbon County Journal*, "Gone Up Higher," (The Penitent "Sick Man" Recovers and Attempts Life of Jailer, An Indignant People Assist Him on His Way up the Golden Stair.), March 24, 1881.
- Ibid. "Coroner's Inquest and verdict on Death of George Parrot…,"
- *Cheyenne Daily Leader*, "Big Nose George," (Attacks the Jailer & tries escape), March 23, 1881.
- *Cheyenne Daily Leader*, "The Last of Big Nose George," March 24, 1881.
- *Cheyenne Daily Leader*, "Sheriff Miller Is cheated out of $100.00 Job on account of Lynch Mob," March 31, 1881.
- *Cheyenne Daily Leader*, "Big Nose George, Widow Wants Certificate of Death Experience," August 20, 1881.
- *Cheyenne Daily Sun*, "Sheriff Miller, of Rawlins is cheated out of a $100.00 Job on account of Lynching of Big Nose George…," March 24, 1881.
- *Laramie Weekly Sentinel*, "The Way of the Transgressor, George Parrott, better known as Big Nose George was hanged…," March 26, 1881.

- *Wyoming State Tribune*, John Charles Thompson Column, "In Old Wyoming," (Dr. John E. Osborne's Rawlins Sept.12, 1928, version of the hanging of Big Nose George), May 4, 1939.
- *Wyoming State Tribune*, John Charles Thompson Column, "In Old Wyoming," (John Milliken owned a saloon in the town of Carbon, related his story of Big Nose George to the Rawlins Republican and then picked up by John Thompson), November 13, 1939.
- *Wyoming State Tribune*, John Charles Thompson Column, "In Old Wyoming," (Agnes Spring Wright's version of discussion with Dr. Lillian Heath Nelson about being the first woman doctor in Wyoming and including the hanging of Big Nose George), June 16, 1950.
- *Wyoming State Tribune,* John Charles Thompson Column, "In Old Wyoming," "Big Nose" George Parrott," (Story of the arrest and hanging of Dutch Charlie and Big Nose George), July 3, 1941.
- *Wyoming State Tribune*, John Charles Thompson Column, "In Old Wyoming," "Among the earliest…Hunger Strike in Wyoming, Big Nose George…," (Retelling of Big Nose George crimes and his lynching.), May, 15, 1942.
- *Wyoming State Tribune*, John Charles Thompson Column, "In Old Wyoming," (Oliver P. Hanna version of Big Nose George's crimes and lynching.), February 14, 1944.
- *Wyoming State Tribune*, John Charles Thompson Column, "In Old Wyoming," (Continuation of Oliver P. Hanna version of Big Nose George's crimes and lynching), February 15, 1944.
- *Wyoming State Tribune*, John Charles Thompson Column, "In Old Wyoming," "Big Nose" George Parrott," (Story of the arrest and hanging of Dutch Charlie and Big Nose George), October 27, 1946.

Internet References:

- John Eugene Osborne. http://politicalgraveyard.com. Accessed October 31, 2005.
- John Eugene Osborne. http://en.wikipedia.org/wiki/John_Eugene_Osborne. Accessed August 19, 2006.
- The Officer Down Memorial Page, Inc., Special Agent Robert Widdowfield. http://www.odmp.org
- The Officer Down Memorial Page, Inc., Special Agent Henry Vincent. http://www.odmp.org
- Ancestry.Com, 1880 United States Federal Census, Robert Rankin. http://ancestry.com
- UW libraries—Wyoming Biography Database search results, Maghee, Thomas G.. Last updated October 20, 2004. http://www-lib.uwyo.edu/db/Bio/single. Asp?Key=4574
- Assistant Surgeon Thomas G. Maghee, The Medical History of Fort Washakie. http://www.windriverhistory.org/exhibits/jkmoore/medhistory.htm

Epilogue: Medical Studies and New Shoes for the Doctor

- *Carbon County Journal*, "Gone Up Higher," (The Penitent "Sick Man" Recovers and Attempts Life of Jailer, An Indignant People Assist Him on His Way up the Golden Stair.), March 24, 1881.
- Ibid. "Coroner's Inquest and verdict on Death of George Parrot…,"
- *The Rawlins Daily Times*, "Skin Game in Wyoming," May 12, 1950.
- *The Rawlins Daily Times*, Jubilee Special,–Reprint of "Lost Towns of Carbon County," (Includes Song/Poem written by Jean Osborne), –"The Lynching Of Big Nose George," January 13, 1965.

Sources

- *The Rawlins Republican and Wyoming Reporter*, "Dr. Osborne Tells of the Hanging of 'Big Nose' George," June 9, 1927.
- Ibid. "To Boone May, for reward of Frank Toll of the murders of Widdowfield and Vincent...,"
- *Cheyenne Daily Leader*, "Sheriff Miller Is cheated out of $100.00 Job on account of Lynch Mob, "March 31, 1881.
- *Cheyenne Daily Leader*, "Big Nose George, Widow Wants Certificate of Death Experience," August 20, 1881.

Internet References:

- John Eugene Osborne. http://politicalgraveyard.com. Accessed October 31, 2005.
- John Eugene Osborne. http://en.wikipedia.org/wiki/John_Eugene_Osborne. Accessed August 19, 2006.
- Ancestry.Com, 1880 United States Federal Census, Thomas G. Maghee. http://ancestry.com
- Ancestry.Com, 1890 United States Federal Census, Thomas G. Maghee. http://ancestry.com
- Ancestry.Com, 1900 United States Federal Census, Thomas G. Maghee. http://ancestry.com
- Ancestry.Com, 1920 United States Federal Census, Thomas G. Maghee. http://ancestry.com
- Ancestry.Com, 1880 United States Federal Census, Evelyn Maghee. http://ancestry.com
- Ancestry.Com, 1890 United States Federal Census, Evelyn Maghee. http://ancestry.com
- Ancestry.Com, 1900 United States Federal Census, Evelyn Maghee. http://ancestry.com
- Ancestry.Com, 1920 United States Federal Census, Evelyn Maghee. http://ancestry.com
- Changing the Face of Medicine, Biography Dr. Lillian Heath Nelson. http://www.nlm.nih.gov/changingthefaceofmedicine/physician/biography_354.html
- Made In Wyoming: (Our Legacy of Success, Dr. Lillian Heath Nelson, Medicine Woman,) http://www.madeinwyoming.net/profiles/nelson.php
- UW libraries—Wyoming Biography Database search results, Maghee, Thomas G., last updated October 20, 2004. http://www-lib.uwyo.edu/db/Bio/single. Asp?Key=4574
- Assistant Surgeon Thomas G. Maghee, The Medical History of Fort Washakie. http://www.windriverhistory.org/exhibits/jkmoore/medhistory.htm

Author's Notes

- *Laramie Weekly Sentinel*, "Held for Trial," January 3. 1879.
- Ibid., "Taken in John Lafever at Green River, Dutch Charley A.K.A. Baylis A.K.A. Davis- "Captured this week...,"
- *Laramie Daily Sentinel*, "Retributive Justice," (The Hanging of "Dutch Charlie" at Carbon), January 10, 1879. [Note: article says Dutch Charley captured two weeks ago!]
- Ibid. "Dutch Charlie," (Taken up on Number 3 last Sunday...)
- *Laramie Daily Sentinel*, "The Pistol" (Frank Howard was shot in altercation with cattleman), January 24, 1879.
- *Laramie Weekly Sentinel*, "Shot at Powder River"—"Not Dead," (Frank Howard reported dead is not dead, but alive and improving), February 7, 1879.
- *Cheyenne Daily Leader*, "Wyoming"—"Another Shooting Affray—Fort McKinney," (Frank Howard Notorious Road Agent & Horse Thief Shot), January 14, 1879.
- *Carbon County Journal*, "Frank Howard Arrested for Murder at Dixon Wyoming," January 6, 1894.
- *Carbon County Journal*, "Court Grinds—Frank Howard—Jury Members," June 2, 1894.
- *Carbon County Journal*, "Frank Howard Found Guilty, Sentenced to Hang," June 9, 1894.

- Ibid. "Public Sympathy Favor Condemned Man,"
- *Carbon County Journal*, "Howard will Hang," (A large number of people have signed petition on behalf of Frank Howard), November 17, 1894.
- *Carbon County Journal*, "Governor Osborne gave 14 day respite to Frank Howard," November 24, 1894.
- *Carbon County Journal*, "Frank Howard Hanged," December 7, 1894.
- Territory Of Wyoming, County of Carbon, District Court, Second Judicial District, No. 339, (State of Wyoming v. Frank Howard), Criminal Arrest Warrant issued June 12, 1880. Trial held June 25, 1880. Verdict: Innocent.
- State Of Wyoming, County of Carbon, District Court, Third Judicial District, No. 339, (State of Wyoming v. Frank Howard) No.339,—Indictment—For Murder: No.339,—Tried for Murder: January 1, 1894. Verdict: Guilty, sentenced to hang , November 23, 1894. No.339,—Motion for new trial: denied. Application for commutation, November 17, 1894; Fourteen-day reprieve given until December 7, 1894. No.339—November 30, 1894, Request for commutation denied. Frank Howard hanged December 7, 1894.
- Court records located: Wyoming State Archives, Barrett Building, 2301 Central Avenue, Cheyenne, WY 82002
- Gorzalka, Ann. *Wyoming Territorial Sheriffs*. 539 Cassa Road, Glendo, Wyoming 82213. High Plains Press, Copyright 1998.
- Meschter, Daniel Y. *The Rankins of Rawlins, a Family Biography*. Albuquerque: Daniel Y. Meschter, 2001.

Internet Sources

- William Wellington Corlett. http://politicalgraveyard.com. Accessed December 5, 2005.
- Jacob B. Blair. http://politicalgraveyard.com. Accessed May 6, 2007.
- John Eugene Osborne. http://politicalgraveyard.com, October 31, 2005.
- John Eugene Osborne. http://en.wikipedia.org/wiki/John_Eugene_Osborne, August 19, 2006.
- Benjamin Franklin Potts, Governor Montana Territory. http://politicalgraveyard.com
- Newspaper Items Utah Northern (Utah & Northern). http://utahrails.net. Accessed December 22, 2005.
- Montana Governors. http://www.invista.com/society/government/leader/ustates/montna.htm
- Northern Pacific Railroad. http://members.aol.com/Gibson0817/npacific.htm
- The Officer Down Memorial Page, Inc., Special Agent Robert Widdowfield. http://www.odmp.org
- The Officer Down Memorial Page, Inc., Special Agent Henry Vincent. http://www.odmp.org
- The Desperados, (Those who rode with the James—Younger Gang,) http://www.islandnet.con/~the-gang/bio.htm
- Trains, Banks, Stagecoaches, (The Daring Exploits of this Band of Lawless Men, A List of robberies attributed to the James -Younger Gang,) http://www.islandnet.con/~the-gang/rob.htm
- Union Pacific Railroad at ALLExperts, Company Officers, President Sidney Dillon (1874–1884). http:/experts.about.com/e/u/un/Union_Pacific_Railroad.htm
- United States Marshals Service, United States Marshals Service: Historical Perspective. http://www.usdoj.gov/marshals/history/index.html
- United States Marshals Service, Oldest Federal Law Enforcement Agency, Historical Perspective. http://www.usdoj.gov/marshals/history/oldest.html
- United States Marshals Service, Civilian Enforcers, Historical Perspective. http://www.usdoj.gov/marshals/history/loyal_community.html

Sources

- United States Marshals Service, General Practitioners, Historical Perspective. http://www.usdoj.gov/marshals/history/general_practitioners.html
- United States Marshals Service, District Marshals—D/Montana, Historical Perspective. http://www.usdoj.gov/marshals/district/mt/general/history/.html
- United States Marshals Service, District Marshals—D/Nebraska, Historical Perspective. http://www.usdoj.gov/marshals/district/ne/general/history/.html
- United States Marshals Service, District Marshals—D/North Dakota, Historical Perspective. http://www.usdoj.gov/marshals/district/nd/general/history/.html
- United States Marshals Service, District Marshals—D/South Dakota, Historical Perspective. http://www.usdoj.gov/marshals/district/sd/general/history/.html
- United States Marshals Service, District Marshals—D/Wyoming, Historical Perspective. http://www.usdoj.gov/marshals/district/wy/general/history/.html
- Ancestry.Com, 1870 United States Federal Census, John Lafever. http://ancestry.com
- Ancestry.Com, 1880 United States Federal Census, James G. Rankin. http://ancestry.com
- Ancestry.Com, 1880 United States Federal Census, Robert Rankin. http://ancestry.com
- Ancestry.Com, 1880 United States Federal Census, Thomas G. Maghee. http://ancestry.com
- Ancestry.Com, 1890 United States Federal Census, Thomas G. Maghee. http://ancestry.com
- Ancestry.Com, 1900 United States Federal Census, Thomas G. Maghee. http://ancestry.com
- Ancestry.Com, 1920 United States Federal Census, Thomas G. Maghee. http://ancestry.com
- Ancestry.Com, 1880 United States Federal Census, Evelyn Maghee. http://ancestry.com
- Ancestry.Com, 1890 United States Federal Census, Evelyn Maghee. http://ancestry.com
- Ancestry.Com, 1900 United States Federal Census, Evelyn Maghee. http://ancestry.com
- Ancestry.Com, 1920 United States Federal Census, Evelyn Maghee. http://ancestry.com
- Ancestry.Com, 1880 United States Federal Census, Millard F. Leach. http://ancestry.com
- Genealogy.com, Robert Widdowfield -1. http://familytreemaker.genealogy.com
- Genealogy.com, Robert Widdowfield -2. http://familytreemaker.genealogy.com
- Frank and Jesse James Family Outline. http:/rootsweb.com
- Chronology of Jesse James. http://www.sptddog.com/sotp/jesse.html. Accessed April 19, 2008.
- Outlaws In-Law, Frank and Jesse James Relatives. http://kinnexions.com/smlfamilt/oitlaws.htm. Accessed April 6, 2008.
- Frank and Jesse James Family Outline. http://rootsweb.com. Accessed October 11, 2006).
- Changing the Face of Medicine, Biography Dr. Lillian Heath Nelson. http://www.nlm.nih.gov/changingthefaceofmedicine/physician/biography_354.html
- Made In Wyoming: Our Legacy of Success, Dr. Lillian Heath Nelson, Medicine Woman. http://www.madeinwyoming.net/profiles/nelson.php
- UW libraries—Wyoming Biography Database search results, Maghee, Thomas G.. Last updated October 20, 2004. http://www-lib.uwyo.edu/db/Bio/single. Asp?Key=4574
- Assistant Surgeon Thomas G. Maghee, The Medical History of Fort Washakie. http://www.windriverhistory.org/exhibits/jkmoore/medhistory.htm

Appendix I

1869 Laws of Wyoming Territory

Article IV, Sheriff

SECTION I. There shall be in each county organized for political purposes, a sheriff who shall be ex-officio county collector, shall hold his office for the term of two years, and until his successor is elected and qualified, or appointed as the case may be, and who shall before he enters on the duties of the office, take an oath to support the constitution of the United States and the act organizing the territory of Wyoming, and to faithfully discharge the duties disposed upon him by the law of such sheriff and ex-officio collector, which said oath shall be endorsed on the back of certificates of election or appointment, and he shall secure a bond to people of the Territory of Wyoming, with sufficient securities, and penal sum of four thousand dollars. To be approved by the board of county commissioners, and conditioned for the faithful performance of the duties by the sheriff as required by law, and that he will pay according to law, all monies which shall come into his possession belonging to the territory, county school fund, or to any person or corporation, such as sheriff, and that he will render just and true account thereof, and shall deliver to his successor in office or to any other person authorized by law to receive them all monies, books, papers, etc. appertaining thereto or belonging to his office as such sheriff, and he shall at the same time execute another bond for the people of the territory of Wyoming, in such penal sum, as may be prescribed by the board of county commissioners, if said sheriff as ex-officio collector, and his deputy or deputies, and all persons employed in his office shall faithfully and promptly perform the duties required of collector by the laws of this territory, to the satisfaction of the board of county commissioners, and if he, the said sheriff and his deputies, shall collect and pay according to law, to the proper officers or person, all monies which shall come to his hands as ex-officio account collector, and shall render a just true account thereof whenever so required by the board of county commissioners for and provisions of law, and shall deliver to his successor in office, or to any other person authorized by law to receive the same, all monies, books, papers and other things appertaining thereto, or belonging to his office, said bond shall be null and void, otherwise to remain in full force and effect, which said bond, together with certificate of his election or appointment, shall be filled in the county clerk's office, and no person shall receive as a surety on said bond who is not worth at least two thousand dollars over and above his just debts and exemptions provided by law; provided, that no person shall be elected sheriff for more than two terms in succession.

SECTION 2. It shall be the duty of the sheriff to appoint an undersheriff who shall qualify as required by law of deputy sheriffs, and who shall be sheriff in case of death, resignation, or other disability of the sheriff

SECTION 3. The sheriff of each county may, after entering upon the duties of his office, appoint in writing, one or more deputies to assist him in performance of his duties required of him by law, as such sheriff and ex-officio county collector, and for whose official acts he shall be responsible, and he may require each of such deputies to enter into bonds to him for the faithful performance of several duties of his office the written appointment of each deputy with usual oath endorsed thereon, shall be filled in the county clerk's office of the proper county each deputy shall hold his office during the pleasure of the sheriff, who shall upon revoking the appointment of any deputy endorse such revocation and the date thereof upon such written appointment, and shall also give ample notice of such revocation. Each sheriff may also appoint special deputies to do particular acts which shall be specified in each of such appointments and for each of whose official acts he shall be responsible, but such appointments are not required to be filled or revoked as in the case of regular deputies. Provided, that no assessor shall be appointed deputy sheriff or collector.

SECTION 4. The sheriff shall have charge and custody of the jails of his county, and of provisions in the same, and shall keep them himself or his deputy or his jailer whom he may appoint especially for that purpose, and for whose acts he and his sureties shall be liable.

SECTION 5. The sheriff in person or by his deputy or deputies, shall serve and execute according to law, all processes, writs, precepts and orders issued out of any court or record in his county and all criminal and civil cases or made by lawful authority and to him directed, and he shall attend upon all courts of record in his county.

SECTION 6. It shall be the duty of the sheriff and deputy sheriff to keep and preserve the peace in their respective counties, and quiet and suppress all affrays, riots, and unlawful assemblies and insurrections, for which purpose and for the service of process in civil and criminal cases, and in apprehending and securing any person for felony of breach of the peace, they, and every corner in constable, may call to their aid such person or persons of their county, as they may deem necessary.

SECTION 7. Every paper required by law to be served on the sheriff, may be served on him in person or left at his office at business hours, and no sheriff or deputy shall appear or advise as attorney or counselor in any case in any court.

SECTION 8. Every sheriff ex-officio county collector shall have and keep in his office, a "cash book" wherein shall be entered and set down every sum of money paid to him by virtue of his office and the date of such payment, and the name of the person paying the same, the account upon which the same was paid, and the nature of the funds so paid to him whether gold, silver, United States treasury notes, bank bills, or territorial; or auditor's warrants or other territorial or county indebtedness, in the amount of each separate kind, and such cash books shall at all reasonable hours of the day be open to the inspection and examination of all persons desiring to inspect or examine the same.

SECTION 9. Upon the payment of any money to him as aforesaid, he shall issue his receipt therefore of the person paying the same, setting forth in such receipt all of the matters prescribed in the preceding section, to be entered in such cash book.

SECTION 10. Every sheriff as sheriff and ex-officio county collector shall faithfully perform all other duties required of him by the laws of this territory, in addition to those specified in this act.

SECTION 11. Every sheriff as ex-officio county collector, who shall fail, neglect or refuse to have and keep in his office such cash book as required by Section 8 of this act, or shall fail, neglect or refuse to set down in this cash book each and every requirement as set forth in this section, or shall make any false deficient entry thereof, or shall fail, neglect or refuse to have and keep said cash book at his office during business hours or shall fail, neglect, or refuse to permit any person to inspect or examine the same at any reasonable hour of the day, or shall fail, neglect or refuse to issue his receipt for any monies collected or received by him, as such collector as required in Section 9 of this article or shall fail to collect and pay over any monies required to be collected and paid over, or fail, neglect or refuse to do any other official act required by him by law; shall in addition to other penalties that may be prescribed by law, be deemed guilty of misdemeanor, and upon conviction thereof shall be fined in the sum of not less than fifty dollars, no more than five hundred dollars, and the court may, as additional penalty, ad that such sheriff be removed from office, this section shall extend to the deputies of every such sheriff.

Appendix II

Posse Comitatus

Posse Comitatus has affected life in the United States, its Territories, and Protectorates since its inception. Bonnie Baker's essay, "The Origins of the Posse Comitatus," provides an excellent explanation of Posse Comitatus. Following is the original Posse Comitatus Act and the first two impetuses cited by Bonnie Baker. This article in its entirety is certainly worth the read: "The Origins of the Posse Comitatus," Bonnie Baker, *Air & Space Power Journal—Chronicles Online.* www.airpower.maxwell.af.mil/airchronicles/cc/baker1.html

The Origins of the Posse Comitatus by Bonnie Baker

The original Posse Comitatus was a rider to an appropriations bill, Chapter 263, Section 15, approved on June 18, 1878.

Chapter 263, Section 15, Army as Posse Comitatus:
From and after the passage of this act it shall not be lawful to employ any part of the Army of the United States, as a posse comitatus, or otherwise, for the purpose of executing the laws, except in such cases and under such circumstances as such employment of said force may be expressly authorized by the Constitution or by act of Congress, and no money appropriated by this act shall be used to pay any of the expenses incurred in the employment of any troops in violation of this section, and any person willfully violating the provisions of this section shall be deemed guilty of a misdemeanor and on conviction thereof shall be punished by fine not exceeding ten thousand dollars or imprisonment not exceeding two years or both such fine and imprisonment.

The impetus for this bill came from two sources. The first was the end of the Civil War Reconstruction. From the beginning of the Republic until the enactment of Posse Comitatus it had been regular practice to station federal troops at polling places to prevent inebriates from voting, and to be certain that those entering the polls were entitled to do so in an era of limited suffrage. After the Civil War, the federal troops were stationed at polls to be sure that universal manhood suffrage was permitted, and that no former Confederate officers voted. All former Confederate officers had been stripped of the right to vote or hold office above state level. The end of the Reconstruction period meant that enforcement of those strictures was no longer necessary.

The second impetus was conditions on the western frontier. Fort commanders were often the only law and order in a region, the only security for the settlers moving west. Most of the frontier was still outside the US proper, and had not been admitted to statehood. Fort commanders had begun to exercise civilian law law-enforcement responsibilities, sometimes in an arbitrary way, to hunt down whomever they believed to be criminals or Indians who were threatening settlers. The argument was that criminality and Indian attacks happened quickly and needed quick action from whatever authority was on the spot. They were, after all, a long way out of communications with Washington, D.C. The results were sometimes violations of the Constitution and conditions otherwise untenable to elected civil officials..."

Source: http://www.windriverhistory.org/exhibits/jkmoore/medhistory.htm

Additional Resources

Books, Periodicals, Newspapers, Court Records, and Internet References

Books

- Abdill, George B. *This Was Railroading*. New York: Bonanza Books, 1958.
- Ambrose, Stephen E. *Nothing Like It in the World: The Men who Built the Transcontinental Railroad 1863–1869*. New York: Simon and Schuster, 2000.
- Berry, Gladys B. *The Front Streets of Laramie City*. Laramie: Jelm Mountain Publications, 1990.
- Bragg, William F. Jr. *Wyoming: Rugged but Right*. Boulder: Pruitt Publishing Company, 1979.
- Bridwell, J.W. *Life and Adventures of Robert McKimie: Alias "Little Reddy" from Texas*. Hillsboro, Ohio: Hillsboro Gazette, 1878.
- Brown, Dee. *Hear That Lonesome Whistle Blow: Railroads In The West*. New York: Simon and Shuster, 1977.
- Dodge, Grenville M., Major General. *Personal Recollections of President Abraham Lincoln, General Ulysses S. Grant, and General William T. Sherman*. Council Bluffs: Monarch Printing Company, 1914.
- Engebretson, Doug. *Empty Saddles Forgotten Names*. Aberdeen, SD: North Plains Press, 1984.
- Evans, Lloyd R. *Ghost Towns Of Albany County: Twice Told Tales*. Laramie: Laramie Plains Museum, 1984.
- Frazer, Robert W. *Forts Of The West*. Norman: University of Oklahoma Press, 1972.
- Frye, Elnora L. *Atlas of Wyoming Outlaws at the Territorial Penitentiary*. Cheyenne: Pioneer Printing, 1990.
- Gorzalka, Ann. *Wyoming Territorial Sheriffs*. Glendo: High Plains Press, 1998.
- Jensen, Oliver. *The American Heritage History: Of Railroads In America*. American Heritage Publishing Company, Inc., McGraw-Hill, 1975.
- Larson, Taft Alfred. *History of Wyoming*. Lincoln and London: University Of Nebraska Press, 1978.
- Meschter, Daniel Y. *The Rankins of Rawlins, A Family Biography*. Albuquerque: Daniel Y. Meschter, 2001.
- Pence, Mary Lou. *Boswell: The Story of a Frontier Lawman*. Cheyenne: Pioneer Printing, 1978.
- Pence, Mary Lou. *The Laramie Story*. Laramie: Mary Lou Pence, 1973.
- Pence, Mary Lou, and Homsher, Lola M. *The Ghost Towns Of Wyoming*. New York: Hastings House Publishers, 1956.
- Rankin, M. Wilson. *Reminiscences Of The Frontier Days*. Denver: Smith-Brooks, 1935.
- Smith, Helena Huntington. *The War On Powder River: The History of an Insurrection*. Bison Book, reproduced by McGraw-Hill, 1966.

- Thybonym, Scott, Robert G. Rosenberg, and Elizabeth Mullett. *The Medicine Bows—Wyoming's Mountain Country*. Caldwell, Idaho: Caxton Printers, 1985.
- Triggs, J.H. *History Of Cheyenne And Northern Wyoming*. Omaha: *The Herald Steam And Job* Printing House, 1876.
- Triggs, J.H. *History And Directory Of Laramie City, Wyoming Territory*. Laramie City: *Laramie City Daily Sentinel Print*, 1875.
- Triplett, Frank. *The Life, Times And Treacherous Death Of Jesse James*: New York: Konecky & Konecky, 1970.
- Williams, John Hoyt. *A Great and Shining Road: The Epic Story of the Transcontinental Railroad*. Lincoln and London: University of Nebraska Press, 1988.
- Wright, Agnes Spring. *The Cheyenne And Black Hills Stage Routes*. Glendale, CA: Arthur H. Clark, 1949.

Periodicals

- "Big Nose George Parottt: 3000 Words." Omaha, Neb. Union Pacific Railroad, Department Of Public Relations.
- Brown and Willard, *The Black Hills Trails: The Killing of Johnny Slaughter, Gang Members Jim Berry, Joel Collins, Frank Towle, Robert "Reddy" McKimie*. Rapid City, SD. *Rapid City Journal* Company, 1924.
- "Death and a Pair Of Shoes," *Adventure Magazine*. Omaha: UPRR Department Of Public Relations, August 1947.
- Felton and Brown, "The Frontier Years. Bright Lights on the Prairie: Story of Big Nose George Parottt and Gang while in Wyoming and Montana." *Chiefs of Police, Cheyenne, Wyoming, 1867–Present*. Cheyenne: Cheyenne Police Department, 2008.
- "Territorial Governors of Wyoming 1869–1890, and State Governors 1890–1953." *Historical Encyclopedia of Wyoming, The*. Cheyenne: Wyoming State Institute.
- Meldrum, John W. "The Taming of Big Nose George." *The Union Pacific Magazine*, November 1926.

Newspapers

- *Anaconda Standard* (Montana)
- *Atlantic Telegraph* (Iowa)
- *Black Hills Daily Times* (Deadwood)
- *Black Hills Daily Journal* (Rapid City)
- *Black Hills Pioneer* (Deadwood)
- *Black Hills Weekly Times* (Deadwood)
- *Carbon County Journal* (Wyoming)
- *Cheyenne Daily Leader* (Wyoming)
- *Cheyenne Daily Sun* (Wyoming)
- *Cheyenne Frontier Index* (Wyoming)
- *Council Bluffs Bugle* (Iowa)
- *Council Bluffs Nonpareil* (Iowa)
- *Denver Post* (Colorado)
- *Denver Rocky Mountain News* (Colorado)
- *Great Falls Tribune* (Montana)
- *Helena Daily Herald* (Montana)

Additional Resources

- *Helena Weekly Herald* (Montana)
- *Laramie Boomerang* (Wyoming)
- *Laramie Daily Sentinel* (Wyoming)
- *Laramie Weekly Sentinel* (Wyoming)
- *Leavenworth Times* (Kansas)
- *Kansas City Daily Journal* (Missouri)
- *Kansas City Times* (Missouri)
- *Miles City Daily Press* (Montana)
- *Omaha Herald* (Nebraska)
- *Pioneer Press* (Minnesota)
- *Rawlins Daily Times* (Wyoming)
- *Rawlins Republican* (Wyoming)
- *Rawlins Republican And Wyoming Reporter* (Wyoming)
- *St. Joseph Daily Gazette* (Missouri)
- *St. Joseph Weekly Gazette* (Missouri)
- *Salt Lake Daily Reporter* (Utah)
- *Salt Lake Desert News* (Utah)
- *Wyoming State Tribune* (Wyoming)
- *Yellowstone Journal* (Miles City, Montana)

Court Records

- Territory of Wyoming, County of Carbon, District Court, Second Judicial District, No. 265 (Territory of Wyoming v. John Minuse)
- April 7, 1879, No 265, Indictment For Murder: John Minuse alias Joe Minuse, George Parrott alias Big Nose George, Frank James alias McKinney, John Wells alias Sandy, Sim Waun, Jack Campbell, Tim Reed, Frank Tool, and Charles Bates alias Dutch Charley, on August 20, 1878, with force of arms did Murder Henry H. Vinsen.
- No. 265 List of Jury, Triers, Witness for Prosecution, and Witness for Defendant, September 9, 1879 Trial, Territory of Wyoming v. John Minuse.
- No. 265 Jury Verdict of "Not Guilty" Delivered September 10, 1879 in the Case of Territory of Wyoming v. John Minuse…
- Court records located: Wyoming State Archives, Barrett Building, 2301 Central Avenue, Cheyenne, WY 82002
- Territory Of Wyoming, County of Carbon, District Court, Second Judicial DistrictNo. 265 (Territory of Wyoming vs George Parrott)
- April 7, 1879, No 265,—Indictment—For Murder: John Minuse alias Joe Minuse, George Parrott alias Big Nose George, Frank James alias McKinney, John Wells alias Sandy, Sim Waun, Jack Campbell, Tim Reed, Frank Tool, and Charles Bates alias Dutch Charley, on August 20, 1878 with force of arms did Murder Henry H. Vinsen…
- No. 265 Testimony in the Case of Territory of Wyoming v. George Parrott, November 18, 1880, Testimony index James Rankin, Pages 1–9; John G. Foote, Pages 9–18; William Daily, Pages 18–31; Jesse Wallace, Pages 31–42; Taylor Pannock, Pages 42 and 43; and M.F. Leech, Pages 41–80.
- No. 265 "Guilty Verdict" Delivered December 15, 1880 in the Case of Territory of Wyoming v. George Parott, George Parott Sentenced to be hanged on April 2, 1881…
- Court records located: Wyoming State Archives, Barrett Building, 2301 Central Avenue, Cheyenne, WY 82002

- Territory Of Wyoming, County of Carbon, District Court, Second Judicial District, No. 339, (State of Wyoming v. Frank Howard) Criminal Arrest Warrant issued June 12, 1880.
- Trial held June 25, 1880, Verdict innocent.
- State Of Wyoming, County of Carbon, District Court, Third Judicial District,
- No. 339, (State of Wyoming v. Frank Howard)
- No.339,—Indictment—For Murder:
- No.339,—Tried for Murder: January 1, 1894. Verdict: Guilty, sentenced to hang, November 23, 1894.
- No.339,–Motion for new trial: denied. Application for commutation, November 17, 1894; Fourteen day reprieve given until December 7, 1894.
- No.339–November 30, 1894, Request for commutation denied. Frank Howard hanged December 7, 1894.
- Court records located: Wyoming State Archives, Barrett Building, 2301 Central Avenue, Cheyenne, WY 82002

Internet References

- Baker, Bonnie. Origins of the Posse Comitatus, *Air & Space Power Journal—Chronicles Online*. www.airpower.maxwell.af.mil/airchronicles/cc/baker1.html.
- "Blair, Jacob B." Political Graveyard, politicalgraveyard.com. Accessed May 6, 2007.
- "Corlett, William Wellington." Political Graveyard, politicalgraveyard.com. Accessed December 5, 2005.
- "Changing the Face of Medicine," Biography Dr. Lillian Heath Nelson. www.nlm.nih.gov/changingthefaceof medicine/physician/biography_354.html. Accessed May 1, 2007.
- "Desperados: Those who rode with the James-Younger Gang," www.islandnet.com/~the-gang/bio.htm. Accessed September 14, 2006.
- Frank and Jesse James Family Outline, rootsweb.com. October 11, 2006.
- Jesse James. Chronology of Jesse James. www.sptddog.com/sotp/jesse.html. Accessed April 19, 2008.
- "Lafever, John." 1870 United States Federal Census, Ancestry.Com, ancestry.com. Accessed June 11, 2007.
- "Leach, Millard F. 1880 United States Federal Census, Ancestry.Com, ancestry.com. Accessed April 30, 2008.
- "Made In Wyoming: Our Legacy of Success, Dr. Lillian Heath Nelson, Medicine Woman." www.madeinwyoming.net/profiles/nelson.php. Accessed May 1, 2007.
- Maghee, Evelyn. 1880 United States Federal Census, Ancestry.Com, ancestry.com. Accessed May 1, 2007.
- Maghee, Evelyn. 1890 United States Federal Census, Ancestry.Com, ancestry.com. Accessed May 1, 2007.
- Maghee, Evelyn. 1900 United States Federal Census, Ancestry.Com, ancestry.com. Accessed May 1, 2007.
- Maghee, Evelyn. 1920 United States Federal Census, Ancestry.Com, ancestry.com. Accessed May 1, 2007.
- Maghee, Thomas G. 1880 United States Federal Census, Ancestry.Com, ancestry.com. Accessed May 1, 2007.
- Maghee, Thomas G. 1890 United States Federal Census, Ancestry.Com, ancestry.com. Accessed May 1, 2007.

Additional Resources

- Maghee, Thomas G. 1900 United States Federal Census, Ancestry.Com, ancestry.com. Accessed May 1, 2007.
- Maghee, Thomas G. 1920 United States Federal Census, Ancestry.Com, ancestry.com. Accessed May 1, 2007.
- "Maghee, Thomas G." UW libraries—Wyoming Biography Database, search results. Last updated October 20, 2004.
- "Maghee, Thomas G., Assistant Surgeon." The Medical History of Fort Washakie. www.windriverhistory.org/exhibits/jkmoore/medhistory.htm. Accessed May 1, 2007.
- May, Boone. D. Boone May—Gunfighter of the Black Hills, William N. Hockett. www.bar-w.com/boonemay.html. Accessed August 17, 2006.
- "Montana Governors." www.invista.com/society/government/leader/ustates/montna.htm
- Northern Pacific Railroad, members.aol.com/Gibson0817/npacific.htm
- "Outlaws In-Law, Frank and Jesse James Relatives," kinnexions.com/smlfamilt/oitlaws.htm. Accessed April 6, 2008.
- Osborne, John Eugene. Political Graveyard, politicalgraveyard.com. Accessed October 31, 2005.
- Osborne, John Eugene. Political Graveyard, en.wikipedia.org/wiki/John_Eugene_Osborne. Accessed August 19, 2006.
- "Potts, Benjamin Franklin, Governor Montana Territory." Political Graveyard. http://politicalgraveyard.com. Accessed October 31, 2005.
- Rankin, James G. 1880 United States Federal Census, Ancestry.Com, ancestry.com. Accessed August 19, 2006.
- Rankin, Robert. 1880 United States Federal Census, Ancestry.Com, ancestry.com. Accessed October 9, 2006.
- "Trains, Banks, Stagecoaches, (The Daring Exploits of this Band of Lawless Men, A List of robberies attributed to the James/Younger Gang)." http://www.islandnet.con/~the-gang/rob.htm. Accessed September 14, 2006.
- United States Marshals Service, Civilian Enforcers, Historical Perspective. www.usdoj.gov/marshals/history/loyal_community.html. Accessed April 23, 2006.
- United States Marshals Service, District Marshals—D/Montana, Historical Perspective. www.usdoj.gov/marshals/district/mt/general/history/.html. Accessed April 23, 2006.
- United States Marshals Service, District Marshals—D/Nebraska, Historical Perspective. www.usdoj.gov/marshals/district/ne/general/history/.html. Accessed April 23, 2006.
- United States Marshals Service, District Marshals—D/North Dakota, Historical Perspective. www.usdoj.gov/marshals/district/nd/general/history/.html. Accessed April 23, 2006.
- United States Marshals Service, District Marshals—D/South Dakota, Historical Perspective. www.usdoj.gov/marshals/district/sd/general/history/.html. Accessed April 23, 2006.
- United States Marshals Service, District Marshals—D/Wyoming, Historical Perspective. www.usdoj.gov/marshals/district/wy/general/history/.html. Accessed April 23, 2006.
- United States Marshals Service, General Practitioners, Historical Perspective. www.usdoj.gov/marshals/history/general_practitioners.html. Accessed April 23, 2006.
- United States Marshals Service, Oldest Federal Law Enforcement Agency, Historical Perspective. www.usdoj.gov/marshals/history/oldest.html. Accessed April 23, 2006.
- United States Marshals Service, United States Marshals Service: Historical Perspective. www.usdoj.gov/marshals/history/index.html. Accessed April 23, 2006.
- United States Marshals Service, United States Marshal Seth Bullock, Historical Perspective. www.usdoj.gov/marshals/history/loyal_community.html. Accessed April 23, 2006.

- "Utah Northern." Newspaper Items, Utah & Northern, utahrails .net. Accessed December 22, 2005.
- "Vincent, Henry H. Special Agent," The Officer Down Memorial Page, Inc.. www.odmp.org. Accessed October 9, 2006.
- Widdowfield, Robert. Genealogy.com, familytreemaker.genealogy.com. Accessed August 19, 2006.
- "Widdowfield, Robert. Special Agent,"The Officer Down Memorial Page, Inc. www.odmp.org. Accessed October 9, 2006.

Index

Abbot and Downing Company, 101
Adams, Joseph B., 1-3,7-8,12-15,81,92,142-143
Anderson, William "Bloody Bill" a.k.a. "Bloody" Bill Anderson, 52,70,191
Andrews, Nelson L. (attorney), 135
Ash, William L. (attorney), 135
Austin and Saylor's Ranch, 9, 10
Aylsworth, Bill, 9
Bair, Howard L. Bair (deputy), 82, 121
Barnes, Thomas, 92
Bellamy, Joseph, 81
Bennett, Ed, xi
Blair, Jacob B. (judge, second judicial district), 89,90,91,127
Blake, Frank ,185
Burgham, J., 101
Beidler, John Xavier, "X" (US deputy marshal), 193,114
Bella Union Theater, 110
Berry, Jim, 61
Bevins, Bill, 61
Bicktold, Grace, 199
Big Horn (steamboat), 105,106,112
Big Nose George Parott a.k.a.:
    Big Nose George Parott, v,xi,59,97,98,110,122,185,187,188,193, 195,203,
    Big Nose George, v,xi,46,55,57,59,60,69,81,97-99, 102-104,107-109,111,112,115, 116-119,121-128,130,134,135,141, 173-176,179,181-188,191-193,195, 199-202
    George Dixon, 97,98,108-111,113, 121,195
    George Francis Warden, 117,121-124,195
    George Parrott, 133,137,143,160,161, 163-165,168,170,185
Birmingham, George, 136

Blydinburg, C. E., 92
Boerum, David (US deputy marshal), 98,102, 103,105-107,111,112
Boswell Nathaniel Kimball (sheriff), 23,28,31, 32,34-41,43-45,47-49,51,53-79,81-87,94, 97,98,102,115,116,121,169,175-177, 191,193,194,196,200
Boswell, Martha, 32,66,72,73
Boswell, Minnie, 32,66
Botkin, Alexander C. (US marshal, District of Montana Territory), 106,108,109
Bowen, E. J., 136
Bragg, William, 92
Bramel, Charles W. (attorney), 126,127,132,133, 173-177
Braner, William,92,93,
Brophy, John R. (sheriff), 23,96
Brown, Erick, 1,2,3
Brown, F., 34
Brown, H.E. "Stuttering", 36
Brown's Park, 59,60,70,84,93,165,167
Borris, Henry, 41
Bullard, (sheriff), 103,106-108
Bullock, Seth, 41,61,62
Butler, Richard (deputy), 72,74-76,85,115,116
Calvert, Kirk (posse),9,12
Calvin, E. E., 84,119
Campbell, Jack, 55,57,59,60,69,70,81,93,97,97, 108,109,116, 118,123,124,166
Cannon, John, 92
Carbon County Museum, v,xi,171,188
Carbon Station,84,86
Carey, Bill, 97,98,103,104,107-112
CAROLINA, NORTH:
    Raleigh,62
CAROLINA, SOUTH:
    Charleston, 62
Carr, Thomas Jefferson, (sheriff), 17,39,40,43, 56,61,63,64,66,72

Chambers, "Persimmon" Bill (see Persimmon Bill)
Chapman, W.W., 136
Cheyenne—Black Hills Stage Line, 23,180
Chinnick, John, 108-110
Citizens Committee, 49,73.76,86,94,98,119
Clarke, Dutch Charley (see: Dutch Charley Clarke)
Calvert, L. (deputy), 119
Chapman, Charles, 132
Collins, Joel, 46,60
COLORADO:
    Leadville, 131
Concord Stagecoach, 101
Condon, Charles "The Kid", 28,31,44,51,53,56,57
Cook, Lewis T. "Tom" (deputy), 93,94,97,119,122,123
Corlett, William Wellington (attorney), 134-139
Coulson Line, 105
Crawford, J. F., 81
Creighton, Thomas, 136
Csoxford, George, 192
DAKOTA TERRITORY:
    Bismarck, 99,105,106,112
    Custer City, 46
    Deadwood, 23,41,45,46,51,53,60,61,67,72,85,103,115,194
    Fargo, 101,112
    Medora, 99
Daley, William (lumber company, funeral parlor, posse and under-sheriff), 7,9,11,15-20,135,149,151-153,171,181,182,185,200
Davenport, Thomas, 93
Davis, Charles, 91-93
Davis, J.C., 185
Dayton, Thomas J. (sheriff), 33,34.36,38,40,41,43-45,49,56,66-60
Death mask, (plaster of Paris),187,188
Dickinson, Ed,(U .P. Superintendant), 1,7,9,12-20,31,32,34,35,39-41,44,45,48,56,59,60,66-68,72,74,81,82,84,92,94,115,116,126,136-138,144,175,
Dixon, George (see: Big Nose George Parott),
Donahue, J. T., (deputy), 32-34,37,38,45,45,48,49,51,56-60,66,68
Dondee, Cameron, 8
Dougan, Tom, (posse), 34,38

Draper, George W. (sheriff), 23,61,63,113-115
Durant, Thomas (bailiff), 92,47,141
Dungsford, Davis, 41
Dustin, George, 129,131
Dutch Charley Clarke a.k.a.:
    Dutch Charley Clarke, 118,179,194,195
    Dutch Charley, 28,46-55,57-61,66,68,69,71,73,75-79,81-86,94,116-119,179,191,194,195
    Dutch Charlie, 81,123-125,165-167,194
    Charles Clarke, 118
    Dutch Charley Bates, 69,81
    Dutch Charley Bayles, 194
    Dutch Charley Davis, 194,232
    Dutch Charley Randall, 59,69,78,194
    One-Winged Charley, 55,59,69
Dykins, John W., (sheriff), 17,196
Eaton, A. W., 136
Eclipse (steamboat), 106
Edgerton, A.G. (coroner), 17,20,186,187
Elk Mountain, Wyoming, v,3,9,13,15,19,20,23,24,28,32,34,39,41,44,46-48,54-59,63,67,68,71,72,76,78,87,97,109,111,118,121,123,125,127,135,138,143-145,149,154,164-167,169,171,173,179,188,191,194,199,200
English, J., 34
Far West (steamboat), 106
Fee, Jack (posse), 36,38
Fierce, Fernando "Jack", 132,139
Finley, J. W. (deputy), 119
Flannagan, A. P., 107
Flavin, H.E. (deputy), 119,131
Fletcher, Campbell (express man/mail piler), 75,79
Foote, John F. (posse), 144-148,150
Fort Abraham Lincoln, Montana Territory, 103
Fort Benton, Montana Territory, 105,106,112
Fort Buford, Dakota Territory, 99,105,106,112
Fort Fetterman, Wyoming Territory, 11,24-26,28,29,36,45,54,55,59,63,93
Fort Keogh, Montana Territory, 103,105,114
Fort Sanders, Wyoming Territory, 85,175
Fort Steele, 9,68,76,87,120,132159
Fort Washakie, 201,
Fortney, Harry (police lieutenant),
France, Walker, 185
Francis, James (attorney), 91
French, Walter, 136

Friend, John C. (editor, *Carbon County Journal*), 122,131,132,165,183,185
Galbraith, Robert, 185
Gault, Thomas, 93
GEORGIA:
Savannah, 62
Gibson, William A. 10-12
Gilmer, Salisbury and Patrick, 46,47,101,180
Grand Central Hotel, 72
Grand Jury, 81-84,86,90,111,127,132,137,139, 173,176,191,199
Hansen, Jens (posse/deputy/sheriff), 8,9,84,199
Hanson, A. C. a.k.a.
Hanson, A.C., 91,92
Ariel, 93
April, 92
Halstead, B., 34
Hamilton, O. A., 136
Hamma, Peter, 72
Harrington, Henry "Hank", 48-53,55-57, 60,67,71
Hathaway, (under-sheriff), 98,102,103,106,107,111,112
Hayes, Pres. Rutherford B., 135
Hayford, James H. "Doc." (Editor, *Laramie Daily Sentinel*), 33,68,71-73,83,85,86,175,194
Heath, Lillian (doctor), xi,187,188,202.203
Heffridge,61
Henry, Charles, 41
Henry, William, 10-12
Hill, Dick H., 10,11
Hobert, Anthony (Private),132
Hocker, M.E. (judge of probate), 132,135
Holcomb, J. F. "Jed," (posse), 34,37
Horn, Charles199
Howard, Frank, 24,25,28,28,40,41,44-46,55, 81, 82,84,87,92,94,102,125,126,179,195,199
Hoyt, John (governor, Wyoming Territory), 61, 97,98,102,125
Huffman, Layton Alton (photographer), 109,110, 114
Hughes, D. P. (attorney/justice of the peace), 185
I. G. Baker and Company, 105,106
Ike, Bill (posse)16,150
IOWA:
    Adair, 53,191
    Council Bluffs, 70,113,188,203
    Des Moines, 53

Irvine, Thomas H. (US deputy marshal), 97,98, 103-108,111,179,196
Irwin, John, 29,39,40,43,45,51-54,56,61, 63-68,111
James, Charles a.k.a,
    Sim James, 192, (also see: Sim Wan)
James, Frank, 52,55,59,70,81,118,166,191,192
James, Jesse,181,193
James, Sim,192
Johnson, J. W. "Jack" (under-sheriff),103, 105-108,111,112
Johnson William A. (sheriff), 91-94
Jones, John S., 92
Jones, Tom (posse), 9,12
Joslyn, (paymaster), 126
Kerns, Ed S. (deputy),34,39,74-77,79,80,83
Kesterton, Charles
Kirk, Ida (wife of I.C. Miller), 179,
Kling, L. W., 136
Knadler, Morgan (posse)34,39
Lafever, John (deputy), 24,25,28,34-36,38,39, 45,47,175,179,194,195,200
Landon, John (jailer),181-183
Laramie River, 4,35,40,76
Lawry, Isaac M. (sheriff), 1,2,7,8,13,14, 17-20,23,41,43,62,68,71-73,82,83,131,142, 144,195,196
Leach, Millard F. (U. P. special agent), 32,41,44, 45,47,53,59-61,66-68,72,73,92,94,128,159-162, 164,165,167,171,175,194
LeRoy, Al (posse),34
Lewis, Samuel T. (attorney), 126,127,129-134, 135,136,139,142,144,146-148,153,157-160, 162,164,167,168,170,171,173,183,185
Maghee, Thomas G. (doctor), 132,139,160, 161-165,180,183,187,188,201,203
Manuse, Joe, See Minuse, Joe
May, Daniel Boone, 23,24,41,47,56,58,61, 65-68,72,103,179,193,194
Mayhall, William, 92
McCarthy, J. (posse), 9
McPherson, J. A. (yardmaster), 192
McDonald, David (town marshal)43,56,64-66
McIntosh, A., 91
McIntosh, H.93
McKimie, Robert "Reddy", 47,60-62
McKinney, Mack,52,55,59,69,70,81,166,168,169,191

Medicine Bow,(see: Wyoming
Medicine Bow River, (see: Wyoming)
Medicine Bow Station, (see: Union Pacific)
Meldrum, John W. (clerk of court),32,89-91, 94,127-129,133,135,137,138,141,174,176
Merchants Hotel, 112,113
Merrill, Homer (attorney/county attorney), 89-94,130,131,135,136,141,148-151, 153-170,174-176,180
Metcalf, Fonse (posse), 34
Miller, Isaac C. (sheriff), 1,130-132,135, 179-182,185,196,200
Miller, S. M., 185,
Mills, James (night guard), 192
MINNESOTA:
    St. Paul, 99,104,112,113,196
Minuse, John a.k.a.
Joe Minuse
Joe Manuse
Missouri River,105,112,113
Moore, Asa, 41,49

MONTANA TERRITORY:
    Helena,97-99,10,102,105-107,111
    Junction City, 26,103,108
    Miles City, 97-99,102-106,109,113, 114,116,123,179,192,196
    Red Rock, 98,99,101
Murray, Frank, 132

NEBRASKA:
    Big Springs, 61
    Kimba,23,32l
    Ogallala, 33,61,62,67
    Omaha, 18,99,105,113,114
Nelson, Lillian Heath, see: Heath, Dr. Lillian (doctor)xi,188,202
Nelson, Louxi,xii,203

NEW HAMPSHIRE:
    Concord,101

NEWS PAPERS:
    Black Hills Daily Times, 47
    Black Hills Journal, 222
    Carbon County Journal, 122-124,131, 132,165,175,183,192193,195
    *Cheyenne Daily Leader,*125
    *heyenne Daily Sun,*194,195
    *elena Daily Herald*105
    *Kansas City Times*191
    Laramie Daily Chronicle, 175,
    Laramie Daily Sentinel, 7 3,83,85,192,194
    Laramie Independent, 175
    *Laramie Weekly Sentinel*216
    Laramie Times, 83,85
    *Leavenworth times*191
    *he pioneer press, St. Paul,MN,*99
    *Rocky Mountain Morning Star,*83
    *The Yellowstone Journal*107,113,114,196
Nottage, Daniel (sheriff), 2,3,14,17,23,24,28, 29,31-33,35,36,39-41,43,45,49,51,56,58,60-62, 66-71,73,143,196

OHIO:
    Hillsboro,61
Old Woman Creek, 32,46,47,53
Olson, Otto,25
Olson's Whiskey House, 25
Ordway, Ed (deputy), 192,
Osborne, John E. (doctor), 180-183,185,187,188, 199,201 203
Overholt, A.G., 91,92
Pannock, Taylor (posse), 16,17,159,196
Peace, Judge (editor, *Laramie Times*), 83,85
Peck, William Ware (judge, third judicial district), 133,135-139,141-143
"Persimmon Bill"43,47,193
Platte River, 9-11,52,87124,166
Pollock, J. E., 92,
Potts, Benjamin (governor, Montana Territory), 97,98,102,111
Prince, W. O., 92
Pumpkin Buttes,59
Quantrill, William Clarke, 191
Quantrill's Raiders,52,70,71

RAILROADS:
    Chicago, Rock Island, and Pacific Railroad, 70
    Northern Pacific Railroad, 99,102, 105,112
    St. Paul & Sioux City Railroad,93,113
    Sioux City and Pacific Railroad,113
    Union Pacific Railroad,ix,19,25,45, 49,64,68,98,113,118,126,138,142,160, 161,181,202
    Utah & Northern Railroad, 98,
Rankin, James G. (sheriff), 1,18-20,23,41,

73,74,79-81,86,87,91,94,98,103,106,107,111, 112,115,117,119,123,124,126,127,132, 141-144,176,196,
Rankin, Joseph196,199
Rankin, Juletta1,119
Rankin, Mary Elizabeth "Lizzie",83,181
Rankin, Newton T. "Newt" (deputy)199
Rankin, Robert (jailer), 87,181,199
Rankin, Rosanna "Rosa" (wife of jailer), 83, 129,180,181
Rattlesnake Canyon,14-16,19,20,57,138
Rattle Snake Canyon, 144-146,149,154, 156,157,159
Rawlins National Bank, 201
Red Canyon, 46
Red Cloud (steamboat), 105-107,112
Reed, Thomas a.k.a.
Thomas Reed, 118,124,166,193
Reed, Tim, 57,59,69,81,193
Reynolds, A. W., 136
Richardson, J.C. (stenographer), 127,171
Robber's Roost, 47
Rocky Mountain Detective Agency, 47,82,
Robie, Frederic, 66,67
Ruby, Fred, 51
Rose, A.O. (engineer), 75,76
Rose Bud (steamboat), 106
Ryan, Andrew (town marshal), 113,115
Schmalsle, Fred, 104-110
Schnitger, (US marshal), 43,56,61,63
Scott, (Laramie City policeman, posse), 34,41
Scribner, Chas, 185
Simms, William (jailer), 181-183,185
Slater, William, 92
Slaughter, Johnny, 60,61,72
Slaughter, Marshal John, 72
Smith, George C. (Carbon County Attorney), 79-81,87,98,113,115-117,119,121,122,126,126-128,130-134,139,141,142,144-148,176
Smith, P. L., 185
Smith, William J., 126,
Spear, Albert, 41
Sturgis, Ben, (doctor, Carbon County coroner), xi,xii
Sumner, J.C., 182
Swassor, George (posse), 16,150
Swazey, E. L., 136
Taylor, Bill, 41

Thayer, Dana, 24,37-31,34,39-69
Thayer, John Milton (governor, Wyoming Territory), 25,135,175-177
Thies, N., 34
Thomas, John R., 10,11,18
Thorp, Russell, 180
Tongue River, 112
Towle, Frank a.k.a.
Frank Towle, 46,47,52-55,57-61,63,65,67,69,70, 72,78,81,94,103,118,168
Frank Tole, 166,167,169,181
Frank Toll, 193,194
Frank Toule, 123-125
Trabing Brothers Store, 24,33,34,44,46,49,54, 55,57
Union Hotel, 103,106
UNION PACIFIC RAILROAD:
    Coal Company, 14,34,36
    Depot, Carbon, 20
    Depot, Cheyenne,63,64
    Depot, Laramie, 35
    Depot, Omaha, 113
    Railroad Museum, v,188,203
    Station, Como142,143
    Station, Look-Out,76
    Station, Medicine Bow,1,8,13-15,24-26, 36,37,86,87,116,123,143,166,191
    Station, Percy, 3,7-9,11,13,15,17-20, 76,144
    Station, Rock Creek,1,24-26,31,32, 34,35,39,55,63,76,86,87,97,142,194
    Station, St. Mary's, 12,76, 192
    Station, Sherman, 66,115
UTAH:
    Ogden, 8,97-99,101
    Salt Lake City, 126
Vassor, John W., 81,92
vigilantes, 49,50,56,68,77,78,84,116-122,139, 165,179,184,191,196
VIRGINIA:
    Richmond, 62
Vincents, Henry H. "Tip" a.k.a.
Vincents, Henry H. "Tip", xi, 7,12-16-18,20,21, 23,34,44,58,63,67,68,71,85,92,94,97,111,118, 127,128,135,138,144,147,148,150,156,158, 171,173,188,195,201,202
Vinson, 22,90,122,124,125
Wadsworth, Tim (posse), 9

Wagner, Con, 49
Wall, James, 61
Wallace, Jesse (posse), 9, 15-17,92,150,154, 156-159
Walter, Frank, 91,92
Wan, Sim, a.k.a.:
    Wan, Sim, 124,166,192,193
    Charles James, 192
    Sim James, 192
    Sim Wahn, 193
    Sim Waun, 52,55,57,59,60,69, 70,81,118,192
Warrant, Joseph (Jas Warran), 93
Warrant, Mrs. J. (Mrs. Jas Warran), 93
Webber, (posse), 9,10
Webster, T.J., 175
Wells, John, a.k.a.:
    Wells, John, 59,81,93,98.102,108,125
    "Sandy", 69
Widdowfield, Ann, 17,19,20,28,78,117,118
Widdowfield, Joseph, 18-20,175
Widdowfield, Robert (deputy), xi,8-116,120,21, 23,334.44.49,49,50,56,58,63,67-69,71,78,85, 90.93,94,97,111,118,123-125,127,128,135, 138,144,153,157,163-165,173,178, 193-195,200,201
Wilson, Big Ned,, 49
Wilson, Lem, 104,107,109
Woods (doctor)
WYOMING TERRITORY:
    Albany County, v,2-4,14,18,23,25,31-3, 43,44,63-66,72,82,86,91,97,143,175, 193,194,196,200
    Carbon County, v,ix,xi,1,2,23,41,47,48, 63,64,71,73,74,76,79,80,84-87,90.91,111, 115,116,121,126,130,132,133-135,141, 143,145-49,154,159,171,173,175,177, 179,180,185,188,191,192-196,199,200
    Carbon, Town of, 3,8,13-21,25,34,36, 70,73,76,69,80-87,90,98,116,119120, 124,126,139,143,144,164,165,175, 188,191,192-194,200
    Cheyenne,113-115,133,134,138,171, 175,180,194,195
    Como Bluffs, 25
    Dixon, 199
    Hanna, 25
    Jackson Hole, 59,93
    Laramie and Laramie City, ix,2,4,7,14,17,18,23,25,26,28,34,35-40, 47-50,61-69,72,78,79,82,84- 87,98,99, 115,116,120,142,143,175,177,192, 193,195
    Laramie County, 23,47,61,63,65,72,115, 116,195
    Green River and Green River City, 4,17, 47,55,59,60,81,84-86,92-94,98, 118,125,194,201
    Medicine Bow1,3,8.9,11,13-15,23-2 6,33,34,44,46,49,53- 55,63,70,76,87,93, 142,143,166,170
    Medicine Bow River9,11
    Rawlins and Rawlins Springs, ix,xi,1,4, 8,12-14,17-21,34,43,48,49,56,64,68,69, 73,76-80,82-86,91,97-99,105,111,112, 114,115,119,122,126,130,139,142,144, 145,149,153,154,157,8,171,176,177, 179,183-188,192-196,199-203
    Rock Creek, 24-26,32,33,35,37-40,41,45, 55,66-76,86,87,92,102,142,195
    Sweetwater County, 91,92,94,194, 196,201
    Territorial Prison, 35,40,49,64,94,95
Warm Springs159
Yates, Frank D., 46,101
Yellowstone River, 112
Young, Long Steve, 49
Zimmerman, John, 23,24,47,67

www.ingramcontent.com/pod-product-compliance
Lightning Source LLC
Chambersburg PA
CBHW081354290426

44110CB00018B/2372